# A Conductor's Guide to Choral-Orchestral Works, Twentieth Century, Part II

*The Music of Rachmaninov through Penderecki*

Jonathan D. Green

The Scarecrow Press, Inc.
Lanham, Md., & London
1998

# SCARECROW PRESS, INC.

Published in the United States of America
by Scarecrow Press, Inc.
4720 Boston Way
Lanham, Maryland 20706

4 Pleydell Gardens, Folkestone
Kent CT20 2DN, England

This work is adapted from the author's doctoral dissertation, "A Conductor's
Guide to Twentieth-Century Choral-Orchestral Works in English," Universtity
of North Carolina–Greensboro, 1992.

British Library Cataloguing in Publication Information Available

**Library of Congress Cataloging-in-Publication Data**

Green, Jonathan D., 1964–
    A conductor's guide to choral-orchestral works / by Jonathan Green.
       p.   cm.
    "Works to be included must be for full chorus and orchestra, containing some
English text, composed between 1900 and 1972"—Introd.
    Revision of author's thesis (D.M.A.)—Universtiy of North Carolina at Greensboro.
    Includes bibliographical references and discography p.
    ISBN 0-8108-3376-X (acid-free paper)
    1. Choruses with orchestra—20th century—Bibliography.
    I. Title
    ML128.C48G7  1994
    016.7825—dc20                      93-6388

ISBN 0-8108-3376-X (cloth : alk. paper)

This book is dedicated to my teacher and friend

William P. Carroll

for whom many of these works are already
familiar friends

# CONTENTS

vi

# PREFACE

The purpose of this text is to provide conductors with the knowledge required to make informed decisions in programming choral-orchestral repertoire, and to introduce all readers to a diverse body of twentieth-century works. This book is a survey of 89 compositions for choir and orchestra. The majority were composed between 1900 and 1972; however, in the case of composers for whom some works corresponded to these dates with additional works preceding 1900, the earlier compositions may have been included.

In the first volume of this on-going project, all of the scores fell strictly between two dates and were of a minimum length and restricted orchestration. In this second volume, I have chosen to include a number of shorter works and some which use non-traditional orchestras, because they are a valuable part of the repertoire and, I believe, are well served in this venue.

For each work the following information is included: a biography and bibliography of the composer, a detailed instrumentation list, performance times, publishers and availability of materials, location of the manuscript (if known), the source of the text, a discography, and a bibliography specific to the composition. Most importantly, for each work there is a detailed description of the performance issues within the score. This includes an evaluation of each solo vocal role, an evaluation of the choral and orchestral parts, and an estimation of their respective difficulties.

There is an appendix which provides brief biographical or historical information about each text source, and it is indexed back to the works themselves. There is a second appendix which gives the addresses and many telephone numbers for publishers and their U.S. distributors. These change frequently, but all were still valid at the time of this writing.

Most of the information for each work was culled directly from the scores. I must thank the publishers and distributors of these pieces for so readily providing me with information and perusal scores. A number of works were secured through the Sweet Briar College Library, where I received significant assistance from L. Joseph Malloy. Additional materials were provided by the libraries of the University of North Carolina at Greensboro, where Sarah Dorsey and Ted Hunter were most helpful.

The owners of Moore Music in Greensboro, Kay and Stuart Fitzpatrick, provided crucial assistance in identifying current distributors of imported scores and helped in securing a number of study scores. I am thankful to the Sweet Briar College Music Department and especially my chairman, Rebecca McNutt, for their support.

Most of all, I must thank my wife, Lynn Buck, for her patience and constant encouragement.

# CHAPTER I

# DEVELOPMENTS AND TRENDS

This text is the second in an on-going series of books studying the symphonic choral repertoire. The first volume, published by Scarecrow in 1994, was an elaboration of my dissertation. It addressed choral-orchestral works written between 1900 and 1972 which contained at least some English text. This volume will address 89 more works by 21 composers without the language delimiter. I have included a few works with English texts, which were not included in the previous volume.

Since nearly all of the works in the first volume were by American and British composers, it was interesting to observe trends within the entire body of repertoire. In the present volume some of the the most compelling generalities have more to do with how these works differ from those in the first volume than what they have in common with each other.

In one review of the first volume by Kerry Barnett in *Choristers Guild Letters*, Volume 47, number 1 (Summer 1995), it was noted with some well-founded distress how few of those important British and American works had ever been recorded. It is encouraging that a number of them have been recorded in the past three years. It is perhaps more significant to observe not only how many of the works in this second volume have been recorded, but also how numerous the recordings of some single works are. Even at the close of the century the prejudice of the music industry persists in favor of the music of continental Europe over that of Great Britain and the United States.

Certain ensembles, foundations, and conductors again distinguished themselves as champions of this repertoire. Ernest Ansermet and Paul Sacher led the premieres of a number of these works. The case of Sacher is unusual for he also commissioned the works that he premiered, and through his foundation, has collected the manuscripts and other archival materials of the entire works of a number of composers, including Stravinsky and Webern. The Sacher Foundation Archive is projected to erect a large modern library in Basle, Switzerland which will be accessible to the public for musicological research. Another overt supporter of composers represented here is the Koussevitsky Foundation.

## General Trends

It should be noted that the most difficult works in this current study have had numerous repeat performances. It is significant to realize that these most challenging pieces have been written and performed in eastern Europe during the era of communist rule. An interesting dichotomy regarding artistic freedom comes into play. In the eastern-bloc countries, composers had the luxury of state-sponsored ensembles and therefore prolonged rehearsal schedules if needed to perform these works which would often be deemed too expensive to effectively mount today in the west.

There are clearly bodies of music which have been conceived for different levels of performance. The works of Penderecki, Ligeti, and Henze are the most experimental of those studied here. Each composer has clearly written his works with a highly trained professional orchestra and choir in mind. In the Soviet Union, Shostakovich and Prokofiev wrote a number of pieces, mostly for state occasions, for which they have written for a professional orchestra and a large amateur choir.

In most of the remaining works it is apparent that the composers have a clear sense of the level of ensemble for which they are writing, especially in the choral portions. Much of this can be seen in the ways in which the accompaniment supports the vocal parts. The composers who had the most experience as choral conductors, such as Britten, Janacek, Martin, and Nielsen, also generally had the most overt support of the vocal lines in their accompaniments.

## Occasional Music

A large number of these works were written to commemorate anniversaries of institutions or historic events. Three academic institutions commemorated the anniversaries of their foundings with appropriate choral works. Penderecki composed *Cantata in honorem Almae Matris Universitatis Iagellonicae* to celebrate the founding of his own *Alma mater*. Britten was commissioned to compose *Cantata Academica* to commemorate the 500th anniversary of the founding of the University of Basle. For this task he used texts from significant documents from the university's history. The third work is Thompson's *Testament of Freedom* which was written to commemorate the 200th birthday of Thomas Jefferson, but clearly with the thought of his having been the founder of the University of Virginia. For this work, Thompson used writings of the former president.

Many of the Soviet works were written for anniversary celebrations of the revolution including Shostakovich's Symphony No. 2, and Prokofiev's *Cantata on the 20th Anniversary of the October Revolution*. Other Soviet works were composed to honor Stalin's birthday, such as Prokofiev's *Zdravitsa*, or to "kick-off" new government projects, as in Shostakovich's *Songs of the Forests*, which was written for the beginning of a new reforestation program.

Other works commemorated significant historical observances, as in Diamond's *This Sacred Ground*, which sets to music Lincoln's *Gettysburg Address* on the centennial year of its delivery. Penderecki's *Kosmogonia* is a musical setting of diverse texts celebrating man's quest for understanding and eventually visiting the heavens, which was his response for a work commissioned to commemorate the 25th anniversary of the founding of the United Nations.

The performance dilemma created by this segment of the repertoire is often the specificity of the texts. In the hands of these great composers, these sometimes unartistic subjects have resulted in wonderful music. In the case of the Soviet works, it is also a body of very accessible works for large inexperienced symphonic choirs and amateur orchestras. Unfortunately, the texts make them unsuitable even in their native Russia in which the political climate has so dramatically changed in recent years.

## Texts

Most of the works contained herein use a single text source. A common practice in many American works of this period, and even more British works of the same time, is the anthological text in which the composer combined numerous text sources to address a single issue. The American and British works in this volume each use only a single text source. The few works which contain multiple text sources include some of the Soviet works for which a number of authors surely had a more proletarian appearance. Orff uses multiple sources from antiquity in *Trionfo di Afrodite* in which he combines Greek and Latin texts, and in so doing helps us to see the lineage of writers addressing common themes throughout the generations. In *Kosmogonia*, Penderecki draws on numerous sources to give us a history lesson in our changing perceptions of the heavens.

## Languages

The clear majority of these works are in the language of the composer. There is an interesting return to Latin for a number of composers. Stravinsky has suggested that the use of Latin helps to internationalize a composition, by making it a second language to all who hear it. The use of Latin and classical Greek provides this same service for Penderecki whose native tongue is far less accessible to non-Polish ensembles.

An interesting exploration of "historic" language for a composer, is Janáček, whose *Glagolithic Mass* is a setting of a translation of the Roman Catholic Latin Mass into Church Slavonic. This process results in universally recognized text themes set in a language far removed even from its original practitioners.

There is yet another body of work composed in the 20th century which uses meaningless texts, or none at all (See: "Voices as Instruments," below.).

## Folkmusic Influences

Many of the composers discussed in this text had a substantial involvement in the collection and cataloguing of folkmusic. Janáček became an expert in Moravian folk music; Holst collected English folksongs with Vaughan Williams; Kodaly and Bartok collaborated on numerous ethnomusicological projects.

In most of the works studied here, the folk influences are merely heard as a shaping force in the various composers' musical style; however, in some works, there are direct uses of folk material. Bartok's *Cantata Profana* and Janáček's *Ridalka* both derive their texts from ethnic sources. And although *Ridalka* does not appear to quote actual folktunes, it is clearly modeled upon them.

Orff imitates medieval popular and sacred music in his *Carmina Burana*. Penderecki directly quotes passages of Eastern Orthodox chants within the atonal framework of his *Utrenja*. Although Kodaly's

*Budavári Te Deum* and *Psalmus Hungaricus* do not directly quote Eastern liturgical music, he has allowed those traditions to influence his musical choices.

## Pitch Organization

As with most music of the 20th century, composers have explored numerous systems of pitch organization in the choral-orchestral repertoire. The works studied here range from the purely diatonic, to modal, free-atonal and serial.

Works from the beginning of the century are almost exclusively in the late-Romantic mold, often being highly chromatic, but always remaining obedient to the principles of the common-practice period. The works of Mahler, Nielsen, as well as Schoenberg's *Gurrelieder*, are all clear examples of this tradition. In the music of the Russian composers this same tonal lineage remains, but especially among the works of Rachmaninov and Prokofiev there is an influence from the scales of Russian folksong and the modes from the Russian Orthodox Church which color much of their chromaticism. This same modal influence can be heard in Shostakovich's works, but in his music there are also many subtle references to Russian Jewish folksongs.

In the works of Debussy, Ravel, and Holst there is a greater preponderance of extended tertian harmonies. In the French works there are some whole-tone and pentatonic scales. In Holst's work, the whole-tone scale appears and there are a number of modal shifts which reflect the composer's involvement with English folksong and Anglican church music.

In Orff's music there are numerous attempts toward primitivism using prolonged pedal figures, pure diatonicism, and modally guided parallel fourths and fifths. These medieval procedures are often used to be evocative of the era whence the text comes. Likewise in his works with texts from antiquity, he often explores uses of classical modes in his music.

There are a number of serial compositions of varied orthodoxy among these works. The later compositions of Schoenberg include serial procedures, but with clear points of departure from the technique, when it no longer serves the composer's needs. It is interesting to note that the creator of the twelve-tone method is often less dogmatic about its use than his followers have been. Webern's works are the most strictly serial, but in his rows he makes some interesting allusions including the sequence B-A-C-H.

In Penderecki's music, the composer often presents all twelve discrete pitches simultaneously, but without a clearly sequential method for organizing his pitch material. Henze uses pure serialism for sections of works, but integrates these passages with others which are guided by other organizational systems including traditional tonality. Both Penderecki and Ligeti use approximate pitches at times. Penderecki also uses quartertones in most of his works.

Stravinsky's late works often use adaptations of the twelve-tone method. While he does sometimes use Schoenberg's technique in its original form, or following the contrapuntal interpretations worked out by Webern, Stravinsky also applies serial procedures to six-note sets, the combinatorial hexachord of which is often a transposition or inversion of his original hexachord.

Perhaps the most original use of the twelve-note row is in Britten's *Cantata misericordium*. This work is in 13 sections each being centered around a different pitch with the final movement being a return to the pitch center of the first movement. Each movement is conspicuously tonal, but contains a statement of the overall-guiding row somewhere within its tonal fabric. A single central movement treats the row more conspicuously in a baroque-inspired contrapuntal exercise.

### Instrumentation

Two interesting developments from an orchestrational point of view have to do with the varied perceptions of the constitution of an orchestra. These works exhibit trends to expand and reduce the instrumentation in the orchestra throughout the century.

The most strikingly original departure from the traditional orchestra is Stravinsky's *Svadebka* [*Les Noces/The Wedding*] in which the orchestra has been reduced to four pianos and percussion. Orff would also exploit similar ensembles in a number of his works. Stravinsky in his *Symphony of Psalms*, which was commissioned to celebrate the 50th anniversary of the Boston Symphony Orchestra, chose to omit the violins and violas, and to replace them with two pianos. Prominent orchestral piano parts are also to be found in Orff's *Carmina Burana*, Honegger's *Roi David*, and the works of Britten, Henze and Martin.

As has been the case in purely orchestral music in the 20th century, there has been a steady increase in the number of percussion instruments to be found in these scores. Orff introduces a number of Asian instruments including trough xylophone and Japanese temple bells. Ligeti's and Penderecki's works feature: wood plate drums, thunder sheets, metal railroad rails, wooden bells, glass and metal wind chimes, rattles, and assorted marimbas, xylophones, and drums.

It is also interesting to note that an electronic instrument appears in only one work in this collection: Honegger used an Ondes Martenot in his *Jeanne d'Arc au bûcher*.

## Voices as Instruments

Three scores use a textless chorus. They are Debussy's *Nocturnes*, Ravel's *Daphnis and Chloe*, and Holst's *The Planets*. In the first of these, the women's voices are supposed to be evocative of the Sirens after whom the movement is named. The use of textless voices in the remaining two works was surely influenced by Debussy's programatically inspired precedent.

Both Ligeti and Penderecki score nonsense texts which have been conceived for their sonic value alone. In the works of each, consonants are often strung together to create percussive effects wholly unrelated to language or to traditional singing. The works of both composers have very effective acoustic results.

One other interesting use of textless singing is in Honegger's *Jeanne d'Arc au bûcher*. In this score the composer has indicated that the string players are to hum as an accompaniment to the vocalists.

## Conclusion

The works studied here reflect most of the trends to be found throughout western music during this period. A clear majority of these works have already secured a prominent position in the standard repertoire. Shifting tastes are causing some of the most celebrated of these works to fall into disuse, especially those which are the most experimental in conception, or politcal in content.

The subjects of the texts and their various treatments are clearly influenced by the historical, cultural, and political climates in which the works were conceived. Most remain universal in their themes and will survive the test of time.

# CHAPTER II

# SURVEY OF WORKS

**Bartók, Béla** (b. Nagyszentmiklós, Hungary, 25 March 1881; d. New York, NY, 26 September 1945)

**Life:** Bartók is one of the most influential composers of the twentieth century. His interest in folk music, his dedication to the meaningful education of amateur musicians, and his experiments with meter and pitch sets in his music have each had a profound impact upon the development of music in the modern era. Bartók's father was a schoolmaster and his mother a capable amateur pianist. Bartók began publicly performing as a pianist at the age of eleven. At eighteen, he enrolled in the Royal Academy of Music in Budapest, studying piano with István Thomán, and composition with Hans Koessler. Shortly after his graduation, he established an important friendship with Zoltan Kodály with whom he collected and published folk music from Hungary, Rumania, Transylvania, and Slovakia. Later ethnomusicological tours would take him through northern Africa. In 1907 he succeeded Thomán as professor of piano at the Royal Academy. He toured as a pianist throughout Europe, the Soviet Union, and the United States often performing his own compositions. In 1934 he resigned his post at the Royal Academy, but continued his research in folk music as a member of the Hungarian Academy of Sciences. Upon the outbreak of the Second World War, he elected to move to the United States where he was the recipient of an honorary doctorate from Columbia University in 1940. He received support for his research in ethnomusicology under the auspices of Columbia University for the year of 1941-1942. During the final three years of his life he rejected some offers to teach composition, and instead taught piano privately. During these years he also completed a number of substantial commissions, including the *Concerto for Orchestra*, which he composed while seeking the recuperative mountain air of Asheville, NC. Bartók's music is distinctive, in part, because of the catholic palette of resources which he would freely combine within a single work. In his compositions can be found a wealth of folk idea (in quotation or spirit), impressionist harmonic language, and highly refined contrapuntal procedures, not unlike those used by the dodecaphonic composers of the Second Viennese School. The lasting strength of his works rests upon the fact that while being highly technical in conception, they remain tuneful even at their most intellectually complex moments.

**Writings:** Bartók's earliest collection of folk songs was published in 1906. He continued to publish collections and commentaries throughout the rest of his life. These are being published in English translations by the New York Bartók Archive, Benjamin Suchoff, editor. They include *Rumanian Folk Music*, volumes I-V; *Turkish Folk Music of Asia Minor*; *Béla Bartók's Essays*; *Yugoslav Folk Music*, volumes I-IV; and *The Hungarian Folk Song*.

**Principal Works:** *opera*: *Bluebeard's Castle* (1911); *ballets*: *The Wooden Prince* (1914-16), *The Miraculous Mandarin* (1918-19); *orchestral*: 3 Piano Concertos (1926, 1930-31, 1945), *Dance Suite* (1923), *Music for Strings, Percussion, and Celeste* (1936), *Divertimento* (1939), *Concerto for Orchestra* (1945); *chamber*: six String Quartets (1908, 1915-17, 1927, 1928, 1934, 1939), Sonata for Two Pianos and Percussion (1937), *Contrasts* for clarinet, violin, and piano (1938); *piano*: 14 Bagatelles (1908), *Allegro barbaro* (1911), Sonata (1926), *Mikrokosmos* (1926-39); *vocal*: numerous folk song arrangements for various choral ensembles.

## Selected Composer Bibliography

Stevens, Halsey: *The Life and Music of Bela Bartok*, revised. New York: Oxford University Press, 1964.

Demény, János, editor: *Bela Bartok Letters*, with a preface by Sir Michael Tippett, translated into English by Péter Balabán and István Farkas, revised by Elisabeth West and Colin Mason. New York: St. Martin's Press, 1971. The Hungarian edition was first published in 1948.

Antokoletz, Elliott: *The Music of Bela Bartok*. Berkeley, California: University of California Press, 1984.

_____: *Bela Bartok: A Guide to Research*. New York: Greenwood Press, 1988.

## Cantata Profana, op. 94 — *A Kilenc csordaszarvas* [The nine enchanted stags] (1930)

**Duration:** ca. 18 minutes

**Text:** The text taken from a Rumanian *colinda*, a Christmas folksong, was arranged and translated into Hungarian by Bartok. The study score from Universal Edition contains singing translations in English and German, but not the original Hungarian.

**Performing Forces: voices:** two SATB choirs, soprano and baritone soloists; **orchestra:** 3 flutes (flute III doubling piccolo), 3 oboes, 3 clarinets in A (clarinet II doubling bass clarinet), 3 bassoons (bassoon II doubling contrabassoon), 4 horns in F, 2 trumpets in C, 3 trombones, tuba, timpani, percussion (2 players — snare drum, bass drum, cymbals, tam-tam), harp, and strings.

**First Performance:** 25 May 1934, London, Trefor Jones, tenor; Frank Phillips, baritone; BBC Symphony and Wireless Chorus, conducted by Aylmer Buesst.

**Edition:** *Cantata Profana* is published by Universal Edition and distributed in the United States through Boosey and Hawkes. The piano-vocal score (10614), choral parts (10615A-D) full score (10613) and miniature score (12760) are available for purchase; orchestral materials are available through rental.

**Autograph:** The first edition is a facsimile of the composer's manuscript.

**Notes:** The score was completed in Budapest on 8 September 1930. While on a folksong collecting tour of Transylvania in April 1914, Bartok recorded two versions of a *colinda*, a Rumanian Christmas ballad. Each of the songs had the same tune, but different words. They are included in his book on Rumanian Christmas Songs first published by Universal Edition in 1935 and reissued in an updated form by Editio Musica and Schott's Söhne in 1968. Bartok sought to have the text translated into a Hungarian poem which he would set to music. This was undertaken by Jósef Erdélyi with the result being published in the literary magazine, *Nyugat*. Bartok was dissatisfied with Erdélyi's versions and wrote his own which appears anonymously in the original score. Bartok did allow a recording to be made of him reading the text on Budapest radio.

**Performance Issues:** There are two-part divisi within each of the choral parts, yielding a sixteen-part chorus in some sections. The choir must be aurally secure as the choral parts are harmonically outlined by the orchestra, but not in a conspicuous, nor direct fashion. The choral textures are also rather complex presenting many obstacles for creating a clear presentation of the text. There are brief SATB choral solos in the first movement. The score utilizes a number of non-traditional scales and folk modes, two of which (d-e-f#-g#-a-b-c-d and d-e-f-g-a$^b$-b$^b$-c-d) help to shape the overall structure of the piece. The presence of two tritone relationships within each of these pitch sets creates a number of challenges for intonation which will require particular attention in rehearsal. The individual instrumental parts are fairly conservatively written, presenting few technical challenges to the players. The difficulties presented in this score include numerous meter changes wherein the value of the pulse changes within tempi where the speed of the beat is awkwardly slow and the value of the subdivision awkwardly fast. There are also many subtle changes of tempo within each movement. Of greatest difficulty is the maintenance of soft dynamics and balance of parts within a large ensemble as about half of the score is marked piano or lower. **Soloists:** tenor - range: f#-c", tessitura: d'-a', although not long, this is a very vocally demanding role because of its sustained persistence within a narrow band of the high range; baritone - range: A$^b$-e', tessitura: c-c', this role requires a strong and clear voice; **Choir:** difficult; **Orchestra:** medium difficult.

**Discography:** Réti, Faragó; Budapest Symphony and Chorus; conducted by Ferencsik. Hungaroton: HCD-12759 [LP].

Lewis, Rothmüller; Hillis Ensemble; conducted by Süsskind. Bartok: 312 [LP].

John Aler, John Tomlinson; Chicago Symphony Chorus (Margaret Hillis, chorus-master), and Chicago Symphony Orchestra; conducted by Pierre Boulez, recorded in Orchestra Hall, Chicago in December 1991. Deutsche Grammophon: D 101210 [DDD].

## Selected Bibliography

Somfai, Laszlo: *Cantata Profana*, preface to the score. Vienna: Universal Edition, 1937; reprint: New York: Boosey and Hawkes, 1955.

Bartok, Bela: *Cantata Profana. A Kilenc csodaszarvas.* Budapest: Zenemükindó Vállalut, 1974. [This is a published facsimile of Bartok's autograph of his essay on the text for this work. The essay is in Rumanian and includes the text in Hungarian.]

Laszlo, F.: "Megjegyzések a Cantata profana szövegéhez, Még egyszer a Cantata profana szövegévöl" [Notes on the text of Cantata Profana ]. *Müvelödés*, 28/ 9: 11 (1975), 49.

Breuer, J.: "Kolinda-ritmika Bartók zezé jeben" [Colinda Rhythms in Bartok's Music]. *Zeneelmélet, stilus elemzés* (Budapest, 1977), 84.

Tallián, Tibor: "Die Cantata Profana: ein 'Mythos des Übergangs.'" *Studia Musicologica*, 23 (1978), 135.

# Bernstein, Leonard (b. Lawrence, MA, 25 August 1918; d. New York, 14 October 1990).

**Life:** Bernstein was educated at the Boston Latin School and Harvard (BA 1939). He entered the Curtis Institute in 1941, where he studied conducting with Fritz Reiner and orchestration with Randall Thompson. He also studied conducting with Serge Koussevitsky and composition with Aaron Copland and Paul Hindemith at Tanglewood (1940-42). He was catapulted to fame as a conductor when he substituted for the ailing Bruno Walter in a national radio broadcast. After a year as joint principal conductor with Dmitri Mitropoulos, he was named sole conductor of the New York Philharmonic (1958-69), retiring as conductor laureate. He was one of the most influential and renowned conductors of this century. His compositions are marked by an inventive integration of jazz with elements of concert music. His melodies are very technically crafted in terms of intervallic organization, while retaining qualities of popular music. Throughout his works there is a common theme of man's struggle with unstable beliefs and the pursuit to find faith. His skills as a communicator were displayed in the many educational programs given on national television with the New York Philharmonic, and through his popular books on musical topics.

**Writings:** *The Joy of Music* (1959), *Young People's Concerts for Reading and Listening* (1962, revised and enlarged 1970), *The Infinite Variety of Music* (1966), *The Unanswered Question* (1976), and *Findings* (1982).

**Principal Works:** *musicals/operas - On the Town* (1944), *Trouble in Tahiti* (1951), *Wonderful Town* (1953), *Candide* (1956, revised 1973), *West Side Story* (1957), *1600 Pennsylvania Avenue* (1976), *A Quiet Place* (1983); *ballets - Fancy Free* (1944), *Facsimile* (1946), Symphony no. 1, "Jeremiah" (1942), Symphony no. 2, "The Age of Anxiety" (1949), Symphony no. 3, "Kaddish" (1961-63); *choral - Mass* (1971); *film music - On the Waterfront* (1954).

## Selected Composer Bibliography

"Bernstein, Leonard," *Current Biography Yearbook*, v (February 1944); xxi (February 1960); New York: H. W. Wilson Company.

Bernstein, Leonard: *The Joy of Music*. New York: Simon and Schuster, 1959.

_____: *The Infinite Variety of Music*. New York: Simon and Schuster, 1966.

_____: *The Unanswered Question*. Cambridge, MA: Harvard University Press, 1976.

_____: *Findings*. New York: Simon and Schuster, 1982.

Hughes, Allen: "Leonard Bernstein: Musical Personality of 1960," *Musical America* (January 1961), 15.

*Leonard Bernstein: A Catalogue of His Works*. New York: Boosey and Hawkes, 1978.

Robinson, Paul: *Bernstein (Art of the Conductor)*. New York: Vanguard Press of Simon and Schuster, 1982.

Peyser, Joan: "Leonard Bernstein," *The New Grove Twentieth-Century American Masters*, 291-306. New York: W.W. Norton, 1986.

_____: *Bernstein: A Biography*. New York: Beechtree Books, 1987.

Ledbetter, Steven, editor: *Sennets and Tuckets: A Bernstein Celebration*. Boston: Boston Symphony Orchestra, 1988.

Fluegel, Jane, editor: *Bernstein Remembered*. New York: Carroll and Graf, 1991.

Burton, Humphrey: *Leonard Bernstein*. New York: Doubleday, 1994.

Burton, William Westbrook, editor: *Conversations About Bernstein*. Oxford: Oxford University Press, 1995.

## Chichester Psalms (1965)

**Duration:** ca. 19 minutes

**Text:** The Psalms in Hebrew

**Performing Forces: voices:** boy soloist, SATB choral solos; SSAATTBB choir; **orchestra:** 3 trumpets in B$^b$, 3 trombones, timpani, percussion (7 players - glockenspiel, xylophone, suspended cymbal, crash cymbals, triangle, temple blocks, wood block, whip, rasp, snare drum, 3 bongos, tambourine, bass drum), 2 harps, and strings.

reduced orchestra version: organ, harp and percussion.

**First Performance:** 15 July 1965; New York; John Bogart; Camerata Singers (Abraham Kaplan, chorus-master), New York Philharmonic Orchestra; conducted by Bernstein.

**Edition:** *Chichester Psalms* is published by Amberson Music, Bernstein's division of G. Schirmer. The piano-vocal and full scores are available for purchase; orchestral materials are available through rental. The first movement is also available separately for performance with piano.

**Notes:** *Chichester Psalms* was commissioned for the Three Choirs Festival at Chichester Cathedral in England where it was performed 31 July 1965. It is dedicated to Cyril Solomon.

The composer states in the score that he conceived the work to be for a male choir, and that although a mixed choir was acceptable, the extended solo in the second movement must be sung by a male treble or a countertenor. Lukas Foss states that the score contains quotes from Beethoven's *Pastoral Symphony*, and from Foss's own *Psalms*.[1]

The score is written in transliterated Hebrew with a guide for pronunciation and a translation. The texts are selected and arranged as follows:

---

[1]   as quoted in Burton, William Westbrook, editor: *Conversations About Bernstein*, 10-11. Oxford: Oxford University Press, 1995.

Movement I
   Psalm 18, verse 2
   Psalm 100, all

Movement II
   Psalm 23, all
   Psalm 2, verses 1-4

Movement III
   Psalm 131, all
   Psalm 133, verse 1

**Performance Issues:** This score is metrically complex utilizing numerous compound meters reflecting Israeli folk music. There is also an element of middle-eastern modality throughout the work reflecting a good amount of chromaticism. The vocal parts are very rhythmic and require a broad palette of dynamics and articulation. The musical prosody of the Hebrew is accessible to singers lacking previous experience in this language. Although the vocal parts are chromatic and involve significant divisi, they are tonally based and tuneful. All four sections of the choir must be vocally strong and musically independent. The two harp parts can be successful negotiated by a single player although the sonority of two harps is preferred. The score is clearly written for seven percussionists, although five good players could execute all of the parts. The score uses the term "frusta" for a whip. While there is only a single cymbal stroke for the percussion in the final movement, a brief pre-rehearsal percussion sectional of the second movement is advisable. The individual orchestral parts are well-written for the instruments. A good harpist is crucial as this part is quite exposed, particularly in the second movement. The first trumpet part has a high tessitura and all of the brass parts require solid players. The string parts are the most accessible, while rhythmic and chromatic, they present few technical difficulties. **Soloists:** boy, range: d'-e", tessitura: e'-c", this solo represents the young psalmist, King David, he sings only in the second movement; the part is well doubled in the accompaniment, which is suitably transparent to not overshadow a young singer. There are four choral soloists with brief solos in the first and third movements: soprano - range: d-a$^{b}$", tessitura: g'-g"; alto - range: d'-d", tessitura: d'-b'; tenor - range: d-a', tessitura: a-d'; bass - range: d$^{b}$-e', tessitura: d-d'. **Choir:** medium difficult; **Orchestra:** medium difficult.

**Discography:** John Bogart; Camerata Singers (Abraham Kaplan, chorus master), New York Philharmonic Orchestra; conducted by Leonard Bernstein. Recorded: 26 July 1965 in the Manhattan Center, New York. Sony: SM3K 47 162 [ADD] and CBS: MK 44710 [ADD].

Estonian National Orchestra, Pacific Chorale; conducted by J. Alexander. Bay Cities: BCD 1035 [DDD].

Vienna Youth Chorus (Günther Teuring, chorus-master), Israel Philharmonic Orchestra; conducted by Leonard Bernstein. Deutsche Grammophon: 415965 [ADD].

Aled Jones; London Symphony Orchestra Chorus, Royal Philharmonic Orchestra; conducted by Richard Hickox. RPO Records: RPO 7007 [DDD], also released as MCA Classics: MCAD-6199.

American Boychoir, American Symphony Orchestra; conducted by James Litton. MusicMasters: 7049-2-C [DDD].

Atlanta Symphony and Chorus; conducted by Robert Shaw. Telarc: CD-80181 [DDD].

version for organ and percussion: Dominic Martelli; Corydon Singers; Thomas Trotter, organ; Rachel Masters, harp; Gary Kettel, percussion; conducted by Matthew Best. Hyperion: CDA-66219 [DDD].

James Bowman. countertenor; King's College Choir; James Lancelot, organ; Osian Ellis, harp; David Corkhill, percussion; conducted by Stephen Cleobury. Angel: CDC-54188 [DDD].

## Selected Bibliography

Gottlieb, Jack: "The Choral Music of Leonard Bernstein, Reflections of Theater and Liturgy," *American Choral Review*, volume 10 (1968), 155-177.

Berger, Melvin: *Guide to Choral Masterpieces: A Listener's Guide*, 63-67. New York: Anchor Books, 1993.

Burton, Humphrey: *Leonard Bernstein*, 347-49, 418-19. New York: Doubleday, 1994.

**Bloch, Ernest** (b. Geneva, Switzerland,  24 July 1880; d. Portland, Oregon , 15 July 1959)

**Life:** Bloch was one of the central figures in the development of Jewish concert music in the twentieth century. From 1894-97 he studied solfeggio with Émile Jaques-Dalcroze and Violin with Louis

Rey. He then went to Brussels to study violin with Eugène Ysaÿe and composition with François Rasse. In 1900 he began studies in music theory with Iwan Knorr at the Hoch Conservatory in Frankfurt, and composition lessons from Ludwig Thuille in Munich. Bloch returned to Switzerland in 1903 and began to support himself as a conductor. He was offered a teaching post at the David Mannes School of Music in New York in 1917. In 1924, Bloch became an American citizen. He served as director of the Cleveland Institute of Music (1920-25) and the San Francisco Conservatory (1925-30). He moved to Switzerland in 1930 and returned to the United States in 1939, teaching at Berkeley (1940-52). Bloch then retired to Portland, Oregon where he spent his final years composing. Around the time of his arrival in the United States, Bloch began a conscious focus upon creating a genre of concert works which reflected his Jewish heritage. His symphonic setting of the *Sacred Service* is the most conspicuously liturgical, but other works, including the *Israel Symphony* and *Schelomo*, combine programmatic themes from Jewish history with melodic elements suggestive of Jewish folk songs and liturgical cantillation. Bloch's musical legacy as a teacher is substantial; his many students include: George Antheil, Ernst Bacon, Elliott Carter, Herbert Elwell, Theodore Chanler, Isadore Freed, Frederick Jacobi, Earl Kim, Leon Kirchner, Douglas Moore, Roger Nixon, Lionel Nowak, Quincy Porter, Bernard Rogers, Roger Sessions, Halsey Stevens, and Randall Thompson.

**Writings:** A number of Bloch's essays and program notes can be found in *Ernest Bloch, Creative Spirit: A Program Source Book.* New York: Jewish Music Council, 1976.

**Principal Works:** *opera* - *Macbeth* (1904-09); *orchestral* - *Israel Symphony* (1912-16), *Schelomo* for cello and orchestra (1916), *America* (1926), *Evocations* (1937), Violin Concerto (1938), *Suite symphonique* (1945), *Suite hébraïque* for viola and orchestra (1952); *chamber* - Suite for Viola and Piano (1919), *Méditation hébraïque* for cello and piano (1925), *From Jewish Life* for cello and piano (1925), 5 String Quartets (1916, 1946, 1951, 1954, 1956), 3 Suites for Unaccompanied Cello (1956), *Suite Modale* for flute and strings (1957).

## Selected Composer Bibliography

Bloch, Suzanne and Irene Heskes, editors: *Ernest Bloch, Creative Spirit: A Program Source Book.* New York: Jewish Music Council, 1976.

Strassburg, Robert: *Ernest Bloch, A Voice in the Wilderness: A Biographical Study.* Los Angeles: Trident Shop Press, 1977.
Kushner, David Z.: *Ernest Bloch and his Music.* Glascow, Scotland: W. MacLellan, 1973.
_____: *Ernest Bloch: A Guide to Research.* New York: Garland Publishing, 1988.

## Avodath Hakodesh [Sacred Service] (1932-34)

**Duration:** ca. 49 minutes

**Text:** The text is from the Jewish liturgy, it is written to be sung in Hebrew or English. The English text was prepared by David Stevens.

**Performing Forces: voices:** narrator (optional), baritone soloist (cantor); SATB choir; **orchestra:** 3 flutes (flute II doubling piccolo), 2 oboes, English horn, 2 clarinets in A, bass clarinet in $B^b$, 2 bassoons, contrabassoon, 4 horns in F, 3 trumpets in C, 3 trombones, tuba, percussion (3 players- snare drum, bass drum, tambourine, cymbals, suspended cymbal, tam-tam, triangle), 2 harps, celeste, and strings (minimum: 10-8-6-6-5).

**First Performance:** 12 January 1934; Turin, Italy; conducted by the composer.

**Edition:** *Avodath Hakodesh* is published by Broude Brothers. The piano-vocal score, choral parts, full score, and study score (23) are available for purchase. The "Benediction" is available separately for performance with piano. Orchestral materials are available for rent. A full score is available for purchase through Carish publishers (21744). The Broude Brothers score is published with an English singing translation, prepared by David Stevens. The Carish edition includes a singing translation in Italian, prepared by Maria Tebaldi-Chiesa.

**Notes:** The melodic material for this work is derived from the ancient cantillation from Jewish liturgical tradition. Bloch takes this ancient melodic material and sets it within a completely modern harmonic surrounding. The score is dedicated to Gerald Warburg. The work divides the service into five parts, which are further subdivided into the separate prayers of the Shabbat service as follows:

Part I

| | |
|---|---|
| Meditation | orchestra only |
| Mah Tovu | How goodly are your tents, O Jacob |
| Borechu | Sing His Praise |
| Shema Yisroel | Hear, O Israel |
| Veohavto | Thou shalt love Him |
| Mi Chomocho | Who is like Thee? |
| Adonoy Timloch | The Lord shall reign |
| Tsur Yisroel | Rock of Israel |

Part II — Kedusha                    Sanctification

| | |
|---|---|
| Nekadesh es shimcho | Thy name is sanctified forevermore |

Part III

| | |
|---|---|
| Silent devotion | orchestra only |
| Yihyu lerozon | May the words of my mouth |
| Seu Sheorim | Lift up your heads, O ye gates |
| Taking the Scroll from the Ark | orchestra only |
| Toroh Tzivoh | Torah given by God through Moses |
| Shema Yisroel | Hear, O Israel |
| Lecho Adonoy | Thine, Lord, is greatness |

Part IV — Returning the Scroll to the Ark

| | |
|---|---|
| Hodo al Eretz | Earth sees His glory |
| Toras Adonoy | The Law of the Lord |
| Etz Chayim | The tree of life |

Part V

| | |
|---|---|
| Vaanachnu | We adore Thee |
| Adon Olom | Eternal Lord |

Benediction

| | |
|---|---|
| Yevorechecho | May the Lord bless and keep you |

**Performance Issues:** All of the Hebrew is transliterated, so that traditional sung Latin will correspond phonetically. The transliteration is in the Ashkenazy dialect. There are brief choral solos (SAATB) for members of the choir. In movement V, the cantor's part is labeled "minister" for a section which is in English only. This is fully notated, but labeled to be spoken, apparently in the manner of *Sprechstimme*. The Hebrew is probably the better choir for the text; however, using Hebrew for the Cantor and English for the choir offers a compelling compromise. Even in the singing English version, there are a few Hebrew words for which no alternative is given, nor is it needed. The choral writing is very diatonic and scalar in construction. The pitch material of the singers is well supported by the orchestra. The orchestral writing contains many chromatic flourishes for the winds and strings. These generally lie well on the respective instruments. Facile players are needed to execute the many rapid ensemble passages. There is a significant amount of rubato called for in this score. Bloch has transcribed much of the tradition of the performance style of liturgical Jewish music in his musical guidelines in the score, which will require great temporal flexibility from the orchestra and choir. If a well-versed cantor is used, the interplay between his part and the accompaniment must be very fluid, and at times improvisatory in the manner of a Mozart recitative. If a conductor is not familiar with the practices of Jewish liturgical music, appropriate research must be done, and observing some conservative, or orthodox services is crucial. It is interesting that Bloch set the cantor's role for baritone, as most of the cantorial repertoire is for tenors. **Soloist:** Cantor (baritone) - range: B-f', tessitura: d-d', this role is chant-like throughout and requires an understanding of the style of traditional Hebrew cantillation; **Choir:** medium easy; **Orchestra:** medium difficult.

**Discography:** Marko Rothmuller, Dorothy Bond, Doris Cowan; London Philharmonic Orchestra and Choir; conducted by Ernest Bloch. London: 5006 [LP].
Berkman; London Symphony Orchestra, Zemel Chorus; conducted by Geoffrey Simon. Chandos: ABR 1001 [DDD].
Robert Merrill; New York Philharmonic Orchestra; conducted by Leonard Bernstein. Sony Classical: SMK 47533 [ADD].

## Selected Bibliography

Davidson, Walter A.: "Ernest Bloch's *Avodath Hakodesh* and the New York Press," *Jewish Music*, 1 (July 1934), 12-13.

Weisser, Albert: *The Modern Renaissance of Jewish Music*. New York: Bloch Publishing, 1949.

Fulton, Alvin W.: *Ernest Bloch's Sacred Service*. Master's Thesis: Eastman School of Music, 1953.

Binder, A. W.: "Ernest Bloch's *Avodath Hakodesh*," *American Guild of Organists Quarterly* (January 1957), 7-9, 34-35.

Bloch, Ernest: "My Sacred Service," in *Ernest Bloch Creative Spirit: A Program Source Book*, Suzanne Bloch and Irene Heskes, editors New York: Jewish Music Council, 1976. Reprinted in *Source Readings in American Choral Music*, edited by David P. DeVenney. Missoula, MT: College Music Society, 1995.

Kushner, David Z.: "The 'Jewish' Works of Ernest Bloch," *Journal of Musicological Research*, volume 3, numbers 3-4 (1981), 259.

Berger, Melvin: *Guide to Choral Masterpieces: A Listener's Guide*, 70-79. New York: Anchor Books, 1993.

## Britten, Benjamin (b. Lowestoft, 22 November 1913; d. Aldeburgh, 4 December 1976).

**Life:** Britten has been this century's most successful composer of opera in English. As a youth, he studied piano with Harold Samuel and composition with Frank Bridge. He attended the Royal College of Music (1930-33), where he was disappointed by an official refusal to allow him to study in Vienna with Alban Berg. His works began to be published in 1930. In 1936 he started writing music for the G.P.O. Film Unit. In 1939, he and life-long companion, Peter Pears, followed W. H. Auden to the United States, staying until 1942. Upon his return to England, he and Pears settled in Aldeburgh where he founded the Aldeburgh Festival in 1948. He was made a Companion of Honour (1953), received the Order of Merit (1965), and was the first composer to be made a Life Peer: Lord Britten of Aldeburgh (1976). His music is characterized by an exceptional lyric gift, innovative rhythms, and a unique extension of tonality through modal exploration. He enjoyed writing music for amateurs that consistently maintains a high level of artistic integrity. Most of all, he had a distinctive sensibility for setting texts. His texts are generally concerned with themes of lost innocence and the relationship between an outsider and society. Both of these themes border upon the autobiographical.

**Principal Works:** *opera* - *Paul Bunyan* (1940-1), *Peter Grimes* (1945), *The Rape of Lucretia* (1946), *Albert Herring* (1947), *Billy Budd* (1951, revised 1960), *Gloriana* (1953), *The Turn of the Screw* (1954), *A Midsummer Night's Dream* (1960), *Owen Wingrave* (1971), *Death in Venice* (1973); **orchestra** - Sinfonietta (1932), Simple Symphony (1934), Variations on a Theme of Frank Bridge (1937), Piano Concerto (1938, revised 1945), Violin Concerto (1939, revised 1958), *Sinfonia da Requiem* (1940), *Young Person's Guide to the Orchestra* (1946), Cello Symphony (1963); **choral** - *Hymn to the Virgin* (1930, revised 1934), *A Boy was Born* (1933, revised 1955), *Ceremony of Carols* (1942), *Hymn to St. Cecilia* (1942), *Rejoice in the Lamb* (1943), *Saint Nicolas* (1948), *Spring Symphony* (1949), *Five Flower Songs* (1950), *War Requiem* (1962), *Children's Crusade* (1968); **solo vocal** - *Les Illuminations* (1939), *Serenade* (1943), *Nocturne* (1958), *Phaedra* (1975); and many folk song arrangements and chamber works.

## Selected Composer Bibliography

"Britten, Benjamin (Edward)," *Current Biography Yearbook*, volume 3 (October 1942); volume 22 (April 1961); obituary, volume 38 (February 1977); New York: H. W. Wilson Company.

Mitchell, Donald, and Hans Keller: *Benjamin Britten*. London: Rockcliff, 1952; reprinted, Westport, Connecticut: Greenwood Press, 1972.

Hansler, George E.: *Stylistic Characteristics and Trends in the Choral Music of Five Twentieth-Century Composers: A Study of the Choral Works of Benjamin Britten, Gerald Finzi, Constant Lambert, Michael Tippett, and William Walton.* New York University: Dissertation, 1957.

*Benjamin Britten: A Catalogue of His Works.* New York: Boosey and Hawkes, 1973.

Kennedy, Michael: *Britten*. London: J. M. Dent and Sons, 1981.

Palmer, Christopher, editor: *The Britten Companion*. London: Faber and Faber, 1984.

Evans, Peter: "Benjamin Britten," *The New Grove Twentieth-Century English Masters*, 239-296. New York: W.W. Norton, 1986.

Mitchell, Donald: *Britten (Edward) Benjamin, Baron Britten (1913-76) The Dictionary of National Biography 1971-80*. Oxford: Oxford University Press, 1986.

Evans, John, Philip Reed, and Paul Wilson: *A Britten Sourcebook*. Aldeburgh, Suffolk: Britten-Pears Library, 1987.

Whittall, Arnold: *The Music of Britten and Tippett: Studies in Themes and Techniques*, second edition. Cambridge: Cambridge University Press, 1990.

Carpenter, Humphrey: *Benjamin Britten: A Biography*. New York: Macmillan, 1992.

## Cantata Academica, carmen basiliense, op. 62
(1959)

**Duration:** ca. 22 minutes

**Text:** The text is in Latin and was compiled by Bernard Wyss from the charter of the University of Basle and other older orations praising the City and University of Basle.

**Performing Forces: voices:** soprano, alto, tenor, and bass soloists; SATB choir; **orchestra:** 2 flutes (flute II doubling piccolo), 2 oboes, 2 clarinets in B$^b$, 2 bassoons, 4 horns in F, 2 trumpets in C, 3 trombones, tuba, timpani, percussion (4 players - glockenspiel, xylophone, bell in C, snare drum, bass drum, tambourine, cymbals, tam-tam, triangle, "chinese block"), 2 harps (harp II is optional), celeste (optional), piano, and strings.

**First Performance:** 1 July 1960; Basle University; Agnes Giebel, Elsa Cavelti, Peter Pears, Heinz Rehfuss; Basle University Chorus, Basler Kammerorchester; conducted by Paul Sacher.

**Edition:** *Cantata Academica* is published by Boosey and Hawkes. Piano-vocal score (LCB 160), choral score (LCB 53), and miniature score (HPS 719) are available for purchase; full score and orchestral material are available for rental. The piano-vocal score was prepared by Imogen Holst.

**Autograph:** The manuscript is in the possession of the Paul Sacher Foundation in Basle, Switzerland, having been purchased prior to sale at an auction at Christie's in London on 23 March 1961.

**Notes:** This work was composed in commemoration of the 500th anniversary of Basle University. Although this work is diatonic with conspicuous triadic formations, each of the first 12 movements feature a unique tonal center and a 12-note tone row which appears in prime form and retrograde forms as a unifying structural device. The work is arranged into 13 movements, with the final movement being a return to the original pitch center, as follows:

Part I

|   | | | |
|---|---|---|---|
| I | Corale | G | tutti |
| II | Alla rovescio | F | choir |
| III | Recitativo | E$^b$ | tenor solo |
| IV | Arioso | E | bass solo |
| V | Duettino | F# | soprano and alto duet |
| VI | Recitativo | A | tenor solo |
| VII | Scherzo | D | tutti |

Part II

|   | | | |
|---|---|---|---|
| VIII | Tema Seriale con Fuga | B$^b$ | choir |
| IX | Soli et Duetto | C | bass and alto duet |
| X | Arioso con Canto Popolare | D$^b$ | soprano solo, TB choir |
| XI | Recitativo | B | tenor solo |
| XII | Canone ed Ostinato | G# | tutti |
| XIII | Corale con Canto | G | tutti |

**Performance Issues:** Britten uses multi-leveled hemioli as a source of temporal momentum. The melodic material is scalar and triadic. Harmonically, the score exploits quartal-quintal relationships. The choral writing is generally diatonic, but with frequently shifting pitch centers. The pitch material for the choir is often static, using pedals or repeated pitch figurations. The choral writing combines block chordal homophonic motion with an assortment of techniques rooted in pervasive imitation procedures from the Renaissance and Baroque eras. The instrumental writing is accessible to less experienced players. It is very accompanimental in nature, using ostinati and sustained harmonies. The most intricate accompaniments are for the recitatives, where the burden is upon the pianist, who should be a player capable of musical independence and able to interplay with the tenor soloist. **Soloists:** soprano - range: e'-b", tessitura: d"-a", this role has a generally high tessitura and frequent melodic leaps; alto - range: b-e", tessitura: d'-d", this is a sustained role with mostly scalar melodic material;  tenor - range: f#-a', tessitura: g-g', this role is rhapsodic, regularly using the entire range and requiring an expressive singer; bass - range: A-e', tessitura: g-d', this role has a lot of sustained singing in the upper range; **Choir:** medium easy; **Orchestra:** medium easy.

**Discography:** London Symphony Orchestra; conducted by George Malcolm. Oiseaux-Lyre: 60037 [LP], rereleasd as London: 452123-2LM [ADD].

### Selected Bibliography

Bradshaw, S.: "Britten's *'Cantata Academica,'*" *Tempo*, numbers 53-54 (1960), 22.
Sadie, Stanley: "Britten's *Cantata Academica*," *Musical Events*, volume 16 (January 1961).
Maack, R. and Percy M. Young: "Report from Germany," *American Choral Review*, volume 14, number 4 (1972).

## Cantata Misericordium (1963)

**Duration:** ca. 20 minutes

**Text:** The text is a Latin dramatization of the parable of the Good Samaritan from the New Testament as adapted by L. Patrick Wilkerson.

**Performing Forces: voices:** tenor and baritone soloists, SATB choir; **orchestra:** timpani, piano, harp, string quartet, and string orchestra.

**First Performance:** 1 September 1963; Geneva, Switzerland; Peter Pears, Dietrich Fischer-Dieskau; Motet de Genève (Jacques Horneffer, chorus-master), Suisse Romande Orchestra; conducted by Ernest Ansermet.

**Edition:** *Cantata misericordium* is published by Boosey and Hawkes. The piano-vocal score, full score, choral score, and miniature score are available for purchase; orchestral materials are available for rental. The piano-vocal score was prepared by Imogen Holst.

**Notes:** This work was composed for the centenary celebrations of the International Red Cross and is dedicated to Fidelity Cranbrook. The score was completed 25 May 1963. The text is dedicated to the responsibility that people have to their neighbors. The majority of it is centered around the parable of the "Good Samaritan" as a metaphor for the role the Red Cross has played in the modern era. Within the parable, the baritone soloist portrays the traveler, and the tenor, the Samaritan.

**Performance Issues:** This is a rhythmically complex, but musically accessible score, riddled with syncopations and frequent alternations between duple and triple divisions of the beat. These duple/triple division changes recur over successive beats in some sections. It is, however, a good work for less-experienced chamber orchestras if strong principal players are available. The string quartet is treated as the concertato section of a concerto grosso. The ripieno string section could be as small as two or three players per part; however, a minimum of two double basses is advisable because of divisi. A total string allocation of 4-4-3-3-2 would be quite effective. The choral writing juxtaposes sections of homophonic writing which are harmonically supported by, but often rhythmically independent of, the accompanying orchestra with highly imitative writing, suggestive of sixteenth-century models, which are directly doubled by the concertato strings. Significant quantities of the choral writing utilize paired doubling and unison singing allowing rehearsal time for the more intricate imitative passages. The harp and piano parts are within the abilities of good amateur players as are the ripieno string parts. The concertato string parts are quite difficult and contrapuntally complex. The more difficult passages for the ripieno players are in tutti passages so that the stronger solo players are able to lead them. The timpani part is written for two chromatic drums and a third drum tuned to a pedal D. The composer indicates that if the latter is unavailable, it may be substituted with a bass drum. This D does function as the harmonic root when played, so its presence is much preferred. **Soloists:** tenor - range: e-a$^{b}$', tessitura: c-g', this is a short and very lyrical role with a fairly high tessitura; baritone - range: B$^{b}$-f#', tessitura: f-d', this role suggests a lyric voice capable of very expressive singing; **Choir:** medium difficult; **Orchestra:** medium easy, with the exception of the principal strings.

**Discography:** Peter Pears, Dietrich Fischer-Dieskau; London Symphony Chorus and Orchestra; conducted by Benjamin Britten; recorded 12 December 1963. London: SXL 6175 [LP], rereleased as London: 425100-2 LH [ADD].

## Selected Bibliography

Mitchell, Donald: "A Memorable Cantata by Britten," *Daily Telegraph* (2 September 1963).
Roseberry, E.: "Britten's *Cantata misericordium* and Psalm 150," *Tempo*, numbers 66-67 (Autumn-Winter 1963).
Evans, John: "Cantata misericordium, Op. 69" *Aldeburgh Festival Program Bulletin* (1983).

## Copland, Aaron (b. New York, NY, 14 November 1900; d. Tarrytown, NY, 2 December 1990).

**Life:** Copland has remained the most internationally recognized American composer of concert music. A tireless champion for American music, he was an influential teacher, composer, and administrator. Copland began his music studies as a piano student of Victor Wittgenstein and Clarence Adler. He studied counterpoint and harmony with Rubin Goldmark (1917-20), and in 1920 entered the American Conservatory at Fontainebleau, near Paris, where he was a composition pupil of Nadia Boulanger. Upon his return to the United States, Copland began to receive a number of important performances of his works. As the depression set in, he began to incorporate more and more folk elements into his music, developing what has been perceived as a very "American" quality. This culminated in his three most celebrated ballets: *Billy the Kid*, *Rodeo*, and *Appalachian Spring*, each of which was centered around frontier American life and included numerous quotations of indigenous music of the eras represented. Copland was active as a musical ambassador to other countries, especially throughout the Americas. He was involved in the League of Composers, American Composers Alliance, Yaddo Festival, and the Koussevitsky Foundation. He led the composition department at the Berkshire Music Center at Tanglewood (1940-65) and served as chairman of the faculty there (1957-65). He lectured extensively, especially important are his talks on *Music and Imagination*, which were presented as the Eliot Norton Lectures at Harvard (1951-52). His honors are numerous including ten honorary doctorates, the Pulitzer Prize, and the Presidential Medal of Freedom. In 1982, the music department of Queens College of the City University of New York became the Aaron Copland School of Music.

**Writings:** *Music and Imagination*, Cambridge, MA: Harvard University Press, 1952. *What to Listen For in Music*, revised edition. New York: McGraw-Hill, 1957. *Copland on Music*. New York:

Harcourt, Brace, and Jovanovich, 1960; reprinted—New York: Da Capo Press, 1976. *The New Music: 1900-1960*, revised edition. New York: W.W. Norton, 1968; and many articles.

**Principal Works:** *opera - The Tenderland* (1954); *ballets - Billy the Kid* (1938), *Rodeo* (1942), *Appalachian Spring* (1945, Pulitzer Prize and N.Y. Critic's Circle Award), *Dance Panels* (1959); *orchestral* - 3 Symphonies (1928, 1932-33, 1944-46), *Music for the Theatre* (1925), Piano Concerto (1926), *Dance Symphony* (1930, N.Y. Critic's Circle Award), *El Salón Mexico* (1933-36), *Music for Radio* (1937), *An Outdoor Overture* (1938), *Quiet City* (1939), *John Henry* (1940), *Lincoln Portrait* (1942), *Music for Movies* (1942), *Fanfare for the Common Man* (1942), *Danzón Cubano* (1944), clarinet concerto (1947-48), *Preamble for a Solemn Occasion* (1949), *Music for a Great City* (1964), *Three Latin American Sketches* (1972); *chamber* - *Vitebsk* (1928), *Threnody I: Igor Stravinsky, In Memoriam* (1971), *Threnody II: Beatrice Cunningham, In Memoriam* (1973); *choral - Las agadachas* (1942), *In the Beginning* (1947); *solo vocal - Twelve Poems of Emily Dickinson* (1949-50), *Old American Songs*, sets I and II (1950 and 1952); *film scores - The City* (1939), *Of Mice and Men* (1939), *Our Town* (1940), *North Star* (1943), *The Cummington Story* (1945), *The Red Pony* (1948), *The Heiress* (1948, Academy Award), *Something Wild* (1961).

### Selected Composer Bibliography

Skowronski, JoAnn: *Aaron Copland: A Bio-Bibliography*. Westport, Connecticut: Greenwood Press, 1985.

Copland, Aaron and Vivian Perlis: *Copland: 1900 through 1942*. New York: St. Martin's Press, 1984.

_____: *Copland since 1943*. New York: St. Martin's Press, 1989.

## Canticle of Freedom (1955)

**Duration:** ca. 13 minutes

**Text:** The text is by John Barbour, in a modern English adaptation of his Middle Scots poem, *Bruce*.

**Performing Forces:** voices: SATB choir; **orchestra:** piccolo, 2 flutes, 2 oboes, English horn (optional), 2 clarinets in $B^b$, 2 bassoons, 4 horns in F, 3 trumpets in $B^b$, 3 trombones, tuba, timpani, percussion (4 players - bells, xylophone, vibraphone, chimes, snare drum, bass drum, suspended cymbal, crash cymbals, gong, tam-tam, triangle, woodblock, slapstock), harp, and strings.

**First Performance:** <u>first version</u>: 8 May 1955; Kresge Auditorium, Massachusetts Institute of Technology, Cambridge, MA; Massachusetts Institute of Technology chorus and orchestra, conducted by Klaus Liepmann.

<u>final version</u>: October 1967, Atlanta, GA; Atlanta Symphony Orchestra and Chorus, conducted by Robert Shaw.

**Edition:** *Canticle of Freedom* is published by Boosey and Hawkes. Study scores and piano-vocal scores are available for purchase; orchestral materials are available through rental.

**Notes:** *Canticle of Freedom* was commissioned by the Massachusetts Institute of Technology for the dedication of its new Kresge Auditorium.

**Performance Issues:** The orchestral writing presents some meter and tempo changes, as well as cross-metric relationships, but all of this is written to remain within the abilities of a student ensemble. With an inexperienced orchestra, the section between mm. 20 and 96 will require specific attention to establish a sense of cohesive ensemble. The first trumpet and first horn parts maintain a fairly high tessitura. There are exposed solo passages for most of the wind and brass players. There are also divisi passages in all of the string parts. The choir appears only in the second half of this work, entering in m. 221. The choral writing is very accessible; it is entirely in unison or two parts with paired doubling between sections of the choir. Most of this is homophonic, while the few contrapuntal vocal sections are in two-part canon. The accompaniment consistently supports the pitch material of the vocal parts, but does not reinforce the vocal rhythms. This score is written so that it is technically within the abilities of many college and youth orchestras, as well as large amateur and student choirs; however, it is also musically worthy of performances from the finest professional ensembles. **Choir:** medium easy; **Orchestra:** medium.

**Discography:** Crane Chorus and Crane Symphony Orchestra (SUNY at Potsdam); conducted by Aaron Copland, recorded in 1978. Vogt: CSRV 2600 [LP].

John Mark Ainsley, Stephen Varcoe; City of London Sinfonia, Britten Singers; conducted by Richard Hickox. Chandos: CHAN 8997 [DDD].

### Selected Bibliography

Durgin, Cyrus: "Illness Causes Fiedler to Miss Opening of Pops 50th Season," *Musical America*, 75 (June 1955), 20 [review of the premiere].

Cowell, Henry: "Current Chronicle: New York," *Musical Quarterly*, 42 (January 1956), 90-92.

White, Chappell: "Atlanta," *American Choral Review*, 10:3 (1968), 135 [review of the premiere of the revised version].

## Debussy, Claude (b. St.-Germaine-en-Laye, 22 August 1862; d. Paris, 25 March 1918)

**Life:** Debussy was one of the most influential composers of the twentieth century. His atmospheric use of non-traditional harmonic structures and his integration of Asian elements in his music established the style which came to be known as impressionism, a style which laid the foundations for many of the important musical developments of the twentieth century. Debussy was admitted to the Paris Conservatory in 1872, there he studied piano with Antoine-François Marmontel, solfeggio with Albert Lavignac, and harmony with Émile Durand. In 1880, he entered Ernest Guiraud's composition class at the Paris Conservatory. In 1884 his *L'Enfant prodigue* won the Grand Prix de Rome. In 1889, Debussy attended the Paris World Exhibition where he was exposed to the music of Asia, including a Javanese gamelan. The non-western scales and unusual timbres of this music had a profound impact upon his developing compositional style. These new sonorities and the exoticism of the impressionist poets of his day converged in his songs and instrumental music throughout the following decade, reaching a critical apex with the opera *Pelléas et Mélisande* which was premiered 30 April 1902 and secured Debussy's position in the first rank of French composers. In later symphonic works he experimented with the organic development of thematic material, as in *La Mer* (1905), and the integration of Spanish folk elements into his music, as in *Images* (1906-1912). It is often noted that Debussy did not accept the term impressionism when applied to his music, but the titles of his works and their musical content are so evocative of the spirit of the poets and painters of this genre, that it is impossible to avoid this categorization. Although celebrated for his uses of parallelisms and exotic scales, Debussy's most important contribution to the development of music in the next generation was his use of musical sonorities purely as aesthetic sound combinations "free from the bonds academic tyranny."

**Writings:** Among the collections of Debussy's writings for the French press which have been published in English translations are: *Debussy on Music: The Critical Writings of the Great French Composer Claude Debussy*. New York, 1977.

**Principal Works:** *opera* - *Pelléas et Mélisande* (1893-1902); *orchestral* - *Prélude à l'après-midi d'un faune* (1892-94), *Nocturnes* (1892-99), *Danse sacréee et Danse profane* for harp and strings (1903), *La Mer* (1903-05), *Images* (1906-12), *Jeux* (1912); *choral* - *l'Enfant prodigue* (1884), *La Damoiselle élue* (1887-89), *Le Martyre de Saint-Sébastien* (1911); *songs* - *Fête galante I*, *Fête galante II*, *Cinq poèmes de Baudelaire*, *Ariettes oubliées*, *Trois chansons de Bilitis*; *piano* - *Deux arabesques* (1880), *Suite bergamasque* (1890-1905), *Estampes* (1903), *Images* I (1905), *Children's Corner* (1906-08), *Images* II (1907-08), *Douze préludes*, book I (1910), *Douze préludes*, book II (1910-13), *Douze études*, books I and II (1915).

## Selected Composer Bibliography

Vallas, Léon: *Claude Debussy et son temps*. Paris: Alcan, 1932; revised as Paris: Albin Michel, 1958. Published in English translation by Maire and Grace O'Brien as *Claude Debussy: His Life and Works*. London: Oxford University Press, 1933; reprinted as New York: Dover, 1973.

Thompson, Oscar: *Debussy: Man and Artist*. New York: Dodd and Mead, 1937.

Dietschy, Marcel: *La Passion de Claude Debussy*. Neuchâtel, Switzerland: Éditions de la Baconnière, 1962.

Lockspeiser, Edward: *Debussy: His Life and Mind*, 2 volumes. London: Cassell, 1962 and 1965; reprinted as Cambridge: Cambridge University Press, 1978.

Lesure, François: *Catalogue de l'œuvre de Claude Debussy*. Geneva: Éditions Minkoff, 1977.

_____: *Debussy*, fifth edition, revised with preface by R. Langham Smith. London: J. M. Dent and Sons, 1980.

Nichols, Roger, with work list by Robert Orledge: "Claude Debussy," in *The New Grove Twentieth-Century French Masters*. New York: W. W. Norton, 1986.
Parks, Richard S.: *The Music of Claude Debussy*. New Haven, Connecticut: Yale University Press, 1989.
Briscoe, James R.: *Claude Debussy: A Guide to Research*. New York: Garland Press, 1990.

**Nocturnes** (1892-99)

**Duration:** ca. 25 minutes

**Text:** none

**Performing Forces: voices:** SSA choir; **orchestra:** movement I: 2 flutes, 2 oboes, English horn, 2 clarinets in $B^b$, 3 bassoons, 4 horns in F, timpani, harp, and strings.

movement II: 3 flutes, oboe, English horn, 2 clarinets in $B^b$, 3 bassoons, 4 horns in F, 3 trumpets in F, 3 trombones, tuba, timpani, percussion (2 players - snare drum, cymbals), 2 harps, and strings.

movement III: 3 flutes, 2 oboes, English horn, 2 clarinets in A, 3 bassoons, 4 horns in F, 3 trumpets in F, 2 harps, and strings.

**First Performance:** movements I and II only: 9 December 1900; Paris; Concerts Lamoureux; conducted by Camille Chevillard.

first complete performance: 27 October 1901; Paris; Concerts Lamoureux; conducted by Camille Chevillard.

first staged performance: [movements I and III only] 5 May 1913; théâtre des Champs-Élysées, Paris; Loïe Full and F. Ochsé, directors; F. Ochsé and Émile Bertin, scenery; conducted by Desiré-Émile Inghelbrecht.

**Edition:** *Nocturnes* was first published by Fromont in 1900 and 1909. An edition was released from Jobert in 1930 and 1964, which reflect changes made to the Fromont edition by the composer. The original version of the score has been published as a reprint from

Peters (1977/78), Dover (1983, in *Three Great Orchestral Works*), Boosey and Hawkes, International, and Kalmus. Orchestral materials may be purchased or rented from Boosey and Hawkes or Kalmus. Parts should be compared to the full score as the sets do not necessarily correspond completely with either the Fromont or Jobert editions. Orchestral materials are also available from Jobert which correspond thoroughly with their revised edition of 1964.

**Autograph:** The principal manuscript is in the collection of Jobert-Georges. A manuscript draft score is in the Library of Congress, and corrected proofs are in the Monteux collection in Hancock, Maine. The Bibliothèque Nationale has a microfilm copy of the corrected Fromont edition which is in the possession of F. Lang in Royaumont, France.

**Notes:** The score is dedicated to Georges Hartmann. The work is in three movements as follows:

| | | | |
|---|---|---|---|
| I | Nuages | Clouds | orchestra only |
| II | Fêtes | Festivals | orchestra only |
| III | Sirènes | Sirens (mythology) | orchestra and choir |

The performance history of this work and the independent spirit of its movements allows for the performance of single movements from the whole.

**Performance Issues:** The third movement uses a women's choir as an orchestral color to represent the sirens from classical mythology. There are no indications as to what vowels are to be used, therefore this must be decided in rehearsal preparation. Since the score indicates varied numbers of singers throughout, it seems logical to use different vowels for various musical contexts. A minimum of 8 singers per part is needed; however, the score's indication of 8 first sopranos, 8 second sopranos, and 8 mezzo-sopranos, seems to indicate these as reduced numbers from a larger whole. Each of the 3 sections of the choir has 2 to 4-part divisi within it. There are divisi within each string section. In movement I there are solo passages for violin I, viola, and cello. The strings have a good amount of soft, controlled playing in the first movement including some important harmonics. The wind parts are practical throughout, remaining within the abilities of better amateur players. Movement two has quite a few octave doublings in the woodwinds that could prove challenging to good intonation.

The woodwinds also have significant passagework in that movement. The two harp parts can be executed by a single player, but the sonority of two instruments should be sought if at all possible. The brass parts in movement III require control of soft playing. This is a work of varied colors and playing styles which is well within the ability of better college and community orchestras. The vocal parts are best suited to the timbre of an adult women's choir. **Choir:** medium easy, **Orchestra:** medium difficult

**Selected Discography:** Orchestre de la Suisse Romande; conducted by Ernest Ansermet, recorded in 1957. London: LL 530 [LP], rereleased as London: 433712-2 [ADD].

Royal Concertgebouw Orchestra, Women's voices of the Collegium Musicum Amstelodamense (Toon Vranken, chorus-master); conducted by Eduard van Beinum, recorded in 1958. Philips: 411 156-4 [LP].

Orchestre Nationale de France; conducted by Désirée-Émile Inghelbrecht, recorded live on 17 December 1963. Disques Montaigne: TCE 8710 [ADD].

Detroit Symphony Orchestra and Chorus; conducted by Paul Paray; Mercury Living Presence: 434306 [ADD].

Leopold Stokowski and "His Orchestra." Victor: LM 1154 [LP].

London Symphony Orchestra, BBC Chorus; conducted by Leopold Stokowski. Seraphim: 4XG-60422 [LP].

Choeurs de l'O.R.T.F and Orchestre National de l'O.R.T.F.; conducted by Jean Martinon, recorded during 1973 in the Salle Wagram in Paris. EMI: CDM 7 69587 2 [ADD].

Philadelphia Orchestra, Temple University Women's Choir; conducted by Eugene Ormandy. CBS: MGT-30950 [ADD].

Philharmonic Orchestra of Strasbourg, Chorus of the Opéra du Rhin; conducted by Alain Lombard. Musical Heritage Society: 6458A [cassette].

Boston Symphony; conducted by Claudio Abbado. Deutsche Grammophon: 415370 [ADD].

Luxembourg Radio Orchestra; conducted by Louis de Froment. Vox Box: CDX 5003 [ADD].

London Symphony Orchestra; conducted by André Previn. Angel: CDD-64056 [DDD].

Royal Concertgebouw Orchestra; conducted by Eliahu Inbal. Philips: 426635-2 [DDD].

London Symphony Orchestra; conducted by Rafael Frühbeck de Burgos. IMP Classics: PCD 915 [DDD].

36 A Conductor's Guide to Choral-Orchestral Works, volume II

Philharmonia Orchestra, Ambrosian Choir; conducted by Michael
    Tilson Thomas. CBS: MDK-44645 [DDD].
Cleveland Orchestra and Women's Chorus; conducted by Vladimir
    Ashkenazy. London: 430732-2 [DDD].
Tanglewood Chorus, Boston Symphony Orchestra; conducted by Colin
    Davis. Philips: 411433-2 PH [DDD].
Montréal Symphony Orchestra and Chorus; conducted by Charles
    Dutoit. London: 425502-2 [DDD].
Royal Concertgebouw Orchestra, Women's voices of the Collegium
    Musicum Amstelodamense; conducted by Bernard Haitink. Philips:
    400023-2 [DDD].
Philharmonia Orchestra and Women's Chorus; conducted by Geoffrey
    Simon, recorded in January 1990. Cala: CACD 1002 [DDD].
Women of the Los Angeles Master Chorale; Los Angeles
    Philharmonic; conducted by Esa-Pekka Salonen. Sony Classical:
    SK 58 952 [DDD].
Orchestre de la Suisse Romande; conducted by Armin Jordan. Erato:
    2292-45605-2 [DDD].
BRT Orchestra; conducted by Alexander Rahbari, recorded in November
    1989. Naxos: 8.550262 [DDD].
Ulster Orchestra, Renaissance Singers and Grosvenor High School
    Choir; conducted by Yan Pascal Tortelier. Chandos: CHAN 8914
    [DDD].
Orchestre du Paris; conducted by Daniel Barenboim. Deutsche
    Grammophon: 4350692 [DDD].

Nuages and Fêtes only:

NBC Symphony Orchestra; conducted by Arturo Toscanini, recorded in
    1952. RCA: (Toscanini Collection, volume 37) 60265-2-RG
    [ADD].
Philadelphia Orchestra; conducted by Eugene Ormandy. Columbia: ML
    4020 [LP].
New York Philharmonic Orchestra; conducted by Guido Cantelli,
    recorded live in Carnegie Hall on 8 May 1955. AS Disc: AS 548
    [ADD mono].
Boston Symphony Orchestra; conducted by Charles Munch. RCA:
    6719-2-RG [ADD].

### Selected Bibliography

Vallas, Léon: *Claude Debussy et son temps*, 204-16. Paris: Alcan,
    1932; revised as Paris: Albin Michel, 1958.

Michel, André: *La Sirène dans l'elément musical.* Paris: Éditions de la Diaspora française, 1970.

Langham Smith, Richard: "Debussy and the Art of the Cinema," *Music and Letters*, volume 54, number 1 (January 1973), 61-70.

Schnebel, Dieter: "Sirènes oder der Versuch einer sinnlichen Musik," *Musik-Konzepte*, volume 1, number 2, Claude Debussy (December 1977), part III.

Fischer, Kurt von: "Claude Debussy und das Klima des Art nouveau: Bemerkungen zur Aesthetik Debusseys und J. McNeil Whistlers," *Art Nouveau, Jugendstil und Musik*, 31-46. Zurich: Atlantis, 1980.

Lang-Becker, Elke: *Claude Debussy: "Nocturnes."* Munich: Fink, 1982.

Stegemann, Michael: "Ausdruck und Eindruck: Claude Debussys missverstandene Ästhetik," *Neue Zeitschrift für Musik*, volume 147, numbers 10 and 11 (October 1986), 8-12; and (November 1986), 13-18.

# Diamond, David Leo (b. Rochester, NY, 9 July 1915).

**Life:** Diamond studied composition at the Cleveland Institute and the Eastman School with Bernard Rogers. He then attended the Dalcroze School in New York (1934-6) where he studied with Roger Sessions and Paul Boepple. This was followed by study in Paris with Nadia Boulanger. In Paris, he made contacts with André Gide, Maurice Ravel, Albert Roussel, and Igor Stravinsky. Diamond served as Fulbright professor at the University of Rome in 1951. Two years later he moved to Florence where he lived until 1965. He has taught at the Harvard Seminar in American Studies, SUNY Buffalo (1961 and 1963), the Manhattan School (1967-8), and since 1973, at the Juilliard School. Of Diamond's music, Virgil Thomson writes: "His string works are idiomatic, his songs melodious, his symphonies romantically inspired. The musical style in general is harmonious, the continuity relaxed. For all its seeming emotional self-indulgence, this is music of artistic integrity and real thought."[2] Since the mid-1980s, there has been a newly invigorated interest in Diamond's music with a number of premieres and a broadening range of performances, which have been led by a recording project undertaken by Gerard Schwartz and the Seattle Symphony. In response to this interest, the composer has maintained a high level of productivity in his eighth and ninth decades.

---

2    Virgil Thomson: *American Music Since 1910*, 138-39. New York: Holt, Rinehart, and Winston, 1971.

**Awards:** National Institute of Arts and Letters, New York Critics' Circle Award for *Rounds* (1944), three Guggenheim Fellowships (1938, 1942, and 1958), William Schuman Award (1985) for lifetime achievement as a composer.

**Principal Works:** 12 Symphonies (1940-1, 1942, 1945, 1945, 1951, 1951-4, 1959, 1960, 1985, 1987, 1992, and 1995), 3 Violin Concertos (1936, 1947, and 1967-8), *Hommage à Satie* (1934), *Elegy in Memory of Maurice Ravel* (1938), *The Enormous Room* (1948), *The World of Paul Klee* (1957), *To Music* (1967), *A Secular Cantata* (1976), many chamber works and songs.

### Selected Composer Bibliography

"Diamond, David," *Current Biography Yearbook*, edited by Charles Moritz (1966); New York: H. W. Wilson Company.

Peyser, Joan: "A Composer who Defies Categorization," *New York Times* (7 July 1985), section N, 16 and 18.

Kimberling, Victoria: *David Diamond: A Bio-Bibliography*. Metuchen, New Jersey: Scarecrow Press, 1987.

Diamond, David: *The Midnight Sleep* (unpublished autobiography).

## This Sacred Ground (1963)

**Duration:** ca. 16 minutes

**Text:** The text is the "Gettysburg Address" of Abraham Lincoln.

**Performing Forces: voices:** baritone soloist; children's choir, mixed choir; **orchestra:** 3 flutes, 3 oboes, 3 clarinets in B$^b$, 3 bassoons, 4 horns in F, 3 trumpets in C, 3 trombones, tuba, timpani, percussion (4 players - chimes, xylophone, snare drum, tom-toms, bass drum, cymbals, tam-tam, whip), harp, and strings.

**First Performance:** 17 November 1963; Buffalo, NY; the Buffalo Philharmonic Orchestra; conducted by Joseph Krips.

**Edition:** *This Sacred Ground* is published by Peer International. The piano-vocal score (61431-122) is available for purchase, all other materials are available for rental.

**Notes:** The score was suggested to the composer by Joseph Krips, to whom it is dedicated. The work was commissioned by the *Buffalo*

*Evening News* and Station WBEN, Inc. to commemorate the centennial of Lincoln's Gettysburg Address (19 November 1863).

**Performance Issues:** The vocal rhythms for the soloist and choir are very logogenic. The choral writing is generally diatonic and scalar. Much of the choral writing is in unison, it is otherwise homophonic with block-chord writing. All of the vocal material is clearly supported by the orchestra. The individual instrumental parts are idiomatic and the scoring is highly effective, exhibiting the characteristic broadness of tonal American works from the middle of the century. There are some surprising chromatic turns which help to perpetuate interest throughout the work. The instrumental parts are highly rhythmic. The principal brass players have some exposed high passages and must be capable of crisp rhythmic articulation throughout the score. The percussion parts can probably be executed by 3 players, but 4 are advisable because of some quick instrument changes. The scoring allows the use of a medium-sized choir, but the nature of the text and the spirit of the score would be best served by a large choir. This is an excellent work for large community or festival choruses and one which provides a useful programming alternative to orchestras. The memorial nature of Lincoln's text and Diamond's triumphant setting of it, make this work suitable for commemorative and patriotic concerts. Musically, this score could be used on classical or pops programs. **Soloist:** baritone - range: A-g#', tessitura: e-e', this is a sustained and declamatory role with exposed passages at the extremes of the range. This solo is more vocally demanding than it first appears. **Choir:** medium easy, **Orchestra:** medium difficult.

**Discography:** Erich Parch; Seattle Girls' Choir, Northwest Boychoir, Seattle Symphony and Chorus; Richard Sparks, director of choirs, conducted by Gerard Schwarz. Recorded: 13 February 1994. Delos: DE 3141 [DDD].

## Selected Bibliography

review of the premiere:
Dwyer, John: in *Buffalo Evening News* (18 November 1963).
UPI review: in *Buffalo Evening News* (18 November 1963).
Cuddihy, Ed: story regarding the premiere in *Buffalo Evening News* (18 November 1963).

other sources
"Composers," *Musical America*, volume 83 (December 1963), 286.

## Duruflé, Maurice (b. Louviers, France, 11 January 1902; d. Paris, 16 June 1986)

**Life:** Duruflé's early musical education was as a student in the choir school of the Rouen Cathedral. At the age of 17 he moved to Paris where he studied organ with Charles Tournemire, Alexandre Guilmant, and Louis Vierne. In 1920, Duruflé entered the Paris Conservatory, there he studied composition with Paul Dukas, counterpoint with Georges Caussade, organ with Eugène Gigout, and harmony with Jean Gallon. From 1919 to 1929, he was assistant organist at St. Clothide in Paris. Duruflé was appointed organist at St. Etienne-du-Mont in Paris in 1930, a post he held until his death. He was succeeded at St. Etienne-du-Mont by his widow, Marie-Madeleine Duruflé-Chevalier. From 1943 to 1969, Duruflé served on the faculty of the Paris Conservatory. His remarkably short list of completed works is a body of highly refined compositions which combine melodic elements of traditional Roman Catholic chant with the harmonic palette of the French impressionists to create a highly individual repertoire.

**Principal Works:** *orchestral* - *Trois Danses*, op. 6 (1936), *Andante et scherzo* (1951); *choral* - Requiem, op. 9 (1947), *Quatre Motets sur des Thèmes Grégoriens*, op. 10 (1960), Mass "Cum jubilo," op. 11 (1967); *organ* - *Scherzo*, op. 2 (1924), *Prélude, adagio et choral varié sur le thème du "Veni Creator,"* op. 5 (1933), *Prélude and Fugue sur le Nom d'Alain*, op. 7 (1942), Fugue, op. 12 (1962), *Prélude sur l'Introit*, op. 13 (1961).

### Selected Composer Bibliography

Beechey, G. : "The Music of Maurice Duruflé," *The Music Review*, volume 32 (1971), 146.
Reynolds, Jeffrey Warren: *The Choral Music of Maurice Duruflé*. University of Illinois at Urbana-Champaign: DMA Thesis, 1990.

## Requiem, op. 9 (1947)

**Duration:** ca. 40 minutes

**Text:** The text is from the Roman Catholic Mass for the Dead.

**Performing Forces: voices:** mezzo-soprano and baritone soloists; SATB choir; **orchestra:** 3 flutes (flutes II and III doubling piccolo), 2 oboes (oboe II doubling as English horn II), English horn, 2 clarinets in $B^b$, bass clarinet in $B^b$, 2 bassoons, 4 horns in F, 3 trumpets in C, 3 trombones, tuba, timpani, percussion (3 players - bass drum, cymbals, tam-tam), celeste, harp, organ, and strings.

**First Performance:** 1947; Paris; conducted by Roger Désmorière.

**Edition:** *Requiem* is published by Durand. An organ-vocal score and study score are available for purchase. The full score of the reduced orchestration is also available for purchase. All other materials are available for rental.

**Notes:** At the time that the publisher Durand approached Duruflé to commission the *Requiem*, he was working on a suite for organ which was based upon the themes of the Gregorian setting of the *Mass for the Dead*. Duruflé used the material he had completed towards this suite as the foundation of the *Requiem*, which he dedicated to the memory of his father. This work, which appears to owe much of its organization to the model of Gabriel Fauré's setting of this service, is arranged in nine movements as follows:

| | | |
|---|---|---|
| I | Introit | choir |
| II | Kyrie | choir |
| III | Domine Jesu Christe | baritone solo and choir |
| IV | Sanctus | choir |
| V | Pie Jesu | mezzo-soprano solo |
| VI | Agnus Dei | choir |
| VII | Lux æterna | choir |
| VIII | Libera me | baritone solo and choir |
| IX | In Paradisum | choir |

**Performance Issues:** The vocal material of this work is at times copied from, and otherwise based upon, the traditional Roman chant settings of these texts. They are therefore vocally quite natural and easily learned by less experienced choirs. The vocal challenges lie in the metric organization of this material into a modern symphonic fabric. The composer has sanctioned the use of the baritones and second tenors of the choir as a replacement for the baritone soloist. He has also indicated that the choral soprano passages in movements III, VIII, and IX may be sung by a children's choir if desired. In movement VI there is an indication of divided soprano and alto parts suggesting an antiphonal treatment. If the size of the choir, or the performance space do not allow these sections to be physically divided, all of the material can be sung by a single section. The instrumentation listed above is correct; however, it is not in the front matter of the score. The most important discrepancy is that the Kyrie has one oboe part and two English horn parts which are very exposed and quite necessary and cannot be played on oboe. There are a number of exposed solo passages for the winds. The bassoon solo in movement VII is especially difficult because of the high tessitura of the part. There is rapid passagework for all of the upper winds. The string parts are generally idiomatic with some intricate scalar figures. The viola section is featured prominently throughout the entire work. An important issue with this work is balance. The chantlike quality of vocal writing benefits from a smaller choir, which must be balanced against a large instrumental contingent. It is advisable to consider dividing the choir in two and placing these halves near the front corners of the stage, even with the strings, and in front of the brass. **Soloists:** mezzo-soprano - range: b$^{\flat}$-f#", tessitura: c'-c", this is a tender and "maternal" solo, requiring a rich and lyrical voice; baritone - range: e-f', tessitura: g-d', this role is sustained and lyric with a cantorial quality; **Choir:** medium difficult; **Orchestra:** difficult (chamber orchestra version: medium difficult).

**Discography:** Kiri Te Kanawa, Siegmund Nimsgern; New Philharmonia Orchestra, Ambrosian Singers and Desborough School Choir (John McCarthy, chorus-master); conducted by Andrew Davis. Columbia: M34547 [Quadrophonic LP].

Judith Blegen, James Morris; Atlanta Symphony Orchestra and Chorus; conducted by Robert Shaw. Telarc: CD-80135 [DDD].

Choir of New College, Oxford; conducted by Edward Higginbotham. CRD: 3466 [DDD].

Ann Murray, Thomas Allen; English Chamber Orchestra, Corydon Singers; conducted by Matthew Best. Hyperion: CDA-66191 [DDD]. third version.

M. Palberg, B. Kämpf; Neuwieder Chamber Orchestra; conducted by B. Kämpf. Motette: CD 50241 [DDD].

Choir and Orchestra of Cologne; conducted by Michel Corboz. Erato: CD45230 [DDD].

## Selected   Bibliography

Rostand, C.: "Un maître normand et son chef d'oeuvre: Maurice Duruflé et son Requiem," *Etudes normandes*, no. 26 (1958).

Robertson, Alec: *Requiem: Music of Mourning and Consolation*, 122-126. New York: Frederick A. Praeger, 1967.

Jarjisian, Peter G.: *The Influence of Gregorian Chant on Maurice Duruflé's Requiem. Op. 9*. University of Wisconsin: Doctor of Musical Arts dissertation, 1991.

Eaton, Robert Powell: *Maurice Duruflé's Requiem. Op. 9: An Analysis for Performance*. University of Hartford: Doctor of Musical Arts dissertation, 1991.

Berger, Melvin: *Guide to Choral Masterpieces: A Listener's Guide*, 108-110. New York: Anchor Books, 1993.

# Finzi, Gerald (b. London, 14 July 1901; d. Oxford, 27 September 1956)

**Life:** Finzi was the son of a ship broker. His early composition study was with Ernest Farrar (1914-16) and Edward Bairstow (1917-22). Upon Holst's advice, Finzi took a course in counterpoint in 1925 under R. O. Morris. This led him to settle in London and to establish himself within a musical circle which included Howard Ferguson, Gustav Holst, Robin Milford, Edmund Rubbra, and Ralph Vaughan Williams. From 1930-33, Finzi taught composition at the Royal Academy of Music. In 1933, he married the artist Joyce Black, and in 1937 the two built a house in the English countryside where Finzi composed and cultivated an orchard of rare trees. He also amassed a fine library including what was probably the finest private collection of English music from the middle of the eighteenth century. In 1939 he established the Newbury String Players which he maintained until his death. With that group he read the works of many aspiring composers and revived numerous eighteenth-century compositions to which he dedicated much editorial time. He gave the 1955 Crees lectures at the Royal College of Music in which he analyzed the history and æsthetics of English song. He died of leukemia, from which he had privately suffered for five years. He continued to make public appearances between medical treatments. His best known works are the songs which are logogenically conceived. He was an authority on English literature with a particular predilection for the works of Thomas Hardy. His music tends to be formally small, tuneful, and meticulously crafted.[3]

**Principal Works:** *orchestral* - *Severn Rhapsody*, op. 3 (1923), *Romance*, op. 11 (1928), Clarinet Concert, op. 31 (1948-9), Grand Fantasia and Toccata, op. 38 (1953), Cello Concerto, op. 40 (1951-5); *choral* - Seven Partsongs, op. 17 (1934-7), *For St. Cecilia*, op. 30 (1947), Magnificat, op. 36 (1956), *In terra pax* (1954); *solo voice with orchestra* - *Dies natalis*, op. 8 (1926-39), *Farewell to Arms*, op. 9 (1940), *Let us garlands bring*, op. 18 (1929-42); *song cycles with piano* - *A Young Man's Exhortation*, op. 14 (1926-9), *Earth and Air and Rain*, op. 15 (1929-32), *Before and After Summer*, op. 16 (1938-49), *Let Us Garlands Bring*, op. 18 (1929-42); *Till Earth Outwears*, op. 19 (1929-56), *I Said to Love* (1928-56).

## Selected Composer Bibliography

Rubbra, Edmund: "Gerald Finzi," *The Monthly Musical Record*, volume 59 (1929), 14.

Ferguson, Howard: "Gerald Finzi (1901-56)," *Music and Letters*, volume 38 (1957), 130.

Hansler, George E.: *Stylistic Characteristics and Trends in the Choral Music of Five Twentieth-Century Composers: A Study of the Choral Works of Benjamin Britten, Gerald Finzi, Constant Lambert, Michael Tippett, and William Walton.* New York University: Dissertation, 1957.

McVeagh, Diane: "Gerald Finzi," *Records and Recording*, volume 23, number 4 (1980), 30.

_____: "Finzi, Gerald," in *The New Grove Dictionary of Music and Musicians*, ed. Stanley Sadie.  20 volumes.  London: Macmillan, 1980, volume 6, 594-97.

McCoy, Jerry Michael: *The Choral Music of Gerald Finzi: A Study of Text/Musical Relationships.* University of Texas at Austin: Dissertation, 1982.

Dressler, John C.: *Gerald Finzi: A Bio-Bibliography.* Westport, Connecticut: Greenwood Press, 1997.

---

3    Diana McVeagh: "Finzi, Gerald," in *The New Grove Dictionary of Music and Musicians*, edited by Stanley Sadie, volume 6, 594-97. 20 volumes.  London: Macmillan, 1980.

# Intimations of Immortality, op. 29 (1936-8, 1949-50)

**Duration:** ca. 43 minutes

**Text:** The text, by William Wordsworth, is in English.

**Performing Forces: voices:** tenor soloist; SATB choir; **orchestra:** 3 flutes (flute II doubling piccolo, flute III optional), 2 oboes, English horn (optional), 2 clarinets in B$^b$, bass clarinet in B$^b$ (optional), 2 bassoons, contrabassoon (optional), 4 horns, 3 trumpets in C, 3 trombones, tuba, timpani, percussion (2 players - xylophone, snare drum, tenor drum, bass drum, tambourine, temple blocks, castanets, triangle), harp, and strings.

**First Performance:** 1950; Three Choirs Festival, Gloucester Cathedral, Gloucester, England; conducted by Herbert Sumsion.

**Edition:** *Intimations of Immortality* is published and distributed by Boosey and Hawkes. The piano-vocal score is for sale; the full score and orchestral materials are available for rental.

**Autograph:** The manuscript is in the possession of the Finzi Trust.

**Notes:** There was an earlier setting of this text by Arthur Somervell which was premiered at the 1907 Leeds Festival, but has fallen into obscurity. Finzi chose to eliminate the seventh and eighth stanzas of Wordsworth's text in his setting which is divided into nine movements as follows:

I   There was a time when meadow, grove, and stream
II   The rainbow comes and goes
III   Now, while the birds thus sing a joyous song
IV   Te blessèd Creatures, I have heard the call
V   Our birth is but a sleep and a forgetting
VI   Earth fills her lap with pleasures of her own
VII   O joy! that in our emberes
VIII   Then sing, ye Birds, sing, sing a joyous song!
IX   And O, ye Fountains, Meadows, Hills, and Groves

In movement IV, there is a shift of pitch center down from B minor to B$^b$ minor, which marks a point at which the poet abandoned the writing of the text for two years, and returned with a more retiscent spirit.

**Performance Issues:** This is a challenging and expressive score by a remarkable composer. There are divisi throughout the choral and the string sections. The scoring is generally motivated by counterpoint more than color, but there are a great number of intricately conceived entrances and intertwinings of melodic material. There is a certain chamber-music quality throughout this symphonically cast score. The choral parts are harmonically supported by the accompaniment, but there is little melodic reinforcement. Elements of pervasive imitation abound within the choral parts. A notable difficulty for the singers is that the voicing of harmonies for the orchestra often differs from that of the choir, so that the pitches for the bass singers are often different chord tones from those present in the lower strings. These differences are often at the interval of a second and may pose significant difficulty if not well reinforced during preparatory meetings of the choir. There is a brief unaccompanied passage which is homophonic. The orchestral parts are conceived felicitously for the respective instruments; however, there are exposed, virtuosic passages in every part. The string parts are particularly idiomatic and very practical bowings have been provided by the composer for the entire work. Much of the score is rooted in a pan-modal vocabulary utilizing many non-functioning seventh and ninth chords. The score is rhythmically complex with great dynamic breadth and a need for flexibility throughout the ensemble in executing musical subtleties. **Soloist:** tenor - range: c-b'; tessitura: a-f'; This sizeable role requires a lyric and powerful voice. The vocal writing for the soloist resembles intimate English art song, except that it must be rendered with a symphonic accompaniment. **Choir:** difficult; **Orchestra:** difficult.

**Discography:** Philip Langrige; Liverpool Philharmonic Choir (Ian Tracey, chorus-master), Royal Liverpool Philharmonic Orchestra; conducted by Richard Hickox, recorded 27 and 28 November 1988. EMI: CDM 7 64720 2 [DDD].

### Selected Bibliography

McCoy, Jerry Michael: *The Choral Music of Gerald Finzi: A Study of Text/Musical Relationships*. University of Texas at Austin: Dissertation, 1982.

Banfield, Stephen: notes for recording booklet of *Intimations of Immortality*. London: EMI, 1989.

**Henze, Hans Werner** (b. 1 July 1926, Gütersloh in Westfalia, Germany)

**Life:** Henze studied with Wolfgang Fortner who introduced him to a variety of technical procedures which were successively integrated into his compositional palette. He scored successes with a number of early operas. With time, the subjects of his works began to reflect his own Marxist ideologies. Concurrently, his music evidenced a gradual change of style involving monumental challenges to performers and listeners alike. From 1942 to 1944, he attended the Braunschweig Musikschule, and then was conscripted into the German army, serving one year on the Russian front. In 1946, he entered the Heidelberg Kirchenmusikalisches Institute and began his private studies with Fortner. He had additional studies in serialism with René Liebowitz in Darmstadt. In the 1950s he moved to Italy where he became a member of the Communist Party. His radical political beliefs have had a significant impact upon his artistic activities and upon the subjects of his compositions. In 1986 he was made International Chair of Compositional Studies at the University of London. A very prolific composer, Henze has combined virtually all of the techniques used in the twentieth century into his works with remarkably convincing results. His works often require non-traditional procedures in their performance, but they remain possible and have maintained an audience throughout the world with seeming disregard to their propogandistic qualities.

**Writings:** *Music and Politics: Collected Writings 1953-81*. Ithaca, NY: Cornell University Press, 1982.

**Principal Works:** *opera - Das Wundertheater* (1948), *Boulevard Solitude* (1951), *König Hirsch* (1952-55), *Elegy for Young Lovers* (1959-61), *The Brassaids* (1965), *The English Cat* (1980-83), *Ödipus der Tyrann oder Der Vater vertreibt seinem Sohn und Schikt die Tochter in die Küche* (1983), *Des verratene Meer* (1990); *radio opera - Ein Landzart* (1951), *Das Ende einer Welt* (1953); *ballet - Ballet Variations* (1949), *Jack Pudding* (1949), *Rosa Silber* (1950), *Labyrinth* (1951), *Der Idiot* (1952), *Maratona* (1956), *Ondine* (1956-57), *We Come to the River* (1974-76), *Orpheus* (1978); *orchestral* - seven Symphonies (1948, 1949, 1951, 1955, 1962, 1969, 1983-84), 2 Piano Concertos (1950, 1967), Violin Concerto (1948), Symphonic Variations (1950), *Ode to the West Wind* for cello and orchestra (1954), *Antifone* (1960), *Doppio Concerto* for oboe, harp and strings (1966), Doublebass Concerto (1967), *Heliogabalus Imperator* (1972), *Cinque piccoli* *concerti* (1980-82), *Sieben Liebeslieder* for cello and orchestra (1984-85), *Allegro brillante* (1989); chamber - 5 String Quartets (1947, 1952, 1976, 1977, 1977), Woodwind Quintet (1952), *Amicizia* for clarinet, cello, and percussion (1976), *Canzona* for seven instruments (1982), *Serenade* for violin (1986); **choral** - 5 Madrigals (1947), *Chorus of the Captured Trojans* (1948), *Cantata della Fiaba Estrema* (1963), Choral Fantasy (1964); *solo vocal* - *Whispers from Heavenly Death* (1948), 5 Neapolitan Songs for baritone and orchestra (1956), *Nocturnes and Arias* (1957), *Being Beauteous* (1964), *El Cimarrón* (1970), *Voices* (1974), *The King of Harlem* (1980).

### Selected Composer Bibliography

Heyworth, Peter: "I can Imagine a Future...: Conversations with Hans Werner Henze," *The Observer* (23 August 1970).

Henderson, R.: "Hans Werner Henze," *The Musical Times*, volume 118 (1976), 566.

Henze, Hans Werner: *Music and Politics: Collected Writings 1953-81.* Ithaca, NY: Cornell University Press, 1982.

Rickards, Guy: *Hindemith, Hartmann, and Henze.* London: Phaidon, 1995.

*Hans Werner Henze: ein Werkverzeichnis 1946-1996.* Mainz: Schott, 1996.

## Novæ de Infinito Laudes (1962)

**Duration:** ca. 50 minutes

**Text:** The text is taken from the Italian writings of Giordano Bruno. The score includes literal translations of the Latin text into English.

**Performing Forces: voices:** soprano, alto, tenor and bass soloists; SATB choir; **orchestra:** 2 flutes (both doubling piccolo), 2 English horns, 2 bassoons, 2 trumpets in D, 2 trumpets in C, 2 bass trumpets in C, 4 trombones, 2 tubas, timpani, 2 lutes (amplified), 2 pianos, 4 cellos, 4 doublebasses.

Members of the choral bass section are to play: crotale in G, tambourine, bells (probably meaning finger cymbals), and castatnets.

**First Performance:** 24 April 1963; Venice; 26th International Festival of Contemporary Music.

**Edition:** *Novae de Infinito Laudes* is published by Schotts. The piano-vocal score (5267) and miniature score (5028) are available for purchase; orchestral materials are available for rental.

**Notes:** *Novæ de Infinito Laudes* was commissioned by the London Philharmonic Society. Using texts from eleven of Bruno's dialogues, the work is divided into six movements which are organized as follows:

| I | I Corpi Celesti | Celestial Bodies |
|---|---|---|

"De l'infinito, universo e mondi" Dialogue III
"La Cena de le Ceneri" Dialogue IV
"La Cena de le Ceneri" Dialogue III
"La Cena de le Ceneri" Dialogue I

| II | I Quattro Elementi | The Four Elements |
|---|---|---|

"De l'infinito, universo e mondi" Dialogue III
"De l'infinito, universo e mondi" Dialogue V

| III | La Continua Mutazione | Continuous Mutation |
|---|---|---|

"La Cena de le Ceneri" Dialogue

| IV | Il Piacere e' nel Movimento | Pleasure of Motion |
|---|---|---|

"Spaccio de la bestia trionfante" Dialogue I
"De gli Eroici fuori" Part I, Dialogue II

| V | Il Sorgere del Sole | The Sunrise |
|---|---|---|

"De la Causa, Principio e Uno" Dialogue I

| VI | Il Sommo Bene | The Ultimate Good |
|---|---|---|

"De la Causa, Principio e Uno" Dialogue V

**Performance Issues:** The altos and sopranos each have six-part divisi, while the tenors and basses divide into three parts. There are two tenor and two bass solos for members of the choir. Henze uses harmonics marks for the male soloists, apparently to indicate falsetto. The score combines passages of free atonality, serialism, and tonality to create a diverse, and remarkably challenging, pitch fabric. The rhythmic language is less difficult, but varied divisions of the beat, frequent meter changes, and numerous fluctuations of tempi all contribute to the hazards for achieving a cohesive ensemble. Much of the choral material is atonal and densely written to heighten the sense of dissonance. The vocal material is not clearly supported by the accompaniment, but the opening pitches of most vocal passages are clearly doubled or immediately preceded by the accompaniment. The score is in C with the doublebasses and lutes sounding an octave lower than written and the piccolos an octave higher. The composer indicates that guitars may be substituted for the lutes. The polyphonic techniques Henze employs for the orchestra interweave melodic lines in a manner which diffuses entrances and often blurs the aural sense of meter. This combined with the disparate pitch relationships between parts will present great obstacles in achieving a sense of ensemble. **Soloists:** soprano - range: c'-c''', tessitura: g'-g'', this solo is vocally demanding and filled with awkward melodic leaps; alto - range: g-e'', tessitura: d'-d'', this role requires a dramatic voice capable of sustained singing in the upper range; tenor - range: B$^b$-a', tessitura: g-g', this is a lyric role with some awkward leaps, the B$^b$ occurs only once, the next lowest pitch is d; bass - range: G-f#', tessitura: d-d', this role requires vocal stamina and musical independence; **Choir:** very difficult; **Orchestra:** very difficult

**Discography:** As of February 1997, there are no commercial recordings available of this work.

### Selected Bibliography

Eimert, H.: "An Hans Werner Henze zur Zeit seiner Giordano-Bruno Kantate," *Melos*, volume 30 (June 1963), 206-207.

Thomas, E.: "Absurdes Theatre und hymnischer Kantate; Berio und Henze auf der venezianischen Biennale," *neue Zeitschrift für Musik*, volume 124, number 6 (1963), 240-241.

Knessl, L.: "Absurdes Musiktheatre und Manierismus in Venedig," *Melos*, volume 30 (Sptember 1963), 309-310.

## Die Muzen Siziliens [Muses of Sicily] (1966)

**Duration:** ca. 60 minutes

**Text:** The text is in Latin by Virgil. The title is taken from his *Eclogue No. 4*, the text of the first part is from *Eclogue No. 9*, the middle part from *Eclogue No. 10*, and the final part from *Eclogue No. 6*.

**Performing Forces: voices:** SATB choir; **orchestra:** 2 flutes
flute II doubling piccolo), 2 oboes, 2 clarinets in B$^b$, 2 bassoons, 4
horns, 2 trumpets in B$^b$, 2 trombones, timpani, and 2 solo pianos.

**First Performance:** 20 September 1966; Berlin, Germany; Berlin
Singakademie.

**Edition:** *Die Muzen Siziliens* is published by Schotts. The miniature
score (5515) is available for purchase. Choral scores and orchestral
materials are available for rental.

**Notes:** *Die Muzen Siziliens* was commissioned by the Berlin
Singakademie to commemorate their 175th anniversary. It is
dedicated to them and their director, Mathieu Lange.

**Performance Issues:** This work is conceived as a "concerto for
voices and instruments," the central element of which is the two
pianos, requiring exceptionally virtuosic playing throughout the
work. The remaining instrumental parts are demanding, but
significantly less so than the pianos. Much of the wind writing is
homophonic, with an abundance of articulation and dynamic
indications. These chordal sections are often voiced at a
disadvantage to good intonation. The vocal parts are somewhat
diatonic in their conception, but the pitch sets shift frequently
creating significant dissonances and numerous cross relations.
There is little reinforcement of the vocal parts from the
accompaniment. The wind parts frequently reflect metric divisions
which are different from those of the remaining parts, and which are
also often at odds with the barlines of the parts themselves. The
final movement is written in a rapid tempo with frequently
changing meters. The non-symmetrical meters are inconsistent in
their successive patterns of two and three beat divisions and the
solo pianos are often conceived in a larger metric form that crosses
barlines within their implied beats. **Choir:** difficult; **Orchestra:**
difficult.[4]

---

4   F. Mark Daugherty and Susan Huneke Simon list this work as
"difficult" in *Secular Choral Music in Print*, 414. Philadelphia,
Pennsylvania: Musicdata, 1987.

**Discography:** As of February 1997, there are no commercial recordings available of this work.

### Selected Bibliography

"New Works: New York," *Music Journal*, volume 28 (January 1968), 82.
Davis, P. G.: "Chicago Symphony (Martinon)," *HiFi / Musical America*, volume 18 (February 1968), 10.

## Das Floss der Medusa [The Raft of the Medusa] (1968)

**Duration:** ca. 120 minutes

**Text:** The libretto was written by Ernst Schnabel using an outline from the composer. The text is in German.

**Performing Forces: voices:** soprano and baritone soloists; narrator; 16-part mixed choir, children's choir; **orchestra:** 4 flutes (flute I and II doubling piccolo, flutes III and IV doubling alto flute), oboe, oboe d'amore, English horn, heckelphone, soprano clarinet in $E^b$, clarinet in $B^b$, alto clarinet in $E^b$ (or bassett horn), bass clarinet in $B^b$, soprano saxophone in $B^b$, tenor saxophone in $B^b$, 2 bassoons, contrabassoon, 4 horns, 1 piccolo trumpet, 2 trumpets in C, bass trumpet in C, alto trombone, tenor trombone, bass trombone, alto ophicleide (may substitute baritone), bass ophicleide (may substitute four-valved trombone), bombardone (may substitute tuba in F), tenor Wagner-tuba, bass tuba, contrabass tuba, timpani, percussion (8 players - vibraphone, marimba, chimes, snare drum, bass drum, 3 bongos, tambourine, wooden drum, 3 suspended cymbals, 5 tam-tams, 3 triangles, 3 steel plates, 2 temple blocks, woodblock, herd cowbells, shell chimes, guiro, maracas, bamboo strip), 2 harps, piano, electric organ, electric guitar, electric bass guitar, and strings (12 violins, 8 violas, 6 cellos, 4 doublebasses).

**First Performance:** 9 December 1968 in a broadcast performance on the North German Radio Network from Hamburg; Edda Moser, soprano; Dietrich Fischer-Dieskau, baritone; Charles Regnier, speaker; North German Radio Orchestra and Chorus; conducted by the composer. A concert performance scheduled for the same time was cancelled because the chorus refused to sing under a red banner installed on the stage at the composer's request.

**Edition:** *Das Floss der Medusa* is published by Schotts. The piano-vocal score (6719) and miniature score (6326) are available for purchase; orchestral materials are available through rental.

**Notes:** The libretto is based upon a true story. King Louis XVIII of France sent a military unit to reclaim Senegal from the English. Just prior to arriving in Africa, the flagship, "Medusa," struck a reef. Abandoning ship, the officers and passengers boarded the lifeboats and placed 150 soldiers, crew, women, and children upon a make-shift raft. In an attempt to secure the lifeboats, the commander ordered that the tow ropes to the raft be cut, leaving its passengers to drift at sea. The raft was eventually spotted and rescued by the "Argus." Only fifteen passengers remained alive, of them only ten would survive. The oratorio features a soprano soloist who personifies Death, a baritone soloist named Jean-Charles a mulatto survivor, a narrator named Charon after the ferryman upon the mythological river Styx. There are two choirs: the "Chorus of the Living" and the "Chorus of the Dead" on opposing sides of the stage. As the drama unfolds, members from the side of the living cross over to the side of the dead. The work is arranged in seventeen sections which are grouped into two larger parts as follows:

Part I — Embarkation for disaster

    1  Charon's Prologue — narrator, unaccompanied
    2  Motto
    3  Order of the day and roll-call
    4  Journal of the passage
    5  An answer
    6  Attempts to save the ship and men
    7  Disembarkation
    8  Ballad of betrayal
    9  Song for new voices
   10  Instruction for the second day

Part II — The ninth night and the morning

   11  Report on the situation — narrator, unaccompanied
   12  Motto

*Das Floss der Medusa* is dedicated to Che Guevara.

**Performance Issues:** This score, notated in C, combines free-atonality with serialism. There are also a few diatonic passages. Some of the narrator's part is specifically notated for rhythm and approximate pitch. There are very brief choral solos for an alto and a bass, and a longer solo for two children. There are *Sprechstimme* passages for the baritone soloist and all of the choral singers. Very little instrumental support is given to the vocal lines. In instances where melodic lines are doubled there are often parallel instrumental parts in seconds to the principal line. The strings divide to one-on-a-part in some sections. Henze uses harmonics notation in the baritone solos to indicate falsetto. All of the instrumental parts are technically demanding. The atonal pitch material combined with a vast orchestral fabric and rhythmic complexities creates a most difficult ensemble work. Some assignments of percussion parts to players are quite clear, but many are not. A pre-rehearsal sectional is advisable to sort out the percussion allocations. The shell chimes are to be strongly amplified. The first-choice instruments, where alternates are provided, should be utilized as the sonorities created in the score with the less-common instruments is quite spectacular. The choirs should be placed at, or near, the front of the staged for visual effect and to assist in balance. This is a remarkably moving and dramatic work exhibiting exceptional technical facility. It is also within the abilities of only the finest ensembles. **Soloists:** soprano - range: g#-c#''', tessitura: g'-g'', this is a sustained role for a sweet and lyrical voice; baritone - range: G-f#' (g#' in falsetto), tessitura: f-e', this is vocally a very demanding role exploiting all of the range with many awkward leaps, it requires a singer capable of great expression and vocal stamina; **Choir:** very difficult; **Orchestra:** very difficult.[5]

5   F. Mark Daugherty and Susan Huneke Simon list this work as "difficult" in *Secular Choral Music in Print*, 414. Philadelphia, Pennsylvania: Musicdata, 1987.

**Discography:** Edda Moser, Dietrich Fischer-Dieskau; Charles Regnier, speaker; North German Radio Orchestra and Chorus; conducted by Hans Werner Henze. Deutsche Grammophon: K 9429 [reel tape].

## Selected Bibliography

Wagner, K: "Untergang bei der Ausreise: Henzes Floss der Medusa Kentert in Hamburg," *Melos* , volume 36 (1969), 19.

Schnabel, Ernst: *Das Floss der Medusa: Text zum Oratorium von Hans Werner Henze: zum Untergang einer Uraufführung—Postscriptum.* Munich: 1969.

Foessel, K: "Nürnberg zeigt Henzes 'Floss' als theatralische Imagination," *Melos* , volume 39 (1972), 232.

Pahlen, Kurt: *The World of the Oratorio*, 182-183. Portland, Oregon: Amadeus Press, 1985.

# Hindemith, Paul (b. Hanau, Germany, 16 November 1895; d. Frankfurt, 28 December 1963).

**Life:** Hindemith studied composition with Arnold Mendelssohn and Bernhard Sekles. He established a reputation for his virtuosity on the viola (he premiered a number of solo works, including Walton's Viola Concerto) and as an important chamber musician. Hindemith left Germany in 1937 following pressure from the Nazi party which forbade the performance of his works (most notably the cancellation of the premiere of *Mathis der Mahler* in 1933). He emigrated to the United States where he taught at Yale University and Tanglewood (where his students included Lukas Foss and Leonard Bernstein); he became a United States citizen in 1945. As the 1949-50 Norton Professor of Poetry at Harvard University, he presented *A Composer's World*. In 1953, he moved his permanent residence to Zürich while maintaining an international career. He mastered all of the orchestral instruments and wrote very practical sonatas and concertos for all of them. His music is always masterfully crafted and practical in its orchestration. His works are an ammalgamation of devices from throughout the history of western music, which are combined in the shadow of Hindemith's theories of harmony based upon his profound understanding of the acoustics of musical sound.

**Writings:** *The Craft of Musical Composition* (1941), *A Concentrated Course in Traditional Harmony*, 2 volumes (1943, 1953), *Elementary*

*Training for Musicians* (1946), *J.S. Bach: Heritage and Obligation* (1952), *A Composer's World: Horizons and Limitations* (1952).

**Principal Works:** *opera* - *Mörder, Hoffnung der Frauen* (1919), *Das Nusch-Nuschi* (1920), *Sancta Susanna* (1921), *Cardillac*, op. 39 (1926), *Hin und Zurück* (1927), *Neues vom Tage* (1928-29), *Mathis der Mahler* (1933-5), *Die Harmonie der Welt* (1956-7), *Das lange Weihnachtsmahl* (1960); *ballets* - *Der Dämon* (1922), *Nobilissima Visione* (1938), *Theme and Variations: The Four Temperaments* (1940); *orchestral* - Cello Concerto (1916), Piano Concerto (1924), *Mathis der Mahler Symphony* (1934), *Der Schwanendreher* for viola and orchestra (1935), Cello Concert (1940), Symphony in E$^b$ (1940), *Symphonic Metamorphosis of Themes by Carl Maria von Weber* (1940-43), Piano Concerto (1945), *Symphonia Serena* (1947), Clarinet Concerto (1947), Sinfonietta (1949), Horn Concerto (1949), Symphony in B$^b$ for Concert Band (1951), *Pittsburgh Symphony* (1958), Organ Concerto (1962-63); *chamber* - 6 String Quartets (1919, 1921, 1922, 1923, 1943, 1946), 2 Violin Sonatas (1918), Viola Sonata (1919), Cello Sonata (1919), Kleine Kammermusik (1922-27), Flute Sonata (1936), Oboe Sonata (1938), Bassoon Sonata (1938), Clarinet Sonata (1939), Horn Sonata (1939), Trumpet Sonata (1939), Harp Sonata (1939), Violin Sonata in C (1939), Viola Sonata in C (1939), Trombone Sontata (1941), English Horn Sonata (1941), Saxophone Sonata (1943), Cello Sonata (1948), Doublebass Sonata (1949), Tuba Sonata (1955); *choral* - *When Lilacs Last in the Dooryard Bloom'd* (1946), *Apparebit Repentina Dies* (1947), 12 Madrigals (1958), *Der Mainzer Umzug* (1962), Mass (1963); *vocal* - *Das Marienleben*, op. 27 for soprano and piano (1922-3), 12 *Madrigals* for choir (1958); as well as a number of significant educational works for developing musicians.

## Selected Composer Bibliography

Kemp, Ian: *Hindemith*. Oxford: Oxford University Press, 1970.

Monroe, Robert C.: *Compositional Techniques in the Choral Works of Stravinsky, Hindemith, Honegger, and Britten.* Northwestern University: Dissertation, 1953.

Skelton, Geoffrey: *Paul Hindemith: The Man Behind the Music.* Taplinger Publishing Company, 1975.

Kemp, Ian: "Paul Hindemith," *The New Grove Modern Masters*, 229-282. New York: W.W. Norton, 1984.

Neumeyer, David: *The Music of Paul Hindemith.* New Haven: Yale University Press, 1986.

Noss, Luther: *Paul Hindemith in the United States*. Champaign-Urbana: University of Illinois Press, 1989.

Skelton, Geoffrey, editor and translator: *Selected Letters of Paul Hindemith*. New Haven, Connecticut: Yale University Press, 1995.

**Der Lindberghflug** (1928) — see entry under Kurt Weill with whom Hindemith collaborated in the original version (p. 272).

## Das Unaufhörliche [The Unceasing] (1931)

**Duration:**   ca. 85 minutes

**Text:** The libretto, by Gottfried Benn, is in German.

**Performing Forces: voices:** soprano, tenor, baritone, bass soloists; two-part boy's choir, SATB choir; **orchestra:** piccolo, 2 flutes, 2 oboes, 2 clarinets in B$^b$, 2 bassoons, contrabassoon (optional), 3 horns in F, 2 trumpets in C, 2 trombones, tuba, timpani, percussion (1 player - snare drum, suspended cymbal with triangle beater, crash cymbals), organ (optional), and strings.

**First Performance:** 21 November 1931; Berlin, Germany; conducted by Otto Klemperer.

**Edition:** *Das Unaufhörliche* is published by Schotts. The piano-vocal score (3258) is available for purchase; other materials are available through rental.

**Notes:** The score is divided into three acts which are subdivided by movements for varied forces as follows:

Act I
- I   choir
- II   soprano and tenor solos
- III   bass solo with men's choir
- IV   soprano solo
- V   soprano, tenor, and bass solos with choir

Act II
- VI   soprano solo and women's choir
- VII   tenor and bass solos
- VIII   Little March—baritone solo with no strings

      IX   soprano and bass solos
      X    bass solo with choir
      XI   tenor solo
      XII  soprano solo with choir

Act III
      XIII   overture—orchestra only
      XIV   soprano, tenor, and bass trio—tenor solo
      XV    double choir
      XVI   baritone solo
      XVII  men's choir and boy's choir
      XVIII choir

**Performance Issues:** This score combines elements of modal and tonal music with quartal-quintal harmonic combinations. It is highly contrapuntal throughout the tutti sections. The choral writing intersperses homophonic and polyphonic textures. The vocal parts are harmonically supported by the orchestra, but they remain melodically and rhythmically independent of the accompaniment much of the time. The inner motion and chromatic language of the choir demands an ensemble of experienced singers. The movements for men's and women's choirs are less musically difficult for the singers. If separate ensembles are used in these movements, they need not be as accomplished. The composer notes that the boys' choir may be reinforced with trumpets if needed. The writing for the boys' choir is fairly diatonic with a true alto part. Hindemith suggests using a string section in proportion to the choral forces employed. There is an optional organ part in movements I, III, and XVIII, which reinforces the orchestra parts. There is no contrabassoon in the instrumentation list, but there is a composer's note which suggests doubling the doublebasses with contrabassoon as deemed appropriate. This appears to be the composer's preference. The score states that a single player may cover the timpani and percussion parts; however, this is not possible in movement XVII. In that movement the suspended cymbal must be played simultaneously with a two-handed timpani part. This cymbal part can be entrusted to a member of the choir, as it is technically simple. The baritone solos may be sung by the bass soloist if necessary. All of the vocal solos are musically challenging. The orchestra parts are chromatic and often filled with rapid passage work. There are exposed solo passages for all of the principal woodwinds. **Soloists:** soprano - range: b-a", tessitura: f'-e", this is a sustained and lyric role; tenor - range: d-g#', tessitura: f-e', this role is lyric with some rapid text declamation; baritone - range: c-f#', tessitura: d-d', this role is sustained and requires a very powerful voice, in movement VIII it is accompanied by the full wind and brass; bass - range: F#-e', tessitura: f-d', this is a sustained role with nearly all of its singing within the listed tessitura; **Choir:** difficult; **Orchestra:** difficult.[6]

**Discography:** Heather Frank, Rich Williams, David Stoffel, Douglas Starr; Symphonic Choir, Chorale, Women's Glee Club, and Symphony Orchestra of Ohio State University; conducted by Maurice Casey. Century Advent Recordings: USR 6220 [LP].

Ulrike Sonntag, Robert Worle, Siegfried Lorenz, Arthur Korn; Berlin Radio Children's Chorus, Chorus, and Symphony Orchestra; conducted by Lothar Zagrosek, recorded 3-8 February 1995. Wergo: WER 6603-2 [DDD]. This recording ends with an introductory reading by Gottfried Benn for a 1932 radio performance of the work.

### Selected Bibliography

reviews of the premiere:
Pringsheim, Heinz: *Allgemeine Musikzeitung* (27 November 1931).
Oboussier, Robert: *Frankfurter Zeitung* (25 November 1931).
Schrenk, Walter: *Deutsche Allgemeine Zeitung* (23 November 1931).

other bibliographic resources:
Benn, Gottfried: *Aus dem Oratorium Das Unaufhörliche.* Hamburg: Otto Rohse Presse, 1970.
Fehn, A.C.: Change and Permanence   [Benn's text for *Das Unaufhörliche*]. Berne, 1977.
Heyworth, Peter: *Otto Klemperer: His Life and Times*, volume 1: 1885-1933, 383-384. Cambridge: Cambridge University Press, 1983.
Pahlen, Kurt: *The World of the Oratorio*, 184-85. Portland, Oregon: Amadeus Press, 1985,.
Skelton, Geoffrey, editor and translator: *Selected Letters of Paul Hindemith*, 63, 67, 68, 81, 168, 233. New Haven, Connecticut: Yale University Press, 1995.

---

6   F. Mark Daugherty and Susan Huneke Simon list this work as "difficult" in *Secular Choral Music in Print*, 426. Philadelphia, Pennsylvania: Musicdata, 1987.

## ITE, ANGELI VELOCES

### Part I — Chant De Triomphe Du Roi David —Triumphgesang Davids [David's Victory Song] (1955)

**Duration:** ca. 25 minutes

**Text:** Paul Claudel and Psalm 17. It is published to be sung in French or German.

**Performing Forces: voices:** alto and tenor soloists; choir and audience; **orchestra:** 2 flutes, 2 oboes, English horn, 2 clarinets in B♭, bass clarinet in B♭, 2 bassoons, contrabassoon, 4 horns in F, 2 trumpets in B♭, 3 trombones, tuba, timpani, percussion (3 players - snare drum, bass drum, suspended cymbal, crash cymbals), organ, and strings.

additional wind ensemble with a minimum of 5 instruments: horn in F, trumpet in B♭, trombone, and optional winds.

**First Performance:**

First complete performance of all three sections: 4 June 1955; Wuppertal, Germany; conducted by Hindemith.

**Edition:** *Chant De Triomphe Du Roi David* is published by Schotts as part of *Ite, Angeli Veloces*. All materials are available through rental.

**Notes:** There are a number of unsettled issues in the score. The brass choir which is labeled "fanfare" is written as a keyboard part on a grand staff with no indication of the independent lines. The passages for the audience, labeled "peuple," are intermittently scattered throughout the opening and closing sections of the piece. These groups return in the third cantata of the set, *Cantique de l'Ésperance.*

**Performance Issues:** The choral writing is quite accessible for less-experienced choirs. Much of the choral writing is in octaves or with paired doubling of soprano with tenor and alto with bass. The vocal parts are clearly supported by the accompaniment. The passages for the audience are always doubled by the brass fanfares. The percussion parts are very easy. If one cymbal is mounted on the bass drum so that the crash cymbals and bass drum are played by one percussionist, then only two players are needed. There are some very unclear indications for the percussionists. In section 5 there is a part labeled "percussion" with no instrument listed. It seems likely that this is meant to be suspended cymbal; however, there are no suspended cymbal parts in the rest of the work. The other orchestra parts are all idiomatically written for the respective instruments. The upper winds and strings all have some rapid and fairly awkward chromatic passage work throughout the piece. The principal winds all have some exposed solo passages. The breadth of the orchestration suggests the use of a large choir. Hindemith's expectations of the musical prowess of his audience to be capable of participating in the singing of this work are not to be found in traditional audiences today. A possibly effective treatment would be to assign the audience parts and fanfare to an antiphonal ensemble in the rear of the hall. **Soloists:** alto - range: b-f#", tessitura: d'-c", this is a lyric role with considerable sustained singing at the top of the range; tenor - range: c#-g#', tessitura: f-e', this role is lyric and articulate; **Choir:** medium easy, **Orchestra:** medium difficult.

**Discography:** As of February 1997, there are no commercial recordings available of this work.

## Selected Bibliography

Lüttwitz, H. von: "Das 109. Niederrheinische Musikfest," *Musica*, volume 9 (July 1955), 318-319.

Stephani, M.: "Hindemiths Kantaten-Trilogie," *Musik und Leben*, volume 8 (July-August 1955), 246-248.

Schab, G.: "Hindemith und Blacher uraufgeführt," *Musik und Leben*, volume 8 (July-August 1955), 269.

Schmidt, H.: "Neue Chorwerke von Hindemith und Blacher," *Melos*, volume 22 (July-August 1955), 230.

Wörner, K.H.: "Hindemith Claudel-Kantate," *Neue Zeitschrift für Musik*, volume 116 (November 1955), 67-70.

Skelton, Geoffrey, editor and translator: *Selected Letters of Paul Hindemith*, 216-220, 224, 228, 236-237. New Haven, Connecticut: Yale University Press, 1995.

## Part II—Custos quid de nocte [Watchman, what of the night?] (1955)

**Duration:** ca. 8 minutes

**Text:** The text is by Paul Claudel. It is published to be sung in French or German.

**Performing Forces: voices:** tenor solo; choir; **orchestra:** flute, oboe, clarinet in B$^b$, bassoon, horn in F, trumpet in B$^b$, trombone, tuba, timpani, and strings.

**First Performance:**

> First complete performance of all three sections: 4 June 1955; Wuppertal, Germany; conducted by Hindemith.

**Edition:** *Castos, Quid De Nocte* is published by Schotts as part of *Ite, Angeli Veloces*. All materials are available through rental.

**Notes:** The title and apparent basis of Claudel's text is taken from Isaiah, chapter 21. This second section of *Ite, angeli veloces* appears to be labeled for tenor and alto soloists in some sources; however, this portion of the work has only a tenor soloist.

**Performance Issues:** The choral writing is very accessible and the choir sings for only thirteen measures. The instrumental parts are all exposed and quite chromatic, but they remain within the abilities of most collegiate-level players. This work is really a short cantata for tenor soloist and chamber orchestra with a brief obbligato choir passage. This is an excellent work to showcase a tenor soloist with a small instrumental ensemble. It is well-suited for performance with only a string quintet. **Soloist:** tenor - range: e-a$^b$', tessitura: a-f', this is a sustained and lyric role; **Choir:** easy; **Orchestra:** medium difficult.

**Discography:** As of February 1997, there are no commercial recordings available of this work.

### Selected Bibliography

Lüttwitz, H. von: "Das 109. Niederrheinische Musikfest," *Musica*, volume 9 (July 1955), 318-319.

Stephani, M.: "Hindemiths Kantaten-Trilogie," *Musik und Leben*, volume 8 (July-August 1955), 246-248.

Schab, G.: "Hindemith und Blacher uraufgeführt," *Musik und Leben*, volume 8 (July-August 1955), 269.

Schmidt, H.: "Neue Chorwerke von Hindemith und Blacher," *Melos*, volume 22 (July-August 1955), 230.

Wörner, K.H.: "Hindemith Claudel-Kantate," *Neue Zeitschrift für Musik*, volume 116 (November 1955), 67-70.

Skelton, Geoffrey, editor and translator: *Selected Letters of Paul Hindemith*, 216-220, 224, 228, 236-237. New Haven, Connecticut: Yale University Press, 1995.

# Part III—Cantique de l'espérance [Canticle of Hope] (1953)

**Duration:** ca. 25 minutes

**Text:** The text is by Paul Claudel. It is published to be sung in French, German, or English.

**Performing Forces: voices:** alto solo; choir and audience; **orchestra:** 2 flutes (flute II optionally doubling piccolo), 2 oboes, English horn, 2 clarinets in B$^b$, bass clarinet in B$^b$, 2 bassoons, contrabassoon, 4 horns in F, 2 trumpets in B$^b$, 3 trombones, tuba, timpani, percussion (1 player - bass drum, cymbals), piano, and strings.

additional wind ensemble with a minimum of 5 instruments: horn in F, trumpet in B$^b$, trombone, and optional winds.

**First Performance:**

First complete performance of all three sections: 4 June 1955; Wuppertal, Germany; conducted by Hindemith.

First United States Performance in English: 19 April 1958; Woolsey Hall, Yale University, New Haven, Connecticut; conducted by Hindemith. This program also included Brahms's *Ein Deutsches Requiem*, conducted by Howard Boatwright. This program was repeated the following day in Carnegie Hall.

**Edition:** Cantique De L'Esperance is published by Schotts as part of *Ite, Angeli Veloces*. All materials are available through rental.

**Notes:** The brass choir which is labeled "fanfare" is written as a keyboard part on a grand staff with no indication of the independent lines. The passages for the audience, labeled "peuple," are intermittently scattered throughout the opening and closing sections of the piece.

**Performance Issues:** This is a straightforward and rhythmically charged work with homophonic motion from the entire ensemble throughout much of the score. As with the first cantata of this set, *Chant de Triomphe du Roi David*, the composer has written passages for audience singing which are beyond the expected abilities of our contemporary audiences. It is therefore recommended that an antiphonal choir be given these few choral interjections. They should be placed with the brass band. The choral writing is diatonic and quite simple with most passages consisting of a single melody sung in octaves, or two levels of melodic material with paired doubling of the tenor with the soprano and the alto with the bass. The orchestral parts are generally within the grasp of moderately experienced amateur players. In the closing section the entire orchestra is in unison on some rapid chromatic passages which may prove awkward for good ensemble and intonation for some groups. The score uses smaller notes for many of the parts, which appears to indicate that they are optional. If these parts are eliminated, the instrumentation becomes identical to the second cantata of the set, *Custos quid de nocte*, see above; however, the fanfare group and the audience parts are still in large notes. It should be observed that this same reduced orchestration does not seem to apply to the first cantata of the set. **Soloist:** alto - range: d'-f#", tessitura: g'-d", this is a lyric and sustained role with some direct text declamation. **Choir:** medium easy, **Orchestra:** medium difficult.

**Discography:** As of February 1997, there are no commercial recordings available of this work.

### Selected Bibliography

Lüttwitz, H. von: "Das 109. Niederrheinische Musikfest," *Musica*, volume 9 (July 1955), 318-319.

Stephani, M.: "Hindemiths Kantaten-Trilogie," *Musik und Leben*, volume 8 (July-August 1955), 246-248.

Schab, G.: "Hindemith und Blacher uraufgeführt," *Musik und Leben*, volume 8 (July-August 1955), 269.

Schmidt, H.: "Neue Chorwerke von Hindemith und Blacher," *Melos*, volume 22 (July-August 1955), 230.

Wörner, K.H.: "Hindemith Claudel-Kantate," *Neue Zeitschrift für Musik*, volume 116 (November 1955), 67-70.

Skelton, Geoffrey, editor and translator: *Selected Letters of Paul Hindemith*, 216-220, 224, 228, 236-237. New Haven, Connecticut: Yale University Press, 1995.

## Holst, Gustav (b. Cheltenham, 21 September 1874; d. London, 25 May 1934)

**Life:** The son of a pianist, Holst learned the instrument from his father and began to compose while a student at the Cheltenham Grammar School where he was virtually self-taught in composition. At 17, he studied counterpoint for a few months at Oxford and entered the Royal College of Music in 1893. There he studied composition with Charles Villiers Stanford. In that same year he made the acquaintance of Ralph Vaughan Williams. The two became life-long friends and regularly criticized each other's sketches. While in London, Holst guest directed the Hammersmith Socialist Choir in the home of William Morris where he was introduced to Hindu philosophy and literature. This led to his later study of Sanskrit at University College in London. He worked for a number of years as an orchestral trombonist. Holst began teaching at James Allen's Girls' School in Dulwich (1903), continuing at St. Paul's Girls' School in Hammersmith (1903-34), the Royal College of Music (1919-25), University College at Reading (1919-25), and he took over the music program at Morley College (1907-24). He remained active in the direction of amateur music ensembles and hosted annual 3-day festivals on Whitsunday in Thaxted. He led the English premieres of a number of Bach cantatas, and the first performance of Purcell's *The Fairy Queen* since 1697. He suffered from ill health most of his life, but particularly after a fall from a podium in 1923. He was ordered to spend the entire year of 1924 at rest in the country. The works which followed this hiatus are marked by a new sparseness and a keener awareness of his Hindu influences. He served as a visiting lecturer at Harvard in 1932, but fell ill the following March and had to return to England where he never truly recovered (although he was able to compose until his death). Like Vaughan Williams, Holst refused official titles of honor including knighthood. Holst's music combines the contrapuntal elegance of Byrd and Weelkes (whose revivals he championed) with the harmonic palette of Stanford and Elgar. His music is imbued with a mystical sense, but is always direct in its approach to the listener. The last decade of his work is marked by an increased presence of Eastern philosophy.[7]

**Awards:** Fellowship of the Royal College of Music, the Gold Medal of the Royal Philharmonic Society (1930), and the Yale University Howland Memorial Prize for distinction in the Arts.

**Principal Works:** *operas* - *Savitri*, op. 25 (1908), *The Perfect Fool*, op. 39 (1920-1), *At the Boar's Head*, op. 42 (1924), *The Wandering Scholar*, op. 50 (1929-30); *orchestral* - *Beni Mora*: oriental suite in E minor, op. 29, no. 1 (1910, revised. 1912), *St. Paul's Suite*, op. 29, no. 2 (1912-3), *The Planets*, op. 32 (1914-6), *Egdon Heath*, op. 47 (1927), *A Moorside Suite* (1928), *Brook Green Suite* (1933); *band* - Suite No. 1 in $E^b$, op. 28a (1909), Suite No. 2 in F, op. 28b (1911), *Hammersmith*, op. 52 (1930-1); *vocal* - *The Mystic Trumpeter*, op. 18 (1904, revised 1912), *3 Choral Hymns from the Rig Veda*, op. 26 (1908-10), *The Cloud Messenger*, op. 30 (1910, revised 1912), *Dirge for 2 Veterans* (1914), *Ode to Death*, op. 28 (1919), Seven Partsongs, op. 44 (1925-6), and *Choral Fantasia*, op. 51 (1930).

### Selected Composer Bibliography

Krone, Max Thomas: *The Choral Works of Gustav Holst*. Northwestern University: Dissertation, 1940.

Boult, Sir Adrian: "Gustav Holst," *Royal College of Music Magazine*, volume 70 (1974), 52.

Holst, Imogen, and C. Matthews, eds.: *Gustav Holst: Collected Facsimile Edition of Autograph Manuscripts of the Published Works*. 4 volumes. London: Faber, 1974-83.

Holst, Imogen: *A Thematic Catalogue of Gustav Holst's Music*. London: Faber and Faber, 1974.

---

7   Imogen Holst: *The Music of Gustav Holst*, third edition; and *Holst's Music Reconsidered*. 1 volume. Oxford: Oxford University Press, 1986.

_____: *The Music of Gustav Holst*, third edition; and *Holst's Music Reconsidered*. 1 volume. Oxford: Oxford University Press, 1986.

_____: "Gustav Holst," *The New Grove Twentieth-Century English Masters*, 145-174. New York: W.W. Norton, 1986.

Short, Michael: *Gustav Holst: The Man and His Music*.  Oxford: Oxford University Press, 1990.

## The Planets, op. 32 (1914-16)

**Duration:** ca. 51 minutes

**Text:** none

**Performing Forces: voices:** 2 SSA choirs; **orchestra:** 4 flutes (flute III doubling piccolo, flute IV doubling piccolo and alto flute in G[8]), 3 oboes (oboe III doubling bass oboe), English horn, 3 clarinets in B$^b$ and A, bass clarinet in B$^b$, 3 bassoons, contrabassoon, 6 horns in F, 4 trumpets in C, 3 trombones, euphonium,[9] bass tuba, 2 timpanists (6 drums), percussion (3 players[10] - glockenspiel, chimes, xylophone, snare drum, bass drum, tambourine, cymbals, gong, triangle), celeste, 2 harps, organ, and strings.

There are cues throughout the score that allow the elimination of flute IV, oboe III, bassoon III, contrabassoon, horns V and VI, trumpet IV, euphonium, and organ.

**First Performance:** Private performance: 29 September 1918, London, choir of St. Paul's Girls's School, New Queen's Hall Orchestra; conducted by Adrian Boult. This performance was a gift to the composer from Balfour Gardiner.

---

[8]   The score uses the British label of bass flute in G.

[9]   The score lists this as tenor tuba in Bb.

[10]  David Daniels recommends 4 percussionists in *Orchestral Music: A Handbook*, third edition. Lanham, Maryland: Scarecrow Press, 1996.

Performance of selected movements: 27 February 1919, London, Royal Philharmonic Society Concert, conducted by Adrian Boult; 22 November 1919, London; 10 October 1920, Birmingham.

Public premiere: 15 November 1920; Queen's Hall, London.

**Edition:** *The Planets* is published by Curwen, Eulenberg, and G. Schirmer. The full score is available for purchase and orchestral materials are available through rental.

**Autograph:** Curwen publishes a facsimile of the composer's manuscript. This facsimile also includes a listing of Holst's own tempi from recordings made under his baton.

**Notes:** Holst portrayed the then-known planets of our solar system, excluding earth, through his musical interpretation of their astrological personifications as follows:

|  |  |
|---|---|
| I | Mars, the Bringer of War |
| II | Venus, the Bringer of Peace |
| III | Mercury, the Winged Messenger |
| IV | Jupiter, the Bringer of Jollity |
| V | Saturn, the Bringer of Old Age |
| VI | Uranus, the Magician |
| VII | Neptune, the Mystic |

**Performance Issues:** The choir is textless and is used as an orchestral effect. The score states that if at all possible, the choir should be placed outside of the concert hall, to be heard through a door which is gradually closed so that the choir truly fades away. Each performance space will require its own interpretation of these instructions. In any case, the two choirs should be quite small, totaling 12 to 18 singers between them. The vocal material is shared between the choir which are usually set in imitation of each other. Both parts are clearly supported by the orchestra. The sonic effect of the voices in the score suggests the use of clear voices, especially in the soprano I parts. The orchestral parts are all quite demanding. The timpanists are given melodies between the players so there must be two executants. Much of the difficulty in performing this work is the general challenge of any work for so large an ensemble. Holst writes very idiomatically for all the instruments, but there are perpetual exchanges of melodic material between sections of the orchestra which present some challenges in synchronization. Movements III, IV and VI are particularly rich with these musical "hand-offs." The brass parts, especially horn I and trumpet I have some prominent sustained high playing which requires strong players. The score exploits the relationships of 2 against 3 and 3 against 4 with overlapping subdivisions of each creating some temporal hazards. The breadth of the orchestration requires a large string section. Although there are compensations made for a reduced instrumentation, it is advisable to do the full version. The tempi are an important performance consideration. The tempi which Holst used are almost always considerably faster than any of the current commercial recordings. The composer's tempi give the work a much different spirit from that heard in most contemporary performances. **Choir:** medium easy, **Orchestra:** difficult.

**Discography:** London Symphony Orchestra; conducted by Gustav Holst, recorded between 1922 and 1924. Pearl: GEMM CD9417 [mono AAD].

Vienna State Opera Orchestra; conducted by Adrian Boult, recorded in 1960. MCA: MCAS2-9813A [ADD].

London Philharmonic Orchestra; conducted by Adrian Boult, recorded in 1978. Angel: CDM-69045 [ADD].

Boston Symphony Orchestra; conducted by William Steinberg. Deutsche Grammophon: 419475-4 GGA [ADD].

Philadelphia Orchestra; conducted by Eugene Ormandy. RCA Victor: 09026612702 [ADD].

London Philharmonic Orchestra; conducted by Bernard Haitink, recorded in 1970. Philips: 6500-072 [LP], rereleased as Philips: 420893-2 [ADD].

New York Philharmonic Orchestra; conducted by Leonard Bernstein, recorded in 1973. CBS: MYT 37226 [LP], rereleased as CBS: MYK-37226 [ADD].

St. Louis Symphony Orchestra, Ronald Arnatt Chorale, Missouri Singers; conducted by Walter Susskind, recorded in 1974. Vox Unique: VU 9035 [ADD].

Concertgebouw Orchestra; conducted by Neville Marriner, recorded in 1978. Philips: 9500-425 [LP].

London Philharmonic Orchestra; conducted by George Solti, recorded in 1979. London: 425152-2 [LP], rereleased as London: 425152-2 LM [ADD].

London Philharmonic Orchestra; conducted by George Solti. London: 414567-2 LH [ADD].

Boston Symphony Orchestra; conducted by Seiji Ozawa, recorded in 1979. Philips: 416456-2 [LP], rereleased as Philips: 416456-2 PH [ADD].

Vienna Philharmonic Orchestra; conducted by Herbert von Karajan. London: 417709-2 [ADD].

Berlin Philharmonic Orchestra; conducted by Herbert von Karajan. Deutsche Grammophon: 400028-2 [DDD].

Berlin Philharmonic Orchestra; conducted by Colin Davis. Philips: 422403-2 PH [DDD].

Los Angeles Philharmonic Orchestra; conducted by Zubin Mehta. London: 417677-2 LC [ADD].

New York Philharmonic Orchestra; conducted by Zubin Mehta. Teldec: 2292-46316-2 [DDD].

London Symphony Orchestra and Chorus; conducted by André Previn. Angel: CDC-47160 [DDD].

Royal Philharmonic Orchestra, Brighton Festival Women's Chorus; conducted by André Previn. Telarc: CD-80133 [DDD].

Montréal Symphony Orchestra and Chorus; conducted by Charles Dutoit. London: 417553 [DDD].

Scottish National Orchestra, Women's Voices of the Scottish National Orchestra Chorus; conducted by Alexander Gibson. Chandos: CD-8302 [DDD], also released as Musical Heritage Society: 416514L [DDD].

Toronto Symphony Orchestra; conducted by Andrew Davis. EMI: CDD-64300 [DDD].

Boston Pops, Tanglewood Chorus; conducted by John Williams. Philips: 420177-2 PH [DDD].

Philharmonia Orchestra; conducted by William Boughton. Nimbus: NI-5117 [DDD].

Chicago Symphony Orchestra and Chorus; conducted by James Levine. Deutsche Grammophon: 429 730-2 GH [DDD].

National Orchestra of France; conducted by Loren Maazel. CBS: MDK-44781 [DDD].

London Symphony Orchestra and chorus; conducted by Richard Hickox. IMP Classics: PCD 890 [DDD].

Dallas Symphony Orchestra and Chorus; conducted by Eduardo Mata. Pro Arte: CDD-542 [DDD].

Hallé Orchestra and Hallé Women's Chorus; conducted by James Loughran. EMC: CDB62811 [DDD].

London Symphony Orchestra; conducted by Geoffrey Simon. London: 31001 [DDD].

Royal Philharmonic Orchestra; conducted by James Judd. Denon: C)75076 [DDD].

### Selected   Bibliography

Shore, Bernard: *Sixteen Symphonies*. London: Longmans Press, 1949.
Greene, Richard: *Gustav Holst and a Rhetoric of Musical Character: Language and Method in Selected Orchestral Works*, chapter 5. New York: Garland Publishing, 1994.
_____: *Holst: The Planets*. Cambridge: Cambridge University Press, 1995.

## Honegger, Arthur (b. Le Havre, 10 March 1892; d. Paris, 27 November 1955)

**Life:** Honegger was an influential French-born composer who maintained dual citizenship in Switzerland because of his Swiss parentage. He was a member of the group of composers know as Les Six, which also included Auric, Durey, Milhaud, Poulenc, and Taillefer. Honegger studied in Switzerland with Kempter and Friederich Hegar, and then at the Paris Conservatory with André Gédalge and Charles-Marie Widor. His early music was marked by a fascination with imitating the sounds of the modern era through music, in works like *Pacific 231*, which imitates a locomotive. He later focused his attentions on absolute music and classical forms. In 1947, he came to the United States to teach at the Berkshire Music Festival, but his visit was abbreviated by illness.

**Writings:** Honegger wrote an autobiography: *Je suis compositeur*. Paris: Éditions du Conquistador, 1951. It has been translated into English by Wilson O. Clough as: *I am a Composer*. London: St. Martin's Press, 1966.

**Principal Works:** *operas* - *Antigone* (1924-27), *Judith* (1925), *L'Aiglon* (1935), ; *oratorios*- *Le Roi David* (1921), *Cris du monde* (1930), *Nicolas de Flue* (1940); *ballets* - *Rose de métal* (1928), *Cantique des cantiques* (1937), *La Naissance des couleurs* (1940); *orchestral* - 5 Symphonies (1929-30, 1941, 1945-46, 1946, 1950), *Mouvement symphonique No. 1 "Pacific 231"* (1923), *Mouvement symphonique No. 2, "Rugby"* (1928), *Mouvement symphonique No. 3* (1932-33); *chamber* - 3 String Quartets (1917, 1936, 1937), *Danse de chèvre* (1919), *Prélude et Blues* for four harps (1925), *Sortilèges* (for ondes martinot (1946); *vocal* - *Cantique de Pâques* (1918), *Une Cantate de Noël* (1941-53).

## Selected Composer Bibliography

Tappolet, Willy: *Arthur Honegger*. Neuchâtel: La Baconnière, 1957.

Landowski, Marcel: *Honegger*. Paris: Éditions du Seuil, 1957.

Honegger, Arthur: *I am a Composer*, translated by Wilson O. Clough. London: St. Martin's Press, 1966.

Feschotte, Jacques: *Arthur Honegger*. Paris, Éditions Sechers, 1966.

*Arthur Honegger Werkverzeichnis*. Zurich: Schweizerisches Musik-Archiv, 1975.

# Le Roi David (1921)

**Duration:** ca. 75 minutes

**Text:** *Le Roi David* is a "Symphonic Psalm" in 3 parts after a drama of René Morax. It is based upon the story of King David as told in Samuel I and II, and Kings I and II in the Old Testament. It was originally composed with a French text, but the premiere concert used a German translation by Hans Reinhart. The E. C. Schirmer score includes singing translations in German and English, or only English, depending on the edition.

**Performing Forces: voices:** narrator, Witch of Endor (female dramatic speaker), soprano, alto, and tenor soloists; SATB choir; **orchestra:** chamber orchestra version: 2 flutes, oboe, 2 clarinets in B♭, bassoon, horn in F, 2 trumpets in C, trombone, timpani (2 drums), percussion (1 player - gong and tam-tam), celeste, harmonium or organ, piano, and doublebass.

symphonic version: 2 flutes (flute II doubling piccolo), 2 oboes (oboe II doubling English horn), 2 clarinets in B♭ and A (clarinet II doubling bass clarinet in B♭), 2 bassoons (bassoon II doubling contrabassoon), 4 horns in F, 2 trumpets in C, 3 trombones, tuba, percussion (4 players - tambourine, bass drum, crash cymbals, tam-tam), timpani, harp, celeste, organ (optional), and strings.

**First Performance:** as theater music: 11 June 1921; Théâtre Jorat; Mézières, Switzerland; conducted by the composer.

as a symphonic psalm: 2 December 1923; Winterthur, Switzerland; conducted by Ernst Wolters, in a German translation.

first staged performance: 21 October 1960; Paris, France; Paris
Grand Opéra.

**Edition:** *Le Roi David* is published by E. C. Schirmer. The piano-
vocal score (1665 French / German / English, or 2707 French /
English), choral score (1666), narrator's part (2707), and study
score (1402) are available for purchase; orchestral materials are
available through rental.

**Notes:** An English singing translation is available. The score,
originally written as functioning incidental music within a play by
Morax for his own outdoor drama company, was begun 25
February and completed 28 April 1921. Two other composers
turned down the commission. With only three months remaining
before the first performance, Morax solicited Honegger on the
recommendation of Ernest Ansermet. Honegger then revised the
work into an entirely concerted "symphonic psalm" during the
summer of 1923. The original 17-member chamber orchestra was
dictated by the size of the orchestra pit. In later life, Honegger
expressed a preference for this smaller orchestration. The libretto
outlines the life of King David as described in the Old Testament.
The work is in three acts organized as follows:

Part I

| I | Introduction | orchestra only |
|---|---|---|
| II | Song of David the Shepherd | alto solo |
| III | Psalm: "All Praise to Him" | choir |
| IIIb | Fanfare and Entrance of Goliath | orchestra only |
| IV | Song of Victory | choir |
| V | March | orchestra only |
| VI | Psalm: "In the Lord I put my faith" | tenor solo |
| VII | Psalm: "O, had I wings like a dove" | soprano solo |
| VIII | Song of the Prophets | men's choir |
| IX | Psalm: "Pity me, Lord" | tenor solo |
| X | Saul's Camp | orchestra only |
| XI | Psalm: "God the Lord shall be my light" | choir |
| XII | Incantation of the Witch of Endor | orchestra and Witch |
| XIII | March of the Philistines | orchestra only |
| XIV | Lament of Gilboa | soloists and women's choir |

Part II

| | | |
|---|---|---|
| XV | Song of the Daughters of Israel | soprano solo and women's choir |
| XVI | The Dance before the Ark | soloists and choir |

Part III

| | | |
|---|---|---|
| XVII | Song: "Now my voice in song up-soaring" | choir |
| XVIII | Song of the Handmaid | alto solo |
| XIX | Psalm of Penitence | choir |
| XX | Psalm: "Behold in evil I was born" | choir |
| XXI | Psalm: "Oh, shall I raise my eyes?" | tenor solo |
| XXII | The Song of Ephraim | soprano solo and women's choir |
| XXIII | March of the Hebrews | orchestra only |
| XXIV | Psalm: "Thee will I love, O Lord" | choir |
| XXV | Psalm: "In my distress" | choir |
| XXVI | The crowning of Solomon | orchestra only |
| XXVII | The Death of David | soprano solo and choir |

**Performance Issues:** The choral portions of this work are well written for accessibility to less experienced singers. Honegger introduces a number of challenging pitch situations in a manner that allows them to be easily learned. The soli roles are somewhat chromatic, and the tenor and soprano sit fairly high in the voice; however, they are well within the grasp of many undergraduate singers.

both versions: The orchestra parts are fairly idiomatic to their instruments. The string parts are particularly accessible, well within the abilities of an average student orchestra. The two oboe parts have a number of exposed, chromatic solo passages including some important solos on the English horn. The trombone I and horn I parts also have prominent solos which are somewhat demanding. The most challenging orchestral parts are the two trumpets which have many exposed passages. These players must also exchange fragments of a single melodic line between them, requiring players of similar timbre. There are a few spots that call for four percussionists; however, if players are limited, this number can be reduced to two if a cymbal is mounted onto the bass drum shell.

symphonic version: There are some awkward passages for the harp. The organ and celeste overlap only on the first beats of two measures, allowing a single player to cover both parts if necessary. In the symphonic version, the organ part is entirely doubled by other instruments and is listed as optional, but its sonority contributes greatly to this orchestration.

**Soloists:** soprano - range: $e^{b'}$-$b^{b''}$; tessitura: d"-g"; this role requires a lyric voice which is asked to portray an angel, but must be able to project over the entire ensemble; contralto - range: b-e"; tessitura: e'-b'; this is a shorter solo role which should timbrally contrast with the soprano soloist; tenor - range: c-a'; tessitura: f-f'; this is a lyric role which requires a beautiful and sweet voice capable of sustained light singing in the upper range. The narrator must be capable of a powerful and dramatic presentation of this text. Because the narrator is asked to portray the voice of Samuel, a male voice should be used. The Witch of Endor, who appears in only one movement, is clearly a theatrical role and is often executed with lighting, costume, and minimal staging. **Choir:** medium easy; **Orchestra:** medium easy to medium difficult.

**Discography:** chamber version: Christiane Eda-Pierre, Jeannine Collard, Eric Tappy, Bernard Petel (David as a child); Simone Valere and Jean Desailly, speakers; Chorale Philippe Caillard (Philippe Caillard, chorus-master), Instrumental Ensemble; conducted by Charles Dutoit, recorded in 1973. Erato: 2292-45800-2 [ADD].

symphonic version:

Micheau, Jeannine Collard, Mullet; Hervé, speaker; Brasseur Choir, French Radio Orchestra; conducted by Arthur Honegger. Westminster: WAL 204 [LP].

Coburn, Kallisch, Blochwitz; Freiburg Collegium Musicum, Frankfurt Kantorei; conducted by Wolfgang Schäfer. Christophorus: CD-74523.

Christiane Eda-Pierre, M. Senn, T. Raffalli; Czech Philharmonic and Chorus; conducted by Serge Baudo. Supraphon: CO-1412/13 [DDD].

Susan Danco, de Montmolin, Hamel; Suisse Romande Orchestra and Chorus; conducted by Ernest Ansermet. London: 425621-2 LM [ADD].

N. Davrath, J. Preston, M. Sorenson; Martial Singher and Madeleine Milhaud, speakers; Utah Symphony Orchestra; conducted by Maurice Abravanel. Vanguard Classics: OVC 4038 [ADD].

B. Fournier, Felicity Palmer, John Elwes, L. Wilson, Y. Théraulaz; Gulbenkian Symphony Orchestra and Chorus; conducted by M. Corboz. Cascavelle: VEL 1017 [DDD].

U. Frühhaber, M. Georg, K. Immer, W. Quadflieg; Dortmund Instrumental Soloists and University Chorus; conducted by W. Gundlach. Thorofon: CTH 2128 [DDD].

### Selected Bibliography

Bass, Claude Leroy: *Phrase Structure and Cadence Treatment in Stravinsky's Symphony of Psalms and Honegger's Le Roi David.* University of Oklahoma: Master's thesis, 1960.

Meyland, Pierre: *René Morax et Arthur Honegger au Théâtre du Jorat.* Lausanne: Éditions du Cervin, 1966.

Baker, H. A.: "Arthur Honegger and *King David*," *Amor artis Bulletin*, volume 7, number 1 (1968), 1, 10.

Berger, Melvin: *Guide to Choral Masterpieces: A Listener's Guide*, 177-178. New York: Anchor Books, 1993.

## Jeanne d'Arc au bûcher (1935-37)

**Duration:** ca. 80 minutes

**Text:** A setting of the story of Joan of Arc written by Paul Claudel; the text is in French.

**Performing Forces: voices:** Joan of Arc (speaker), Brother Dominic (speaker), King of France (speaker), King of England (speaker), Regnault de Chartres (speaker), Guillaume de Flavy (speaker), Duke of Bedford (speaker), Duke of Burgundy (speaker), Jean de Luxembourg (speaker), Perrot (speaker), Mother of Barrels (speaker), Grinder Trusty (speaker), Priest (speaker), Asinus the Donkey (speaker), Harold III (speaker), the Seven Deadly Sins (7 speakers/dancers), Holy Virgin (soprano), St. Margaret (soprano), St. Catherine (alto), Porcus the Swine (tenor), peasant (tenor), peasant (bass), Harold I (tenor), Harold II (bass), a child's voice; SATB choir and children's choir; **orchestra:** 2 flutes (flute II doubling piccolo), 2 oboes, soprano clarinet in $E^b$, clarinet in $B^b$, bass clarinet, 3 alto-saxophones in $E^b$, 3 bassoons, contrabassoon, trumpet in D, 3 trumpets in C, 3 trombones, bass trombone or tuba, timpani, percussion (2 players), celeste, 2 pianos, Ondes Martenot, and strings.

**First Performance:** concert version: 12 May 1938; Basle, Switzerland; Chamber Orchestra of Basle, conducted by Paul Sacher; Ida Rubinstein played Joan. partially staged version: May 1939; Orléans, France; as part of the Jeanne d'Arc Festival. fully staged version: 13 June 1942; Zürich.

**Edition:** *Jeanne d'Arc au Bûcher* is published by Salabert. Piano-vocal and choral scores are available for purchase; orchestral materials are available through rental.

**Autograph:** The manuscript of the score is in the possession of the Paul Sacher Foundation in Basle, Switzerland.

**Notes:** A musical composition based upon Claudel's *Jeanne d'Arc au Bûcher* was suggested to Honegger by Ida Rubinstein in 1935. The score was completed 30 August 1938.

**Performance Issues:** The score allows for this work to be performed with six solo singers and five speakers; however, the story could be made clearer if each role were done by a different person. The multiple parts for the male singers are all short and varied so that members of the choir could be used. The one exception is the character Porcus, which has a number of sustained high passages. The ranges of all the other tenor solos fall within the range of c#-e'. Dividing the parts one by one, creates 14 spoken roles, and 11 sung roles. The score includes some rhythmic recitation for the choir. All of the reciters must be able to follow the score as their integration into the work must be somewhat independent. The choral writing is generally diatonic. It incorporates unison singing, four-part homophonic chorale style, and some imitative writing. There are a number of chromatic passages with contrary motion that will be difficult to make clear. The majority of the vocal pitch material is supported by the orchestra. The orchestral parts are idiomatic and well-conceived for balance. Much of the instrumental writing is typical of theater music, which this is. The score integrates many popular dance figurations and effective polymetric elements. **Soloists:** Jeanne - range: b-a', tessitura: b-a', this is primarily a spoken role, but she has one brief sung passage; Holy Virgin (soprano) - range: e'-b", tessitura: d"-g", this role requires a bright, pure voice; St. Margaret (soprano) - range: e'-a", tessitura: g'-f", this is a lyric role; St. Catherine (alto) - range: g-e#", tessitura: d'-c", this is a lyric and diatonic role; tenor (Porcus the Swine, a voice, Harold I) - range: c#-b", tessitura: g-g', this role must be capable of sustained singing in the upper range; bass (a voice, Harold II, a countryman) - range: G-e', tessitura: B$^b$-d, this role requires a contrast of timbres from character to character; child's solo - range: d'-d", tessitura: d'-b', this is a brief, diatonic solo; **Choir:** medium difficult; **Orchestra:** medium difficult.

**Discography:** Frances Yeend, Martha Lipton, Robert Lloyd, K. Smith; Zorina, speaker; Temple University Choir, St. Peter's Boy Choir, Philadelphia Orchestra; conducted by Eugene Ormandy. Columbia: SL 178 [LP].

C. Château, A-M Rodde, H. Brachet, P. Proenza, Z. Jankovsky, F. Loup; Czech Philharmonic Orchestra and Chorus; conducted by Serge Baudo, recorded in 1974. Supraphon: 11 0557-2 [AAD].

### Selected Bibliography

Berger, Melvin: *Guide to Choral Masterpieces: A Listener's Guide*, 178-179. New York: Anchor Books, 1993.

## Janácek, Leos (b. Hukvaldy, Moravia, 3 July 1854; d. Moravská Ostrava, 12 August 1928)

**Life:** Janácek was one of the most significant of all Czech composers. He distinguished himself from his native forbears with his attentiveness to the natural music of the Czech language, which may have been influenced by his interest in Moravian folk music. This sensitivity to language combined with a profound understanding of the dramatic process led him to create a remarkably rich repertoire which is best distinguished in his operatic works. He was born into a musical family and received his early musical education as a chorister at the Augustinian Queen's Monastery. His further education was in Brno and Leipzig where his teachers included Oskar Paul, Leo Grill, and later Franz Krenn at the Vienna Conservatory. He returned to Brno where he was engaged as an organist and choirmaster. His music is marked by a distinctive use of dissonant harmonies and innovative rhythmic patterns which are probably the result of logogenesis.

**Writings:** There have been posthumous publications of the studies: *Folk Song and Folk Music* (1955) and *Music Theory Works*, 2 volumes (1968, 1974).

**Principal Works:** *operas - Jenufa* (1903), *The Cunning Little Vixen* (1923), *The Makropolous Affair* (1925), *From the House of the Dead* (1928); *orchestral - Taras Bulba* (1915-18), *Sinfonietta* (1926) Violin Concerto (1926); *choral - Hospodine* (1896), *Amarus* (1897), *Na Soláni Carták* (1911), *Vecné evangelium* (1914), and many part-songs and motets.

### Selected Composer Bibliography

Stedron, Bohumir: *Leos Janacek: Letters and Reminiscences.* Prague: Artia, 1955.

Vogel, Jaroslav: *Leos Janácek: Leben und Werk.* Kassel: Hamlyn, 1958. Published in English as: *Leos Janácek: His Life and Works*, second edition. London: Orbis, 1980.

Hollander, Hans: *Leos Janácek.* London: John Calder, 1963.

Horsbrugh, Ian: *Leos Janácek: The Field that Prospered.* New York: Charles Scribner's Sons, 1981.

## Msa Glagskaja [Glagolithic Mass] (1926)

**Duration:** ca. 45 minutes[11]

**Text:** This is a setting of the Eastern Orthodox Mass in Old Church Slavonic, written in Glagolithic script. It is published in a Czech/German edition and a Latin/English edition.

**Performing Forces:** **voices:** soprano, alto, tenor, and bass soloists; SATB choir; **orchestra:** 4 flutes (flutes I, II, and III doubling piccolo), 2 oboes, English horn, 3 clarinets in $B^b$ (clarinet III doubling bass clarinet in $B^b$), 3 bassoons (bassoon III doubling contrabassoon), 4 horns in F, 4 trumpets in F, 3 trombones, tuba, timpani, percussion (3 players - glockenspiel, snare drum, cymbals, tam-tam, triangle), 2 harps, celeste, organ, and strings.

---

[11] The score lists a duration of 45 minutes; however, the Masur recording is 37 minutes and 17 seconds with tempi comparable to those indicated in the score.

**First Performance:** 5 December 1927; Brno; Brno Opera Orchestra and Chorus; conducted by Jaroslav Kvapil.

**Edition:** *Msa Glagskaja* is published by Universal Edition. The choral/vocal score (9544 in German and Czech, and 9544A in Latin and English), full score (9541), and miniature score (13 366) are available for purchase; orchestral materials are available through rental.

**Autograph:** The manuscript of the later authorized version and some early sketches are in the Janácek Archive in Prague. The manuscript of the original authorized version is in the Österreichische Nationalbibliothek in Vienna. An incomplete set of string and orchestra parts from the premiere are housed in the archive of the Brno State Philharmonic.

**Notes:** This was the last concert work completed by Janacek. The score, which is dedicated to the Archbishop, Dr. Leopoldu Precanovi, was written between 5 August and 15 October 1926. A symphonic setting of these texts is particularly interesting since all music on the Eastern Orthodox Rite is, by tradition, *a cappella*.

Janacek organized the Mass as follows:

    I    Uvod (Introduction)
   II    Gospdodi pomiluj (Kyrie eleison)
  III    Slava (Gloria)
   IV    Veruju (Credo)
    V    Svet Gospod (Sanctus)
   VI    Agnece Bozij (Agnus Dei)
  VII    organ solo
 VIII    Intrada

The composer saw the *Glagolithic Mass* as a nationalist undertaking, an expression of his culture and heritage.[12] Although the score does not use any borrowed materials, the dramatic compositional style of this work is highly influenced by a sense of ethnic identity and Janacek's operatic tendencies.

---

12 Kurt Pahlen: *The World of the Oratorio*, 196. Portland, Oregon: Amadeus Press, 1985.

**Performance Issues:** There are instances of whole-tone melodies, non-traditional scalar patterns and occasional polytonal sections. There are two-part divisi in all of the choral parts. Much of the vocal material is initially challenging because of the rather unique style of Janacek's choral writing in this work. With some exposure, the choral writing becomes quite logical and accessible. Most of the vocal material is clearly supported by the accompaniment and entrance pitches for singers are well prepared. The orchestral writing is practical, but is intended for secure players. There are many sections which exploit the temporal juxtaposition of 6 against 4 and 4 against 3. The brass parts are demanding and exposed. The trumpet I part is especially difficult with many important high passages. Trumpets I, II, and III have extended sections of unison playing. The horns and trombones have some endurance challenges as they play much of the time. The woodwinds have some very high passages for all of the players, most notably in movement VI, where the voicing of the winds will be problematic to successful intonation. The string parts are chromatic and rhythmically articulate, but are quite practical. This piece requires a skilled organist. The seventh movement is an unaccompanied organ solo with significant technical demands, for which a large romantic instrument is desirable. The organ has some exposed passages in other movements as well. The orchestration of this work demands a sizeable choir to achieve a successful balance. This is an extraordinarily dramatic work which will provide challenges to professional ensembles and yet provides the opportunity for an orchestra with moderate string proficiencies and strong brass and wind to successfully program a virtuoso symphonic choral work. **Soloists:** soprano - range: $g^{b\prime}$-$b^{b\prime\prime}$, tessitura: b'-g", this is a sustained and powerful role; alto - range: $a^b$-$d^{b\prime\prime}$, tessitura: d'-b', this role appears in only 10 measures of the entire work; tenor - range: $d^b$-b', tessitura: d'-a', this role is the largest and most difficult of the four, it is a legitimate heldentenor part; bass - range: $d^b$-e', tessitura: a-d', this role is really a baritone part, its is sustained and remains within the tessitura almost exclusively, it appears in only 25 measures of the entire composition; **Choir:** medium difficult, **Orchestra:** difficult

**Discography:** Moravian Mixed Chorus, Brno Radio Symphony Orchestra; conducted by Bakala. Urania: URLP 7072 [LP].

Brewer, Simpson, Dent, Roloff; Atlanta Symphony Orchestra and Chorus; conducted by Robert Shaw. Telarc: CD-80287 [DDD].

Lear, Rössel-Majdan, Haefliger, Crass; Bavarian Radio Symphony Orchestra and Chorus; conducted by Rafael Kubelik. Deutsche Grammophon: 429182-2 GGA [ADD].

Palmer, Benacková, Lakes, Kotcherga; London Symphony Orchestra and Chorus; conducted by Michael Tilson Thomas. Sony Classical: SK 47182 [DDD].

Czech Philharmonic Orchestra and Chorus; conducted by Karl Ancerl. Supraphon Collection: 110609 [ADD].

Elisabeth Söderström, Drobková, Livora, Novak; Czech Philharmonic Orchestra and Chorus; conducted by Charles Mackerras. Supraphon: 10 3575-2 [DDD].

Venceslava Hruba, Rosemarie Lang, John Mitchinson, Theo Adam; Czechoslovak Chorus of Prague, Gewandhaus Orchestra of Leipzig; conducted by Kurt Masur, recorded live in the Gewandhaus of Leipzig in January 1991. Philips: D 110358 [DDD].

### Selected Bibliography

Vecerka, R.: "K historii textu Janáckovy Hlaholské mse," *Sbornik praci filosofické fakulty brnenské university* (1957), 64.

Horsbrugh, Ian: *Leos Janácek: The Field that Prospered*, 8, 9, 24, 60, 62, 105, 157, 197, 213-221, 228, 246. New York: Charles Scribner's Sons, 1981.

Pahlen, Kurt: *The World of the Oratorio*, 195-198. Portland, Oregon: Amadeus Press, 1985.

Wingfield, Paul: *Janácek: Glagolithic Mass*. Cambridge: Cambridge University Press, 1992.

Berger, Melvin: *Guide to Choral Masterpieces: A Listener's Guide*, 183-185. New York: Anchor Books, 1993.

## Ridalka [Nursery Rhymes] (1925, revised 1927)

**Duration:** ca. 15 minutes

**Text:** The texts are traditional children's nursery rhymes in Czech. The published score includes a singing translation in German.

**Performing Forces: voices:** choir of 9 solo voices (SSAATTT BB); **orchestra:** ocarina, 2 flutes (flute II doubling piccolo), 2 clarinets in B$^b$ (both doubling soprano clarinet in E$^b$ and clarinet in A), 2 bassoons (bassoon II doubling contrabassoon), percussion (1 player - toy drum), piano, and doublebass.

**First Performance:** <u>original version</u>: 26 October 1925; Brno, Czechoslovakia; female ensemble; Stanislav Krticka, clarinet; Jaroslav Kvapil, piano.

> <u>revised version</u>: 25 April 1927; Brno, Czechoslovakia; Moravian Composers Club.

**Edition:** *Ríkadla* is published by Universal Edition. The full score and piano-vocal score are available for purchase; orchestral materials are available through rental.

**Autograph:** The manuscripts are housed in the Janácek Archive of the Moravian Museum of Brno.

**Notes:** The orginal version of 1925 consisted of only eight songs, and was scored for 3 female voices, clarinet, and piano. The revised score of 1927 is divided into 19 brief movements each conveying a single nursery rhyme. It is arranged as follows:

| | | |
|---|---|---|
| 1 | Introduction | instruments only |
| 2 | The Beet Wedding | SATB |
| 3 | Spring Sun | tenor solo |
| 4 | Mole and Hamster | SA |
| 5 | Karel in Hell | SA |
| 6 | Raggedy Trousers | S |
| 7 | Bully Franz Plays the Bass | T |
| 8 | Our Little Dog | SA |
| 9 | Lovely, Lovely Sermon | SA |
| 10 | Sorcery | S |
| 11 | Ho, Ho, Cows Are Here | SA |
| 12 | Little Doll Soup | T |
| 13 | Difficult Crawl in the Brush | S |
| 14 | Fruit Picking | S |
| 15 | Country Bumpkin | B |
| 16 | A Goat Basks in the Sunshine | SA |
| 17 | Vasek, Pasek, Bubeník | A |
| 18 | The Little Chick | SA |
| 19 | The Bear Sits on a Stump | SATB |

**Performance Issues:** The vocal parts are almost entirely unison, in a folksong style. There are occasional divisi, but even sections labeled for two sopranos and two altos, are generally a single melodic line. The movements assigned to the tenors feature two-part writing the most frequently. Movements 2, 9, and 19, are vocally polyphonic. The pitch material for the singers is chromatic and reflects the composer's familiarity with a number of Czech folk-music scales. These pitch sets will prove troublesome in learning the vocal melodies. The vocal parts are harmonically supported by the accompaniment, but rarely doubled directly. The instrumentation varies from movement to movement. The percussion and flute parts are involved in only a few movements and are technically accessible to most undergraduate-level players. The piano is prominent throughout the work and is quite difficult in terms of cross-rhythmic material and rapid passage work. The two clarinet parts are very challenging, especially in some quick chromatic unison passages. The composer has indicated that the ocarina, used only in movements 1 and 10, may be substituted with an alto flute; although it is a very easy part which anyone could play, which justifies finding one. It must have these pitches, in this octave: g, $a^b$, $c^{b'}$. This is a delightful and varied composition for small vocal and instrumental ensembles, which seems intended more for adult audiences than children. It is most effective if sung in the language of the audience. **Choir:** medium difficult; **Orchestra:** medium difficult.

**Discography:** Vienna Philharmonic Orchestra; conducted by Charles Mackerras. London: 430375-2 LH2 [DDD].

chamber version (1925-26):
Caramoor Festival Orchestra; conducted by Julius Rudel. Phoenix: PHCD 109 [ADD].

### Selected Bibliography

Horsbrugh, Ian: *Leos Janácek: The Field that Prospered*, 117, 202-203. New York: Charles Scribner's Sons, 1981.


**Kodály, Zoltán** (b. Kecskemét, Hungary, 16 December 1882; d. Budapest, 6 March 1967)

**Life:** Kodály was an important composer, folk-song collector, and a highly influential figure in the development of music education in the 20th century. He began composing as a child. He attended the University of Budapest where he studied composition with Hans Koessler. He received a Ph.D. in 1906 with the focus of his scholarship being Hungarian folksong. He established a strong friendship with his classmate, Bartók. The two young composers undertook a series of landmark projects collecting eastern European folkmusic. In 1907, Kodály was appointed to the faculty of the Royal Academy of Music in Budapest. His *Psalmus Hungaricus*, which was composed to commemorate the 50th anniversary of the union of Buda and Pest brought him international attention as a composer. Beginning in the 1930s he dedicated much of his compositional work to pieces for student performances, especially children's choir. He developed a series of educational methods which stressed the importance of singing in a complete education. Many of his teaching methods were centered around solmization. He received international honors including: the Gold medal of the Royal Philharmonic Society of London (1967), and honorary memberships in the Moscow Conservatory (1963), and the American Academy of Arts and Sciences (1963). The International Kodály Society was founded in 1975.

**Writings:** Kodály published a number of volumes on folkmusic including collaborative work with Bartok. An anthology of his writings has been published: *The Selected Writing of Zoltán Kodály*. London: Boosey and Hawkes, 1974.

**Principal Works:** *orchestral* - *Háry János Suite* (1927), *Dances from Galanta* (1933), *Peacock Variations* (1939), Concerto for Orchestra (1940); *choral* - *At the Martyr's Grave* (1945), *The Music Makers: An Ode* (1964); *chamber* - Cello Sonata (1909), 2 String Quartets (1909, 1918), and numerous works for students.

## Selected Composer Bibliography

Dickinson, A.E.F.: "Kodály's Choral Music," *Tempo*, number 15 (1946).

Eösze, László: *Zoltán Kodály: His Life and Work*. Boston: Crescendo Publishing Company, 1962.

Young, Percy M.: *Zoltán Kodály: A Hungarian Musician*. London: Ernest Benn Limited, 1964.

Stevens, Halsey: "The Choral Music of Zoltan Kodaly," *The Musical Quarterly*, liv (1968), 147.

Kodály, Zoltán:*The Selected Writing of Zoltán Kodály*. London: Boosey and Hawkes, 1974.

# Psalmus Hungaricus, op. 13 (1923)

**Duration:** ca. 23 minutes

**Text:** The text is a Hungarian adaptation of the 55th Psalm written by Mihály Vég during the 16th century. The score also includes singing translations in English by Edward J. Dent, and German by Bence Szabolcsi.

**Performing Forces: voices:** tenor soloist; SATB choir and optional children's choir; **orchestra:** 3 flutes, 2 oboes, 2 clarinets in A, 2 bassoons, 4 horns in F, 3 trumpets in C, 3 trombones, timpani, percussion (1 player - cymbals), harp, organ (optional), and strings.

**First Performance:** 19 November 1923; Budapest; in a concert of works commissioned to celebrate the fiftieth anniversary of the union of Buda and Pest. It was also performed with Honegger's *Le Roi David* on 18 June 1926 as part of the Fourth Festival of the International Society for Contemporary Music in Zürich, Switzerland.

**Edition:** *Psalmus Hungaricus* is published by Universal Edition. The piano-vocal score (8463), choral score (8463a), and miniature score (PH.233) are available for purchase; orchestral materials are available through rental.

**Autograph:** The manuscript is in the possession of the Budapest Székesföváros Közönségének.

**Notes:** *Psalmus Hungaricus* was one of three works commissioned for a concert celebrating the fiftieth anniversary of the union of Buda and Pest. The other pieces were Ernst von Dohnányi's *Festival Overture* and Béla Bartok's *Five Dances*. Kodály includes a section of unison pentatonic chant imitating ancient Magyar practices as musical hommage to the history of the city to which this piece is dedicated. This work was the first to draw international attention to the composer.

**Performance Issues:** This work requires a large orchestra and chorus. There are divisi among all of the choral parts including the children's choir which in some sections becomes SSAA. The children's choir exists for color only, as all of its material is doubled by the adult choir. While not necessary, the effect of the children's voices contributes to the overall spirit of the piece. It was probably included by the composer because of the festival nature of the first performance and the celebratory nationalist character of the work. The score includes the following note on that subject:

> It is strongly recommended to employ a children's chorus (boy's voices) for the passage **14** to **16**, especially if the female voices are not sufficiently strong in the middle register to balance the men's voices. When a very efficient children's chorus is available, it may be employed to reinforce the sopranos and altos from **33** to **35** and from **36** to **40**.

There are a number of *a cappella* sections. The choral writing is generally scalar or modal with chromatic inflections frequently repeated and supported by the harmonic environment. The vocal writing in general reflects Kodály's intimate knowledge of choral music. Interestingly, the final passage for the choir, which is primarily comprised of chant in octaves, ends with the second basses on an AA. The choral textures are often dense, but melodically generated and accessible to singers of moderate experience. The orchestra must be an ensemble of experienced players. The instrumental writing is rhythmically complex with much cross-accented material between sections of the ensemble. The principal flute should have a low-B foot. The greatest contrapuntal complexities are to be found between divisi parts within single sections of the strings. Perhaps the greatest performance issue in this work is the choice of language. The work is so profoundly tied to the rhythm and stress of the Hungarian that it becomes difficult to condone singing it in translation. **Soloist:** tenor - range: c#-b', tessitura: e-f#', this is a heldentenor role also requiring great clarity of diction; **Choir:** difficult; **Orchestra:** difficult.

**Discography:** Krebs; Radio Berlin Orchestra and Chorus; conducted by Rother. Urania: URLP 7014 [LP].

L Kozma; Brighton Festival Chorus; conducted by Istvan Kertész. London: 433080-2 LM [LP].

Komlóssy; London Symphony Orchestra and Chorus; conducted by Istvan Kertész. London: 421810-2 LM2 [ADD].

Simándy; Hungarian State Orchestra, Buda mac paest Chorus; conducted by Antal Dorati. Hungaroton: HCD-11392 [ADD].

Simándy; Stockholm Philharmonic Orchestra; conducted by Antal Dorati, recorded live on 16 December 1967. 8-Bis: CD-421/424 (mono/stereo) [ADD].

## Selected Bibliography

Eösze, László: *Zoltán Kodály: His Life and Work*, 156-160. Boston: Crescendo Publishing Company, 1962.

Young, Percy M.: *Zoltán Kodály: A Hungarian Musician*, 74-81. London: Ernest Benn Limited, 1964.

Pahlen, Kurt: *The World of the Oratorio*, 198-199. Portland, Oregon: Amadeus Press, 1985.

Berger, Melvin: *Guide to Choral Masterpieces: A Listener's Guide*, 189-190. New York: Anchor Books, 1993.

# Budavári Te Deum (1936)

**Duration:** ca. 20 minutes

**Text:** The text is the "Te Deum laudamus," a 4th-century Ambrosian song of praise in Latin, which is one of the principal canticles of the Roman Catholic rite of Morning Prayer.

**Performing Forces: voices:** soprano, alto, tenor, and bass soloists; SATB choir; **orchestra:** 2 flutes, 2 oboes, 2 clarinets in A, 2 bassoons, 4 horns in F, 3 trumpets in C, 3 trombones, tuba, timpani, organ (optional), and strings.

**First Performance:** 11 September 1936[13]; Budapest.

**Edition:** *Te Deum* is published by Universal Edition. The piano-vocal score (10849), choral score (10849a), and miniature score (PH.276) are available for purchase; orchestral materials are available through rental.

**Notes:** This work was composed to commemorate the 250th anniversary of the city of Buda being successfully defended from invading Turks. The work combines "the pentatonic modes of

---

[13] Kurt Pahlen: *The World of the Oratorio*, 205. Portland, Oregon: Amadeus Press, 1985.

immemorial Pannonia with devotional ecclesiastical tropes set in freely modulating triadic harmonies."[14]

**Performance Issues:** The solo passages are very brief, in fact, the bass and alto soloists sing in fewer than eight measures. The soprano solo is the most important, but still represents only two dozen measures of singing. The chorus has two-part divisi in each section. This work is scored for a very large chorus. The soprano and tenor sections have some very high sustained passages. All of the vocal parts are forceful and sustained, suggesting the use of a mature choir. The choral material is functionally tonal with some folk-music-inspired modal inflections. The melodic material is triadic and scalar. The vocal passages are thoroughly supported by the accompaniment. There are a number of rapid chromatic passages for the woodwinds and the strings which are fairly idiomatic. The brass section is engaged in fanfare-like material throughout most of the work. Stamina for the brass players must be a consideration in programming and rehearsal scheduling. Also of programming consideration is that for all of its grandeur and bombast, this work ends pianissimo. **Soloists:** soprano - range: c#'-bb", tessitura: e'-e", this is a declamatory solo with broad melodic leaps; alto - range: d'-bb', tessitura: d'-bb', this is a very brief solo; tenor - range: g#-bb', tessitura: a-f', this is a declamatory solo with some sustained high singing; bass - range: c-bb, tessitura: c-bb, this is a brief solo; **Choir:** medium difficult; **Orchestra:** medium difficult.

**Discography:** Hungarian Radio Orchestra and Chorus; conducted by János Ferencsik. Hungaroton: MK-11397 [LP].
Jurinac, Wagner, Christ, Poell; Vienna Choir and Vienna Symphony Orchestra; conducted by Henry Swoboda. Westminster: WL 5001 [LP].

### Selected Bibliography

Eösze, László: *Zoltán Kodály: His Life and Work*, 163-166. Boston: Crescendo Publishing Company, 1962.
Young, Percy M.: *Zoltán Kodály: A Hungarian Musician*, 101-103. London: Ernest Benn Limited, 1964.

---

[14] Nicolas Slonimsky: *Music Since 1900*, fifth edition, 398. New York: Schirmer Books, 1994.

Pahlen, Kurt: *The World of the Oratorio*, 200-201. Portland, Oregon: Amadeus Press, 1985.
Berger, Melvin: *Guide to Choral Masterpieces: A Listener's Guide*, 190-191. New York: Anchor Books, 1993.

## Missa brevis (1944)

**Duration:** ca. 32 minutes

**Text:** The text is in Latin and is taken from the Roman Catholic communion liturgy.

**Performing Forces: voices:** SATB choir; **orchestra:** 3 flutes (flute III doubling piccolo), 2 oboes, 2 clarinets in B$^b$, 2 bassoons, 4 horns in F, 3 trumpets in C, 3 trombones, tuba, timpani, organ (optional), and strings.

**First Performance:** 11 February 1945; Budapest.

**Edition:** *Missa Brevis* is published by Boosey and Hawkes. The piano-vocal score (LCB 12), choral score (LCB 39), full score (FSB 56), and miniature score (HPS 702) are available for purchase; orchestral materials are available through rental.

**Notes:** The score is dedicated *"Coniugi et consorti carisimae in anniversario XXXV —* Beloved spouses and companions upon the thirty-fifth anniversary." The work is divided into eight movements as follows:

    I    Introitus (orchestra only)
    II   Kyrie
    III  Gloria
    IV   Credo
    V    Sanctus
    VI   Benedictus
    VII  Agnus Dei
    VIII Ite missa est

**Performance Issues:** This entire mass is contrapuntally conceived and reveals Kodály's appreciation for sixteenth-century imitative procedures, which are combined with a twentieth-century harmonic palette colored by the modal language of traditional Hungarian music. The work primarily uses a four-part choral texture, but there are two-part divisi for all sections of the choir. There are three-part soli for the sopranos. The uppermost of these parts goes up to c''' a number of times. The choral parts are thoroughly doubled by the orchestra throughout the work. There are divisi for all strings except the cellos. The doublebasses must be able to play down to CC#. The instrumental writing is conservative and well-conceived for the individual instruments. There is significant doubling between the sections of the orchestra and very little exposed playing for any single instrument. Flute I and bassoon I have the most prominent solo passages. All of the organ material is doubled within the orchestra, but its timbre greatly enhances the overall effect of the piece as the organ part is present throughout most of the work. If an organ is used, a strong player must be engaged. Also, because of the pervasive nature of the organ part, forethought must be given to the selection of registrations. A pre-rehearsal consultation with the organist is strongly recommended. The manner in which the choral parts are doubled by the orchestra is likely to create balance troubles. Care must be taken to combat the dense texture of the orchestra with unusually clear vocal articulations. It may also prove helpful to place the choir in front, or along the sides, of the orchestra in an attempt to separate the sounds of the two ensembles. **Choir:** medium difficult; **Orchestra:** medium difficult.

**Discography:** Hungarian Radio Orchestra and Chorus; conducted by Ferencsik. Hungaroton: MK-11397 [LP].
Brighton Festival Chorus; conducted by L. Heltay. London: 433080-2 LM [LP].

with organ accompaniment:

National Presbyterian Church Choir of Washington, DC; conducted by Schaefer. WCFM: WCFM 4 [LP]. This is the choir which gave the first performance of this work in the United States.[15]

### Selected Bibliography

Seiber, Matyas: "Kodály: Missa Brevis," *Tempo*, number 4 (1947), 3.
Eösze, László: *Zoltán Kodály: His Life and Work*, 161-163. Boston: Crescendo Publishing Company, 1962.

---

15 Miller, Philip L.: *The Guide to Long-Playing Records: Choral Music*, 128. New York: Alfred A. Knopf, 1955.

Young, Percy M.: *Zoltán Kodály: A Hungarian Musician*, 127-130. London: Ernest Benn Limited, 1964.
Berger, Melvin: *Guide to Choral Masterpieces: A Listener's Guide*, 191-192. New York: Anchor Books, 1993.


## Ligeti, György (b. Dicsöszentmárton, Transylvania, 28 May 1923)

**Life:** Ligeti's music is quite distinctive for its use of sonority as a structural element over motive through procedures which he calls micropolyphony. He studied at the Kolozsvar Conservatory with Ferenc Farkas, and privately with Pál Kadosa. He continued his studies at the Budapest Academy of Music (1945-49), studying again with Farkas, and with Lajos Bárdos, Pál Járdányi, and Sándor Veress. He taught at the Budapest Academy from 1950 until 1956 when he fled Hungary following the unsuccessful revolution of that year. He worked for North German Radio and taught at the Music School of Stockholm and the summer institute at Darmstadt until 1973 when he joined the faculty of the Hamburg Hochschule für Musik. His works are often quite experimental, but have achieved a broad audience, in part, because of the inclusion of the *Kyrie* from his *Requiem* into the soundtrack of the film *2001: A Space Odyssey*. He has received many awards including: an honorary membership in the American Academy and Institute of Arts and Letters (1984), and the Grawemeyer Award (1986).

**Principal Works:** *opera* - *Le Grand Macabre* (1977); *orchestral* - *Apparitions* (1959), *Atmosphères* (1961), *Lontano* (1967), *Ramifications* (1969), Piano Concerto (1988); *chamber* - 2 String Quartets (1954, 1968); *keyboard* - *Hungarian Rock* (1978), *Passacaglia ungherese* (1978); *choral* - *Cantata for Youth* (1949), *Lux aeterna* (1966), *Drei Phantasien* (1983).

### Selected Composer Bibliography

Nordwall, Ove: "György Ligeti," *Tempo*, volume 88 (1969), 22.
_____: *György Ligeti: Eine Monographie*. Mainz: B. Schotts Söhne, 1970.
Griffiths, Paul: *György Ligeti*. London: 1983.
Soria, D.: "György Ligeti: Distinguished and Unpredictable," *Musical America* (September 1987).

# Requiem (1963-65)

**Duration:** ca. 27 minutes

**Text:** The text is from the Roman Catholic Mass for the Dead.

**Performing Forces: voices:** soprano and mezzo-soprano soloists, 2 SMATB choirs; **orchestra:** 3 flutes (flutes II and III doubling piccolo), 3 oboes (oboe III doubling English horn), 3 clarinets in $B^b$ (clarinet II doubling bass clarinet in $B^b$, clarinet III doubling contrabass clarinet in $B^b$, one of the clarinets doubling soprano clarinet in $E^b$), 2 bassoons, contrabassoon, 4 horns in F, 3 trumpets in C, bass trumpet in $E^b$ or C, tenor trombone, "tenor-bass" trombone, contrabass trombone, tuba, percussion (3 players - glockenspiel, xylophone, snare drum, bass drum, tambourine, suspended cymbal, large tam-tam, whip), harp, harpsichord, celeste, and strings.

The score suggests a minimum of 60 singers in choir I, but a preference for 80 to 100. This group has 20 independent parts in some passages with 4-part divisi in each choral section. A minimum of 120 singers is recommended for choir II.

The minimum strings possible is 12-12-10-8-6.

**First Performance:** 14 March 1965; Stockholm. It was also performed on 21 September 1968 in Warsaw as part of the 42nd Festival of the International Society for Contemporary Music.

**Edition:** *Requiem* is published by Peters. The piano-vocal score (8152) and full score (P4841) are available for purchase only; orchestral materials are available through rental.

**Autograph:** The full score is a facsimile of the composer's manuscript.

**Notes:** *Requiem* was commissioned by Swedish Radio. The full score is accompanied by a 23-page booklet of translations, page-by-page, of the indications in the score. There are additional performance indications in the front matter of the score which greatly enhance the utility of the score. In this work, Ligeti has selected portions of the *Missa pro defunctis* which he has organized into four movements as follows:

| | | |
|---|---|---|
| I | Introitus | soloists, choir I |
| II | Kyrie eleison | choir I |
| III | De die judicii sequentia (Dies irae) | soloists, choirs I and II |
| IV | Lacrimosa | soloists |

**Performance Issues:** Kurt Pahlen writes of the *Requiem*, "It exceeds in difficulty of performance almost anything written for voices, instruments, and the perfecting of their combined effects."[16] The score is in C with octave displacements for doublebasses, piccolo, and contrabassoon, but not xylophone. The score also states that the glockenspiel sounds one octave higher than written, but the composer probably intended the normal two-octave transposition. The flute II must have a low-B foot. The bassoons and contrabassoon are asked to use mutes in the Kyrie, for this, the composer suggests the use of a handkerchief. The bass trumpet part is printed for both C and $E^b$ instruments. It will be necessary to acquire a mute for the bass trumpet. The double basses must be capable of playing down to BBB. The composer's notes state that the barlines are for synchronization of parts, and are not meant to imply any metric organization. There are *Sprechstimme* parts which combine approximate pitch and whispers. There are numerous rhythmic features which present substantial challenges including as many as two changes of subdivision per player in a single measure, and compound subdivisions of the beat into 9, 8, 7, 6, 5, 3, and 2 parts simultaneously from diverse sections of the ensemble. The pitch material is highly chromatic with craggy leaping melodic passages for all singers and players. There are also many dense tone-clusters with the constituents in a constant state of flux. The choral material for choir I is extremely difficult with numerous densely voiced passages and some tremendously difficult rhythms. The choir II writing is much less confounding and occupies only about five minutes of the work. That portion could be executed by a large collegiate or community chorus. Most of the choral material is doubled by the orchestra; however, the textures are often dense enough to render supporting lines indistinguishable. The individual orchestra parts are quite difficult due to extremes of

---

[16]  Kurt Pahlen lists 2 September 1936 as the premiere date in *The World of the Oratorio*, 200. Portland, Oregon: Amadeus Press, 1985.

range, sudden dynamic contrasts, and rapid, non-conventional leaps for all players. The literalness of some of Ligeti's notation makes it difficult to discern some of the rhythms. It may be prudent to indicate the placement of beats within the measures of movement III in the instrumental parts to clarify the rhythmic organization of the score. The overall sonic effect of the score is tremendous, and although fiercely difficult, all of the indications are possible and reveal the composer's remarkable understanding of the sounds and methods of the orchestral and choral palettes. The intensity of this score and the challenges presented within it demand that it be programmed with music of a much different style. **Soloists:** soprano - range: b-d'''(optional e$^{b}$'''), tessitura: c'-b", this role is filled with broad leaps, one exceeding two octaves, with little support from the accompaniment, this soloist must be capable of soft and sustained singing at the top of the range; mezzo-soprano - range: g-a", tessitura: b-f", this role is comprised of broad atonal leaps and sustained high singing; **Choir:** very difficult; **Orchestra:** very difficult.

**Discography:** Poli, Ericson; Hesse Radio Symphony Orchestra and Chorus; conducted by Michael Gielen. Wergo: WER-60045-50 [ADD].

### Selected Bibliography

Salmanhaara, E.: *Das musikalishe Material und seine Behandlung in den Weihen "Apparitions," "Atmospheres," "Aventures," and "Requiem" von Gyorgy Ligeti.* Helsinki and Regensberg, 1969.

## Uhren und Wolken [Clocks and Clouds] (1972-73)

**Duration:** ca. 13 minutes

**Text:** The text is a collection of syllables chosen by the composer for their sound qualities.

**Performing Forces: voices:** SSSSMMMMAAAA choir or soloists; **orchestra:** 5 flutes (flute I doubling alto flute; flutes 3, 4, and 5 doubling piccolo), 3 oboes, 5 clarinets in B$^{b}$ (clarinet V doubling bass clarinet in B$^{b}$), 4 bassoons (bassoon IV doubling contrabassoon) , 2 trumpets, percussion (2 players - glockenspiel, vibraphone), 2 harps, celeste, 4 violas, 6 cellos, 4 doublebasses.

**First Performance:** 15 October 1973; Graz.

**Edition:** *Uhren und Wolken* is published by Schott. All materials are available through rental.

**Autograph:** The full score is a copy of the composer's manuscript.

**Notes:** *Uhern und Wolken* is dedicated to the memory of Harold Kaufmann. It was composed for the "Musikprotokoll" program of the Steiermark studio of Austrian Radio in Graz.

**Performance Issues:** The score is notated in C. Those instruments with octave transpositions (piccolo and doublebass, etc.) are indicated at traditional written pitch rather than in the sounding octave. There are quarter-tone passages for the singers and the instrumentalists. The singers are given nonsense syllables throughout, which are spelled in the International Phonetic Alphabet. There appears to be a numeralogical significance to the presence of 13 vowel and 13 consonant sounds in this text. The presence of twelve singers appears to be significant to the title as well. The composer suggests that for the balance to be successful, a large chorus may be placed behind the instruments, but if a small chorus is employed it should be placed evenly with, or in front of the instruments. For this configuration, Ligeti recommends placing the singers in the areas vacated by the violins who do not play in this work. One of the most significant challenges facing conductors of this work is the marginal legibility of the score. Not only is the orchestration often dense and complex, but the manuscript is inconsistent and, at times, wholly illegible. The score requires the doublebass IV to have a five-string instrument with the lowest string tuned to low BB. Each of the string players has an independent part. All of the instrumental parts are virtuosic. The strings, harp, flutes, oboes, and bassoons are asked to play some sections in harmonics. There are regularly occuring staggered entrances throughout the ensemble on uneven divisions of the beat. The instrumental pitch material often consists of rapid overlapping chromatic scales, creating dense clusters of vertical quarter and half steps. The pitch material of the choir begins as a unison which is supported by the orchestra. Through a gradual unfolding of quarter-tone scales, the singers achieve a very dissonant tonal sonority. The beat is divided into 2, 3, 4, 5, 6, 9, 10, 15, and 16 even parts with as many as five different divisions occuring simultaneously.

The overall sonic effect is remarkable and dramatic with a great variety of colors and textures creating a very logical overall shape; however, the internal workings of the piece which create this effect are fiercely difficult to achieve accurately. **Choir:** very difficult; **Orchestra:** very difficult.

**Discography:** As of February 1997, there are no commercial recordings available of this work.

### Selected Bibliography

Sandner, W.: "Graz: Musikprotokoll beim 'Steirer Herbst' 1973," *Neue Zeitschrift für Musik*, volume 134, number 12 (1973), 800-802.

"Urauffuehrungen," *Schweizerische Musikzeitung*, volume 113, number 6 (1973), 378.

"First Performances," *The World of Music*, volume 16, number 1 (1974), 69.

Brunner, G.: "Musikprotokoll 73," *Musica*, volume 28, number 1 (1974), 69.

Polaczek, D.: "Reife Freuchte und saure Trauben beim Musikprotokoll in Graz," *Melos*, volume 41, number 1 (1974), 38-42.

## Mahler, Gustav (b. Kalischt, Bohemia, 7 July 1860; d. Vienna, 18 May 1911)

**Life:** Mahler was regarded as the greatest virtuoso conductor of his generation, and he was one of the most influential composers in the transition from the Romanticism of the 19th century into the Expressionism of the early 20th century. Following his death, many of his works fell into neglect, only to be reintroduced in performances led by Dmitri Mitropolous and Leonard Bernstein during the 1950s and 1960s. Bernstein stated that Mahler had brought the development of the symphonic form to its logical conclusion. Mahler studied philosophy and history at the University of Vienna and music at the Vienna Conservatory with Robert Fuchs and Franz Krenn. He received his first conducting appointment in 1880 and gradually rose through the ranks of German, Austrian, Czech, and Hungarian opera houses, being appointed assistant to Nikisch in Leipzig in 1888, principal conductor in Hamburg in 1891, and music director of the Vienna State Opera from 1897-1907. He also served as director of the Vienna Philharmonic from 1898 to 1901. In Vienna he established an unprecedented level of quality in his productions. He became music director of the Metropolitan Opera in New York in 1907 and the New York

Philharmonic in 1909. He resigned both posts in 1911 following disputes with the boards of directors, returning to Austria where he died of a heart attack. Even Mahler's works without texts are given programmatic titles or inscriptions. He often incorporates musical themes which recur in successive works almost as life-long leitmotives. There is an element of autobiography in much of his music, which as a reflection of his generation includes remarkable contrasts between humor and despair.

**Principal Works:** *orchestral* - 10 Symphonies (1883-88, 1887-94, 1893-96, 1899-1901, 1901-02, 1903-05, 1904-06, 1906-07, 1909-10, unfinished f.p. 1960); *vocal - Das klagende Lied* (1878-80), *Lieder eines fahrenden Gesellen* (1883-85), *Das Knaben Wunderhorn* (1892-1901), *Rückert Lieder* (1901-03), *Kindertotenlieder* (1901-04), *Das Lied von der Erde* (1907-09).

## Selected Composer Bibliography

Walter, Bruno: *Gustav Mahler*, translated by James Galston. New York: Greystone Press, 1941; reprinted New York: Vienna House, 1973.

Mahler, Alma: *Gustav Mahler: Memories and Letters*, translated by Basil Creighton. New York: Viking Press, 1946.

La Grange, Henry-Louis de: *Mahler*, volume I. Garden City, NY: Doubleday and Co., 1973.

_____: *Gustav Mahler: Vienna: The Years of Challenge (1897-1904)*. Oxford: Oxford University Press, 1995.

Cooke, Deryck: *Gustav Mahler: An Introduction to his Music*. Cambridge: Cambridge University Press, 1980.

Bauer-Lechner, Natalie: *Recollections of Gustav Mahler*. Cambridge: Cambridge University Press, 1980.

Filler, Susan M.: *Gustav and Alma Mahler: A Guide to Research*. New York: Garland Publishing, 1989.

Kennedy, Michael: *Mahler*, revised. New York: Schirmer Books, 1990.

## Das klagende Lied (1878-80; rev 1888, 1893-1902)

**Duration:** ca. 40 minutes

**Text:** The text, in German, is by Mahler, derived from a fairy-tale by Ludwig Bechstein.

**Performing Forces: voices:** soprano, alto, and tenor soloists; SATB choir; **orchestra:** 3 flutes (flute III doubling piccolo), 3 oboes (oboe III doubling English horn), 3 clarinets in $B^b$ (clarinet III doubling bass clarinet in $B^b$), 2 bassoons, contrabassoon, 4 horns in F, 4 trumpets in F, 3 trombones, tuba, timpani, percussion (3 players - bass drum, cymbals, tam-tam, triangle), 2 harps, and strings.

additional "distant orchestra": piccolo, 2 flutes, 2 oboes, 4 clarinets in $B^b$, 4 horns in F, 2 trumpets in F, timpani, percussion (2 players - cymbals, triangle).

**First Performance:** 17 February 1901; Vienna; Vienna Philharmonic Orchestra and Chorus, conducted by the composer.

first performance of Waldmärchen: 26 November 1934; radio broadcast from Brno; conducted by Alfred Rosé.

**Edition:** *Das klagende Lied* is available in multiple editions. The piano-vocal score, full score, and orchestral materials are available from Kalmus (A5603) for purchase. The full score is available from Universal Edition (51 16814) for purchase. An edition of the "Waldmarchen" movement is available with optional piano reduction from Rolf Budde Musikverlag through rental; a study score of this edition is available for purchase from Belwin. The "Waldmarchen" movement is also available from Universal Edition and Kalmus, although Kalmus has only the full score and not the orchestral materials.

**Autograph:** The autograph of the sketches and orchestral draft of the second movement are in the Stadts und Landesbibliothek, Vienna. Portions of the sketches for the final movement are in the collection of J. Bruck in New York. The copyist's fair copies with autograph corrections and the autograph fair copy are in the Pierpont Morgan Library in New York.

**Notes:** This cantata is a dramatic presentation of the tale of a young prince who murders his elder brother to gain direct succession to the throne. His crime comes back to haunt him when a shepherd makes a flute from one of the discarded bones of the murdered sibling. The flute miraculously sings the story revealing the crime. The score was originally conceived in three sections, but was revised, omitting the *Waldmärchen* portion. Most recent scholarship leans in favor of the belief that the composer's preferred version was the original in three parts, although many performances have been given of the two-sectioned version. In its original form the work was arranged in three movements as follows:

| I | Waldmärchen | Forest Legend |
| II | Der Spielmann | The minstrel |
| III | Hochzeitstück | Wedding Piece |

**Performance Issues:** The tam-tam does not appear in the instrumentation list at the beginning of the score. The choral parts are directly supported by the orchestra throughout the score. There are some divisi for each of the sections of the choir. The choral writing is primarily homophonic, and it is tonally centered at all times. The breadth of the orchestration and the dramatic nature of the work demand a large choir. The orchestral parts are all somewhat technically challenging, especially the string parts which have a lot of filigree work. The brass parts are virtuosic with demands of endurance, range, and flexibility for all of the players. The placement of the "distant orchestra" will be problematic in most halls. It is important that they be able to see the podium, and the size of the group prohibits their being placed off-stage with a monitor. The temporal integration of this group with the on-stage orchestra and choir will present some difficulties, which will be rewarded in the stunning aural effect. An important consideration in performing this work is whether to include the *Waldmärchen* movement, which adds 28 minutes to the work. In the *Waldmärchen* movement, Mahler asks that the two harp parts have three players each. There is also a baritone solo in this movement. **Soloists:** soprano - range: $b^b$-b'', tessitura: g'-g'', very sustained with some prolonged passages in the upper part of the range; alto - range: a-e'', tessitura: d'-a', this role should be sung by a voice significantly darker than that chosen for the soprano soloist; tenor - range: e-b$^{b'}$, tessitura: a$^b$-f', this is a lyric and sustained role; **Choir:** medium difficult; **Orchestra:** difficult.

**Discography:** Steingruber, Wagner, Majkut; Vienna Chamber Choir, Vienna Symphony Orchestra; conducted by Fekete. Mercury: MG 10102 [LP].

Harper, Procter, Hollweg; Royal Concertgebouw Orchestra, Netherlands Radio Chorus; conducted by Bernard Haitink. Philips: 420113-2 PH2 [ADD].

E. Lear, E. Söderström, G. Hoffman, S. Burrows, E. Haefliger, G. Nienstedt; London Symphony Orchestra and Chorus; conducted by Pierre Boulez. Sony Classical: SK 45841 [DDD].

Zyliz-Gara, Reynolds, Kaposy; New Philharmonia Orchestra, Ambrosian Singers; conducted by Wyn Morris, recorded in 1967. Nimbus: NI-5084 [AAD].

Susan Dunn, Brigitte Fassbaender, Markus Baur, Werner Hollweg, Andreas Schmidt; Städtischer Musikverein Düsseldorf (Hartmut Schmidt, chorus-master), Berlin Radio Symphony Orchestra; conducted by Riccardo Chailly. London: D101231 [DDD].

### Selected Bibliography

Diether, Jack: "Mahler's *Klagende Lied*: Genesis and Evolution," *Music Review*, 29 (1968), 268-287.

_____: foreward for Gustave Mahler: *Waldmärchen/A Forest Legen (Das klagende Lied), I*. Melville, NY: Belwin-Mills, 1973.

Mitchell, Donald: "Mahler's Waldmärchen: The Unpublished First Part of 'Das klagende Lied,'" *Musical Times*, 111 (1970), 375-379.

La Grange, Henry-Louis de: *Mahler,* volume I, 729-738. Garden City, NY: Doubleday and Co., 1973.

Stephan, Rudolf: "Vorwort und Revisionsbericht" for Gustav Mahler: *Das Klagende Lied*, volume 12 of the *Kritische Gesamtausgabe*. Vienna: Universal Edition, 1978.

Zenk, Martin: "Mahlers Streichung des "Waldmärchen' aus dem 'Klagende Lied': zum Verhältnis von philosophischer Erkenntnis und Interpretation," *Archiv für Musikwissenschaft*, 38 (1981), 179-193.

Fiske, Richard Allen: *Mahler's Klagende Lied: A Conductor's Analysis of the Original Tripartite Manuscript and Its Bipartite Revisions*. Indiana University: Doctor of Musical Arts project, 1983.

## Symphony No. 2 (1884-94, revised 1910, f.p. 1895)

**Duration:** ca. 80 minutes

**Text:** The German text is a compilation of "Uhrlicht" from *Des Knaben Wunderhorn*, "Auferalsteh'n" by Friederich Klopstock, and "O glaube, mein Herz, o glaube" by Gustav Mahler.

**Performing Forces: voices:** soprano and alto soloists; SATB choir; **orchestra:** 4 flutes (flutes I, II, III, and IV doubling piccolo), 4 oboes (oboe III and IV doubling English horn), 3 clarinets in B♭, A, and C (clarinet III doubling bass clarinet in B♭), 2 E♭ clarinets (one doubling clarinet in B♭ and A), 4 bassoons (bassoon IV doubling contrabassoon), 6 horns in F, 4 trumpets in F and C, 4 trombones, tuba, 2 timpanists (3 drums each), percussion (5 players - glockenspiel, 3 large chimes, snare drum, bass drum, cymbals, large and small tam-tams, triangle), 2 harp parts (several players/part if possible), organ, and strings.

offstage ensemble: 4 horns in F, 4 to 6 trumpets in F and C, timpani (one drum), percussion (bass drum, cymbals, triangle, switch).

The composer states that one should utilize the largest contingent of strings possible. Some of the doublebasses must have a low CC.

**First Performance:** 4 March 1895; Berlin (movements 1, 2, and 3); first complete performance: 13 December 1895; Berlin; conducted by the composer.

**Edition:** Symphony No. 2 is available in multiple editions. The choral score (2936), miniature score, and individual choral parts (2935A-D) are available for purchase from Universal Edition; the orchestral materials for this edition are available through rental. The full score is available for purchase from Dover (0-486-25473-9). These full scores are identical, both being reprints of the original edition published by Josef Weinberger in Vienna in 1897. The full score and orchestral parts are available for purchase from Kalmus (A1686); a study score is also available from Kalmus (154). The second movement is available through rental in an arrangement for reduced orchestration by Erwin Stein from Boosey and Hawkes and Universal Edition. The third movement is available through rental for reduced orchestration from Boosey and Hawkes, as is the fifth movement from Carl Fischer.

A facsimile of the fair-copy manuscript is published concurrently by New York: Kaplan Foundation, and London: Faber and Faber, 1986. The score is accompanied by relevent documents and annotations prepared by Edward Reilly.

**Autograph:** The autograph fair copy of the entire score and the sketches of the "In ruhig fliessender Bewegung" are in the Pierpont Morgan Library in New York. The autograph fair copy of the

"Urlicht" is in the British Library in London. The sketch of the original version of the "Allegro maestoso" is in the Jewish National and University Library in Jerusalem.

**Notes:** There were two revised versions of this score published by Universal Edition following the composer's death. Both make changes to the orchestration, but not to the composition. The work is divided into five movements with a five-minute pause indicated between movements I and II. The movements are disposed as follows:

| | | |
|---|---|---|
| I | Allegro maestoso. Mit durchaus ernstem und feierlichem Ausdruck | orchestra only |
| II | Andante moderato. Sehr gemächlich. Nie eilen. | orchestra only |
| III | In ruhig fliessender Bewegung | orchestra only |
| IV | "Uhrlicht," Sehr feirlich, aber schlicht | alto solo |
| V | Im Tempo des Scherzo's. Wild herausfahrend.— "Aufersteh'n" | soprano, alto and chorus |

**Performance Issues:** There are divisi for all of the sections of the choir. The orchestration demands that the choir be very large. The score includes a number of BB$^b$'s for the second basses in the choir, which the composer notes may not be realistically audible. As with all of Mahler's orchestral work, the score is filled with musical instructions. The Dover score includes a translation table for these indications. The choral writing is diatonic and well supported by the orchestra except for a brief *a cappella* passage at 31. The most significant choral issue is balancing the choir against the huge orchestral mass. The actual choral part is quite musically accessible to an amateur ensemble, but it requires vocal fortitude and numbers. The orchestration is thinned for the solo passages, especially the alto. All of the instrumental parts are technically demanding. The woodwinds have many involved chromatic passages. There is important solo material for all of the principal winds and brass. There is also a lengthy solo for violin. The clarinet I and E$^b$ clarinet I have some awkward exposed passages. All of the brass parts are demanding technically and a test

of endurance, especially horns I, III, and V. The integration of the
offstage material presents the usual logistical problems of pitch and
time. The off-stage group will probably need to tune slightly
sharp. These off-stage parts are as difficult as their on-stage
counterparts, except for endurance, and cannot be entrusted to lesser
players. The harp parts are difficult and should be doubled if at all
possible. The orchestra must remain buoyant and temporally fluid
despite its size, which requires an experienced orchestra familiar
with each other. This is an example of giant chamber music filled
with musical nuances that must be expressed from the podium and
sensitively executed. **Soloists:** soprano - range: $a^b$-$g^{b''}$, tessitura:
e'-e", this is a very sustained role; alto - range: $b^b$-e", tessitura: e'-
b', this role is lyric, sustained, and lightly accompanied; **Choir:**
medium easy; **Orchestra:** difficult.

**Discography:** G. Bindernagel, E. Leisner; Berlin State Opera
Orchestra and Chorus; conducted by Oskar Fried, recorded in 1923.
Pearl: GEMM CDS 9929 (mono) [AAD].

Rössl-Majdan; Vienna Symphony Orchestra; conducted by Otto
Klemperer. Vox: PL 7010 [LP].

Leontyne Price, Brigitte Fassbaender; London Symphony Orchestra and
Chorus; conducted by Leopold Stokowski. Victrola: ALK2-5392
[LP].

Cundari, Forrester; New York Philharmonic Orchestra, Westminster
Choir; conducted by Bruno Walter. CBS: M2K-42032 [AAD], also
released as Odyssey: YT-30848 and CBS: M3P-3-635.

Donath, Finnilä; Stuttgart Radio Symphony Orchestra and Choruses;
conducted by John Barbirolli, recorded live on 19 June 1970.
Arkadia: 719 [ADD].

J. Vincent, K. Ferrier; Royal Concertgebouw Orchestra; conducted by
Otto Klemperer, recorded  on 12 July 1951. Verona: 27062/63
(mono) [AAD].

A. Finley, A. Hodgson; New Philharmonia Orchestra and Chorus;
conducted by Otto Klemperer, recorded live on 16 May 1971.
Arkadia: 2 CDHP 590 [ADD].

Schwarzkopf, Rössl-Majdan; Philharmonia Orchestra and Chorus;
conducted by Otto Klemperer. Angel: CDM-69662 [ADD].

Selig, Zareska; Orchestra Nationale de Paris and chorus; conducted by
Schuricht, recorded live on 20 February 1958. Melodram: CD
27504 (mono) [AAD].

B. Sills, F. Kopleff; Utah Symphony Orchestra; conducted by Maurice
Abravanel, recorded in 1967. Vanguard Classics: OVC 4004
[ADD].

M. Coertse, L. West; Philharmonic Symphony Orchestra of London, Vienna Academy Chorus; conducted by Hermann Scherchen. MCA Classics: MCAD2-99833 [AAD].

Mathis, Procter; Bavarian Radio Symphony Orchestra; conducted by Rafael Kubelik. Deutsche Grammophon: 413149-4 GW.

E. Ameling, A. Heynis; Royal Concertgebouw Orchestra; conducted by Bernard Haitink. Philips: 420234-2.

Sheila Armstrong, Janet Baker; London Symphony Orchestra, Edinburgh Festival Chorus; conducted by Leonard Bernstein. CBS: M2K-42195.

Barbara Hendricks, Christa Ludwig; New York Philharmonic Orchestra, Westminster Choir; conducted by Leonard Bernstein. Deutsche Grammophon: 423395-2 GH 2 [DDD].

Harper, Watts, Chicago Symphony Orchestra and Chorus; conducted by Georg Solti. London: 421161-4 LJ2.

Harper, Watts, London Symphony Orchestra and Chorus; conducted by Georg Solti. London: 425005-2 LM2 [ADD].

Buchanan, Zakai; Chicago Symphony Orchestra and Chorus; conducted by Georg Solti. London: 410202-2 LH2 [DDD].

Cotrubas, Ludwig; Vienna Philharmonic Orchestra, Vienna State Opera Chorus; conducted by Zubin Mehta. London: 414538-2 LH2 [ADD].

Neblett, Horne; Chicago Symphony Orchestra and Chorus; conducted by Claudio Abbado. Deutsche Grammophon: 427262-2 GGA2 [ADD].

Plowright, Fassbaender; Philharmonia Orchestra and Chorus; conducted by Giuseppe Sinopoli. Deutsche Grammophon: 415959-2 GH2 [DDD].

Greenberg, Quivar; Israel Symphony Orchestra; conducted by Zubin Mehta, recorded live at Masada on 18 October 1988. Pickwick: PWK 1136 [DDD].

Kiri Te Kanawa, Marilyn Horne; Boston Symphony Orchestra, Tanglewood Festival Chorus; conducted by Seiji Ozawa. Philips: 420824-2 PH2 [DDD].

Arlene Augér, Janet Baker; City of Birmingham Symphony and Chorus; conducted by Simon Rattle. Angel: CDCB-47962 [DDD].

Kathleen Battle, Maureen Forrester; St. Louis Symphony and Chorus; conducted by Leonard Slatkin. Telarc: CD-80081/82 [DDD].

F. Lott, J. Hamari; Oslo Philharmonic Orchestra and Chorus; conducted by Mariss Jansons. Chandos: CHAN 8838/39 [DDD].

Eva Martón, Jessye Norman; Vienna Philharmonic Orchestra, Vienna State Opera Chorus; conducted by Loren Maazel. CBS: M2K-38667 [DDD].

Benita Valente, Maureen Forrester; London Symphony Orchestra and Chorus; conducted by G. Kaplan. MCA Classics: MCAD-11011 [DDD]. This recording is accompanied by a booklet containing translations of texts from ninety letters in which Mahler discusses the second symphony.

Sylvia McNair, Jard van Nes; Dallas Symphony Orchestra and Chorus; conducted by Eduardo Mata, recorded in September 1989. Pro Arte: CDD 479 [DDD].

### Selected Bibliography

Nodnagel, Ernst Otto: "Gustav Mahlers zweite Sinfonie: technische Analyse mit 25 Notenbeispielen," *Die Musik*, 2 (1903), 337-353.

Casella, Alfredo: "Gustav Mahler et sa deuxième symphonie," *Revue Société Internationale de Musique*, 6 (1910), 238-250.

Specht, Richard: *Gustav Mahler: Symphonie II c-moll (thematische Analyse)*. Vienna: Universal Edition, 1916.

Grant, William Parks: "Mahler's Second Symphony," *Chord and Discord*, 2 (1958), 76-85.

La Grange, Henry-Louis de: *Mahler,* volume I, 780-794. Garden City, NY: Doubleday and Co., 1973.

Danzinger, Gustav: *Die zweite Symphonie von Gustav Mahler*. University of Vienna: Ph.D. dissertation, 1976.

Stephan, Rudolf: *Mahler II. Symphonie c-moll: Meisterwerke der Musik: Werkmonographien zur Musikgeschichten*, 21. München: Wilhelm Fink, 1979.

Hefling, Stephen E.: *The Making of Mahler's "Todtenfeier": A Documentary and Analytical Study*. Yale University: Ph.D. dissertation, 1985.

Floros, Constantin: "Symphonie No. 2," in *Gustav Mahler: The Symphonies*, translated by Vernon Wicker, 52-82. Portland, Oregon: Amadeus Press, 1993.

## Symphony No. 3 (1895-96, f.p. 1902)

**Duration:** ca. 94 minutes

**Text:** The text is a compilation of "Nachtwandrers Lied" from *Also Sprach Zarathustra* by Friedrich Nietzsche; and *Des Knaben Wunderhorn*.

**Performing Forces: voices:** alto soloist; women's SSMMAA choir and boys' choir "in a high gallery"; **orchestra:** 4 flutes

(flutes I, II, III, and IV doubling piccolo), 4 oboes (oboe IV doubling English horn), 3 clarinets in B$^b$ and A (clarinet III doubling bass clarinet in B$^b$), 2 clarinets in E$^b$ (E$^b$ clarinet II doubling clarinet in B$^b$ and A), 4 bassoons (bassoon IV doubling contrabassoon), 8 horns in F, 4 trumpets in F and B$^b$, 4 trombones, tuba, 2 timpanists (3 drums each), percussion (5 players - 2 glockenspiels, snare drum, bass drum, tambourine, suspended cymbal, 2 pairs of crash cymbals, tam-tam, triangle), 2 harps and strings.

in the distance: flugelhorn in B$^b$, several snaredrums.

in a high gallery (with the boy choir): 4 tuned bells (c', d', f', and g').

reduced orchestration: 3 flutes, 3 oboes, 3 clarinets, 3 bassoons, 4 horns, 3 trumpets, 3 trombones, tuba, 2 timpanists, percussion (4 players - 2 glockenspiels, snare drum, bass drum, tambourine, suspended cymbal, 2 pair of crash cymbals, tam-tam, triangle), 2 harps and strings.

Benjamin Britten's re-orchestration: 2 flutes, 2 oboes, 2 clarinets, 2 bassoons, 4 horns, 3 trumpets, 1 trombone, percussion, harp, and strings.

**First Performance:** 9 March 1897; Berlin (movements I, II, and VI); first complete performance: 9 June 1902; Krefeld; conducted by the composer.

**Edition:** Symphony No. 3 is available in multiple editions. The choral score (02942) is available for purchase from Universal Edition; the orchestral materials for this edition are available through rental. The full score is available for purchase from Dover (0-486-26166-2). These full scores are identical. Another reprint is available from Kalmus (A2399) for which the full score and orchestral parts are available for purchase, as is a companion study score (449). A reduced orchestration is available for rental from Universal Edition of which a study score may be purchased (950). The second and third movements have also been transcribed for a reduced orchestra by Benjamin Britten, which are available through rental from Boosey and Hawkes.

**Autograph:** The autograph fair copy and most sketches are in the Pierpont Morgan Library in New York. The piano-vocal draft is in the Library of Congress in Washington, DC.

**Notes:** The score is subtitled *Ein Sommermorgentraum*, "a summer morning dream." The manuscript has the following programmatic inscriptions:

### Part I

I  Kräftig. Entschieden                                        orchestra only

*Abtheilung: Pan erwacht*
[Introduction: Pan Awakes]
*Der Sommer marschiert ein*
[Summer marches in]

### Part II

II  Tempo di Menuetto. Grazioso                    orchestra only

*Was mir die Blumen auf der Wiese erzählen*
[What the flowers of the field tell me]

III  Comodo. Scherzando.                                orchestra only
Ohne Hast

*Was mir die Tiere im Walde erzählen*
[What the animals of the woods tell me]

IV  "O Mensch! Gib Acht!"                                    Alto solo
[O Man! Give Attention!]

*Was mir der Mensch erzählt*
[What man tells me]

V  "Es sungen drei Engel"                    alto solo and choirs
[Three angels sang it]

*Was mir die Engel erzählen*
[What the angels tell me]

VI   Langsam. Ruhevoll.                              orchestra only
     Empfunden

*Was mir die Liebe erzählt*
[What love tells me]

There was originally a movement VII, subtitled *Was mir das Kind erzählt* [What the child tells me], which was deleted in June of 1896 and may have become the final movement of the Symphony No. 4.[17]

**Performance Issues:** The boy choir is written in one and two parts. It has broad leaps, but is tuneful and well supported by the accompaniment. Although the boys are to be placed in a distant gallery, much of their crucial pitch cues come from the chimes which are placed with them. The choral writing is sustained and diatonic throughout. The choral movement is only between four and five minutes in length. It is scored so that a choir of medium size could be used successfully. There is a prominent violin solo for the concert master. The strings are asked to play *col legno* in some passages. In movement IV, Mahler asks that only doublebasses with a low CC play. As in Symphony No. 2, Mahler indicates that there be a long pause following Part I. The score indicates that the glockenspiel sound an octave higher than written, but it is really two octaves higher. The composer indicates that, if possible, the clarinet I part be doubled throughout the score, and the clarinets in E$^b$ be doubled in movement V. He also suggests adding 2 more high trumpets, and using cornet in E$^b$ for the trumpet I part in a passage in movement I. The orchestral writing is virtuosic much of the time with involved rapid passagework for all of the winds, especially the clarinet I and clarinet in E$^b$ I. The brass writing is often sustained and high. Strong players must be used through the section. The trumpet I is very difficult, especially at the end of movement I. The string section must be very large to achieve the indicated sonorities and  to balance the rest of the orchestra. The final movement requires controlled intensity at a very slow tempo and subdued dynamic level. While the choral portions of this composition are accessible to most amateur choirs, the orchestral writing is demanding of the finest symphonic

---

[17]   La Grange, Henry-Louis de: *Mahler*, volume I, 797. Garden City, NY: Doubleday and Co., 1973.

ensembles. **Soloist:** alto - range: a-f", tessitura: e'-e", this role is musically simple, it is very sustained and tender and may be successfully sung by a dramatic soprano; **Choir:** medium easy; **Orchestra:** very difficult.

**Discography:** Krebs; New York Philharmonic Orchestra; conducted by Dmitri Mitropoulos, recorded live in Carnegie Hall on 15 April 1956. Arkadia: 557 [AAD].

Rössl-Majdan; Vienna Philharmonic; conducted by Adler. SPA 20/1/2 [LP].

C. Krooskos; Utah Symphony Orchestra and Chorus; conducted by Maurice Abravanel, recorded in 1969. Vanguard Classics: OVC 4005/6 [ADD].

L. West; Berlin Philharmonic Orchestra, St. Hedwig's Cathedral Choir; conducted by John Barbirolli, recorded live on 8 March 1969. Arkadia: 719 [ADD].

Procter; London Symphony Orchestra, Ambrosian Singers, Wandsworth School Boys' Choir; conducted by Jascha Horenstein. Unicorn-Kanchana: UKCD-2006/07 [ADD].

Martha Lipton; New York Philharmonic Orchestra, Schola Cantorum, Boys' Choir; conducted by Leonard Bernstein. CBS: M2K-42196.

Christa Ludwig; New York Philharmonic Orchestra, New York Choral Artists, Brooklyn Boys' Choir; conducted by Leonard Bernstein. Deutsche Grammophon: 427328-2 GH2 [DDD].

Maureen Forrester; Royal Concertgebouw Orchestra and Netherlands Radio Women's Chorus; conducted by Bernard Haitink. Philips: 420113-2 PH2 [ADD].

Janet Baker; London Symphony Orchestra and Chorus; conducted by Michael Tilson Thomas. CBS: M2K-44553 [DDD].

Agnes Baltsa; Vienna Philharmonic Orchestra and Chorus; conducted by Loren Maazel. CBS: M2K-42403 [DDD].

Jessye Norman; Vienna Philharmonic Orchestra, State Opera Chorus, Vienna Boys Choir; conducted by Claudio Abbado. Deutsche Grammophon: 410715-2 GH2 [DDD].

Helen Watts; London Symphony Orchestra, Ambrosian Singers, Wandsworth School Boys' Choir; conducted by Georg Solti. London: 414254-2 LM2 [ADD].

Dernesch; Chicago Symphony Orchestra and Chorus, Glen Ellyn Children's Chorus; conducted by Georg Solti. London: 414268-2 LH2 [DDD].

Christa Ludwig; Czech Philharmonic Orchestra and Chorus; conducted by Vaclav Neumann. Supraphon: C37-7288/89 [DDD].

Marilyn Horne; Chicago Symphony Orchestra and Chorus; conducted
by James Levine. RCA: RCD2-1757 [DDD].
Soffel; Frankfurt Radio Symphony Orchestra, Chorus; conducted by
Eliahu Inbal. Denon: C37-7828/9 [DDD].
A. Gjevang; Danish National Radio Symphony Orchestra and Choir;
conducted by L. Segerstam. Chandos: CHAN 8970/71 [DDD].

### Selected Bibliography

Nodnagel, Ernst Otto: *Gustav Mahlers III. Symphonie; Analyse.*
Darmstadt: Editions Rother, 1904.
Specht, Richard: *Gustav Mahler: Symphonie III d-moll (thematische
Analyse.* Vienna: Universal Edition, 1919.
La Grange, Henry-Louis de: *Mahler,* volume I, 795-811. Garden City,
NY: Doubleday and Co., 1973.
Franklin, Peter: "The Gestation of Mahler's Third Symphony," *Music
and Letters,* 58 (1977), 439-446.
Werck, Isabelle: *La symphonie de la terre et du ciel: 7 variations sur la
troisième symphonie de Gustav Mahler.* Lyon: Éditions à Coeur
Joie, 1985.
Floros, Constantin: "Symphonie No. 3," in *Gustav Mahler: The
Symphonies,* translated by Vernon Wicker, 83-108. Portland,
Oregon: Amadeus Press, 1993.
Franklin, Peter: *Mahler: Symphony No. 3.* Cambridge: Cambridge
University Press, 1991.

## Symphony No. 8 (1906-7)

**Duration:** ca. 90 minutes

**Text:** The text is a combination of "Veni creator spiritus," a traditonal
ninth-century Latin hymn; and the final scene from *Faust* by
Goethe, which is in German.

**Performing Forces: voices:** 3 soprano, 2 alto, tenor, baritone,
and bass soloists; boy choir, 2 large SSAATTBB choirs;
**orchestra:** 2 piccolos (several per part with piccolo I doubling
flute V), 4 flutes, 4 oboes, English horn, soprano clarinet in E$^b$
(doubled throughout), 3 clarinets in B$^b$ and A, bass clarinet in B$^b$
and A, 4 bassoons, contrabassoon, 8 horns in F, 4 trumpets in F
and B$^b$, 4 trombones, tuba, timpani, percussion (3 players -
glockenspiel, "deep" bells (A and A$^b$), bass drum, crash cymbals,

suspended cymbal, tam-tam, triangle), 2 harps (several players per part), celeste, harmonium, piano, organ, mandolin (several players), strings.

off-stage instruments: 4 trumpets in F (the composer recommends several players on the trumpet I part), 3 trombones.

reduced orchestration: 3 flutes, 3 oboes, 3 clarinets, 3 bassoons, 4 horns in F, 4 trumpets in F and B$^b$, 4 trombones, tuba, timpani, percussion (3 players - glockenspiel, "deep" bells (A and A$^b$), bass drum, crash cymbals, suspended cymbal, tam-tam, triangle), harp, celeste, harmonium, piano, organ, mandolin, strings.

**First Performance:** 12 September 1910; Exposition Concert Hall, Munich; conducted by the composer.

**Edition:** Symphony No. 8 is available in multiple editions. The piano-vocal score (2660) and individual choral parts (2661A-D) are available for purchase from Universal Edition; the orchestral materials for this edition are available through rental. The full score is available for purchase from Izdatel'stvo Muzyka which has been reprinted with English notes by Dover (0-486-26022-4). The reduced orchestration is available through rental from Universal Edition, of which a study score may be purchased (3000).

**Autograph:** The autograph fair copy is in the Bayerische Staatsbibliothek in Munich.

**Notes:** Mahler dedicated the score to "My beloved wife, Alma Maria." This work has been nicknamed the "Symphony of a Thousand," and there were in fact, 1003 performers involved in its premiere. The score is divided into two large parts, the first being the "Veni Creator Spiritus" and the second, the conclusion of Goethe's *Faust* as adapted by the composer. The soloists are assigned characters from *Faust*, as follows:

| | |
|---|---|
| soprano 1 | Magna Peccatrix |
| soprano 2 | Una pœnitentium |
| soprano 3 | Mater gloriosa |
| alto 1 | Mulier Samaritana |
| alto 2 | Maria Ægyptiaca |
| tenor | Doctor Marianus |
| baritone | Pater ecstaticus |

bass                    Pater profundus

The singer who portrays the "Mater gloriosa" is the only soloist who does not appear in Part I of the symphony. Hers is also the shortest role in Part II.

**Performance Issues:** The boy choir is written in one and two parts with a range of a-f" and frequent melodic leaps. The melodic contours are well supported by the accompaniment. The two mixed choirs have two-part divisi in each section. The choral writing is generally diatonic, with scalar and triadic melodic material. Mahler combines block chordal textures with traditional imitative procedures to foster a varied choral palette. In the most dense choral passages, the two choirs double each other. The choral parts are accessible to most amateur singers, although the tessituras of the first soprano and first tenor parts are consistently high and quite vocally taxing. Of greatest importance for the success of the choral contingent of this work is the formation of a truly enormous vocal ensemble with a substantial core of trained singers. The score indicates that when large choirs and string sections are employed, the principal woodwind parts should be doubled. The boy choir should also be large if possible. The brass parts are sustained, high, and difficult, especially the trumpet I. There are numerous exposed solos for the horn I. The woodwinds have a number of challenging passages, especially the oboe I, clarinet I and the clarinet in $E^b$ I. The string writing is technically challenging throughout the score. The most difficult performance issues are balance and musical fluidity from this enormous ensemble. **Soloists:** soprano 1 / Magna Peccatrix - range: a-c''', tessitura: a'-c''', this is a vocally demanding role with sustained singing at the top of the range; soprano 2 / Una pœnitentium - range: c'-c''', tessitura: a'-c''', this is a vocally demanding role with sustained singing at the top of the range; soprano / Mater gloriosa - range: $b^b$'-$b^b$", tessitura: $b^b$'-$b^b$", this is a very sustained and brief role; alto 1 / Mulier Samaritana - range: b-g", tessitura: e'-e", this is a lyric role which moves freely throughout the range; alto 2 / Maria Ægyptiaca - range: a-g", tessitura: e'-e", this is a lyric role which moves freely throughout the range; tenor / Doctor Marianus - range: e-b', tessitura: a-a', almost all of this role remains within the listed tessitura, it is a true heldentenor part; baritone / Pater ecstaticus - range: $A^b$-g', tessitura: e-e', this is a lyric role requiring flexibility and endurance in the top of the range; bass / Pater profundus - range: C-g', tessitura: d-d', this is a powerful and sustained role, the entire range falls between $A^b$ and g' except for a single passage at **32** in movement I; **Choir:** medium difficult; **Orchestra:** difficult.

**Discography:** Philharmonic Symphony Orchestra, Westminster Choir; conducted by Leopold Stokowski, recorded live in Carnegie Hall on 6 April 1950. Arkadia: CDGI 761.1 [ADD].

Vienna Symphony Orchestra; conducted by Hermann Scherchen. Columbia: SL 164 [LP].

Bavarian Radio Symphony Orchestra and Chorus; conducted by Rafael Kubelik. Deutsche Grammophon: 419433-2 GH [ADD].

London Symphony Orchestra, Leeds Festival Chorus; conducted by Leonard Bernstein. CBS: M3K-42199.

Price, Blegen, Zeumer, Schmidt, Baltsa, Riegel, Prey, van Dam; Vienna Philharmonic Orchestra, Vienna State Opera Chorus, Vienna Boy Choir; conducted by Leonard Berstein, recorded at the Salzburg Festival in 1975. Deutsche Grammophon: 435102-2 GH2 [ADD].

Heather Harper, Lucia Popp, Arlene Augér, Yvonne Minton, Heather Watts, René Kollo, John Shirley-Quirk, Martti Talvela; Chicago Symphony Orchestra, Vienna State Opera Chorus, Vienna Boy Choir; conducted by Georg Solti, recorded in 1971. London: 414493-2 LH2 [ADD].

Royal Concertgebouw Orchestra, Choruses; conducted by Bernard Haitink. Philips: 420543-2 PH2 [ADD].

London Philharmonic Orchestra and Chorus, Tiffin School Boys' Choir; conducted by Klauss Tennstedt. Angel: CDCB-47625 [DDD].

Vienna Philharmonic Orchestra, Choruses; conducted by Loren Maazel. Sony Classical: S2K-45754 [DDD].

Atlanta Symphony Orchestra and Choruses; conducted by Robert Shaw. Telarc: CD-80267 [DDD].

Czech Philharmonic Orchestra and Choruses; conducted by Vaclav Neumann. Supraphon: C37-7307/08 [DDD].

Boston Symphony Orchestra; conducted by Seiji Ozawa. Philips: 410607-2 PH2 [DDD].

Frankfurt Radio Symphony Orchestra, Choruses; conducted by Eliahu Inbal. Denon: CO-1564/65 [DDD].

### Selected Bibliography

Specht, Richard: *Gustav Mahler: Symphonie VIII Bb-dur (thematische Analyse): mit einer Einleitung, biographischen Date und dem Porträt Mahlers*. Vienna: Universal Edition, 1912.

Engel, Gabriel: "Mahler's Eighth: The Hymn to Eros," *Chord and Discord*, 2 (1950), 12-32.

Cooke, Deryck: "The Word and the Deed: Mahler and His Eighth Symphony," in *Vindications: Essays on Romantic Music*. London: Cambridge University Press, 1982.

Breig, Werner, herausgegeben:*Schütz-Jahrbuch*, band 4/5. Kassel: Bärenreiter, 1983. This volume contains four essays on various aspects of this symphony — Frieheim Krummacher: "Fragen zu Mahlers VIII. Symphonie," Adolf Nowak: "Mahlers Hymnus," Rudolf Stephan: "Zu Mahlers Komposition der Schluss-szene von Goethes Faust," and Stefan Strohm: "Die Idee der absoluten Musik aus ihr (angesprochenes) Programm."

Floros, Constantin: "Symphonie No. 8," in *Gustav Mahler: The Symphonies*, translated by Vernon Wicker, 213-240. Portland, Oregon: Amadeus Press, 1993.

Berger, Melvin: *Guide to Choral Masterpieces: A Listener's Guide*, 194-197. New York: Anchor Books, 1993.

**Martin, Frank** (b. Geneva, 15 September 1890; d. Naarden, Netherlands, 21 November 1974)

**Life:** Martin has come to be regarded as one of the most important Swiss composers. He was a student of Joseph Lauber, Hans Huber, and Frederic Klose. He traveled through Europe in the early 1920s, returning to Switzerland in 1926 where he taught at the Jaques-Dalcroze Institute (1927-38). He founded his own school, the Technicum Moderne de Musique (1933-39). He also taught at the Cologne Hochschule für Musik (1950-55). He was president of the Association of Swiss Composers (1942-46) after which he settled in the Netherlands. His works explore a number of procedures, all with confidence and assiduous technical mastery.

**Writings:** *Responsabilité du compositeur*. Geneva: 1966. *Un compositeur médite sur son art*. Neuchâtel: 1977.

**Principal Works:** *operas - Der Sturm* (1954), *Monsieur de Pourceaugnac* (1962); **orchestral** - 2 Piano Concertos (1934, 1969), *Rythmes* (1926), *Symphony with Jazz Instruments* (1937), *Petite symphonie concertante* (1945), *Les Quatre Éléments* (1964), *Erasmi monumentum* (1969), *Polyptique* (1973); **vocal** - *Les Dithyrambes* (1918), Mass for double choir (1922), *Psaumes de Genève* (1958), *Le Mystère de la Nativité* (1929-59), *Pilate* (1964), *Requiem* (1972).

## Selected  Composer  Bibliography

Klein, Rudolf: *Frank Martin: sein Leben und Werk*. Vienna: 1960.
Tappolet, Willy: "Frank Martin und die religiöse Musik," *Schweizerische Musikzeitung/Revue Musicale Suisse*, c (1960), 278.
Martin, Frank: *Un Compositeur médite sur son art*. Neuchâtel: A la Baconnière, 1977.
King, Charles W.: *Frank Martin: A Bio-Bibliography*. New York: Greenwood Press, 1990.

# Le Vin Herbé (1938-41)

**Duration:** ca. 93 minutes

**Text:** The text, taken from three chapters of the *Roman de Tristan et Iseult* by Joseph Bédier, is in French. The score includes a German singing translation prepared by Rudolf Binding.

**Performing Forces: voices:** 3 solo sopranos, 3 solo altos, 3 solo tenors, 3 solo basses; **orchestra:** 2 solo violins, 2 solo violas, 2 solo cellos, doublebass, and piano.

**First Performance: first complete performance:** 28 March 1942; Zürich; Züricher Madrigalchor; Robert Blum, conductor.

part I premiered separately: 16 April 1940; Zürich; by same forces.

staged premiere: 15 August 1948; Salzburg; Ferenc Fricsay, conductor; in German as *Der Zaubertrank*.

**Edition:** *Le Vin Herbé* is published by Universal Edition. The choral-vocal score (11311) is available for purchase; orchestra materials are available through rental.

**Autograph:** The Martin Archive is in the possession of the Paul Sacher Foundation in Basle, Switzerland.

**Notes:** This work is based upon the legend of Tristan and Iseult. It is arranged as follows:

Prologue
    Act One             The Love Potion
    Act Two            The Forest of Morois
    Act Three          The Death
Epilogue

**Performance Issues:** This work is intended to be sung by a chamber ensemble of twelve singers, each of whom has some solo singing. The roles labeled Tristan (tenor 2), and Iseult (soprano 2), are the most pervasive. The ensemble writing is entirely homophonic with numerous passages of unison singing, or two-part writing in parallel octaves. The harmonic material is functionally tonal, but quite chromatic. The melodic configurations are scalar or triadic throughout; however, they are consistently exploring chromatic variants over often static pedal figures in the accompaniment. All of the vocal material is clearly supported by the accompaniment. The instrumental writing is idiomatic and conservative. This is an attractive work which is accessible to many ensembles and provides solo opportunities for all of the singers and players. It is a concert length work on a secular theme which involves only 20 musicians. **Soloists:** Only the following two roles have enough exposed singing to warrant description here. Iseult (soprano): range: c'-bb", tessitura: g'-g", this is a lyrical role with some very sustained high passages; Tristan (tenor): range: d-b', tessitura: g-g', this role is declamatory and somewhat dramatic; **Choir:** medium easy; **Orchestra:** medium easy.

**Discography:** Chamber Ensemble; Frank Martin, piano; conducted by Victor Desarzens, recorded September 1961. Westminster: XWN2232/ WST232 [LP].

### Selected Bibliography

Martin, Frank: "A propos du 'Vin Herbé,'" *Schweizerische Musikzeitung. Revue Musicale Suisse*, 82 (March 1942), 73-75.

Daniel, Oliver: "Antiquity Updated," *Saturday Review*, 45 (March 1962), 39.

Frankenstein, Alfred: "Le Vin herbé: What Debussy planned now consummately achieved," *High Fidelity*, 12 (May 1962), 66.

Cremers, Adrienne: *De legende vom Tristan en Isolde bej Richard Wagner en Frank Martin.* University of Leide: Ph.D. dissertation, 1963.

Tupper, Janet Eloise: *Stylistic Analysis of Selected Works by Frank Martin.* Indiana University: Ph.D. dissertation, 1964.

Gugliemo, Ecoardo: "Le Vin herbé," *Accademia musicale Chigiana, Siena, Estate musicale Chigiana* (21 August 1986).

## In terra pax (1944)

**Duration:** 45 minutes

**Text:** The text is a French translation of portions of the *Revelations of St. John*, and the Lord's Prayer and Beatitudes from the *Gospel of St. Matthew*, as organized by the composer. The score includes a German singing translation by Romana Segantini.

**Performing Forces: voices:** soprano, alto, tenor, baritone, and bass soloists; 2 SATB choirs; **orchestra:** 2 flutes (flute II doubling piccolo), 2 oboes (oboe II doubling English horn), 2 clarinets in B$^b$ (clarinet II doubling bass clarinet in B$^b$), 2 bassoons, 4 horns in F, 2 trumpets in B$^b$, 3 trombones, tuba, timpani, percussion, celeste, 2 pianos, and strings.

**First Performance:** 7 May 1945; Geneva, Switzerland; Orchestre de la Suisse Romande, conducted by Ernest Ansermet for a radio performance on Radio Genève.

first concert performance: 31 May 1945; Geneva, Switzerland; Madeleine Dubuis, Nelly Grétillat, Ernst Haefliger, Paul Sandoz, Fernando Corena; Orchestre de la Suisse Romande, conducted by Ernest Ansermet.

**Edition:** *In terra pax* is published by Universal Edition. The piano-vocal score (11984) and choral score (11985) are available for purchase; orchestra materials are available through rental.

**Autograph:** The Martin Archive is in the possession of the Paul Sacher Foundation in Basle, Switzerland. The piano-vocal score is a facsimile of the composer's fair copy.

**Notes:** *In terra pax* was commissioned by Radio Genève to be broadcast on armistice day. The texts were chosen in reaction to

World War II, which was taking place around Martin's native Switzerland. The composition is derived from a number of historic models: The organization of recitatives, arias, and choruses is reflective of the classical era. The baritone soloist serves the equivalent role of Evangelist and the choir often functions like the critical turba of Baroque oratorios. He also initiates sections of antiphonal chant between the two choirs harkening back to medieval liturgical practices. The score is arranged into four subdivided parts as follows:

Part I

| I | Lorsque l'agneau | baritone, choir I |
|---|---|---|
| II | Mon Dieu, pourquoi | choir II |
| III | Malheur au peuple chargé de péchés | bass, choir I |
| IV | Eternel, Dieu de mon Salut | tutti |

Part II

| V | Sentinelle, que dis-tu de la nuit | tenor, choirs I and II |
|---|---|---|
| VI | Mais le ténèbres | soprano, tenor, and bass |
| VII | Consolez mon peuple | tutti |

Part III

| VIII | Voici mon serviteur | alto |
|---|---|---|
| IX | Heureux les affligés | tenor |
| X | Nôtre Père | choirs I and II |

Part IV

| XI | Puis je vis un nouveau ciel | tutti |
|---|---|---|

**Performance Issues:** The baritone solos are written in the tenor-treble clef. The choral writing features paired doubling, in octaves, between the men's and women's parts. There is also a significant amount of unison singing for the choir. The harmonic material of the choir is chromatic, with an emphasis on parallel fourths and hidden-fourth relationships. The final movement has a line labeled mezzo-sopranos with the note "a chorus of young girls." The choral parts are written to be accessible to amateur choirs. The orchestral parts are conservatively written and well within the abilities of most amateur orchestras. The level of chromaticism in this work is the only potential snare for inexperienced ensembles. This score provides church choirs with a good twentieth-century selection for use as a Good Friday Passion setting which is both musically accessible to less-experienced ensembles and of high musical integrity. **Soloists:** soprano - range: $e^{b\prime}$-b″, tessitura: g′-g″, this is a lyric and often parlando solo; alto - range: g-f#″, tessitura: g′-e″, this is a lyric role, the solo in section VIII alternates between phrases at the top of the range, and phrases at the bottom of the range; tenor - range: f#-b′, tessitura: a-g′, this is a sustained and lyric role; baritone - range: $B^b$-f′, tessitura: e-c′, this is a declamatory and powerful role; bass - range: $G^b$-f′, tessitura: f-d′, this role must be a strong and dark voice, it is interesting that Martin labels this solo bass, as its tessitura is consistently higher than that of the baritone soloist, there is only one $G^b$ and it is in an ensemble section; **Choir:** easy; **Orchestra:** medium easy.

**Discography:** Ursula Buckel, Marga Höffgen, Ernst Haefliger, Pierre Mollet, Jakob Stämpfli; L'Orchestre de la Suisse Romande; Ernest Ansermet, conductor; recorded 20-23 October 1963. Communauté de Travail: CT64-12, Decca: SXL6098/ LXT6098, London: OS25847/Ol5847, and Decca: DPA593-4[LP].

N. Okada, B. Baileys, R. Marcais, P. Huttenlocher, M. Brodard; Gulbenkian Foundation Orchestra and Chorus; conducted by M. Corboz, recorded in 1990. Cascavelle: VEL 1014 [ADD/DDD].

## Selected Bibliography

Paychère, Albert: "In terra pax, oratorio breve de Frank Martin," *Schweizerische Musikzeitung. Revue Musicale Suisse*, 85 (1945), 272-273.

Martin, Frank: "In terra pax," in *Alte und neue Muzik — Das Basler Kammerorchester unter Leitung von Paul Sacher 1926-1951.* Zürich: Atlantis, 1952.

Pahlen, Kurt: *The World of the Oratorio*, 213-215. Portland, Oregon: Amadeus Press, 1985.

Shigihara, Susanne: "In terra pax Anmerkungen zu Frank Martins Oratorium," *Beiträge zur Geschichte des Oratoriums seit Händel, Festschrift Günther Massenkeil zum 60. Geburtstag*, 514-532. Bonn: Voggenreiter Verlag, 1986.

## Golgotha (1945-48)

**Duration:** ca. 85 minutes

**Text:** The text is an arrangement, by the composer, of French translations of selections from the *Confessions* of St. Augustine and the four Gospels of the *New Testament*. The score includes a German singing translation.

**Performing Forces: voices:** soprano, alto, tenor, baritone, and bass soloists; SATB choir; **orchestra:** 2 flutes (flute II doubling piccolo), 2 oboes (oboe I doubling oboe d'amore [optional] and oboe II doubling English horn), 2 clarinets in B$^b$, 2 bassoons, 4 horns in F, 2 trumpets in B$^b$, 3 trombones, timpani, percussion, organ, piano, and strings.

**First Performance:** 29 April 1949; Geneva, Switzerland; Renée Defraiteur, Nelly Grétillat, Ernst Haefliger, H. B. Etcheverry, Heinz Rehfuss; Société de Chant Sacré, Orchestre de la Suisse Romande, conducted by Samuel Baud-Bovy.

**Edition:** *Golgotha* is published by Universal Edition. The piano-vocal score (11949) and individual choral parts (11950A-D) are available for purchase; orchestra materials are available through rental.

**Autograph:** The Martin Archive is in the possession of the Paul Sacher Foundation in Basle, Switzerland. The piano-vocal score is a facsimile of the composer's fair copy.

**Notes:** This work has many neo-Baroque features. As in its predecessor, *In terra pax*, Martin has used five soloists, in this case the bass sings the Evangelist role and the baritone portrays Christ. The score is dated 8 June 1948, Amsterdam. The work is in two subdivided parts as follows:

Part I

| | | |
|---|---|---|
| I | Père! Père! | choir |
| II | Les Rameaux | tutti |
| III | Le Discours au Temple | soprano, Jesus, choir |
| IV | La Sainte Cène | tenor, Jesus, bass |
| V | Géthsémané | tutti |

Part II

| VI | Que dirai-je? | alto, choir |
|---|---|---|
| VII | Ils menèrent Jésus | tutti |
| VIII | Jésus devant Pilate | tenor, bass, choir |
| IX | Le Calvaire | tenor, Jesus, ATB choir |
| X | O mort! où est ton aiguillon? | tutti, except for Jesus |

**Performance Issues:** There are two-part divisi for each male section of the choir and three-part divisi for the women's sections. The score indicates that some brief passages be sung by a few members of their section of the choir. There are some solo notes for Jesus which are labeled with a harmonic circle in a range not consistent with the use of falsetto (for example two measures before 5 in section IV. The choral writing uses quite a bit of unison singing. Much of the choral writing is in homophonic four-, eight-, or ten-part block chord writing. In the broad divisi sections, Martin doubles the men and women in parallel octaves. The harmonic material is based upon relationships of perfect fifths and fourths in chromatic successions. The vocal pitches, both solo and choral, are well supported by the orchestra. The instrumental writing is conservative and well within the ability of most amateur orchestras. The choral writing is accessible to large church choirs. This work is well conceived for use as a Passion service for Good Friday or Palm Sunday. The second section, "Les Rameaux" is, in fact, a telling of the procession over the palms into Jerusalem. **Soloists:** soprano - range: c#'-b", tessitura: g'-f", this is a lyric role with few vocal demands; alto - range: g-f#", tessitura: d'-d', this role is dramatic and exploits the upper range; tenor - range: d-b', tessitura: g-g', this is a lyric and sustained role; Jesus (baritone) - range: A-f', tessitura: d-d', a dramatic and lyrical role; bass - range: G-f', tessitura: d-d', this role is declamatory and forceful; **Choir:** medium easy; **Orchestra:** medium easy.

**Discography:** Walli Staempfli, Marie-Lise Montmollin, Eric Tappy, Pierre Mollet, Philippe Huttenlocher; André Luy, organ; Symphony Orchestra and Chorus of Lausanne; Robert Faller, conductor; recorded November 1968. Erato: STU70407/98 and Musical Heritage Society: MHS1337/38 [LP].
Martina von Bargen, Margit Hungerbühler, Friedhelm Decker, Joachim Gebhardt, Martin Blasius; Chor der Erlöserkirche of Bad Homburg, Offenbacher Kammerorchester, Frankfurter Bläservereinigung;

Hayko Siemens, conductor; recorded 1 April 1988. Vengo 3544002/3 [LP].

## Selected Bibliography

Martin, Frank: "Golgotha," *Schweizerische Muzikzeitung, Revue Musicale Suisse,* volume 90 (1950), 205-209.

Baud-Bovy, Samuel: "Sur le Gogotha de Frank Martin," *Schweizerische Muzikzeitung, Revue musicale suisse,* volume 90 (1950), 252-255.

Cowell, Henry: "Current Chronicle," *Musical Quarterly,* volume 38 (1952), 291-294.

Rochester, Mark: *Frank Martin at Golgotha: Frank Martin's Compositional Technique as Shown by his Passion Oratorio, "Golgotha."* University of Wales: Master's of Music thesis, 1976.

Hutcheson, Robert Joseph, Jr.: *Twentieth-Century Passion Settings: An Analytic Study of Max Baumann's "Passion," Op. 63; Frank Martin's "Golgotha;" Krzysztof Penderecki's "St. Luke Passion;" and Ernest Pepping's "Passionsbericht des Mattäus."* Washington University of St. Louis, Missouri : Ph.D. thesis, 1976.

Pahlen, Kurt: *The World of the Oratorio,* 215-217. Portland, Oregon: Amadeus Press, 1985.

Melroy, Marcia: *Frank Martin's "Golgotha."* University of Illinois: Doctor of Musical Arts dissertation, 1988.

## Nielsen, Carl (b. Sortelung, Denmark, 9 June 1865; d. Copenhagen, 3 October 1931)

**Life:** Nielsen is the most celebrated of all 20th-century Danish composers. He studied composition privately with Orla Rosenhoff, and was a student at the Royal Conservatory in Copenhagen where he studied music theory with Rosenhoff and J.P.E. Hartmann and music history with Niels Gade. Having learned to play the violin and cornet as a child, he played in a variety of bands and orchestras including the Royal Chapel Orchestra of Copenhagen (1889-1905). He also conducted at the Royal Theater (1908-14) and the Musikforeningen (1915-27). His works, while tonally centered are highly experimental with significant explorations of dissonance and attempts toward musical expressionism. His works only entered the standard repertory years after his death.

**Writings:** *Levende musik.* Copenhagen: Edition Wilhelm Hansen, 1925; in English translation as: *Living Music.* London: Edition Wilhelm Hansen, 1953. *Min fynske barndom.*Copenhagen: Edition

Wilhelm Hansen, 1927; in English translation by Reginald Spink, as: *My Childhood*. London: Edition Wilhelm Hansen, 1955.

**Principal Works:** *opera - Saul og David*, op. 25 (1901), *Maskarade*, op. 39 (1906); *orchestral* - six Symphonies (op. 7, 1892; op. 16, 1902; op. 27, 1911; op. 29, 1916; op. 50, 1922; op. 116, 1926), Violin Concerto, op. 33 (1911), Flute Concerto, op. 119 (1926), Clarinet Concerto, op. 57 (1928); *vocal - Hyldest til Holberg*, op. 102 (1922), *Hymne til Kunsten*, op. 141 (1929), many songs, and occasional cantatas.

## Selected Composer Bibliography

Nielsen, Carl: *Levende musik*. Copenhagen: Edition Wilhelm Hansen, 1925; in English translation as: *Living Music*. London: Edition Wilhelm Hansen, 1953.

_____: *Min fynske barndom.*Copenhagen: Edition Wilhelm Hansen, 1927; in English translation by Reginald Spink, as: *My Childhood*. London: 1955.

Simpson, Robert: *Carl Nielsen: Symphonist 1865-1931*. London: J. M. Dent and Sons, 1952.

Sørensen, Søren: "The Choral Works," translated by Ruth Bantzen, in *Carl Nielsen: Centenary Essays*, Jürgen Balzer, editor. London: Dennis Dobson, 1966; originally published in Danish by Nyt Nordisk Forlag, 1965.

Miller, Mina F.: *Carl Nielsen: A Guide to Research*. New York: Garland Publishing, 1987.

# Hymnus Amoris, op. 12 (1896)

**Duration:** ca. 25 minutes

**Text:** At Nielsen's request, the text was initially written by Axel Olrik in Danish and translated into Latin by Johan Ludvig Heiberg.

**Performing Forces: voices:** soprano, tenor, baritone, and bass soloists; children's choir (optional), SATB choir; **orchestra:** 3 flutes (flute III doubling piccolo), 3 oboes (oboe III doubling English horn), 2 clarinets in A, 2 bassoons, 4 horns in F, 3 trumpets in C, 3 trombones, tuba, timpani, percussion (2 players - glockenspiel, triangle), and strings.

**First Performance:** 27 April 1897; Copenhagen.

**Edition:** *Hymnus Amoris* is published by Wilhelm Hansen Musik-Forlag. The piano-vocal score is available for purchase; orchestral materials are available through rental. A reprint of the Hansen edition is available for purchase from Kalmus.

**Notes:** The inspiration for *Hymnus amoris* came from a Titian painting of a man murdering his lover out of jealousy. Nielsen saw this painting in Padua while honeymooning in 1891. He chose to set a Latin text to signify the "monumental and universal nature of the theme: Love's power over our lives." The text is divided into "Childhood," "Youth," "Manhood," and "Old Age." The children's choir is used to portray youth. Nielsen indicates that a women's sub-section of the choir may sing this section. The women of the choir also represent the mother in a dialogue with the child, which reinforces the advantage of using a children's choir. The "Manhood" portion is sung by the men of the choir, and in the conclusion of the work, the choirs combine to represent a choir of angels with the children (SSAA), and a choir of mankind (AATB). The three male soloist serve as a trio portraying old age. The full score includes a forward by the composer and Olrik's original Danish text paired with the Latin translation used in the score and also a German translation.

**Performance Issues:** The use of a children's choir is imperative in creating a clear sense of the text. The children's voices serve as children and angels while the adult singers portray mankind, allowing the sometimes simultaneous roles to be clearly perceived. There are passages assigned to the children which are *a cappella* in four parts. All of the vocal writing is tonally centered and follows common-practice voice-leading procedures. With the exception of the previously mentioned unaccompanied passages, the choral material is very clearly supported by the accompaniment. Nielsen uses a variety of choral textures, usually maintaining three or four levels of rhythmic activity for the singers. Much of the work is heavily orchestrated so a large choir is preferable. The orchestra parts are accessible to players of moderate experience. The brass parts have some fairly sustained playing. There are some peculiar harmonic notations for the viola which use bass clef with the C string tuned down to A. The players are asked to tune down to A and back up to C during the performance. Nielsen's methods of overlapping levels of melodic material may present some challenges in achieving clarity between the parts. **Soloists:**

soprano - range: c'-b♭", tessitura: g'-g", this is the most substantial of the solo roles, it is quite sustained and dramatic; tenor - range: e-g', tessitura: f-f', this role is sustained and lyric; baritone - range: A-d', tessitura: c-c', this is a brief solo in an ensemble texture; bass - range: G#-c', tessitura: B-a, this is a brief solo in an ensemble texture; **Choir:** medium easy, **Orchestra:** medium easy.

**Discography:** I. Nielsen, P. Elming, A. Elkrog, P. Hoyer, J. Ditlevsen; Danish National Radio Symphony Orchestra and Chorus, Copenhagen Boys' Choir; conducted by Leif Segerstam. Chandos: 8853 [DDD].

### Selected Bibliography

Doctor, David Reinhardt: *Choral music in Denmark 1900-1960: Repertory and Stylistic Trends.* University of Minnesota: Ph.D. dissertation, 1976.

Krenek, Thomas Bradley: *An Examination and Analysis of the Choral Music of Carl Nielsen.* University of Cincinnati: Doctor of Musical Arts dissertation, 1984, part I.

Christiansen, Cheryl Ann: *An Analysis of Carl Nielsen's Choral-Symphonic Works: Fynsk forar, opus 42; Hymnus amoris, opus 12; and Søvnen, opus 18.* University of Texas at Austin: Master's of Music thesis, 1996.

## Søvnen, op. 18 [Sleep] (1904)

**Duration:** ca. 20 minutes

**Text:** The text by Johannes Jørgensen is in Danish and was written at the request of the composer. The score includes a German singing translation prepared by C. Rocholl.

**Performing Forces: voices:** SATB choir; **orchestra:** 3 flutes (flute III doubling picolo), 2 oboes, 2 clarinets in A, 2 bassoons, 4 horns in F, 3 trumpets in C, 3 trombones, tuba, timpani, percussion (1 player - glockenspiel), and strings.

**First Performance:** 21 March 1905.

**Edition:** *Søvnen* is published by Wilhelm Hansen Musik-Forlag (number 1288). The piano-vocal score is available for purchase, all other materials are available through rental.

**Notes:** This work is tripartite with the first and third sections portraying the calm and restfulness of sleep interrupted by the nightmare of the second section.

**Performance Issues:** Nielsen uses a variety of choral textures, including some imitative procedures. The largest portions utilize homophonic block-chord writing and paired doubling. These pairings are usually tenor with bass and soprano with alto. These divisions make this an unusually suitable work to select for a program in which a men's choir and a women's choir are to be combined shortly before a joint performance. There are two-part divisi for each of section of the choir. The harmonic language of this work is functionally tonal throughout. The vocal harmonies are triadic with scalar and triadic melodic motion. There are some interesting passages which have an element of polytonality with opposed tonal centers in the treble and bass registers. Some of these are spelled with chromatic cross relations. The choral parts are very lyrically conceived and are readily accessible to less experienced ensembles. All of the vocal material is well supported by the orchestra. The instrumental parts are very idiomatic and conservatively written. The choral and orchestral parts are appropriate for average community ensembles. **Choir:** medium easy, **Orchestra:** medium easy.

**Discography:** I. Nielsen, P. Elming, A. Elkrog, P. Hoyer, J. Ditlevsen; Danish National Radio Symphony Orchestra and Chorus, Copenhagen Boys' Choir; conducted by Leif Segerstam. Chandos: 8853 [DDD].
selections: Aksel Schiøtz, tenor; orchestra; HMV X 6612 [78].

### Selected Bibliography

Doctor, David Reinhardt: *Choral music in Denmark 1900-1960: Repertory and Stylistic Trends.* University of Minnesota: Ph.D. dissertation, 1976.

Krenek, Thomas Bradley: *An Examination and Analysis of the Choral Music of Carl Nielsen.* University of Cincinnati: Doctor of Musical Arts dissertation, 1984, part II.

Christiansen, Cheryl Ann: *An Analysis of Carl Nielsen's Choral-Symphonic Works: Fynsk forar, opus 42; Hymnus amoris, opus 12; and Søvnen, opus 18.* University of Texas at Austin: Master's of Music thesis, 1996.

## Fynsk Foraar, op. 42 [Springtime in Funen] (1921)

**Duration:** ca. 18 minutes

**Text:** The text by Aage Bernsten is in Danish (see under notes below). The Hansen edition distributed outside of Denmark is published with singing translations in English (by C. Rocholl) and German (by K. Tindall), but without the original Danish.

**Performing Forces: voices:** soprano, tenor, and baritone soloists; SATB choir; **orchestra:** 2 flutes (flute II doubling piccolo), 2 oboes, 2 clarinets in A and B$^b$, 2 bassoons, 4 horns in F, 2 trumpets in C, timpani, percussion, and strings.

**First Performance:** 8 July 1922; Danish Choral Society.

**Edition:** *Fynsk Foraar* is published by Wilhelm Hansen Musik-Forlag. All materials are available through rental.

**Notes:** Funen is the name of Nielsen's native island. The poet was also a native of Funen. The text was the first-place winner of a poetry contest on the theme of Danish life. Nielsen chose to set it to music a few years later. The work is divided into four movements with the first serving as an introduction and the remaining three presenting scenes from rural Danish life as follows:

I   Springtime in Funen
II  The Blind Minstrel
III The Old Folks          *a cappella* men's TTBB choir
IV  Dance Piece

**Performance Issues:** The choral writing is entirely in homophonic, block-chord style. The rhythms are very logogenic. The rhythmic similarities of Danish to German and English make the singing translations read fairly well. The pitch material of the choir is functionally tonal and generally diatonic. The *a cappella* movement is quite short and musically very accessible even to inexperienced choirs, with narrow ranges for each part. There are two brief solos for a boy and girl in movement II, each is about eight measures long with a range from e' to e". This movement also has very brief passages which are labeled "girls" and "boys," which would be most effectively  sung by a children's group, but which could be sung by members of the adult choir if necessary. There are minimal divisi for the sopranos and a four-part movement for the men, but no divisi for the altos. The orchestral writing is very accessible and quite conservative. It appears to be a score which the composer envisioned being played by provincial community orchestras, and it is well-conceived for such use. This is a charming and light-hearted secular work which is within the means of most ensembles and which could provide a useful contrast to many other symphonic choral works on a larger program. **Soloists:** soprano - range: b-a", tessitura: a'-f', this is a lyric and scalar role with sustained passages in the upper range; tenor - range: e-g#', tessitura: f#-e', this role is lilting and folksong-like; baritone - range: A-e$^{b'}$, tessitura: d-b, this role is a light and lyric baritone part which is notated in treble clef with the obvious intention of sounding down an octave; **Choir:** easy, **Orchestra:** medium easy.

**Discography:** I. Nielsen, P. Elming, A. Elkrog, P. Hoyer, J. Ditlevsen; Danish National Radio Symphony Orchestra and Chorus, Copenhagen Boys' Choir; conducted by Leif Segerstam. Chandos: 8853 [DDD].

## Selected Bibliography

Schousboe, Torben: "Samtale med Emil Telmanyi," *Dansk Musik Tidsskrift* 40:4 (May 1965), 95-100.

Krenek, Thomas Bradley: *An Examination and Analysis of the Choral Music of Carl Nielsen.* University of Cincinnati: Doctor of Musical Arts dissertation, 1984, part III.

Christiansen, Cheryl Ann: *An Analysis of Carl Nielsen's Choral-Symphonic Works: Fynsk forar, opus 42; Hymnus amoris, opus 12; and Søvnen, opus 18.* University of Texas at Austin: Master's of Music thesis, 1996.

## Orff, Carl (b. Munich, 10 July 1895; Munich, 29 March 1982)

**Life:** Orff was an innovative composer of remarkable pieces of musical theater, and a highly influential figure in music education. The "O Fortuna" movement from his *Carmina Burana* has become one of the most recognized themes in all western music. Orff attended the Munich Academy of Music where he studied with Anton Beer-Walbrunn and Hermann Zilcher. Following World War I, he had additional studies with Heinrich Kaminski. In 1924, with Dorothee Günther, he founded the Günther School where he began his life-long devotion to the musical education of youth. He developed a collection of "Orff instruments" which were based upon various Asian and African percussion models. These instruments were designed to be easily played with satisfying musical results. Integrating the teaching of Émile Jaques-Dalcroze, he compiled a body of original compositions entitled *Schulwerk* (1930-35). Orff's large-scale compositions borrowed heavily from Greek theater and medieval music, both of which were tempered by contemporary musical processes to create highly dramatic works of musical pageantry in the form of operas and scenic oratorios.

**Principal Works:** *Carmina Burana* (1937), *Der Mond* (1938), *Die Kluge* (1942), *Catulli Carmina* (1943), *Die Bernauerin* (1945), *Antigonæ* (1948), *Trionfo di Afrodite* (1951), *Œdipus der Tyrann* (1958), *Prometheus* (1967), *Rota* (1972).

### Selected Composer Bibliography

Wagner, Wieland, and Wolfgang E. Schäfer: *Carl Orff zum 60. Geburstage.* Bayreuth, Germany: Bayreuther Festspiel, 1955.
*Carl Orff, ein Bericht in Wort und Bild*, second edition. Mainz: B. Schotts Söhne, 1960.
Liess, Andreas: *Carl Orff*, translated to English by Adelheid and Herbert Parkin. London: Calder and Boyars, 1966.
*Carl Orff: sein Leben und sein Werk in Wort, Bild, und Noten*, edited by H. W. Schmidt. Cologne: 1971.

## Carmina Burana, cantiones profanae (1935-36)

**Duration:** ca. 65 minutes

**Text:** Selected by Orff from the Benedictbeuren Collection, the texts are in Latin and Middle High German.

**Performing Forces: voices:** soprano, tenor, baritone soloists; choir, semi-choir, unison children's choir; **orchestra:** 3 flutes (flutes II and III doubling piccolo), 3 oboes (oboe III doubling English horn), clarinet in $E^b$ and $B^b$, 2 clarinets in A and $B^b$, 2 bassoons, contrabassoon, 4 horns, 3 trumpets in $B^b$ and C, 3 trombones, tuba, timpani (5 and timp-piccolo), celeste, 2 pianos, percussion (5 players - 3 glockenspiels, xylophone, castanets, rattle or maraca, sleigh bells, triangle, 2 crotales (no pitch indicated), 4 cymbals (suspended and crash), tamtam, 3 bells (f, c', f'), chimes, tambourine, 2 snare drums, and bass drum), and strings.

**First Performance:** 8 June 1937; Frankfurt am Main, Germany.

**Edition:** *Carmina Burana* is published by Schotts. The piano-vocal score (2877), miniature score (4425), full score (4920), and choral parts are available for purchase; orchestral materials are available through rental.

**Notes:** The texts are from a collection of manuscripts in the Beuren monastery. They focus on the activities of the Goliards who were bacchanalian poets in the middle ages. This is the first of three works which the composer would later group together as *Trionfi — Trittico Teatrale*. It would be useful to compare this work with Stravinsky's *Svadebka* (all) and Honegger's *Le Roi David* (XXIII) as part of the score study. The score is organized into sections as follows:

FORTUNA IMPERATRIX MUNDI

   I O Fortuna - choir
   II Foturne plango vulnera - choir

Act I — PRIMO VERE
   III Veris leta facies - semi-choir
   IV Omnia Sol temperat - baritone
   V Ecce gratum - choir

UF DEM ANGER

   VI Tanz - orchestra
   VII Floret silva - choir
   VIII Chramer, gip die varwe mir - soprano, choir
   IX Reie Swaz hie gat umbe - choir
     Chume, chum geselle min - semi-choir
     Swaz hie gat umbe - choir
   X Werediu werlt alle min - choir

## Act II — IN TABERNA

> XI    Estuans interius - baritone
> XII   Olim lacus colueram - tenor, TB choir
> XIII  Ego sum abbas - baritone, TB choir
> XIV   In taberna quando sumus - TB choir

## Act III — COUR D'AMOURS

> XV     Amor volat undique - soprano, treble choir
> XVI    Dies, nox et omnia - baritone
> XVII   Stetit puella - soprano
> XVIII  Circa mea pectora - baritone, choir
> XIX    Si puer cum puella - TTTBarBB choir
> XX     Veni, veni, venias - double-choir
> XXI    In trutina - soprano
> XXII   Tempus est iocundum - soprano, baritone, treble choir
> XXIII  Dulcissime - soprano

## BLANZIFLOR ET HELENA

> XXIV   Ave formosissima - choir

## FORTUNA IMPERATRIX MUNDI

> XXV   O Fortuna - choir

**Performance Issues:** The main choir should be large and capable of rhythmic precision. Ranges of all choral parts extend fairly high and there are two-part divisi for each choral section. There are also extended sections which move in parallel diatonic triads. The score is primarily diatonic with much paired doubling between the men's and women's parts. The vocal material is thoroughly supported by the orchestra. The singers must be well prepared to execute rapid changes of tempo and dynamics. The children's choir parts are quite easily learned. There are some passages where the children's choir is in unison with the soprano soloist, or the adult choir, which suggests placing them on stage; however, they only sing in movements XV and XXII. The nature of the score would allow them to enter the stage between movements XIV and XV. The scoring suggests a large symphonic choir. There are a few movements which are labeled for small choir. These movements are, conveniently, the more difficult to learn so a subgroup of stronger singers can be assigned these parts. In movement XX it is advisable to assign this stronger small choir to the choir II parts. The most difficult choral movement is XIX, which is for six-part men's choir, *a cappella*, and this is written in parallel triadic motion throughout. The orchestral parts are generally accessible to moderately experienced players. There is a solo for bassoon I in movement XII which is high and quite difficult. Movement VI is an orchestral dance which has frequent meter changes with exchanges between diverse instruments on the downbeats of new meters which can create some temporal hesitation. The two piano parts are very prominent and require secure players. The piano material frequently doubles the woodwinds, which may be considered when selecting the placement of the pianos on stage. The percussion parts require experienced players. Especially important are the timpanist, and the presence of at least one strong mallet player. **soloists:** soprano - range: d'-d''', tessitura: a'-a'', this is a coquettish role which must be effortless at the top of the range; tenor - range: c'-d'', tessitura: c'-d'', this role is sometimes given to countertenors, but the drama of the singer portraying a dying swan on a spit is best served with a tenor; baritone - range: B-a' (b' in falsetto), tessitura: e-g'', this role must have a falsetto that carries over a moderate accompaniment, endurance in the high range, and a strong stage presence; **Choir:** medium easy; **Orchestra:** medium difficult.

**Discography:** Elfride Trötschel, Paul Kuen, Hans Braun and Karl Hoppe; Bavarian Radio Chorus and Orchestra; conducted by Eugen Jochum. Decca: DL 9706 [LP].

Giebel, Cordes, Kuen; Cologne Radio Symphony Orchestra, West German Radio Chorus; conducted by Wolfgang Sawallisch, recorded in 1956. Angel: CDM-64237 [ADD].

Söderström, Bäckelin, Svanholm; Stockholm Philharmic and Chorus; conducted by Schmidt-Isserstedt, recorded live 26 November 1954. 8 Bis: CD-421/424 [AAD].

June Anderson, Philip Creech, Bernd Weikl; Chicago Symphony and Chorus; conducted by James Levine. Deutsche Grammophon: 415136-2 GH [DDD].

Armstrong, English, Allen; London Symphony and Chorus, St. Clement Danes Boys' Choir; conducted by André Previn. Angel: CDC-47411 [DDD].

Sheila Armstrong, John Graham Hall, Rayner Cook; Hallé Orchestra and Chorus; conducted by Maurice Handford. Angel: CDB-62005 [ADD].

Auger, Van Kesteren, Summers; Philharmonia Orchestra and Chorus; conducted by Riccardo Muti. Angel: CDC-47100 [DDD].

Judith Blegen, Kenneth Riegel, Peter Binder; Cleveland Orchestra and Chorus (Robert Page, chorus-master); conducted by Michael Tilson Thomas. CBS: MK-33172 [ADD].

Judith Blegen, William Brown, Håkan Hagegård; Atlanta Symphony Orchestra and Chorus; conducted by Robert Shaw. Telarc: CD-80056 [DDD].

Norma Burrowes, Louis Devos, John Shirley-Quirk; Royal Philharmonic, Brighton Festival Chorus; conducted by Antal Dorati. London: 417714-2 LM [ADD].

Sylvia Greenberg, James Bowman, Stephen Roberts; Berlin Radio Symphony and Chorus; conducted by Riccardo Chailly. London: 411702-2 LH [DDD].

Edita Gruberova, John Aler, Thomas Hampson; Berlin Philharmonic, Shinyukai choir, Berlin Cathedral Boys' Choir; conducted by Seiji Ozawa. Philips: 422363-2 PH [DDD].

Janice Harsanyi, Rudolf Petrak, Harve Presnell; Philadelphia Orchestra and Rutgers Univ. Chorus; conducted by Eugene Ormandy. CBS: MYK-37217 [ADD].

Barbara Hendricks, John Aler, Håkan Hagegård; London Symphony and Chorus; conducted by Riccardo Muti. RCA: RCD1-4550 [DDD].

Janowitz, Stolze, Fischer-Dieskau; German Opera Orchestra and Chorus; conducted by Eugen Jochum. Deutsche Grammophon: 423886-2 GGA [ADD].

Barbara Hendricks, Michael Chance, Jeffrey Black; London Philharmonic Orchestra and Chorus, St. Alban's Cathedral Choristers; conducted by Franz Welser-Möst. Angel: CDC-54054 [DDD].

Evelyn Mandac, Stanley Kolk, Sherrill Milnes; Boston Symphony and New England Conservatory Chorus; conducted by Seiji Ozawa. RCA: 6533-2-RG [ADD].

Popp, Unger, Wolansky, Noble; New Philharmonia Orchestra and Chorus; conducted by Frühbeck de Burgos. Angel: CDM-69060 [CD].

Subrtova, Tománek, Srubar; Czech Philharmonic Orchestra and Chorus; conducted by Smetácek. Supraphon Gems: 2SUP-0025 [ADD].

Jenisová, Dolezal, Kusnjer; Czechoslovak Radio Symphony Orchestra and Chorus; conducted by S. Guzenhauser. Naxos: 8.550196 [DDD].

Walmsley-Clark, Hall, Maxwell; London Symphony and Chorus, Southend Boys' Choir; conducted by Richard Hickox. MCA Classics: MCAD-25964 [DDD].

Bareva, Kamenov, Yanukov; Sofia Philharmonic Orchestra and Chorus; conducted by G. Robev. Forlane: UCD-16556 [DDD].

Casapietra, Hiestermann, Stryczek; Leipzig Radio Symphony Orchestra; conducted by Herbert Kegel. Philips: 420713-2 [DDD].

Regina Klepper, Ulrich Ress, James Taylor, Dietrich Henschel; München Motettenchor, Residenzorchester München; conducted by Hans Rudolf Zobeley. Caligari: CAL 50938 [DDD].

Lisa Griffiths, Ulrich Ress, Thomas Mohr; Kinderchor Frankfurt, Kinderchor des Goethegymnasium, Figuralchor Frankfurt, Frankfurt Singakademie, Frankfurt Kantorei; conducted by Muhai Tang, recorded 3 October 1993 in the Grosser Saal of the Alte Oper, Frankfurt. Wergo: WER 6275-2 [DDD].

with synthesized orchestra: Deis, Cody, Pedrotti; Jeffrey Reid Baker, synthesizers; New York Choral Society; conducted by Robert DeCormier. Newport Classics: NCD-60052 [DDD].

### Selected Bibliography

Schadewaldt, Wolfgang: "Carl Orff Trionfi, die Idee des Werks;" Ruppel, K. H.: "Trionfi, zur Geschichte ihrer Entstehung und Erneuerung durch Carl Orff," and "Carl Orff, Trionfi, Werk und Wirkung," booklet published in French, English, and German, with the complete recording of *Trionfi* by Deutsche Grammophon in 1957.

Schadewaldt, Wolfgang: "Carl Orff—Trionfi," in *Hellas und Hesperin*. Zurich: Artemis Verlag, 1960.

Pahlen, Kurt: *The World of the Oratorio*, 253-255. Portland, Oregon: Amadeus Press, 1985.

Berger, Melvin: *Guide to Choral Masterpieces: A Listener's Guide*, 232-233. New York: Anchor Books, 1993.

## Catulli Carmina, ludi scaenici (1942)

**Duration:** ca. 45 minutes

**Text:** The texts are chosen from the Latin writings of Catullus.

**Performing Forces: voices:** soprano and tenor soloists; SATB choir; **orchestra:** 4 pianos; timpani (4 drums), percussion {10-12 players - xylophone, tenor trough-xylophone (may be substituted by marimba), 2 glockenspiels, metalophone (may be subsituted by vibraphone with the motor off), lithophone (optional), wooden sticks or wood blocks,[18] maracas, 3 tambourines, triangle, bass drum, crotales, crash cymbals, suspended cymbals, tam-tam}, and castanets played by a dancer.

**First Performance:** 6 November 1943; Leipzig, Germany.

**Edition:** *Catulli Carmina* is published by Schotts. The piano-vocal score (3990), miniature score (4565), and choral parts are available for purchase; orchestral materials are available through rental.

**Notes:** *Catulli Carmina* is a musico-theatric work in which the soloists represent Catullus and Clodia (Lesbia) who caution the younger people, represented by the chorus, about the perils of love. Lesbia becomes unfaithful and Catullus is left folorn, yet their younger audience is not turned away from their amorous pursuits. The courtship of Catullus and Lesbia is to be pantomimed by two dancers. The composer envisioned this work to be performed with the chorus and orchestra in the pit and the soloists and dancers on stage. This is the second of three works which the composer would later group together as *Trionfi — Trittico Teatrale*.

**Performance Issues:** This work was conceived of in theatrical terms and is best presented in this fashion. As music for pantomime it could be an effective and dramatic score. As absolute music it is limited. The vocal parts are very easily learned, featuring straightforward rhythms and a narrow pitch palette. The chorus often intones a single pitch for pages of the score. Melodic material is diatonic and most figures are treated as ostinati. The legitimate challenge for the singers is the tessitura of certain sections, lending itself to inevitable vocal fatigue. The sections labeled Acts I, II, and III are unaccompanied, but are fairly static in the sense of pitch centricity. There is a brief section at [47] where a portion of the basses are asked to sing an exposed pedal D. The instrumental parts, including the pianos, are quite accessible to less experienced players. This is a very practical work for a collaborative effort

---

18  Orff indicates "legni" in the list of instruments, which can be used to indicate wood blocks or wooden sticks; however, he does not include the term within the score, except to describe types of beaters.

between collegiate or community music and dance programs, although some institutions may take exception to the forthright sexuality of the text. **Soloists:** soprano - range: f#'-b''; tessitura: a'-e''; this is a minor vocal role of only a dozen measures, but the singer must be capable of a pianissimo high b-natural; tenor - range: d-a'; tessitura: a-g'; this role is chant-like with some soft sustained high notes which would be best in a strong falsetto, it is more of a dramatic effort than a musical one. **Choir:** medium easy; **Orchestra:** medium easy.

**Discography:** Elisabeth Roon, Hans Loeffler; Vienna Chamber Choir; Walter Kamper, Eduard Mrazek, Michael Gielen, and Walter Klein, pianists; conducted by Heinrich Hollreiser, recorded in 1954. Vox: PL 8640 [LP].

S. Crowder, P. Bologna; Choral Guild of Atlanta; conducted by W. Noll. Newport Classics: NCD 60118 [DDD].

E. Stoyanove, K. Kaludov; Bulgarian Radio and Television Symphony Orchestra and Chorus; conducted by M. Milkov, recorded live in Sofia in 1988. Forlane: UCD 16610 [DDD].

Regina Klepper, Ulrich Ress, James Taylor, Dietrich Henschel; München Motettenchor, Residenzorchester München; conducted by Hans Rudolf Zobeley. Caligari: CAL 50938 [DDD].

Lisa Griffiths, Thomas Dewald; Figuralchor Frankfurt, Frankfurt Singakademie, Frankfurt Kantorei; Alois Ickstadt, Elisabeth Kramer, Karl Rarichs, and Fritz Walter-Lindquist, pianists; conducted by Wolfgang Schäfer, recorded 3 October 1993 in the Grosser Saal of the Alte Oper, Frankfurt. Wergo: WER 6275-2 [DDD]; also released as Koch Schwann: 314 021 [DDD].

## Selected Bibliography

Schadewaldt, Wolfgang: "Carl Orff Trionfi, die Idee des Werks;" Ruppel, K. H.: "Trionfi, zur Geschichte ihrer Entstehung und Erneuerung durch Carl Orff," and "Carl Orff, Trionfi, Werk und Wirkung," booklet published in French, English, and German, with the complete recording of Trionfi by Deutsche Grammophon in 1957.

Schadewaldt, Wolfgang: "Carl Orff—Trionfi," in *Hellas und Hesperin*. Zurich: Artemis Verlag, 1960.

Pahlen, Kurt: *The World of the Oratorio*, 255. Portland, Oregon: Amadeus Press, 1985.

# Trionfo di Afrodite:  Concerto scenico (1950-51)

**Duration:** ca. 45 minutes

**Text:** Taken from the writings of Catullus, Sappho, and Euripides, the texts are in Latin and Greek.

**Performing Forces: voices:** 1 or 2 soprano, 1 or 2 tenor, and bass soloists; soprano choir, tenor choir, large choir, and dancing choir; **orchestra:** 3 flutes (flute III doubling piccolo ), 3 oboes oboes II and III doubling English horn), clarinet in E$^b$, 2 clarinets in B$^b$, 3 bassoons (bassoon III doubling contrabassoon), 6 horns, 3 trumpets, 3 trombones, 2 tubas, percussion {11 players - 6 timpani, 3 glockenspiels, xylophone, marimba, tenor trough-xylophone (marimba is the closest substitute), chimes, tambourine, snare drum with snare, snare drum without snare, 2 bass drums, 4 maracas, 4 wood blocks, castanets, crash cymbals, 2 suspended cymbals, tam-tam, triangle), 2 harps, 3 pianos, 3 guitars, and strings.

**First Performance:** <u>concert performance</u>: 13 February 1953; Teatro La Scala; Milan, Italy. <u>staged performance</u>: 10 March 1953; Stuttgart.

**Edition:** *Trionfo di Afrodite* is published by Schotts. The piano-vocal score (4306) is available for purchase; orchestral materials are available through rental.

**Notes:** This is the third of three works which the composer would later group together as *Trionfi — Trittico Teatrale*. Like its companion pieces, it was intended to be performed as a scenic drama.

**Performance Issues:** This work is scored for an enormous ensemble. The choral writing is more adventurous than in Orff's *Catulli Carmina*, but he maintains his use of diatonic pitches, ostinati, unison singing, and parallel motion of like triads to keep the musical material within the grasp of amateur singers. Although Orff often pairs the sopranos and tenors in octaves, and likewise the altos and basses, there are sections where this pattern is altered with chromatic cross-relations which may prove difficult to tune. Two harps are necessary for the proper effect. At times the score has each harp playing the same material, but using a contrasting technique. Both harp parts require strong players. The composer suggests 12-14 players for violin I, 12-14 for violin II, 12 for viola, 12 for cello, and 8 doublebasses; this is surely for sound mass alone. The string parts are very simple, and represent only a portion of the work's total duration. The principal challenge in successfully presenting this work is the coordination of its many disparate elements, as well as the potential difficulties confronted by theatrical situations. This is a remarkably modern interpretation of the classical theater of Ancient Greece and Rome. The directness of the text toward sexual issues may present non-musical obstacles toward a successful performance as well. **Soloists:** soprano - range: $g-b^{b''}$; tessitura: $g'-g''$; this role requires vocal agility and dynamic control at the top of the staff, it include numerous leaps in excess of an octave; tenor - range: $B^b-c^{b''}$; tessitura: $c'-g'$; this is a high, florid, and very ornamented role; bass - range: $G-e'$, tessitura: $c-c'$; this is a declamatory and powerful role. **Choir:** medium difficult; **Orchestra:** medium easy.

**Discography:** Annelies Kupper, Richard Holm; Bavarian Radio Chorus and Orchestra; conducted by Eugen Jochum. Deutsche Grammophon: LPM 18485 [LP].
Susan Roberts, Thomas Dewald, Ulrich Ress; Figuralchor Frankfurt, Frankfurt Singakademie, Frankfurt Kantorei, Cäcilienchor; conducted by Muhai Tang, recorded 3 October 1993 in the Grosser Saal of the Alte Oper, Frankfurt. Wergo: WER 6275-2 [DDD].

## Selected Bibliography

Schadewaldt, Wolfgang: "Carl Orff *Trionfi*, die Idee des Werks;" Ruppel, K. H.: "*Trionfi*, zur Geschichte ihrer Entstehung und Erneuerung durch Carl Orff," and "Carl Orff, *Trionfi*, Werk und Wirkung," booklet published in French, English, and German, with the complete recording of *Trionfi* by Deutsche Grammophon in 1957.
Schadewaldt, Wolfgang: "Carl Orff—*Trionfi*," in *Hellas und Hesperin*. Zurich: Artemis Verlag, 1960.
Pahlen, Kurt: *The World of the Oratorio*, 255. Portland, Oregon: Amadeus Press, 1985.

# Die Sänger der Vorwelt (1955)

**Duration:** ca. 11 minutes

**Text:** The text, by Friedrich Schiller, is in German.

**Performing Forces:** voices: ST choir; **orchestra:** timpani, percussion (9 players - glockenspiel, xylophone, marimba, 5 crotales (written: c", e", g", c''', e'''), bass drum, tambourine, crash cymbals, suspended cymbal, triangle), 2 harps, 2 pianos (or more if available), and doublebasses.

**First Performance:** 3 August 1956; Stuttgart, Germany; as part of the XIV Deutscher Sänger-Bund Festival; Philharmonischer Choir; conducted by Fritz Mende.

**Edition:** *Die Sänger der Vorwelt* is published by Schotts. The piano-vocal score (4367), full score (4699), and choral parts are available for purchase; orchestral materials are available through rental. The full score and performance materials are combined with *Nänie und Dithyrambe*, under the single title, *Dithyrambe*. This score was newly revised in 1981.

**Notes:** *Die Sänger der Vorwelt* was commissioned by the Deutscher Sänger-Bund for their 1956 festival in Stuttgart.

**Performance Issues:** The vocal writing is exclusively homophonic from beginning to end. The soprano and tenor parts are identical except for the octave transposition throughout. These parts are in unison and two- or three-part divisi. The ranges are appropriate for the use of altos and basses on the lower divisions. The vocal parts are well-supported by the accompaniment, and often directly doubled. The harp part is very prominent and could be executed by a single player, but the sonority of the two players in unison is desirable. There must be two pianists and two instruments despite a fair quantity of doubling between the two parts. The doublebass part is very simple, as are the percussion parts. There are numerous meter and tempo changes, which are logical and may be executed with little difficulty. The harp and piano parts are the foundation of the orchestra so secure players are crucial; however, this is an entirely white-note work so many of the usual technical difficulties are abated. This is a very accessible work which displays a strong connection with Orff's educational works. **Choir:** easy, **Orchestra:** medium easy.

**Discography:** Regina Klepper, Ulrich Ress, James Taylor, Dietrich Henschel; München Motettenchor, Residenzorchester München; conducted by Hans Rudolf Zobeley. Calig: CAL 50938 [DDD].

### Selected Bibliography

Liess, Andreas: *Carl Orff*, translated to English by Adelheid and Herbert Parkin, 136-137. London: Calder and Boyars, 1966.

## Nänie und Dithyrambe (1956)

**Duration:** ca. 7 minutes and 4 minutes, respectively

**Text:** The text, by Friedrich Schiller, is in German.

**Performing Forces: voices:** SATB choir; **orchestra:** 6 flutes, 3 trombones (optional), timpani, percussion (7 players - glockenspiel, vibraphone, xylophone, marimba, crotale (written: c'), dobaci (Japanese temple bell in c'), bass drum, tambourine, crash cymbals, suspended cymbal, large tam-tam, castatnets), 2 harps, 4 pianos (16 hands).

**First Performance:** 4 December 1956; Bremen, Germany; Philharmonische Gesellschaft Bremen; conducted by Hellmut Schnackenburg.

**Edition:** *Nänie und Dithyrambe* is published by Schotts. The choral parts (4939) and full score are available for purchase; orchestral materials are available through rental. The full score and performance materials are combined with *Die Sänger der Vorwelt*, under the single title, *Dithyrambe*. This score was newly revised in 1981.

**Notes:** The score is dedicated to the Philharmonische Gesellschaft Bremen. Schiller's *Nänie* has also been set for choir and orchestra by Johannes Brahms (op. 82, 1881). Orff's setting is very minimalist in the true sense of the term. The writing is very sparse. During the first minute of the score only the pitch c has been heard. The treatment of the text is original and quite dramatically effective. There is a good English poetic translation of *Dithyrambe* in *The Fischer-Dieskau Book of Lieder*.[19]

**Performance Issues:** The score calls for a dobaci on c', which is generally as low as they are made. Some performances have substituted gong for the dobaci, but a better solution is to find a large brake drum of the correct pitch set on a non-damping ring with the open side up. Strike the brake drum on the outside of the rim with a large padded stick. It should be noted that this sound occurs three times in four measures near the end of the *Nänie* movement. Throughout the two movements there are only six measures of polyphonic writing for the voices, in fact nearly all of the vocal material is in unison. In the few passages with vocal harmonies, the sopranos and altos are doubled an octave lower by the men's voices. There are some unexpected chromaticisms in the vocal melodies which are set against pedal points in the accompaniment. The vocal writing is very rhythmic, but with significant repetition of most rhythmic figures. The six flutes are in unison throughout, and are often doubled by the pianos. The four pianists are playing two identical four-hand piano parts. These parts are only moderately challenging; however, the integration with the flutes will present some difficulties in controlling the tempo. This is a very dramatic and musically accessible work. It is well-suited to include dancers. **Choir:** easy; **Orchestra:** medium easy.

**Discography:** Regina Klepper, Ulrich Ress, James Taylor, Dietrich Henschel; München Motettenchor, Residenzorchester München; conducted by Hans Rudolf Zobeley. Caligari: CAL 50938 [DDD].

### Selected Bibliography

Liess, Andreas: *Carl Orff*, translated to English by Adelheid and Herbert Parkin, 137-140. London: Calder and Boyars, 1966.

---

[19]  Dietrich Fischer-Dieskau: *The Fischer-Dieskau Book of Lieder*, George Bird and Richard Stokes, translators, 190-191. New York: Limelight Books, 1984.

# Penderecki, Krsysztof (b. Debica, Poland, 23 November 1933)

**Life:** Penderecki is one of the most innovative and acclaimed of all living composers. He attended Jagellonian University in Krakow and the State Higher School of Music. His teachers included Artur Malawski, Skolyszewski, and Wiechiwicz. In 1959 he won all three composition prizes in the Warsaw Autumn Festival. He joined the faculty of the State Higher School of Music in 1958, remaining there after it became the Academy of Music, and serving as Rector (1972-87). Additional teaching posts have included the Essen Folkwang Hochschule and Yale University. In his music, he has sought innovative sound resources which were often achieved using extended techniques for which he developed specialized notational procedures. He received early international recognition with his *Threnody to the Victims of Hiroshima* (1960). Penderecki has received numerous awards including the Herder Prize (1977), the Grand Medal of Paris (1982), the Sibelius Prize (1983), and memberships in the Royal Academy of Music in London (1975), the Royal Academy of Music in Stockholm (1975), and the East Geman Academy of Arts (1975).

**Principal Works:** *opera - Paradise Lost* (1978), *Die schwarze Maske* (1986), *Ubu Rex* (1991); **orchestral** - *Anaklasis* (1960), *Threnody to the Victims of Hiroshima* (1960), *Polymorphia* (1961), *Fluorescences* (1962), *De natura sonoris*, no. 1 (1966), *De natura sonoris*, no. 2 (1968), Symphony no. 1 (1973), Violin Concerto (1976), *Christmas Symphony* (1980), ; **other choral** - *Psalms of David* (1958), *Stabat Mater* (1962), *De profundis* (1977), *Te Deum* (1980), *Agnus Dei* (1981), *Polish Requiem* (1984), *Song of the Cherubim* (1987).

## Selected Composer Bibliography

Linthicum, David Howell: *Penderecki's Notation: A Critical Evaluation*. University of Illinois: Doctor of Musical Arts thesis, 1972.

Erhardt, Ludwik: *Spotkania a Krzysztofem Pendereckim*. Krakow: Polskie Wydawnictwo Muzyczne, 1975.

Felder, David and Mark Schneider: "Conversations with Krzysztof Penderecki," *The Composer*, volume 7 (1976-77), 8-20.

Schwinger, Wolfram: *Penderecki: Begegnungen, Lebensdaten, Werkkomentare*. Stuttgart: Deutsche Verlagsantalt, 1979.

Published in English translation by William Mann as: *Krzysztof Penderecki: His Life and Work*. London: Schott, 1989.

Robinson, Ray: *Krsysztof Penderecki: A Guide to His Works*. Princeton, New Jersey: Prestige Publications, 1983.

# Wymiary czasu i ciszy [Dimensions of Time and Silence] (1960)

**Duration:** ca. 15 minutes

**Text:** According to Slonimsky,[20] this work is an attempt to create a musical equivalent to the visual artwork of Paul Klee. He also states that the text is syllables derived from the Latin palindromic square:

> SATOR
> AREPO
> TENET
> OPERA
> ROTAS

"Creative thirst keeps labor turning."

However, the composer removed the section which contained this Latin text in his revision of the score for a 1961 performance. The remaining text is an agglomeration of vocal sounds.

**Performing Forces: voices:** a choir of 40 solo voices: 10 sopranos, 10 altos, 10 tenors, and 10 basses; **orchestra:** percussion (7 players - glockenspiel, vibraphone, xylorimba, chimes, 2 snare drums, 2 bongos, 6 tom-toms, 4 timpani, 3 wood drums, 4 cymbals [graduated], gong, tam-tam, triangle, 3 cowbells, claves, 2 metal blocks, 4 glasses), harp, celeste, piano, and strings (6 violins, 4 violas, 4 cellos, and 2 doublebasses).

**First Performance:** 18 September 1960; Warsaw, Poland; Krakow Philharmonic Chorus and Orchestra; conducted by Andrzej Markowski. The concert also included the premiere of Boguslaw

---

[20]  Nicolas Slonimsky: *Music Since 1900*, fifth edition, 689. New York: Schirmer Books, 1994.

Schaeffer's *Tertium datur*, as part of the Fourth International Festival of Contemporary Music, "The Warsaw Autumn."

**Edition:** *Wymiary czasu i ciszy* is published as *Dimensions der Zeit und der Stille* by Moeck (5005) and co-published by Polskie. The full score is available for purchase; performance materials are available through rental.

**Autograph:** The published score is derived from the composer's manuscript.

**Notes:** The published edition of the score omits the Latin "magic square" shown above, which is also known as the Cirencester word square, that was written as an *a cappella* choral section near the end of the work. This same text was used as an illustration by Anton Webern in a lecture which was not published until 1960.[21] At the time of composition, Penderecki was not familiar with Webern's association to the text. It might prove interesting to consider restoring this passage for performance.

**Performance Issues:** The score includes quarter-tone writing, sections of indeterminate pitch and rhythm, with many of these elements conveyed through graphic notation. Players and singers are asked to make the highest and lowest possible pitches they can. String players are also directed to play on the tailpiece, between the bridge and tailpiece, to strike the strings with the palm of the hand, and to strike the body of their instruments with their bows and fingers. The singers have only a few pitched moments. In these they are to sing random pitches within a cluster, or to sing a melodic contour of indefinite pitch. The majority of the choral "singing" involves the rhythmic pronunciation of various consonants and occasional whistling. The design of the vocal parts makes them much less difficult than most of Penderecki's symphonic-choral works. Although, while the independent parts are very accessible, the interplay between these parts and the overall function within the score will demand careful rehearsal. The score is in C. The composer indicates that the doublebasses sound an octave lower, and the xylorimba, celeste, and glockenspiel an octave higher than written; however, the notation for the

---

21   Anton Webern: *The Path to the New Music*, edited by Willi Reich, 56-58. London and Bryn Mawr, Pennsylvania: Theodore Presser, 1963.

glockenspiel suggests that it is to follow traditional notational practice, sounding two octaves higher than written. Each of the string parts is for a solo player. There are a number of intricate melodic passages outlined note-by-note between disparate instruments. The pianist must play inside the piano with a variety of percussion beaters. The passages which utilize the interior of the piano are of indefinite pitch. Sectional rehearsals of the percussion with harp and piano will be necessary before the first tutti rehearsal in order to clarify a number of the unusual techniques employed, and to coördinate instrument assignments and the interplay between the percussionists. Some sources catalogue this work with four percussionists; however, it cannot be done with fewer than seven, each of whom must be a savvy and independent player. While presenting numerous ensemble problems, this work is an excellent point of entry for less experienced ensembles to explore the devices and notations of the important body of Polish avant-garde repertoire. **Choir:** medium difficult; **Orchestra:** medium difficult.

**Discography:** Warsaw National Philharmonic Orchestra and Chorus; conducted by Andrzej Markowski, recorded in 1972. Disco: M 0781 [LP]. Rereleased as Muza: PNCD 017 A [AAD].

### Selected Bibliography

Schwinger, Wolfram: *Krzysztof Penderecki: His Life and Work*, translated by William Mann, 194-197. London: Schott, 1989.

# Cantata in honorem Almae Matris Universitatis Iagellonicae: sescentos abhinc annos fundatae [Cantata in honor of my alma mater, the Jagellone University, 600 years after its foundation] (1964)

**Duration:** ca. 6 minutes

**Text:** The text is in Latin, taken from the University's charter.

**Performing Forces:** voices: 2 SATB choirs; **orchestra:** contrabassoon, 4 horns in F, 4 trumpets in B♭, 3 trombones, tuba. 2 timpanists, percussion ( players - chimes, bongos, 2 tom-toms, bass drum, 2 cymbals (graduated), tam-tam, gong, triangle, rattle), piano, organ, 6 doublebasses.

**First Performance:** 10 May 1964; Warsaw, Poland; Warsaw Philharmonic Chorus and Orchestra; conducted by Witold Rowicki.

**Edition:** *Cantata in honorem Almae Matris Universitatis Iagellonicae* is published by Polskie. The full score is available for purchase; performance materials are available through rental.

**Autograph:** The published score is derived from the composer's manuscript.

**Notes:** This piece was written to commemorate the 600th anniversary of the Jagellonian University of Krakow. In his sketches Penderecki nicknamed it the "drumstroke" cantata because of the recurrent drumbeat figure.

**Performance Issues:** This work is the most musically conservative of Penderecki's works for choir and orchestra in that it is thoroughly notated. The notation is primarily traditional. Temporal organization is based upon clear metrical foundations. Pitches are also notated specifically. The choir uses repeated consonant sounds as a percussive effect. Much of the choral work is rhythmically spoken text or speech sounds. In passages where the choir sings, each part repeats a single pitch for the duration of the phrase so that a single section of the choir must find only six or seven successive pitches in the entire work, and the first of these is a unison D which is clearly prepared in the opening bars of the orchestra. In subsequent entrances the choral pitches are not supported, nor introduced by the orchestra. The harmonic material of the second choral entrance includes eleven discrete pitches with the remaining combinatorial pitch being sounded by most of the orchestral instruments in unison. Some members of the choir are also asked to whistle. There are a number of freely repeating pizzicato passages for the doublebasses which are of indeterminate rhythm. Each of the doublebasses must be able to play down to CC. The pianist is directed to play within the piano with an assortment of percussion beaters. Although not labeled so, the full score is in C. This score presents significantly fewer problems of time integration and ensemble than the other Penderecki scores presented here; however, more traditionally vertical construction of this score presents many more challenges for intonation. **Choir:** difficult; **Orchestra:** medium difficult to difficult.

**Discography:** Philharmonic Orchestra and Chorus of Krakow; conducted by Jerzy Katlewicz. Polish Nagrania: SXL 1151 [LP].

### Selected Bibliography

Schwinger, Wolfram: *Krzysztof Penderecki: His Life and Work*, translated by William Mann, 32-34. London: Schott, 1989.

## Passio Et Mors Domini Nostri Iesu Christi Secundum Lucam  [Passion According to St. Luke] (1963-66)

**Duration:** ca. 80 minutes

**Text:** This Latin text is taken from the *Gospel of St. Luke*, chapters 22 and 23; *Gospel of St. John*; *Lamentations of Jeremiah*; *Psalms*; and the Roman Catholic Passion Liturgy.

**Performing Forces: voices:** speaker, soprano, baritone, and bass soloists; three SATB choirs, SA children's choir; **orchestra:** 4 flutes (flutes I and II doubling piccolo, flute IV doubling alto flute), bass clarinet in B$^b$, 2 alto saxophones in E$^b$, 3 bassoons, contrabassoon, 6 horns in F, 4 trumpets in B$^b$, 4 trombones, tuba, percussion (5 players - vibraphone, chimes, timpani (4 drums), snare drum, 2 bongos, 6 tom toms, bass drum, 4 woodblocks, guiro, claves, whip, ratchet, 4 graduated cymbals, large tam-tam, medium tam-tam, chinese gong, javanese gong), harp, harmonium, organ, piano, and strings (24 violins, 10 violas, 10 cellos, 8 doublebasses).

**First Performance:** 30 March 1966; Münster Cathedral, Münster, Germany; Stefania Woytowicz, Andrzej Hiolski, Bernard Ladysz, Rudolf Jürgen Bartsch; Cologne Radio Chorus (Herbert Schernue, chorus-master), Tölzer Boys Choir (Gerhard Schmidt, chorus-master), Cologne Radio Orchestra; conducted by Henryk Czyz.

**Edition:** *Passio et Mors Domini Nostri Iesu Christi Secundum Lucam* is published by Moeck (5028); it is co-published with Polskie. The full score is available for purchase; performance materials are available through rental. "Two Choruses from *Passio et Mors Domini Nostri Iesu Christi Secundum Lucam*" containing the "In Pulverem Mortis" and "Miserere" for 3-part choir *a cappella* is also available for purchase from Moeck.

**Autograph:** The published score is a facsimile of the composer's manuscript.

**Notes:** *Passio et Mors Domini Nostri Iesu Christi Secundum Lucam* was commissioned to commemorate the 700th anniversary of the Münster Cathedral. The score includes a subtle hommage to J. S. Bach through a number of statements of his musical motto B-A-C-H, first in retrograde in the organ on the first page of the score, and lastly at the beginning of the final section in the baritone solo. It is a dramatic and fiercely atonal work which closes with a climactic cadence to E major on the text, "In manus tuas commendo spiritum meum: Domine, Deus veritatis (Into your hands I commend my spirit: Lord, God of truth.)."

**Performance Issues:** This is a remarkably expressive and innovative composition, which is accessible only to the most advanced vocal and instrumental ensembles. The score, written in sounding pitch, very effectively integrates traditional notation with modern graphic symbology where non-traditional techniques are employed. Much of the pitch material is serially conceived. The choral pitches are sometimes supported by the accompanying instruments, but there are substantial *a cappella* sections. The voicing of harmonies within each choir is helpful to the performers, but at times all twelve discrete pitches are being sounded by the singers simultaneously. Additionally there are portions which call for pitch divisions in quarter tones. Penderecki's orchestrational palette is rich and he often creates orchestral arpeggios of great rhythmic complexity. There are passages in which the composer requests a degree of rhythmic freedom within the section. In sections which are devoid of a conspicuous pulse, numerous entrances are entirely dependent upon cues or carefully guided patterns of chance. At times the singers employ *Sprechstimme*. There are divisi within each choral part, at times yielding 48 independent vocal parts. The numbers of strings are critical as divisi are indicated by player number. In some sections orchestra members are asked to play the highest or lowest possible sounds on their instruments. There are a number of aleatoric devices including random tone clusters, non-pitched "scat" singing, free repetition of musical figures, and non-specific notational devices. Some non-traditional notational symbols which are used within the score do not appear in the explanatory table in the front materials. The pianist is asked to play inside the piano with percussion mallets. The organ part includes a glissando from diminished pressure, requiring an instrument which can sound with the blower turned off. The singing soloists occasionally recite text. **Soloists:** narrator, the narrator's entrances are non-precise and there are no rhythmic recitations, but the complexity of the score surrounding that text make this much more accessible to a person with musical training; soprano, range: b$^b$-c''', tessitura: c'-e'', these solos are very florid and riddled with pitch challenges, the soprano must have flexibility and wide dynamic control throughout the entire range; baritone, range: A$^b$-b$^b$', tessitura: c-c', this role requires a declamatory and flexible voice; bass, range: F-e', tessitura: B-b, this part requires a clear, focused, and lyrical voice capable of wide leaps; **Choir:** very difficult; **Orchestra:** very difficult.

**Discography:** Stefania Woytowicz, Andrzej Hiolski, Bernard Ladysz, Leszek Herdegen; Krakow Philharmonic Orchestra and Chorus; conducted by Henryk Czyz, recorded in 1966. Polish Gramophone: SXL 0325/6 [LP]. Rereleased as Muza: PNCD 017 A [AAD].
Stefania Woytowicz, Andrzej Hiolski, Bernard Ladysz, Leszek Herdegen; Cologne Radio Orchestra and Chorus; conducted by Henryk Czyz. RCA: VICS-6015 [LP].

### Selected Bibliography

Hutcheson, Robert Joseph, Jr.: *Twentieth-Century Passion Settings: An Analytic Study of Max Baumann's "Passion," Op. 63; Frank Martin's "Golgotha;" Krzysztof Penderecki's "St. Luke Passion;" and Ernest Pepping's "Passionsbericht des Mattäus."* Washington University of St. Louis, Missouri : Ph.D. thesis, 1976.
Pahlen, Kurt: *The World of the Oratorio*, 266-267. Portland, Oregon: Amadeus Press, 1985.
Schwinger, Wolfram: *Krzysztof Penderecki: His Life and Work*, translated by William Mann, 200-214. London: Schott, 1989.

## Dies Irae (1967)

**Duration:** ca. 22 minutes

**Text:** The text is taken from *Revelation of St. John the Divine*, the Psalms, I Corinthians, and poems of Louis Aragon, "Auschwitz;" Broniewski, "Bodies;" Ròzewich, and "A Pigtail;" and Paul Valery,

"Le Cimitière riarin;" translated into Latin by Tytus Gorski. Additional texts are extracted from *The Eumenides* of Aeschylus in Greek.

**Performing Forces: voices:** soprano, tenor/baritone, and bass soloists; choir; **orchestra:** 4 flutes (flutes I and II doubling piccolo), 3 oboes, 2 alto saxophones in $E^b$, baritone saxophone in $E^b$, 3 bassoons, contrabassoon, 6 horns in F, 4 trumpets in $B^b$, 4 trombones, 2 tubas, percussion (8 players - 6 timpani, chimes, 2 bongos, 2 military drums, field drum, bass drum, 6 cymbals, 2 chinese gongs, javanese gong, 2 tam-tams, ratchet, guiro, whip, metal block [anvil], siren, iron chains, and thunder sheet), harmonium, piano, 10 cellos, 8 doublebasses (no violins or violas).

**First Performance:** concert premiere: 14 April 1967; Krakow, Poland. Its official premiere was 6 April 1967[22]; Oswiecim (Auschwitz), Poland; Delfina Ambroziak, soprano; Wieslaw Ochman, tenor; Bernard Ladysz, bass; Krakow Philharmonic Orchestra and Chorus, conducted by Krzysztof Missona; for the unveiling of the International Monument to Victims of Fascism on the sight of the Nazi concentration camps.

**Edition:** *Dies Irae* is published by Moeck (5043) and co-published by Polskie. The full score is available for purchase; performance materials are available through rental.

**Autograph:** The published score is derived from the composer's manuscript.

**Notes:** This work is dedicated to the memory of those exterminated by the Nazis in Auschwitz. It is organized into three sections as follows:

    I   Lamentatio
    II  Apocalypsis
    III Apotheosis

---

[22] Nicolas Slonimsky lists 17 April for this premiere in *Music Since 1900*, fifth edition. The 16th is indicated in the published score. Slonimsky is also the source for the performance in Krakow, which is not noted in the score.

Penderecki also composed a setting of this text for his *Polish Requiem* (1980-84).

**Performance Issues:** The entire full score is written in sounding pitch. The entire composition is unmetered and written in an amalgamation of graphic and traditional notations. Some of the pitch material is serially generated, but the score includes so many clusters and free-pitch passages that this becomes an inconspicuous feature. The over-all effect of this work is as a sound composition of great dramatic effect requiring careful attention to timbre and dynamics. There are numerous aleatoric devices including free repetition, free rhythm, indications of approximate pitch, absence of meter, and imprecise notation. Players are asked to engage in a number of extended techniques. There are string divisi by chair. The lack of metrical organization within this score requires substantial rehearsal time in order to coördinate complex, but unrhythmed interplay between diverse sections of the orchestra. There are six-part divisi within each section of the choir. Much of the choral material is *a cappella*, and in those sections with orchestra, little of the choral material is in anyway supported by the accompaniment. Despite the quantity of imprecisely notated passages for the choir, this score remains accessible to only the most advanced ensembles. The composer's exploitation of the upper ranges in the choral parts will require cautious rehearsal planning for the singers. The vocal solos are all difficult, exposed, and relatively short. The composer calls for a "lastra" among the percussion instruments which, given the notation, he must mean a thundersheet. **Soloists:** soprano - range: c'-d$^b$''', tessitura: g'-f#'', this role requires vocal flexibility to accommodate very broad and awkward leaps; tenor - range: c-a', tessitura: g-a$^b$', this role is declamatory and triumphant; bass - range: F-e', tessitura: c#-b$^b$, filled with awkward leaps and a number of quarter-tone pitch indications; **Choir:** very difficult, **Orchestra:** very difficult.

**Discography:** Stefania Woytowicz, Wieslaw Ochman, Bernard Ladysz; Krakow Philharmonic Orchestra and Chorus, conducted by Henryk Czyz. Philips 839/701 LY [LP]. Rereleased as Muza: PNCD 021 [AAD].

Szwajgier, Jankowski, Mroz; Polish Radio and Television Symphony Orchestra and Chorus; conducted by S. Kawalla. Conifer: CDCF 185 [DDD].

## Selected Bibliography

Marinelli, C: "Review of K. Penderecki: Dies Irae," *La Revue internationale de la musique*, volume 2 (1967), 436.

Schwinger, Wolfram: *Krzysztof Penderecki: His Life and Work*, translated by William Mann, 214-217. London: Schott, 1989.

# UTRENJA

## Part I—Grablegung Christi [The Entombment of Christ] (1969-71)

**Duration:** ca. 50 minutes

**Text:** This is a setting of a traditional liturgical text in old Slavonic.

**Performing Forces:** voices: soprano, mezzo-soprano, tenor, bass, and basso profundo soloists; double choir; **orchestra:** 4 flutes (flutes I and II doubling piccolo, flute IV doubling alto flute in G), 3 oboes, 3 clarinets in $B^b$ (clarinet III doubling soprano clarinet in $E^b$), bass clarinet in $B^b$, 2 alto saxophones in $E^b$, 2 baritone saxophones in $E^b$, 3 bassoons, contrabassoon, 6 horns in F, 4 trumpets in C, 4 trombones, 2 tubas, timpani, percussion (6 players - vibraphone, marimba, chimes, wood bells,[23] snare drum, 2 bongos, 4 tom-toms, large wood-plate drum, 4 cymbals, 2 [Chinese] gongs, Javanese gong, 2 tam-tams, 2 triangles, 2 rattles, guiro, claves, slapstick, Chinese wood blocks), piano, organ, bass guitar, and strings (24 violins, 10 violas, 10 cellos, 8 doublebasses).

**First Performance:** 8 April 1970; Cathedral of Altenburg, Germany; Stefania Woytowicz, Krystyna Szczepanska, Louis Devos, Bernard Ladysz, Boris Carmeli; North German Radio Choir of Hamburg (Helmut Franz, chorus-master), West German Radio Choir of Cologne (Herbert Schernus, chorus-master), Radio Symphony Orchestra of Cologne; conducted by Andrzej Markowski.

---

[23] The wood bells are available on rental from the publisher, B. Schott's Söhne, Mainz.

**Edition:** *Grablegung Christi* is published by Schotts in a co-edition with Polskie. The miniature score (6314) is available for purchase; performance materials are available through rental.

**Autograph:** The published score is derived from the composer's manuscript.

**Notes:** The score is dedicated to Eugene Ormandy. The work is divided into five untitled movements.

**Performance Issues:** The score is written in C. The composer uses a number of graphic devices to introduce elements of indeterminacy. Players and singers are asked to execute their highest and lowest possible pitches; rapid, unmeasured repetitions of single sounds; passages of indeterminate pitch; and unmeasured free repetion of melodic passages. String players are asked to play between the bridge and tailpiece. Some sections of the score use quarter-tones. Penderecki indicates that the two choirs should be placed as far from each other as possible. At times the choirs share the same material, which may be rhythmically active, so that this spatial separation will present aural incongruities which appear to be an intended musical effect. Individual sections of each choir are subdivided into as many as twelve parts. The harmonic material of both the choirs and orchestra include dense, often specifically notated, clusters, which often include all twelve discrete pitches. Every instrumental part is technically demanding in terms of facility and range. Each brass part involves sustained playing at the upper and lower extremities of playing range. There are extended *a cappella* sections, including the entire third movement. The choir is directed to whisper and speak text, to whistle, and to percussively repeat consonant sounds in and out of rhythm. **Soloists:** soprano - range: b$^\flat$-c''', tessitura: g'-a'', this part requires rapid articulation, wide melodic leaps, and the ability to sustain prolonged pitches at the top of the range; mezzo-soprano - range: g#-a'', tessitura: d'-d'', this part exploits the entire range and requires frequent, awkward melodic leaps; tenor - range: c-e''(optional c''), tessitura: d'-a', this soloist must be capable of sustained singing in the uppermost range; bass - range: G-f#', tessitura: d-d', this solo includes sustained passages in the bottom of the range; basso profundo - range: C#-d', tessitura: D-d, this soloist must be able to project clearly below the staff; **Choir:** very difficult; **Orchestra:** very difficult.

**Discography:** Delfina Ambroziak, Krystyna Szczepanska, Kazimierz Pustelak, Adam Denysenko, Boris Carmeli; Warsaw National Philharmonic Orchestra and Chorus, Pioneer Choir; conducted by Andrzej Markowski, recorded in 1973. Polish Gramophone SXL 0889 [LP]. Rereleased as Muza: PNCD-018 [AAD].

Stefania Woytowicz, Kerstin Meyer, Seth McCoy, Bernard Ladyz, Peter Lagger; Temple University Chorus (Robert Page, chorus-master), Philadelphia Orchestra; conducted by Eugene Ormandy. RCA: LSC 3180 [LP].

### Selected Bibliography

Schwinger, Wolfram: *Krzysztof Penderecki: His Life and Work*, translated by William Mann, 217-224. London: Schott, 1989.

## Part II — Auferstehung Christi [The Resurrection of Christ] (1970-71)

**Duration:** ca. 36 minutes

**Text:** This is a setting of a traditional liturgical text in old Slavonic.

**Performing Forces: voices:** soprano, alto, tenor, and 2 bass soloists[24]; 2 mixed choirs and boys' choir; **orchestra:** 4 flutes (flutes I and II doubling piccolo, flute IV doubling alto flute in G), 4 oboes (oboe IV doubling English horn), 4 clarinets in $B^b$ (clarinet III doubling soprano clarinet in $E^b$, clarinet IV doubling bass clarinet in $B^b$), 3 bassoons, contrabassoon, 6 horns in F, 4 trumpets in C (trumpet IV doubling trumpet in D), 4 trombones, 2 tubas, timpani, percussion (10 players - glockenspiel, chimes, small bells, sanctus bells, bells [small ship's or school], plate bells, crotales, xylophone, bass xylophone [or second marimba], marimba, 2 bongos, 4 tom-toms, bass drum, large wood-plate drum, 6 cymbals, 2 gongs, 2 tam-tams, 2 triangles, 2 claves, 2 hyoshigi [Japanese concussion blocks], wooden bells,[25] glass chimes, piece of railway rail, thunder sheet), celeste, harmonium, piano, and strings (24 violins, 10 violas, 10 cellos, and 8 double basses).

---

24   There is a solo role for a child soprano which is not indicated in the front matter of the score.

25   The wooden bells are available for rent from the publishers.

Members of the choirs are also asked to play hyoshigi, rattles, wooden bells, and small bells.

**First Performance:** 28 May 1971, Münster Cathedral, Germany; Stefania Woytowicz, Krystyna Szczepanska, Louis Devos, Bernard Ladysz, Boris Carmeli; Cologne Radio Chorus (Herbert Schernue, chorus-master), North German Radio Chorus of Hamburg (Helmut Franz, chorus-master), Tölzer Boys Choir (Gerhard Schmidt, chorus-master), Cologne Radio Orchestra; conducted by Andrzej Markowski.

**Edition:** *Auferstehung Christi* is published by Schotts in a co-edition with Polskie. All materials are available through rental.

**Autograph:** The published score is a facsimile of the composer's manuscript.

**Notes:** The score was commissioned by West German Radio in Cologne.

**Performance Issues:** This score uses a wide variety of graphic notational devices including indications for highest and lowest possible pitches, free repetition, quickest possible repetition, and indeterminate pitches. There are some additional graphic indications for extended instrumental techniques including playing between the bridge and the tailpiece, slapping the brass mouthpieces, blowing through wind instruments without phonating, overblowing, and arpeggiating the harmonic sequence. And there are some uses of quartertone notation which are clearly explained in an opening table; however, there are a number of graphic figures in the score which are not defined within the score and which are not in broad use. The full score uses Italian for instrumental labels and instructions which are not graphically indicated, but the Slavonic text is written in the Cyrillic alphabet. The score suggests that the two mixed choirs be placed as far from each other as possible. Each mixed choir divides to SSSAAATTTBBB, and the children's choir is divided to SSSSAAAA. Each of these divisions at some point has an independent percussion part, which is sometimes integrated with a simultaneously sung passage. If possible, the chorus members may be at their best advantage with music stands. If this is not practical, the percussion assignments may be given to alternating members of the choir, with the non-playing singers holding the score. Much of the choral writing is spoken, or of unspecified pitch, but there are some passages with dense pitch clusters that are not clearly supported by the instruments. All of the instrumental parts are quite difficult in terms of extreme range, extended techniques, and most of all, the integration of the independent parts into the whole score. It is crucial that there be sectional rehearsals of each section of the orchestra with the conductor before the entire ensemble meets, as there are numerous organization decisions which must be made within each section. Also, Penderecki has treated the sections of the orchestra as integrated units which have unified musical figures that are more in synchrony with each other than with the rest of the orchestra. The layout of the percussion section should be carefully planned and a detailed list of player assignments throughout the score should be made and distributed before the first sectional rehearsal. This is a remarkable score which, through its use of high-pitch percussion and broad sonic spectrum, creates a very dramatic musical depiction of the resurrection. It is fiercely difficult and remains within the abilities of only the finest ensembles, but is very deserving of more frequent performances than it receives. It would be an interesting pairing with a baroque Easter work, or Beethoven's *Christus am Oelberge*. **Soloists:** soprano - range: $b^b$-c''', tessitura: a'-a'', this role combines very sustained passages with rapidly articulated figures containing broad melodic leaps; alto - range: g-a', tessitura: b-d'', this is a sustained role with exposed passages at both extremes of the range; tenor - range: g'-e'', tessitura: g'-e'', most of this role is sustained and requires a strong and clear falsetto; baritone - range: A-c'', tessitura: b-g', this role has extended passages in the highest range which must be in a strong falsetto; basso profundo - range: C-d', tessitura: G-g, this is a very sustained role which requires a clear pedal C; child soprano - range: e''-g#'', this role is fairly brief, exposed, and very sustained. There is little support for providing the starting pitch for the soloist. **Choir:** very difficult, **Orchestra:** very difficult.

**Discography:** Stefania Woytowicz, Krystyna Szczepanska, Kazimierz Pustelak, Bernard Ladysz, Peter Lagger; Warsaw National Philharmonic Orchestra and Chorus, Pioneer Choir; conducted by Andrzej Markowski, recorded in 1973. Polish Gramophone SXL 0890 [LP]. Rereleased as Muza: PNCD-018 [AAD].

Stefania Woytowicz, Kerstin Meyer, Seth McCoy, Bernard Ladyz, Peter
    Lagger; Temple University Chorus (Robert Page, chorus-master),
    Philadelphia Orchestra; conducted by Eugene Ormandy. RCA: LSC
    3180 [LP].

## Selected Bibliography

Schwinger, Wolfram: *Krzysztof Penderecki: His Life and Work*,
    translated by William Mann, 217-224. London: Schott, 1989.

## Kosmogonia (1970)

**Duration:** ca. 17 minutes

**Text:** Taken from Copernicus, Lucretius, the Book of Genesis,
    Sophocles, Ovid, Leonardo da Vinci, Giordano Bruno, Yuri
    Gagarin, and John Glenn; the text is in Greek, Latin, Italian,
    Russian, and English.

**Performing Forces: voices:** soprano, tenor, and bass soloists; 20-
    part mixed choir; **orchestra:** 4 flutes (flutes I and II doubling
    piccolo), 4 oboes, 3 clarinets in B$^b$, bass clarinet in B$^b$, 2 alto
    saxophones in E$^b$, baritone saxophone in E$^b$, 3 bassoons,
    contrabassoon, 6 horns in F, 4 trumpets in C (trumpet I doubling
    trumpet in D), 4 trombones, 2 tubas, timpani, percussion (9
    players - glockenspiel, chimes (2 sets), snare drum, 2 bongos, 4
    tom-toms, bass drum, 4 cymbals (graduated), 2 tam-tams, 2 gongs
    [Chinese?], Javanese gong, cowbells [listed as cencerros], claves,
    rattle, wooden wind chimes, glass wind chimes, slapstick,
    flexatone, thunder sheet), harp, celeste, harmonium, piano, organ,
    bass guitar, and strings (24 violins, 10 violas, 10 cellos, 8
    doublebasses).

**First Performance:** 24 October 1970; United Nations, New York;
    Joanna Neal, Robert Nagy, Bernard Ladysz; Rutgers University
    Choir (F. Austin Walter, chorus-master), Los Angeles
    Philharmonic; conducted by Zubin Mehta.

**Edition:** *Kosmogonia* is published by Schotts in a co-edition with
    Polskie. The miniature score (6324) is available for purchase;
    performance materials are available through rental.

**Autograph:** The published score is derived from the composer's manuscript.

**Notes:** The work is in two parts; the first, *Arche* (beginning), describes the foundations of the universe; the second, *Apeiron* (infinity), praises the genius of man and the exploration of space. It was commissioned by the Secretary General of the United Nations to commemorate that body's twenty-fifth anniversary.

**Performance Issues:** This is a fiercely difficult score which incorporates a broad selection of avant-garde techniques. Each instrument and voice part is presented with significant technical challenges and the pitch material for the choir is in no way supported by the orchestra. The overall effect of the score is a stunning array of musical sounds, the coördination of which is within the ability of only the finest ensembles. The score is in C with the traditional one- and two-octave transpositions for the contrabassoons, doublebasses and mallet percussion. At **22**, trumpet I is instructed to return from D to B$^b$ trumpet, but surely the composer intended this to be a return to trumpet in C. The score uses quarter-tone notation, and various graphic-notation devices to indicate approximations of pitch and rhythm and freedom of tempo. The pianist must play inside the piano with an assortment of percussion beaters. Most sections of the orchestra are occasionally assigned consecutive semitones to produce clusters within each instrumental choir. The choir has numerous entrances on specifically notated dense pitch clusters which are often not clearly prepared by the accompaniment. Members of the choir are also asked to whistle sustained pitches with semitone clusters. The choir is also used percussively through rhythmic repetition of consonant sounds. In fully-notated melodic passages the choir is often responsible for electing the syllabification of prolonged melismas. All of the instrumention labels are Italian abbreviations, but the instrumentation tables are in German and English causing the less common orchestral instruments to be difficult to identify on first reading of the score. The most difficult examples include "cht" for bass guitar, "vtr" for glass wind chimes, "cpc" for wood wind chimes, "cpl" for glockenspiel, "cpn" for chimes, "frs" for rattle, "fxf" for flexatone, and "lst" for thunder sheet. **Soloists:** soprano - range: b-c'''; tessitura: d'-a'', this role moves repeatedly throughout the entire range, the singer must be capable of very wide melodic leaps; alto - range: e-g''; tessitura: b-e'', this is a sustained melodically awkward role; tenor - range: d-b$^b$'; tessitura:

d'-a', this is a short but very sustained solo; bass - range: G-f';
tessitura: d-e', this role requires a flexible and declamatory singer;
**Choir:** very difficult; **Orchestra:** very difficult.[26]

**Discography:** Stefania Woytowicz, Kazimierz Pustelak, Bernard
Ladysz; Choir and Orchestra of the National Polish Philharmonic;
conducted by Andrzej Markowski. Philips: 6500/683 [LP].

### Selected  Bibliography

Schwinger, Wolfram: *Krzysztof Penderecki: His Life and Work*,
translated by William Mann, 224-225. London: Schott, 1989.

# Canticum  Canticorum  Salomonis  [Song  of  Songs]
(1971-72)

**Duration:** ca. 17 minutes

**Text:** The text is taken from the Latin translation of the *Song of
Solomon* found in the Old Testament of the Bible.

**Performing Forces: voices:** SSSSAAAATTTTBBBB choir;
**orchestra:** 2 flutes (flute II doubling alto flute in G), 2 oboes,
English horn, soprano clarinet in E$^b$, bass clarinet in B$^b$, bassoon,
horn in F, trumpet in B$^b$, 2 trombones, percussion (7 players -
celeste, glockenspiel, chimes, vibraphone, marimba, 4 wooden
drums, 2 bongos, 5 tom-toms, 6 graduated cymbals, gong, 2 tam-
tams, 2 triangles, 4 crotales [no pitches specified], 4 wood blocks,
2 metal blocks, claves, whip, 3 conch shells, musical saw), harp,
harmonium, guitar, and strings (9 violins, 4 violas, 3 cellos, and 1
doublebass).

It also provides the option of using two dancers.

---

26  F. Mark Daugherty and Susan Huneke Simon list this work as
"difficult" in *Secular Choral Music in Print*, 763. Philadelphia,
Pennsylvania: Musicdata, 1987.

**First Performance:** 5 June 1973; Lisbon, Portugal; NCRV Vocal Ensemble, Percussion Ensemble of Strasbourg, Orchestra of the Gulbenkian Foundation; conducted by Werner Andreas Albert.[27]

**Edition:** *Canticum Canticorum Salomonis* is published by Schotts in a co-edition with Polskie; the full score is available for purchase (PWM 7604); all other materials are available through rental.

**Autograph:** The published score is derived from the composer's manuscript.

**Performance Issues:** The score is written in C with the traditional octave transpositions. There are indications for approximate pitches, improvised pitches, quarter tones, rapid unmeasured repetitions, and the highest and lowest possible notes from respective voices and instruments. There are a number of choral effects which include notated breathing, whistling, laughter, speaking, and the use of falsetto. There is no music in this score which is metrically organized in a measured sense, although there are some note groupings which are set into repetition. Much of the ensemble nature of the work is the integration of temporally free and independent events. the pitch material for the choir is exceptionally dense, often containing all twelve discrete pitches at once. Some of the vocal parts involve the rapid repetition of consonant sounds. If the conch shells are unavailable, the composer has indicated that each may be replaced with two ocarinas. The instrumental parts are written with great freedom, but the material presented to each player is difficult by itself, and more so in the context of its neighbors. There are numerous dense clusters in the extreme ranges. The choral material is not supported by the orchestra in any fashion. The overall arrangement of this work is, in many ways, the most free of the Penderecki scores surveyed here; however, he has created a series of melodic lines which travel through the ensemble in an apparently uninterrupted flow while the other parts are involved in temporally non-specific passages. **Choir:** very difficult;   **Orchestra:** very difficult.

**Discography:** Philharmonic Orchestra and Chorus of Krakow; conducted by Jerzy Katlewicz. Polish Nagrania: SXL 1151 [LP].

---

27   Nicholas Slonimsky states that the premiere was led by the composer in his *Music Since 1900*, fifth edition, 852. New York: Schirmer Books, 1994.

Polish Radio Symphony Orchestra and Chorus; conducted by Krzysztof Penderecki. EMI Electrola: C 065-02484 [LP].

## Selected Bibliography

Schwinger, Wolfram: *Krzysztof Penderecki: His Life and Work*, translated by William Mann, 226. London: Schott, 1989.


**Poulenc, Francis** (b. Paris, 7 January 1899; d. Paris, 30 December 1963)

**Life:** Poulenc was a gifted pianist and one of the greatest composers of French mélodies. Born into a wealthy family, he was first educated in music by his mother. Upon the encouragement of Satie, Poulenc became involved with the concerts of the *Nouveaux Jeunes*, which led to his being named a member of *Les Six*, with Auric, Durey, Honegger, Milhaud, and Taillefer. After service in the military, he studied composition with Charles Koechlin (1921-24). His aptitude for song composition can be attributed to the same gift in his teacher, and his long-time association as accompanist to the French singer, Pierre Bernac. His music is always cosmopolitan, using classical forms, extended tertian harmonies, and flavorings from cabaret music.

**Writings:** *Emmanuel Chabrier*. Paris: La Palatine, 1961. *Moi et mes amis*. Paris: La Palatine, 1963; published in English translation by James Harding as: *My Friends and Myself*. London: Dennis Dobson, 1978. *Journal de mes Mélodies*. Paris: Éditions Bernard Grasset, 1964; published in English translation byWinifred Radford as: *Diary of My Songs*. London: Victor Gollancz, 1985.

**Principal Works:** *opera* - *Les Mamelles de Tirésias* (1944), *Dialogues des Carmelites* (1956), *La Voix humaine* (1958); *orchestral* - Concerto for 2 Pianos (1932), Concerto for Organ (1938), Sinfonietta (1947), Piano Concerto (1949); *chamber* - *Suite française* (1935), Violin Sonata (1943), Cello Sonata (1948), Flute Sonata (1957), Oboe Sonata (1962), Clarinet Sonata (1962); *vocal* - Mass in G (1937), *Figure humaine* (1943), *Un Soir de neige* (1944), *Sept répons des ténèbres* (1961), and many motets and songs.

## Selected  Composer  Bibliography

Poulenc, Francis: *Moi et mes amis*. Paris:   La Palatine, 1963; published in English translation by James Harding as: *My Friends and Myself*. London: Dennis Dobson, 1978.

_____: *Journal de mes Mélodies*. Paris: Éditions Bernard Grasset, 1964; published in English translation byWinifred Radford as: *Diary of My Songs*. London: Victor Gollancz, 1985.

Daniel, Keith W.: *Francis Poulenc: His Artistic Development and Musical Style*. Ann Arbor, MI: University of Michigan Press, 1982.

Keck, George R.: *Francis Poulenc: A Bio-Bibliography*. New York: Greenwood Press, 1990.

Mellers, Wilfrid: *Francis Poulenc*. Oxford: Oxford University Press, 1993.

Ramezani, M. and T. Vilbert: *Francis Poulenc: 1899-1963. Catalogue des œuvres*. Paris: Salabert, 1993.

Schmidt, Carl B.: *The Music of Francis Poulenc (1899-1963): A Catalogue*. Oxford: Clarendon Press, 1995.

## Sécheresses (The Droughts) (1937)

**Duration:** ca. 18 minutes

**Text:** The text is in French by Edward James. Two of the four poems are from James's *Trois Secheresses* which appeared in *Minotaur* with illustrations by Salvador Dali. There has been an English singing translation made by Doda Conrad for Robert Shaw.

**Performing Forces: voices:** SATB choir; **orchestra:** piccolo, 2 flutes, 2 oboes, English horn, 2 clarinets in $B^b$, 2 bassoons, 4 horns in F, 2 trumpets in C, 3 trombones, tuba, timpani, percussion (3 players - military (snare) drum, bass drum, tambourine, suspended cymbal, tam-tam), celeste, harp, and strings.

**First Performance:** May 1938; Concerts Colonne, Paris; Chanteurs de Lyons; conducted by Paul Paray.

**Edition:** *Sécheresses* is published by Durand. The piano-vocal score, full score, and choral parts are available for purchase; orchestral materials are available through rental.

**Autograph:** The composer's manuscripts are in the archives of the publisher, Durand.

**Notes:** The score is dedicated to Yvonne Marchessa de Casa Fuerte and was written for the Chanteurs de Lyon. It is organized into four sections which are entitled as follows:

| | |
|---|---|
| Les Sauterelles | The Grasshoppers |
| Le village abandonné | The abandonned village |
| Le faux avenir | The false prospects |
| Le squelette de la mer | The skeleton of the sea |

**Performance Issues:** The style of this work is much different from that of Poulenc's better-known *Stabat Mater* and *Gloria*. The anguish and tragedy of these despair-ridden texts are effectively conveyed in this ascerbic and dramatic setting. Of Poulenc's three symphonic choral works, this is the most challenging for the choir, but it is also more like his serious song settings than the two sacred works. Much of the pitch material is derived from an interplay between minor and major seconds and non-functional melodic uses of the tritone. The choral writing is exclusively homophonic. The vocal textures are varied through the use of one, two, or four parts. There are a few brief divisi for each choral section. The harmonic language is created through traditional part motion, but the resulting chords are often quite dissonant and difficult to tune. Fortunately, the harmonic tempo is slow, with single chords persisting for measures at a time. Many of the most concentrated harmonies are supported by the orchestra, but at times a single vocal line will be placed a minor second from the accompanying instruments. There are a number of *a cappella* passages for the choir which are generally more traditionally diatonic than the accompanied passages. The percussion section divides into three parts in measures 332 and 333, this can be effectively played by two executants. Much of the varied orchestral textures are derived from simultaneous use of staccato and legato playing between sections. Poulenc also frequently exchanges notes of a single melodic line between instruments in a hocket-like manner. Beyond these ensemble challenges there are few elements in the score of great technical difficulty, making this an excellent work for introducing a good college or community orchestra to the cosmopolitan style of French music in the 1930s; however, a strong choir is a necessity. **Choir:** difficult; **Orchestra:** medium difficult.

**Discography:** Alexander Carpentier; Maitrise de la Sainte-Chapelle, Choeurs de Radio France, Nouvel Orchestra Philharmonique de Radio France; conducted by Georges Prêtre, recorded 22-23 October 1983 in the Salle Wagram, Paris. EMI: CDM 7 64279 2 [DDD].

### Selected Bibliography

Flanner, Janet: "Letter from Paris," *New Yorker*, volume 29 (21 November 1953), 187-92.

Faure, G.: "Francis Poulenc: *Sécheresses*," *Musiciens français contemporains*, volume 2 (1956), 122.

Cutler, Helen Miller: "Freshened Repertoire Marks 66th Ann Arbor May Festival," *Musical America* volume 79 (June 1959), 2-5.

Daniel, Keith W.: *Francis Poulenc: His Artistic Development and Musical Style*, 358. Ann Arbor, MI: University of Michigan Press, 1982.

Keck, George R.: *Francis Poulenc: A Bio-Bibliography*, 33-34. New York: Greenwood Press, 1990.

Mellers, Wilfrid: *Francis Poulenc*, 77-79. Oxford: Oxford University Press, 1993.

Schmidt, Carl B.: *The Music of Francis Poulenc (1899-1963): A Catalogue*, 272-76. Oxford: Clarendon Press, 1995.

## Stabat Mater (1950)

**Duration:** ca. 35 minutes

**Text:** The text is in Latin from the Roman Catholic liturgy.

**Performing Forces: voices:** soprano soloist; SATBB choir; **orchestra:** piccolo, 2 flutes, 2 oboes, English horn, 2 clarinets in $B^b$, bass clarinet in $B^b$, 3 bassoons, 4 horns in F, 3 trumpets in C, 3 trombones, tuba, timpani, 2 harps, and strings.

**First Performance:** private performance: November 1950; London; Poulenc at the piano for the staff of the BBC.

first public performance: 13 June 1951; Musical Festival of Strasbourg, France; Geneviève Moizan, soprano; The Choirs of Saint-Guillaume and Municipal Orchestra of Strasbourg; conducted by Fritz Münch.

**Edition:** *Stabat Mater* is published by Salabert. The piano-vocal score, choral parts, and miniature score are available for purchase; orchestral materials are available through rental.

**Autograph:** The manuscript of the piano-vocal score is in a private collection. The manuscript of the full score is in the archives of the publisher, Salabert.

**Notes:** *Stabat Mater* is dedicated to the memory of Christian Bérard. The text is divided into twelve movements as follows:

| | | |
|---|---|---|
| I | Stabat mater dolorosa | SATBB |
| II | Cujus animam gementem | SATBB |
| III | O quam tristis | SATBBB |
| IV | Quae moerebat | SATBB |
| V | Quis est homo | SATBB |
| VI | Vidit suum | soprano solo, SATBB |
| VII | Eja mater | SATBBB |
| VIII | Fac ut ardeat | SAT |
| IX | Sancta mater | SATBBB |
| X | Fac ut portem | soprano solo, SATBB |
| XI | Inflammatus et accensus | SATBB |
| XII | Quando corpus | soprano solo, SATBB |

**Performance Issues:** The basses and baritones have divisi which yield three-part bass writing for the choir in movements III, VII, and IX, as indicated above. The choral writing is almost entirely homophonic, and although the harmonic language embraces some non-functional sevenths and ninths, the overall pitch conception is obedient to functional tonality. The vocal writing is well-conceived for singing, and the choral material is clearly supported by the orchestra with the exception of *a cappella* passages in movements III, VIII, XI, and XII. These unaccompanied passages are harmonically conservative and well prepared by the preceding orchestral music. The orchestration is typical of cosmopolitan French music of this era, although less "flashy" than Poulenc's *Gloria*, which is surely due to the subject of the text. The brilliance of the *Gloria* has eclipsed this moving and impeccably well-crafted work. It is an excellent concert work, and is also well-suited for use in a symphonic lenten program. The choral writing is accessible to a strong church choir. The orchestration requires a substantial choral contingent, with a strong male foundation. The orchestration is suitable for a reduced string section if space within a liturgical space is limited. **Soloist:** soprano - range: b-c$^{b'''}$, tessitura: f'-f', this is a delicate and lyrical solo for a clear and penetrating soprano voice; **Choir:** medium easy; **Orchestra:** medium difficult.

**Discography:** Regina Crespin; conducted by Georges Prêtre. Angel: S 36121 [LP], also released as HMV: ALP 2034.

Michèle LaGrange; Choeur et Orchestre National de Lyon; conducted by Serge Baudo, recorded in 1985. Harmonia Mundi: HMC 405149 [LP], rereleased as HMC 90519 [ADD].

Jacqueline Brumaire; conducted by Louis Frémaux. Westminster: XWN1842 [LP], rereleased as Westminster: W9618.

Kathleen Battle; Boston Symphony Orchestra, Tanglewood Festival Chorus; conducted by Seiji Ozawa. Deutsche Grammophon: 427304 [DDD].

Gabriela Benacková; Czech Philharmonic Orchestra and Chorus; conducted by Libor Pesek. Supraphon: CO-1090 [DDD].

### Selected Bibliography

Poulenc, Francis: "Tributes to Christian Bérard [dedicatee]," *Ballet* (April 1949) 30-31.

Barraud, Henry: "Contrasting Modern Opera Hold Parisian Stages," *Musical America*, volume 71 (October 1951), 6.

_____: "French Religious Music: Precursors and Innovators," *Musical America*, volume 72 (February 1952), 26.

Ebensberger, Gary Lee: *The Motets of Francis Poulenc.* University of Texas: Doctor of Musical Arts dissertation, 1970.

Daniel, Keith W.: *Francis Poulenc: His Artistic Development and Musical Style*, 362. Ann Arbor, MI: University of Michigan Press, 1982.

Keck, George R.: *Francis Poulenc: A Bio-Bibliography.* New York: Greenwood Press, 1990.

Mellers, Wilfrid: *Francis Poulenc*, 140-146. Oxford: Oxford University Press, 1993.

Schmidt, Carl B.: *The Music of Francis Poulenc (1899-1963): A Catalogue*, 406-412. Oxford: Clarendon Press, 1995.

## Gloria (1959)

**Duration:** ca. 24 minutes

**Text:** The text of the Gloria is from the Ordinary of the Mass. It is in Latin with an optional singing English translation.

**Performing Forces: voices:** soprano soloist; choir; **orchestra:** piccolo, 2 flutes, 2 oboes, English horn, 2 clarinets in B$^b$, bass clarinet in B$^b$, 2 bassoons, contrabassoon, 4 horns in F, 3 trumpets in C, 3 trombones, tuba, timpani, harp, and strings.

**First Performance:** 20 January 1961; Boston, MA; Adele Addison, soprano; Boston Symphony Orchestra and Pro Musica Chorus; conducted by Charles Munch.

European premiere: 14 February 1961; Paris; Rosanna Carteri, soprano; l'Orchestre National and the Choirs of the R.T.F.; conducted by Georges Prêtre.

**Edition:** *Gloria* is published by Salabert. The piano-vocal score and choral parts are available for purchase; orchestral materials are available through rental.

**Autograph:** The composer's manuscript of the full score is in the Library of Congress in Washington, DC.

**Notes:** *Gloria* was commissioned by the Koussevitsky Foundation and is dedicated to the memory of Serge and Natalie Koussevitsky. The work is divided into six movements as follows:

| I | Gloria | choir |
|---|---|---|
| II | Laudamus Te | choir |
| III | Domine Deus | soprano and choir |
| IV | Domine fili unigenite | choir |
| V | Domine Deus, Agnus Dei | soprano and choir |
| VI | Qui sedes ad dextram Patris | soprano and choir |

**Performance Issues:** The choral writing is vocally conceived. The harmonic material is diatonic and reflects common-practice part-writing techniques. Poulenc's harmonic palette incorporates ninth and eleventh chords, but is always treated through traditional horizontal procedures. Much of the choral work is in four-part block homophonic writing. Imitative procedures for the choir are limited to two independent layers at a time. In those passages, the composer uses imitation between paired choral parts. The orchestration is typical of cosmopolitan French music of the first half of the twentieth century. It is colorful and very effective. All of the instrumental parts are idiomatically conceived. There are sections of exposed and intricate passagework for all parts, especially the winds and brass. Movements I and IV will require particular attention in coördinating these intertwining, disparate parts. All four horns and trumpets I and II require strong players as they have many exposed passages with rapid articulation and frequent melodic leaps. The tessitura of trumpet I remains in the top fourth of the staff and therefore becomes rather taxing. The harp is an integral part of the score, and care must be taken for it to be heard. Placement of that instrument must be carefully considered. If a large section is used, the string parts are accessible to a less-experienced section, as the string writing is not technically demanding, but there are some very high, exposed passages. The pitch language is fairly diatonic for the orchestra as well as the chorus, and the orchestra clearly supports the choir throughout. There are divisi in all of the string sections, which are clearly assigned. All transposing instruments use only accidentals and no key signature, including the clarinets. **Soloist:** range: e'-a", tessitura: c"-g"; This role requires a clear and penetrating voice capable of carrying over the entire ensemble in sustained passages. The narrow compass listed for the tessitura actually represents the range of over half this role. It dwells almost exclusively in the passaggio. **Choir:** medium easy to medium difficult; **Orchestra:** medium difficult.

**Discography:** Rosanna Carteri; l'Orchestre National and the Choirs of the R.T.F.; conducted by Georges Prêtre. Angel: 35953 [LP], rereleased as Angel: CDC 47723 [AAD].

Sylvia Greenberg; Suisse Romande Radio Choir, Lausanne Pro Arte Choir, Orchestre Suisse Romande; conducted by Jésus López-Cobos, recorded in 1982. Argo: ZRDL 1010 [ADD].

Judith Blegen; New York Philharmonic Orchestra, Westminster Choir; conducted by Leonard Bernstein. CBS: MK-44710 [ADD].

Kathleen Battle; Boston Symphony Orchestra, Tanglewood Festival Chorus; conducted by Seiji Ozawa. Deutsche Grammophon: 427304 [DDD].

Donna Deam; City of London Sinfonia, Cambridge Singers; conducted by John Rutter. Collegium: COLCD-108 [DDD].

### Selected Bibliography

Durgin, Cyrus: "Poulenc Premiere," *Musical America*, volume 81 (March 1961), 24.

Kolodin, Irving: "Music to My Ears: Poulenc's *Gloria,*" *Saturday Review,* volume 44 (22 April 1961), 30.

"Carter, Foss, and Poulenc Works Get Music Critics Circle Awards," *New York Times* (19 April 1961), 34.

Sabin, Robert: "Unashamed Beauty," *Musical America,* volume 81 (August 1961), 47-48.

Valante, Harry Robert: *A Survey of French Choral Music of the 20th Century With a Performance and Interpretive Analysis of Selected Works,* Columbia University: Ed.D dissertation, 1968.

Daniel, Keith W.: *Francis Poulenc: His Artistic Development and Musical Style,* 363. Ann Arbor, MI: University of Michigan Press, 1982.

Keck, George R.: *Francis Poulenc: A Bio-Bibliography,* 32. New York: Greenwood Press, 1990.

Mellers, Wilfrid: *Francis Poulenc,* 146-150. Oxford: Oxford University Press, 1993.

Berger, Melvin: *Guide to Choral Masterpieces: A Listener's Guide,* 238-241. New York: Anchor Books, 1993.

Schmidt, Carl B.: *The Music of Francis Poulenc (1899-1963): A Catalogue,* 486-94. Oxford: Clarendon Press, 1995.

**Prokofiev, Sergei** (b. Sontsovka, Russia, 27 April 1891; d. Moscow, 5 March 1953)

**Life:** Prokofiev was one of the most important and innovative of all modern Russian composers. As a youth, he studied composition with Reinhold Glière, and at the age of 13 entered the St. Petersburg Conservatory where he was a pupil of Anatoli Liadov, and later Nikolai Rimsky-Korsakov. Upon graduation, he was awarded the Anton Rubinstein Prize. In 1918, Prokofiev left Russia for the United States, and in 1920, settled in Paris where he became associated with Sergei Diaghilev and the Ballets Russes. He returned to Russia a number of times for concert appearances, and in 1933 chose to remain in his homeland. His return to Russia coincided with a number of "reforms" in Soviet music which often made Prokofiev's music the subject of criticism as formalistic music not serving the needs of the state. The one outlet which proved to be satisfactory for his music within the Soviet regime was that written for films. Prokofiev's death preceded that of Stalin by only a few hours.

**Principal Works:** *operas - Love for Three Oranges* (1921), *The Fiery Angel* (1919), *Semyon Kotko* (1939), *War and Peace* (1952); *ballets - Romeo and Juliet* (1936), *Cinderella* (1944), *A Tale of the*

*Stone Flower* (1950); *film scores* - *Lt. Kijé* (1933), *Alexander Nevsky* (1938), *Ivan the Terrible* (1945); *orchestral* - 7 Symphonies (1916, 1924, 1928, 1930, 1944, 1947, 1952), 5 Piano Concertos (1912, 1913, 1921, 1931 [left hand alone], 1932), 2 Violin Concertos (1917, 1935), *Sinfonia Concertante* for cello and orchestra (1952), *Scythian Suite* (1914), *Peter and the Wolf* (1936) *A Summer Day* (1941), *A Summer Night* (1950); *piano* - 9 Sonatas (1909, 1912, 1917, 1917, 1923, 1940, 1942, 1944, 1947), Toccata (1912), *Visions fugitives* (1917).

### Selected Composer Bibliography

*Sergei Prokofiev: Autobiografiya*, ed. M. G. Kozlova Moscow: Sovetskii kompositor, 1973. Published in English as *Prokofiev by Prokofiev: A Composer's Memoir*, edited by David H. Appel and translated by Guy Daniels. New York: Doubleday, 1979.

Seroff, Victor: *Sergei Prokofiev: A Soviet Tragedy*. London: Frewin, 1969.

Blok, Vladimir, editor: *Sergei Prokofiev: Materials, Articles, Interviews*. Moscow: Progress Publishers, 1978.

McAllister, Rita: "Sergei Prokofiev," *The New Grove Dictionary of Music and Musicians*, edited by Stanley Sadie. London: MacMillan, 1980.

Robinson, Harlow: *Sergei Prokofiev*. New York: Viking, 1987.

## Cantata on the 20th Anniversary of October Revolution, op. 74 (1937)

**Duration:** The work is divided into ten large sections; however, the duration of the entire work is unavailable.

**Text:** Karl Marx, Friedrich Engels, Vladimir Ilyich Lenin, and Joseph Stalin.

**Performing Forces: voices:** 2 SATB choirs; **orchestra:** standard orchestra, military band, accordions, and percussion. This work was Prokofiev's most blatant attempt at social realism in his music, incorporating real sirens and gunshots. The orchestration was conceived for an ensemble of over 500 musicians.

**First Performance:** 5 April 1966; Moscow.

**Edition:** Currently no commercial editions of this score have been published.

**Autograph:** The manuscript is in the Russian Archives of Literature and Art in Moscow.

**Notes:** This work was determined to be ideologically and musically inadequate by the Soviet government, and therefore withdrawn from its intended first performance. At its premiere, twenty-nine years later, the portions on texts of Stalin were deleted in keeping with the then current policy of de-Stalinizing Soviet Art. This first performance was a musical success:

> It may have been naive on Prokofiev's part to set texts of such fundamental ideological importance, but he responded to their drama with music which is both haunting and emotionally stirring, comparable with his best of that time. The build-up of its ten large sections is evidence, once more, of the composer's sure sense of dramatic effect and the direct appeal of his creative ideas...it is surely only the somewhat unexportable nature of its subject that has prevented its international recognition.[28]

**discography:** RSFSR Russian Choirs, Moscow Philharmonic; conducted by Kirill Kondrashian. Melodiya: SR 40129 [LP].

# Songs of Our Days [Pesni nashikh dney], op. 77
(1937)

**Duration:** ca. 25-30 minutes

**Text:** The text, in Russian, is from several sources listed below under notes.

**Performing Forces: voices:** mezzo-soprano and baritone soloists; SATB choir; **orchestra:** 2 flutes, 2 oboes, 2 $B^b$ clarinets, 2 bassoons, 4 horns in F, 3 trumpets, 3 trombones, tuba, percussion (4 players - snare drum, bass drum, tambourine, cymbals, triangle, woodblock), harp, and strings.

---

[28] Rita McAllister: "Sergei Prokofiev" in *The New Grove Russian Masters 2*, 149. New York: W. W. Norton, 1986.

**First Performance:** 5 January 1938; Moscow.

**Edition:** *Songs of Our Days* is published and distributed in the United States by Belwin Mills.

**Autograph:** The manuscript is in the Russian Archives of Literature and Art in Moscow.

**Notes:** This work is divided into nine sections as follows:

| | | |
|---|---|---|
| I | March | orchestra only |
| II | Over the bridge | A. Prichelyitz |
| III | Be healthy | A. Rusak |
| | | translated from White |
| | | Russian |
| | | by M. Isakovskogo |
| IV | Golden Ukraine | folk text |
| V | Brother for Brother | V. Lebedev-Kumach |
| VI | Maidens | A. Prichelyitz |
| VII | The 20-year-old | Samuel Marshak |
| VIII | Lullaby | V. Lebedev-Kumach |
| IX | From border to border | Yvgeny Dolmatovsky |

**Performance Issues:** The full-score is notated in C. The harmonic material is diatonic and firmly grounded in common-practice techniques built around folk-like melodies. The choral parts are diatonic melodies sung by soli sections of the choir, in pairs, or in choral unisons, with occasional four-part writing in a purely homophonic texture. The brass have some sustained playing, but within a practical range for most players. The flute I part has some rapid triadic arpeggios. This is a tuneful and musically accessible work well within the abilities of most amateur ensembles. **Soloists:** mezzo-soprano - range: d'-f", tessitura, d'-d", this is a melodic, and vocally easy solo role which occurs in only two of the movements; baritone - range: c-g', tessitura, g-e', this role is diatonically melodic and declamatory, it appears throughout the work; **Choir:** easy, **Orchestra:** medium easy.

**Discography:** As of February 1997, there are no commercial recordings available of this work.

## Selected Bibliography

Robinson, Harlow: *Sergei Prokofiev*, 339, 341, 352. New York: Viking, 1987.

# Alexander Nevsky, op. 78 (1938-39)

**Duration:** ca. 38 minutes

**Text:** Written by Stikhi V. Lugovskoi and Prokofiev, the text is in Russian.

**Performing Forces: voices:** mezzo-soprano solo; choir (SATTBBB); **orchestra:** piccolo, 2 flutes, 2 oboes, English horn, 2 clarinets in $B^b$ and A, bass clarinet in $B^b$, 2 bassoons, contrabassoon, tenor saxophone in $B^b$, 4 horns in F, 3 trumpets in $B^b$, 3 trombones, tuba, timpani, percussion (7 players - glockenspiel, chimes, xylophone, snare drum, bass drum, tambourine, cymbals, tamtam, triangle, wood block, maracas), harp, and strings.

**First Performance:** 17 May 1939; Moscow; V. Gagarina; conducted by the composer.

**Edition:** *Alexander Nevsky* is widely available; publishers include: Mez Kniga, Kalmus (6380), Dover (in *Four Orchestral Works* 20279-8) all of whom produce the full score for purchase. Kalmus, MCA, Éditions Chant du Monde, and Staff Music (714) have piano vocal scores for purchase. Orchestral materials may be purchased from Kalmus. It is no longer under United States copyright.

**Autograph:** The manuscript is in the Russian Archives of Literature and Art in Moscow.

**Notes:** This work is based on the music for Eisenstein's film of the same name which was produced in 1938, and was completed in concert form on 7 February 1939. The film took place in 13th-century Russia. There are several brass fanfares played offstage by players who must at other times play onstage. The orchestra predominates in this piece and many of its parts are technically demanding. It is organized into seven movements as follows:

I     Russia Beneath the Yoke of the Mongols - orchestra only
II    Song About Alexander Nevsky - ATB choir
III   The Crusader in Pskov - ATTBBB choir
IV    Arise, People of Russia" - SATB choir
V     The Battle on the Ice - ATTTBBB choir
VI    The Field of the Dead - mezzo-soprano solo
VII   Alexander's Entry into Pskov - choir

**Performance Issues:** Movements III and V are in Latin with V containing the text of III with elaborations. The sopranos do not sing much, but their tessitura is very high. The full-score is notated in C with the traditional octave displacements. The choral writing is primarily homophonic in two and three-part textures. The harmonic language is triadic and mostly following the principals of functional tonality with occasional dissonances which though not of the common practice period are none-the-less traditionally prepared and resolved. The vocal material is clearly reinforced by the accompaniment throughout the score. There are a number of off-stage passages for the brass which are intended for the same players as are on-stage, so their access in and out must be considered. The bass clarinet has a sounding low C. If this note is unavailable, the composer has suggested covering it with the contrabassoon. The "Battle on the Ice" movement is the largest and most difficult for the orchestra. It has a wide variety of textures and extensive passagework for the woodwinds and strings. Throughout the cantata, the vast majority of the most active passages for the strings are in unison and built upon traditional scale patterns. The brass section has some prolonged passages of sustained playing, but recovery time is provided by well-placed tacets. The breadth of the orchestration demands a large symphonic chorus. If the string players are capable of the intricate passages of movement V, this work will be within the ability of a good college or community orchestra. The choral sections are quite accessible to a large community chorus. **Soloist:** mezzo-soprano - range: c'-e$^{b}$", tessitura: d'-d", this is a dramatic and fairly brief role, it is quiet and sustained; **choir:** medium easy; **orchestra:** medium difficult.

**Discography:** Jennie Tourel; Westminster Choir, Philadelphia Orchestra; conducted by Eugene Ormandy. Columbia: ML 4347 [LP].

Iriarte; Vienna State Opera Chorus and Orchestra; conducted by Rossi. Vanguard: VRS 451 [LP].

Lili Chookasian; New York Philharmonic; conducted by Thomas Schippers. Odyssey: YT-31014 [LP].

Rosalind Elias; Chicago Symphony; conducted by Fritz Reiner. (in English) RCA: 5605-2-RC [ADD].

Elena Obraztsova; London Symphony and Chorus; conducted by Claudio Abbado. Deutsche Grammophon: 419603-2 GH [ADD] also released as 435151-2 GX3.

Claudine Carlson; St. Louis Symphony; conducted by Leonard Slatkin. Vox: CT-2182 [ADD].

Linda Finnie; Scottish National Orchestra and Chorus; conducted by Neeme Järvi. Chandos: CHAN-8584 [DDD].

Irina Arkhipova; Cleveland Orchestra and Chorus; conducted by Riccardo Chailly. London: 410 164-2 LH [DDD].

Christine Cairns; Los Angeles Philharmonic and Master Chorale; conducted by André Previn. Telarc: CD-80143 [DDD].

Smetchuk; Danish National Radio Symphony Orchestra and Chorus; conducted by Dmitri Kitaenko. Chandos: CHAN 9001 [DDD].

Jard van Nes; Montréal Symphony Orchestra and Chorus; conducted by Charles Dutoit. London: 430506-2 LH [DDD].

### Selected Bibliography

Swallow, Norman: *Eisenstein: A Documentary Portrait*. New York: Dutton, 1977.

Berger, Melvin: *Guide to Choral Masterpieces: A Listener's Guide*, 242-246. New York: Anchor Books, 1993.

## Zdravitsa [Hail to Stalin], op. 85 (1937)

**Duration:** ca. 15 minutes

**Text:** The text, probably authored by a committee to honor Stalin, is in Russian.

**Performing Forces: voices:** SATB choir; **orchestra:** piccolo, 2 flutes, 2 oboes, English horn, 2 clarinets in B$^b$, bass clarinet in B$^b$, 2 bassoons, contrabassoon, 3 trumpets in B$^b$, 4 horns in F, 3 trombones, tuba, timpani, percussion (4 players - glockenspiel, xylophone, snare drum, wooden drum, bass drum, tambourine, cymbals, tam-tam, triangle), harp, piano, and strings.

**First Performance:** 21 December 1939; Moscow.

**Edition:** *Zdravitsa* is published and distributed in the United States by Belwin Mills.

**Autograph:** The manuscript is in the Russian Archives of Literature and Art in Moscow.

**Notes:** This work was written to commemorate Joseph Stalin's sixtieth birthday. This is an attractive and well-crafted score which has a bold and celebratory quality. The specific nature of the text renders it obsolete for modern concert use. If a suitable alternate text could be inserted, this could become a viable symphonic choral work for less experienced ensembles.

**Performance Issues:** The full-score is written in C with the English horn notated in alto clef. The harmonic language is in the diatonic/modal cast of the bulk of Prokofiev's middle and late works. The choral parts are thoroughly doubled by the orchestra. The choral material is primarily homophonic with some paired doubling. In the end of the work, portions of a single melodic line are exchanged between sections of the choir. The harmonic material for the choir is almost exclusively diatonic. Some metric interest is introduced wherein fairly square phrases are truncated by a single beat. The instrumental parts are well within the abilities of amateur ensembles. The principal winds have some rapid passage work which follows traditional scales and arpeggios. The flute I part has a number of brief exposed solos. If the timpanist doubles some battery percussion parts, the number of percussionists may be reduced by one. The percussion section will need one experienced mallet player, as there are a number of fairly rapid exposed passages in the xylophone part. A second mallet player is needed for the glockenspiel part which occurs in the final pages of the score; however, this part is not as difficult. **Choir:** medium easy; **Orchestra:** medium easy.

**Discography:** Choral Ensemble of Russia, National Orchestra of the USSR; conducted by Evgeny Svetlanov. Melodiya: 33SM-02147/8 [LP].

## Selected Bibliography

McAllister, Rita: "Sergei Prokofiev," *The New Grove Russian Masters 2*, edited by Stanley Sadie, 151. New York: W.W. Norton, 1986.

## Ballad of a Boy Who Remained Unknown [Ballada o mal'chike ostavshemya neizvestnïm], op. 93
(1944)

**Text:** The text is in Russian by Pavel Antokol'sky.

**Performing Forces:** soprano and tenor soloists, choir and orchestra.

**First Performance:** 21 February 1944; Moscow.

**Notes:** This work was written as a memorial oratorio during the Second World War. It appears in all of the major works lists for Prokofiev; however, there appears to be no published edition of it currently available. The listings create the impression that this was a large-scale composition. With the significant changes in the artistic culture of Russia, perhaps a revival of this work can be mounted in the reasonable future. Harlow Robinson describes it as "an intensely patriotic work."[29]

## Ivan the Terrible, op. 116  (1942-45; 1961)

**Duration:** ca. 65 minutes

**Text:** The narrator's text is by Serge Eisentstein and the sung text is by Stikhi V. Lugovskoi. All texts are in Russian.

**Performing Forces: voices:** narrator, contralto and "Fyedor" - baritone soloists; children's choir (optional), SATB choir; **orchestra:** piccolo, 2 flutes (flute II doubling piccolo II), 2 oboes, English horn, soprano clarinet in E$^b$, 3 clarinets in B$^b$ (clarinet I also plays clarinet in A), bass clarinet in B$^b$, alto saxophone in E$^b$, tenor saxophone in B$^b$, 3 bassoons, contrabassoon, 4 horns in F, 5 trumpets in B$^b$, 3 trombones, 2 tubas, percussion (5 players - timpani, xylophone, glockenspiel, Russian bells, snare drum, wooden tom tom, bass drum, tambourine, cymbals, tam-tam, triangle, and whip), 2 psalteries (optional), 2 harps, piano, and strings.

---

29  Robinson, Harlow: *Sergei Prokofiev: A Biography*. New York: Viking, 1987.

**First Performance:** world premiere: 23 March 1961; The Great Hall of the Tchaikovsky Conservatory, Moscow; conducted by Abram Stasevich.

premiere outside of the Soviet Union: 29 March 1968; Saint Louis, Missouri ; Saint Louis Symphony Orchestra and Chorus; conducted by Abram Stasevich.

**Edition:** *Ivan the Terrible*, as arranged in oratorio form by Abram Stasevich, was published by Soviet Composers of Moscow in 1972. The full score is available for purchase; parts are available through rental. This edition is now available from Kalmus.

**Autograph:** The manuscript is in the Russian Archives of Literature and Art in Moscow.

**Notes:** Because of the success achieved from converting Prokofiev's score for Serge Eisenstein's film, *Alexander Nevsky*, into a concert oratorio, Abram Stasevich derived this concert version of *Ivan the Terrible* in 1961, from the score which Prokofiev had composed in 1942 and 1945 for another of Eisenstein's films, this one in two parts. The first film was premiered in 1946 and the second was not released until 1958, five years after Prokofiev's death and ten after Eisenstein's. The delay of this second release is due to its being banned by Stalin. This censorship demoralized Eisenstein who died two years later, having worked on no further projects. This controversy dissuaded Prokofiev from developing a concert work from the film score. Stasevich had been the conductor for the recording of Prokofiev's music for the film. When the film was restored to acceptance during the Kruschev era, Stasevich proceeded to assemble an oratorio incorporating narration and music from the film, as well as music composed for, but not included in the film. The choral text for the oratorio was written for Stasevich by Lugovsky who had been the librettist who collaborated with Prokofiev on *Alexander Nevsky*. In *Ivan the Terrible*, Prokofiev utilizes a number of traditional melodies including the hymn, "God Preserve Thy People," which is featured prominently in Tchaikovsky's *1812 Overture*.

**Performance Issues:** This score is dramatic and exhibits a wide variety of orchestral textures, using each instrument to good and accessible effect. It requires endurance from the brass, especially the trumpets who have substantial sustained passages and a good deal of high playing with repeated tonguing patterns. The size of the wind and brass sections, coupled with the generally high tessitura of the upper woodwinds requires a fairly large string section for there to be an adequate balance. The overall score is practical and presents few substantial technical difficulties for the instrumentalists. The violin parts have extended sections of rapid accompanimental figures employing numerous mode shifts in high-pitched sections which may elicit some intonation problems. The E$^b$ clarinet part is somewhat virtuosic and often exposed. The psaltery parts are cued to the harp parts throughout. To cover all parts, the timpanist must be included as one of the five percussionists, and will need to cover some other percussion instruments. The choral parts are generally homophonic with some paired doublings between sections in two-part counterpoint. They are chromatic, but clearly tonal-centric. Most choral passages are well supported and often directly doubled by the orchestra. The few passages that are *a cappella* are carefully prepared, often including foreshadowings of the choral material in the preceding instrumental sections. The men of the chorus have some short sections of rhythmically spoken text. Although the score calls for a single narrator, spoken passages are labeled for a narrator and the character "Ivan." **Soloists:** The narrator's part is cued to general places in the score, but is not rhythmically notated, nor specifically aligned with musical gestures. contralto - range: a-f', tessitura: e'-a', this role is slow and sustained throughout; baritone - range: e$^b$-f', tessitura: a$^b$-e$^b$', this role has only one solo of about three minutes length which is declamatory and folklike; **Choir:** medium difficult; **Orchestra:** difficult.

**Discography:** Levko, Makarenko; USSR Symphony and Chorus; conducted by Abram Stasevich. Chant du Monde: LDC-278390 [LP].

Claudia Carlson, Samuel Timberlake; Saint Louis Symphony Orchestra and Chorus; conducted by Leonard Slatkin, originally recorded in 1979. Vox: CDX 5021 [ADD].

Zorova, Stanchev, Morgounov; Rousse Philharmonic Orchestra, Danube Sounds Choir; conducted by A. Naydenov. Forlane: UCD-16530 [CD].

performing version adapted by Christopher Palmer: L. Finnie, N. Storojev; Philharmonia Orchestra and Chorus; conducted by Neeme Järvi. Chandos: CHAN 8977 [DDD].

Selected   Bibliography

Szneerson, Grigori: "List z Moskwy," *Ruch Muzyczny*, volume 5, number 10 (1961), 19.

"Oratoriya: *Ivan Groznyy*," Sovetskaya Muzyka, volume 25 (May 1961), 129-130.

# Flourish, Our Mighty Land [Rastsvetay, moguchiy kray], op. 114 (1947)

**Duration:** ca. 5 minutes

**Text:** The original Russian text was the poem, *Rastsvetay, moguchiy kray*, by Yevgeny Dolmatovsky. A later edition substitutes a text by A. Mashistov.

**Performing Forces: voices:** SATB choir; **orchestra:** piccolo, 2 flutes, 2 oboes, English horn, 2 clarinets in $B^b$, bass clarinet in $B^b$, 2 bassoons, contrabassoon, 4 horns in F, 3 trumpets in $B^b$, 3 trombones, tuba, timpani, percussion (4 players - snare drum, bass drum, tambourine, cymbals, triangle, castanets), harp, piano, and strings.

**First Performance:** 12 November 1947; Moscow; Russian Federal S.S.R. Choir (A.S. Stepanov, chorus-master), State Symphony Orchestra; conducted by N.P. Anosov.

**Edition:** *Flourish, Our Mighty Land* is published and distributed in the United States by Belwin Mills.

**Autograph:** The first edition of 1947 was a facsimile of the composer's manuscript. The manuscript is in the Russian Archives of Literature and Art in Moscow.

**Notes:** This work was composed for the thirtieth Anniversary of the October Revolution.

**Performance Issues:** The full-score is written in C. This work is basically a fanfare for choir and orchestra. The harmonic material is diatonic with some chromatic inflections evocative of Russian folksong. The choral texture is homophonic throughout. There are two-part divisi for each section of the choir and there are two eight-measure *a cappella* passages. The orchestral writing is well within the grasp of most amateur ensembles with the possible exception of the brass parts which are sustained and rhythmically concise. The principal trumpet part has a particularly high tessitura. **Choir:** easy; **Orchestra:** medium easy.

**Discography:** As of February 1997, there are no commercial recordings available of this work.

### Selected  Bibliography

Robinson, Harlow: *Sergei Prokofiev*, 458, 461. New York: Viking, 1987.

# On Guard for Peace [Na strazhe mira], op. 124
(1950)

**Duration:** ca. 30 minutes

**Text:** The text is in Russian by Samuel Marshak.

**Performing Forces: voices:** narrator, contralto and boy alto soloists; SSAA boy's choir, SATB choir; **orchestra:** piccolo, 2 flutes, 2 oboes, English horn, soprano clarinet in $E^b$, 2 clarinets in $B^b$, bass clarinet in $B^b$, 2 bassoons, contrabassoon, 4 horns in F, 3 trumpets in $B^b$, 3 trombones, tuba, timpani, percussion (5 players - glockenspiel, xylophone, snare drum, bass drum, tambourine, wooden drum, cymbals, tam-tam, triangle), harp, celeste, piano, and strings.

**First Performance:** 19 December 1950; Moscow; conducted by Samuil Samosud.

**Edition:** *On Guard for Peace* is published and distributed in the United States by Belwin Mills.

**Autograph:** The manuscript is in the Russian Archives of Literature and Art in Moscow.

**Notes:** The work is divided into ten movements as follows:

    I   Scarcely had the earth recovered
   II   To those who are ten years old
  III   Stalingrad, city of glory
  IV   May indestructable peace be the hero's reward
   V   We do not want war
  VI   Dove of Peace
 VII   Lullaby
VIII   Festive march of the fighters
  IX   Attack on the air (narrator only)
   X   The whole world will wage war on war

**Performance Issues:** This score is more chromatic than the other propogandistic choral-orchestral works of Prokofiev. It is also more technically demanding than his other contributions to this repertoire. The orchestration demands a large adult choir. The boy choir is accompanied in a lighter fashion. The narrator must be musically literate as much of the spoken material is rhythmically notated. The choral writing is homophonic often with paired doubling between the soprano and tenor, and the bass and alto parts. There are two-part divisi for each of the choral sections. While somewhat chromatic, the choral material is still scalar and triadic in conception and well reinforced by the accompanying instruments. All of the orchestral parts are technically challenging. There are numerous virtuosic passages for each of the wind players. The final movement is the most challenging in terms of ensemble as there are some awkward three against four figures between the winds and strings, as well as some rapid chromatic passagework doubled between varied pairs of instruments from disparate sections of the orchestra. The harp, celeste, and piano players must be very strong players. These three instruments play a prominent role throughout the entire oratorio, and each part is technically quite difficult. A single mallet player can cover both the xylophone and glockenspiel parts. The string writing is idiomatic and the least difficult of the instrumental choirs. The brass parts are quite sustained, but breaks are provided with some regularity. If only three percussionists are available, the timpani part allows that player to cover the few spots which require four players. This work is ideal for a strong orchestra that wishes to feature a large amateur choir with limited experience. **Soloists:** contralto - range: a-f", tessitura: e'-d", this role suggests a dramatic voice capable of wide melodic leaps; boy alto - range: c'-d", tessitura: e'-c", this is an accessible role containing two solos; **Choir:** medium easy; **Orchestra:** difficult.

**Discography:** Dolukhanova, Talanov; USSR Orchestra and Chorus; conducted by Samuil Samosud. Vanguard: VRS 6003 [LP].

### Selected Bibliography

Robinson, Harlow: *Sergei Prokofiev*, 487, 491. New York: Viking, 1987.


**Rachmaninov, Sergei** (b. Semyonovo, 1 April 1873; d. Beverly Hills, California, 28 March 1943)

**Life:** In addition to being one of the most celebrated piano virtuosos of the modern era, Rachmaninov was also a gifted conductor. Although he composed in all genres, as a composer he is best remembered for his piano works and symphonies. He attended the Moscow Conservatory (1885-91) where he studied counterpoint with Sergei Taneyev and harmony with Anton Arensky. Following the unsuccessful premiere of his first symphony, he became despondent and attempted to overcome his depression and resulting creative block through hypnosis. This treatment was followed immediately by the composition of his Second Piano Concerto which remains one of his most popular works. He toured the United States in 1909 as soloist in his own works. Following the 1917 Revolution in Russia, Rachmaninov left Russia, touring the United States and Europe regularly as a pianist and conductor. In 1939, he settled permanently in the United States, becoming a citizen shortly before his death. His music combines the techniques of the late Russian Romantics with a certain sensitivity to indigenous Russian modes and a personal rhapsodic style which is clearly identifiable in all of his works.

**Principal Works:** *operas - Aleko* (1892), *Francesca da Rimini* (1900); *orchestral* - 3 Symphonies (1895, 1908, 1936), 4 Piano Concertos (1891, 1901, 1909, 1926), *The Isle of the Dead* (1909), *Rhapsody on a Theme of Paganini* for piano and orchestra (1934), *Symphonic Dances* (1940); *vocal - Liturgy of St. Chrysostom* (1910), *Vespers* (1915), *Russian Songs* for men's chorus and orchestra (1926), and many songs and motets.

## Selected Composer Bibliography

Serroff, Victor: *Rachmaninov*. London: Cassell and Co., Ltd., 1951.

Bertensson, Sergei, and Jay Leyda: *Sergei Rachmaninov: A Lifetime in Music*. New York: New York University Press, 1956.

Piggott, Patrick: *Rachmaninov Orchestral Music*. London: BBC, 1974.

Norris, Geoffrey: *Rakhmaninov*. London: J. M. Dent and Sons, 1976.

Threfall, Robert and Geoffrey Norris: *A Catalogue of the Compositions of Sergei Rachmaninov*. London: Scolar Press, 1982.

Palmieri, Robert: *Sergei Vasil"evich Rachmaninov: A Guide to Research*. New York: Garland Publishing, 1985.

Martyn, Barrie: *Rachmaninov: Composer, Pianist, Conductor*. Aldershot, England: Scolar Press, 1990.

## Vesna [Spring], op. 20 (1902)

**Duration:** ca. 15 minutes

**Text:** The text is a poem by Nikolai A. Nekrasov. The published edition of this score also includes a singing German translation prepared by Vladimir Shumikov. There is also a literal English translation by Andrew Huth among the front matter.

**Performing Forces: voices:** baritone soloist; SATB choir; **orchestra:** 3 flutes (flute III doubling piccolo), 2 oboes, English horn, 2 clarinets in A, bass clarinet in B$^b$, 2 bassoons, 4 horns in E, 3 trumpets in A, 3 trombones, tuba, timpani (3 drums), percussion (3 players - bass drum, cymbals, tam-tam, triangle), harp, and strings.

**First Performance:** 24 March 1902[30]; Moscow; Alexander Vasileyvich Smirnov, soloist; Moscow Philharmonic Society; conducted by Alexander Ziloti.

**Edition:** *Vesna* is published as *Der Frühling* by Kalmus (5446). The piano-vocal score, full score, and orchestral parts are available for purchase; orchestral materials are also available through rental. It is also published as *Spring Cantata* by Boosey and Hawkes, study

---

[30] Robert Threfall and Geoffrey Norris list the premiere date as 11 March 1902 in *A Catalogue of the Compositions of Sergei Rachmaninov*.

score (HPS 1250); all materials are available through rental. The Boosey and Hawkes materials are a reproduction of the original Gutheil edition.

**Notes:** This score is dedicated to Nikita S. Morozov and was first published under the auspices of Serge and Natalie Koussevitsky.

The text for this work is somewhat peculiar. The chorus sings of the coming of spring, followed by a narrative from the soloist recounting an act of infidelity by his wife and his growing desire throughout the winter to murder her. The coming of spring breaks the murderous spell and he wishes to forgive her as his love is awakened by spring.

**Performance Issues:** This score requires a large orchestra and chorus. The choir has much unison and two-part singing, much of which is full and declamatory with some divisi in all parts. The pitch material of the choir is well supported by the accompanying orchestration; however, they are at times rhythmically at odds with the orchestra and must be articulate and independent in their execution of rhythms. There is a section of the work for textless chorus, which serves as part of the accompaniment for the soloist. The choral material is very accessible, making this an excellent choice for a moderately skilled symphonic choir. There are divisi in all of the string parts, including a three-part division for violin I. There is significant chromatic passagework for all of the woodwinds, involving rapid unison playing throughout the section. The passages for oboe I are the most exposed. The brass scoring is mostly in block harmonic motion, giving shape to the more fluid wind and string parts. This work is brilliantly scored with demanding, soloistic passages for all members of the orchestra. Rich orchestral textures are achieved through the juxtaposition of diverse simultaneous divisions of the beat using the same harmonic material. Achieving clarity between these contrasting rhythms will demand experienced, secure players, or a significant amount of careful rehearsal. **Soloist:** range: B-g'; tessitura: d-d'; This is a declamatory solo which represents about a third of the work's length. The singer must be able to project clearly over a sizeable ensemble. **Choir:** medium easy; **Orchestra:** difficult.

**Discography:** John Shaw; Cathedral Choir of St. Ambrose, John McCarthy, choirmaster; New Philharmonia Orchestra; conducted by Igor Buketoff, recorded in 1968. RCA: LSC-3051 [LP].

Jorma Hynninen;  Danish National Radio Symphony Orchestra and Chorus; conducted by Dmitri Kitaenko. Chandos: CHAN 8966 [DDD].

Arnold Voketaitis; St. Louis Symphony Orchestra and Chorus; conducted by Leonard Slatkin, recorded in 1980. Vox: CD3X 3002 [ADD].

### Selected Bibliography

Rubinstein, Arthur: *My Young Years*, 479. New York: Alfred A. Knopf, 1973.

Martyn, Barrie: *Rachmaninov: Composer, Pianist, Conductor*, 136-140. Aldershot, England: Scolar Press, 1990.

## Kolokola [The Bells], op. 35 (1913)

**Duration:** ca. 35 minutes

**Text:** The text is a  Russian translation by Konstantin Balmont of Edgar Allan Poe's poem, "The Bells." There is a singing English retranslation by Fanny S. Copeland.

**Performing Forces: voices:** soprano, tenor, and baritone soloists; SATB choir; **orchestra:** piccolo, 3 flutes, 3 oboes, English horn, 3 clarinets in $B^b$ and A, bass clarinet in $B^b$ and A, 3 bassoons, contrabassoon, 6 horns in F, 3 trumpets in $B^b$, 3 trombones, tuba, timpani, percussion (5 players - glockenspiel, chimes, snare drum, bass drum, tambourine, cymbals, tam-tam, triangle), harp, celeste, piano, organ (optional), and strings.

The score indicates the use of an upright piano.

**First Performance:** 13 December 1913[31]; St. Petersburg, Russia; A. D. Aleksandrov, E. I. Popova, P. Z. Andreyev; Mariinsky Theatre Chorus; conducted by Rachmaninov.

---

31  Robert Threfall and Geoffrey Norris list the premiere date as 30 November 1913 in *A Catalogue of the Compositions of Sergei Rachmaninov.*

**Edition:** *The Bells* is published by Boosey and Hawkes. The piano-vocal score is available for purchase; all other materials are available through rental. This edition is also available for purchase from Kalmus.

**Autograph:** Autographs of Rachmaninov's corrections to the first edition are in the archives of Boosey and Hawkes in London.

**Notes:** The score was completed 9 August 1913. In this work, Rachmaninov uses the Gregorian chant tune of the "Dies Irae," which also appears in a number of his other compositions, including: *Isle of the Dead, Rhapsody on a Theme of Paganini,* and the *Symphonic Dances.* The work is caste in a traditional symphonic form of four movements as follows:

| I | Allegro ma non tanto | tenor, chorus, and orchestra |
| II | Lento | soprano, chorus, and orchestra |
| III | Presto | chorus, and orchestra |
| IV | Lento lugubre | baritone, chorus, and orchestra |

**Performance Issues:** There are a number of published variants of this score. The original edition published by Gutheil in 1920 serves as the basis of all full scores. The 1920 piano-vocal score, prepared by Aleksandr Goldenweiser, deviates from the full score in a number of places, notably: movement I at **18**; movement III at **63-64, 71-73,** and **88**; and movement IV from **116** to **117.** For an English performance in 1936, significant rewriting was done to the choral parts. Rachmaninov made additional changes to the vocal parts in the 1936 piano-vocal edition, copies of which are in the Boosey and Hawkes archives. Some later piano-vocal editions were exact duplicates of the original version. A 1967 edition of the full-score, from Muzyka, which is also a copy of the original edition, includes annotations explaining the choral variants in the various piano-vocal editions, but not the composer's changes of 1936. In any case, it is important to compare the full score and piano-vocal scores before rehearsals begin to sort out discrepancies at the rehearsal numbers listed above. The current edition from Boosey and Hawkes presents both versions clearly; however, the simplified version includes a singing text in Russian and English, while the foot-noted original version is in Russian only. The choral writing is well supported by the accompaniment of the orchestra. There are 3-part divisi for each section of the choir. The individual orchestral parts are quite difficult. There is intricate passagework for the strings and woodwinds, and a substantial amount of playing for the brass, especially the horns. Clarinets I and II have numerous exposed and awkward passages. The percussion parts are written for five players, but it is possible to cover all of the instruments with four. The harp, celeste, and piano parts are integral to the score and fairly difficult. These three instruments would be at their best advantage placed near each other. The size of the orchestra, and the breadth of Rachmaninov's orchestral palette demand that a large choir be utilized. The greatest choral challenge is sheer force. This is an ideal work for a large festival chorus. **Soloists:** soprano - range: e'-a", tessitura: a'-f", this is a sustained and lyric role; tenor - range: a$^b$-a$^{b'}$, tessitura: a$^b$-a$^{b'}$, this role is declamatory and uses its one-octave range evenly; baritone - range: B-f', tessitura: e-e', this role is lyric and has a somewhat high tessitura; **Choir:** medium difficult; **Orchestra:** difficult.

**Discography:** Moscucci, Anthony, Malfatti; Rachmaninov Chorus and Orchestra; conducted by Rachmilovich. Rachmaninov Society: RS 8 [LP].

Marianna Christos, Walter Planté, Arnold Voketaitis; St. Louis Symphony Orchestra and Chorus; conducted by Leonard Slatkin, recorded in 1980. Vox: CD3X 3002 [ADD].

Mikhailova, Larin; Moscow Philharmonic Orchestra, Bolshoi Theater Chorus; conducted by Dmitri Kitaenko. Melodiya: MCD-116 [DDD].

Elena Ustinova, Kurt Westi, Jorma Hynninen; Danish National Radio Symphony Orchestra and Chorus; conducted by Dmitri Kitaenko. Chandos: CHAN 8966 [DDD].

Suzanne Murphy, Keith Lewis, David Wilson-Johnson; Scottish National Orchestra and Chorus; conducted by Neeme Järvi. Chandos: CHAN-8476 [DDD].

G. Pisarenko, A. Maslennikov, S. Yakovenko; USSR Symphony, Yurlov Choir; conducted by Yevgeni Svetlanov. Mobile Fidelity / Melodiya: MFCD-900 [ADD].

Troitskaya, Karczykowski, Krause; Royal Concertgebouw Orchestra and Chorus; conducted by Vladimir Ashkenazy. London: 414455-2 LH [DDD].

Alexandrina Pendachanska, Kaludi Kaludov, Sergei Leiferkus; Choral Arts Society of Philadelphia (Seán Deibler, chorus-master), Philadelphia Orchestra; conducted by Charles Dutoit, recorded in Memorial Hall, Philadelphia during January 1992. London: D 105682 [DDD].

## Selected Bibliography

Waldo, Fullerton: "Rachmaninov's *The Bells*," *Outlook*, volume 124 (25 February 1920), 318-319.

Hull, Robert: "Rachmaninov's *The Bells*," *Monthly Musical Record* (October 1936), 171-172.

Leonard, Richard A.: *A History of Russian Music*, 227-230. New York, MacMillan, 1957.

Evans, Mary Garrettson: *Music and Edgar Allen Poe: A Bibliographic Study*. Baltimore: Johns Hopkins Press, 1939; reprinted New York: Greenwood Press, 1968.

Calvocoressi, Michel Dmitri: "The Bells," *The Listener*, volume 17 (3 February 1937), 244.

Martyn, Barrie: *Rachmaninov: Composer, Pianist, Conductor*, 241-248. Aldershot, England: Scolar Press, 1990.

Berger, Melvin: *Guide to Choral Masterpieces: A Listener's Guide*, 255-257. New York: Anchor Books, 1993.

## Ravel, Maurice (b. Cibourne, Basses-Pyrénées, France, 7 March 1875; d. Paris, 28 December 1937)

**Life:** Ravel first attended the Paris Conservatory as a pianist and began composing when he had completed those studies in 1895. He returned two years later to pursue an education in composition for which his teacher was Gabriél Fauré. He also studied counterpoint and orchestration with André Gédalge. He made four successive attempts to win the Grand Prix de Rome, which were each unsuccessful. His elimination in the preliminary rounds, in 1905, became a *cause célèbre* which brought about a resignation from Dubois as director of the conservatory. Ravel dedicated himself solely to composition, making occasional performance tours in his own music. His works combine many of the exotic elements found in the works of Debussy, with whom he is often paired, with a keen appreciation of Classical and Baroque forms. His works all exhibit impeccable craftsmanship and a remarkable sensitivity to instrumental timbres. Most of his orchestral works were first composed as piano solos. In his final years he suffered from increasing paralysis and aphasia, completing his final works through an amanuensis.

**Principal Works:** *opera* - *L'Heure espagnole* (1909), *L'Enfant et les Sortilèges* (1925); *ballets* - *Ma Mère l'Oye* (1911), *Daphnis et*

*Chloé* (1912), *Le Tombeau de Couperin* (1920), *La Valse* (1920), *Boléro* (1928); *orchestral - Pavane pour une infant défunte* (1910), *Alborado del gracioso* (1919), *Tzigane* (1924), Piano Concerto in D for Left Hand Alone (1930), Piano Concerto in G (1931); *chamber - Introduction and Allegro* (1905); *vocal - Trois poèmes de Stéphane Mallarmé* (1913), *Chansons madécasses* (1926), *Don Quichotte à Dulcinée* (1933); and many songs and piano solos.

### Selected Composer Bibliography

Roland-Manuel: *Maurice Ravel*, translated into English by Cynthia Jolly. London: Dennis Dobson, 1947.

Goss, Madeleine: *Bolero: The Life of Maurice Ravel*. New York: Henry Holt and Co., 1940.

Demuth, Norman: *Ravel*. London: J.M. Dent and Sons, 1947.

Seroff, Victor I.: *Maurice Ravel*, New York: Henry Holt and Company, 1953.

Jankélévitch, Vladimir: *Ravel*, translated by Margaret Crosland. London: John Calder, 1959.

Myers, Rollo H.: *Ravel: Life and Works*. London: Gerald Duckworth and Co., 1960.

Orenstein, Arbie: *Ravel: Man and Musician*. New York: Columbia University Press, 1975.

Nichols, Roger: *Ravel Remembered*. New York: W. W. Norton, 1987.

Orenstein, Arbie, editor: *A Ravel Reader: Correspondence, Articles, Interviews*. New York: Columbia University Press, 1990.

## Daphnis et Chloe (1909-12)

**Duration:** ca. 50 minutes

There were two suites made of material from the ballet, their durations are:

|           |                |
|-----------|----------------|
| Suite No. 1 | ca. 12 minutes |
| Suite No. 2 | ca. 18 minutes |

**Text:** none.

**Performing Forces: voices:** SATB choir, **orchestra:** piccolo, 2 flutes in C, alto flute in G, 2 oboes, English horn, soprano clarinet in E$^b$, 2 clarinets in B$^b$ and A, bass clarinet in B$^b$, 3 bassoons, contrabassoon, 4 horns in F, 4 trumpets, in C, 3 trombones, tuba, timpani, percussion (8 players - glockenspiel, xylophone, crotales, snare drum, tenor drum, bass drum, tambourine, cymbals, tam-tam, triangle, castanets, wind machine), celeste, 2 harps, and strings.

on-stage (in the ballet): piccolo, soprano clarinet in E$^b$.

off-stage: horn in F, trumpet in C.

**First Performance:** entire ballet: 8 June 1912; Théâtre Chatelet, Paris; Ballets Russes; conducted by Pierre Monteux; produced by Serge Diaghilev; choreographed by Michel Fokine; scenery and costumes by Leon Bakst. The dancers were as follows:

| | |
|---|---|
| Chloé | Thamara Karsavina |
| Daphnis | Vaslav Nijinsky |
| Lyceion | Frohman |
| Dorcon | Adolf Bolm |
| 1st Nymphe | Marie Piltz |
| 2nd Nymphe | Lubov Tchernicheva |
| 3rd Nymph | Kopatzynska |
| Lammon | Enrico Cecchetti |
| Bryaxis | Fedorow |

premiere of Suite No. 1: 2 April 1911; Colonne Orchestra; conducted by Gabriel Pierné.

**Edition:** *Daphnis et Chloe* is published by Durand and Kalmus. The full score is available for purchase and orchestral materials are available through rental. The full score is also available for purchase from Dover.

**Autograph:** The manuscript of the piano score, which was completed in 1910, is in the private collection of Madame Alexander Taverne. The manuscript of the full score is in the archives of Durand and Company.

**Notes:** There are instrumental cues provided in the orchestra parts if a chorus is unavailable; however, these cues do not appear in the full score. Directions to integrate the music with the staging are found throughout the score.

There were two orchestral suites made from the complete score. They appeared as follows:

Suite No. 1 (1911)
Nocturne
Interlude
Danse guerrière

Suite No. 2 (1913)
Lever du Jour
Pantomime
Danse générale

**Performance Issues:** Ravel uses a textless chorus as an orchestral color for his instrumentation of this ballet score, an idea which was probably inspired by Debussy's use of the women's choir in *Nocturnes*. In the score, he indicates mouths closed (humming), and mouths open; however, for the latter, he has not indicated a choice of vowels, so these must be decided in rehearsal preparation. It is advisable to vary them according to the musical context, both for timbral variety and to prevent vocal fatigue. The score indicates that the choir be placed behind the staging. In a concert situation, traditional seating is entirely appropriate. The vocal material is derived from non-functional tertian relationships and quartal-quintal combinations. While the vocal material is harmonically supported by the orchestra most of the time, it is generally rhythmically independent. Some passages are unaccompanied for which orchestral alternatives are provided. There are two-part divisi for each section of the choir. The size of the wind and brass sections requires a large contingent of string players. There are also divisi for all of the string parts. The general percussion parts are not very difficult, but eight players are needed in the final sections of the work. The glockenspiel player must be skilled as there are some four-mallet passages for the glockenspiel. All of the brass parts are demanding in terms of endurance. The trumpet I and horn I are particularly exposed with some challenging solo passages. The flutes, oboes and clarinets all have numerous extended virtuosic passages combining arpeggiations and chromatic passagework. The flutes also have significant exposed sections which require slow beautiful playing. All of the string writing is very idiomatic and exceptionally challenging technically.   Ravel achieves many shimmering sonic effects through brilliant orchestral gestures which are the amalgammation of numerous detailed figures. The two harp parts are quite independent and must be done by two players. The timbral effect of the chorus is probably most effective with a large vocal ensemble. The chorus must be musically independent and the orchestra flexible and virtuosic. **Choir:** difficult, **Orchestra:** very difficult.

**Discography:** There was an Aeolian Pianola Roll made of the entire piano reduction by the composer. It is TL22514/8-TL22548/9.

<u>complete ballet</u>

Orchestre de Paris; conducted by Jean Martinon, recorded in 1975. VSM: 2C 165-02583/7 [LP].
Orchestre de la Suisse Romande, Motet Choir of Geneva (Jacques Horneffer, chorus-master); conducted by Ernest Ansermet, recorded in Victoria Hall, Geneva in 1953. Decca: LXT2775 [LP], released in the United States as London: LL693.
Orchestre du Théâtre des Champs-Elysées, Choeur et Maîtrise de la Radio et Télévision Française; conducted by Désiré-Emile Inghelbrecht, recorded in 1954. Ducretet-Thomson: 320C015 [LP].
Boston Symphony Orchestra, Chorus of the New England Conservatory and Alumni (Robert Shaw, chorus-master, assisted by Lorna Cooke de Varon); conducted by Charles Munch, recorded in 1955. RCA-Victor: LSC 1893 [LP].
London Symphony Orchestra, Chorus of the Royal Opera House, Covent Garden (Douglas Robinson, chorus-master); conducted by Pierre Monteux, recorded in 1959. Decca: SXL2312 [LP], released in the United States as London: CS6248.

<u>second version</u>

Boston Symphony Orchestra, Chorus of the New England Conservatory (Lorna Cooke de Varon, chorus-master); conducted by Charles Munch, recorded in 1961. RCA-Victor: LSC 2568 [LP].
Orchestre de la Suisse Romande, Chorus of Romande Radio, Lausanne (André Charlet, chorus-master); conducted by Ernest Ansermet, recorded in Victoria Hall, Geneva in 1965. Decca: SXL6204 [LP], released in the United States as London: CS6456, rereleased in 1984 as Decca: 414046-2 [ADD].

excerpts

Orchestre de la Société des Concerts du Conservatoire; conducted by
    Charles Munch, recorded in 1949. Decca: GAG 1584/6 [78],
    released in the United States as London: set LA225.

Suite No. 1

L'Orchestre de la Société des Concerts du Conservatoire; conducted by
    Piero Coppola, recorded in Paris in 1934. Victor: 11882 [78].
San Francisco Symphony Orchestra, San Francisco Municipal Choir;
    conducted by Pierre Monteux, recorded in 1947. RCA-Victor:
    119683/4 [78], rereleased as RCA-Camden: CAL 156 [LP].
Philadelphia Orchestra; conducted by Eugene Ormandy. Columbia: ML
    4316 [LP].
Boston Symphony Orchestra, Chorus of the New England Conservatory
    and Alumni (Robert Shaw, chorus-master, assisted by Lorna Cooke
    de Varon); conducted by Charles Munch, recorded in 1955. RCA-
    Victrola: VICS 1271 [LP].

Suite No.2

Orchestre des Concerts Straram; conducted by Philippe Gaubert,
    recorded in 1930. Columbia: 67827/8D [78].
Concertgebouw Orchestra; conducted by Willem Mengelberg, recorded
    on 6 October 1938. Released in 1977 as Educational Media:
    RR506 [LP].
Boston Symphony Orchestra; conducted by Serge Koussevitsky,
    recorded in 1929. Victor: 7143/4 [78].
Berlin Philharmonic Orchestra; conducted by Wilhelm Furtwängler,
    recorded on 20 and 22 March 1944. Released in 1985 as Melodiya:
    459490008 [LP].
Boston Symphony Orchestra; conducted by Serge Koussevitsky,
    recorded in 1946. Victor: 118747/8 [78]. second version
Boston Symphony Orchestra; conducted by Serge Koussevitsky,
    recorded privately in 1948. Released in 1975 as SID: 711 [LP].
    third version
N.B.C. Symphony Orchestra; conducted by Arturo Toscanini, recorded
    in Carnegie Hall, New York on 21 November 1949. RCA: LM
    1043 [LP].
Philadelphia Orchestra; conducted by Eugene Ormandy. Columbia: ML
    4316 [LP].

Boston Symphony Orchestra, Chorus of the New England Conservatory and Alumni (Robert Shaw, chorus-master, assisted by Lorna Cooke de Varon); conducted by Charles Munch, recorded in 1955. RCA-Victrola: VICS 1271 [LP].

Detroit Symphony Orchestra; conducted by Paul Paray, recorded between 1956 and 1962. Philips: 6768230 [LP].

Chicago Symphony Orchesta; conducted by Jean Martinon, recorded in 1965. RCA-Victrola: LSC2806 [LP].

### Selected Bibliography

reviews of the premiere:

Vuillemin, Louis: "Daphnis et Chloé" in *Comœdia* (10 June 1912).
Carraud, Gaston: "Daphnis et Chloé" in *La Liberté* (11 June 1912).
Lalo, Pierre: "Daphnis et Chloé" in *Le Temps* (11 June 1912).

other sources:

"Composer and Impressario, M. Maurice Ravel versus M. Diaghilev" in *Comœdia* (18 June 1914).
Haskell, Arnold: *Diaghileff: His Artistic and Private Life*, 167, 194, 218, -219, 320. New York: Simon and Schuster, 1935. Reprinted as New York: DaCapo Press, 1978.
Orenstein, Arbie: *Ravel: Man and Musician*, 60-61, 69-70, 177-179, 215-216, 231-232, 261-262. New York: Columbia University Press, 1975.
_____, editor: *A Ravel Reader: Correspondence, Articles, Interviews*, 147-148, 217-218, 574-581, 586. New York: Columbia University Press, 1990.

## Schoenberg, Arnold (b. Vienna, 13 September 1874; d. Los Angeles, 13 July 1951)

**Life:** As a composer, theorist, painter, and pedagogue Schoenberg was one of the most significant intellectual figures of the twentieth century. His development of the twelve-tone system of composition exercised a remarkable influence upon the succeeding generations of composers. Schoenberg studied counterpoint with his future brother-in-law, Alexander Zemlinsky. He established a reputation as a composer of promise through early works which continued the tonal Romantic traditions of Wagner and Strauss, the latter of whom help Schoenberg secure his first teaching engagement. Schoenberg gained the support of Mahler in 1903. At this time, he and Zemlinsky established a concert series for new music, and Schoenberg developed æsthetic ties to the Expressionist movement. He attracted a circle of like-minded pupils who included Alban Berg and Anton Webern. During the second decade of this century, Schoenberg began to explore new venues of pitch organization which traversed free atonality and reached an apex in the Suite for Piano (1921-23), which is the first work to be systematically organized via Schoenberg's twelve-note serial method. In 1925, he joined the faculty of the Prussian Arts Academy, but was dismissed from that post by the Nazis due to his Jewish heritage, and was forced to flee. In 1933, in Paris, Schoenberg reconverted to Judaism out of empathy for those now being persecuted in his homeland. The Schoenberg family settled in the United States. For one year, Schoenberg taught at the Malkin Conservatory in Boston, then moving to California, he taught at the University of Southern California (1935-36) and the University of California at Los Angeles (1936-44). In addition to a highly original body of music, Schoenberg produced a series of texts elucidating the processes of musical composition which expose his profound understanding of the inner workings of the music of the common practice period.

**Writings:** *Harmonielehre.* Vienna: Universal Edition, 1911; translated into English as *Theory of Harmony.* Berkeley, California: University of California Press, 1978. *Models for Beginners in Composition.* New York: 1942. *Style and Idea: Selected Writings of Arnold Schoenberg,* edited by Leonard Stein with translations by Leo Black. Berkeley, California: University of California Press, 1975. *Structural Functions of Harmony.* New York: W.W. Norton, 1954. *Preliminary Exercises in Counterpoint.* London: Faber and Faber,1963. *Fundamentals of Music Composition.* London: Faber and Faber, 1967.

**Principal Works:** *stage works - Erwartung,* op. 17 (1909), *Die glückliche Hand,* op. 18 (1913), *Von Heute auf Morgen,* op. 32 (1929), *Moses und Aron* (1930-32, 1951); *orchestral - Pelleas und Melisande,* op. 5 (1903), *Kammersymphonie,* op. 9 (1906), 5 Pieces for Orchestra, op.16 (1916), *Variations* , op. 31 (1928), Violin Concerto, op. 36 (1936); *chamber* - 4 numbered String Quartets (op. 7, 1905; op. 10, 1908; op. 30, 1927; op. 37, 1936),*Verklärte Nacht,* op. 4 (1899), *Die eiserne Brigade* (1916), Serenade, op. 24 (1923), *Ode to Napoleon* (1942); *choral - Friede auf Erden,* op. 13 (1907), *Dreimal Tausend Jahre,* op. 50a (1949); *solo vocal - Das Buch der hängenden Gärten,* op. 15 (1909), *Pierrot Lunaire,* op. 21 (1912).

## Selected Composer Bibliography

Rufer, Josef: *The Works of Arnold Schoenberg: A Catalogue of his Compositions, Writings, and Paintings*, translated by Dika Newlin. New York: Free Press of Glencoe, 1963.

Schoenberg, Arnold: *Style and Idea: Selected Writings of Arnold Schoenberg*, edited by Leonard Stein with translations by Leo Black. Berkeley, California: University of California Press, 1975.

_____: *Arnold Schoenberg: Letters*, selected and edited by Erwin Stein with translations by Eithne Wilkins and Ernst Kaiser. London: Faber and Faber, 1964; reissued as Berkeley, California: University of California Press, 1987.

# Gurrelieder (1900-11)

**Duration:** ca. 130 minutes

**Text:** The text is taken from the poetry of Jens Peter Jacobsen, translated from Danish to German by Robert Franz Arnold.

**Performing Forces: voices:** speaker, Tove—soprano, Waldtaube—mezzosoprano or alto, Waldemar—tenor, Klauss-Narr—tenor, and Bauer—bass soloists; 3 TTBB men's choirs and SSAATTBB choir; **orchestra:** 8 flutes (flutes I, II, III, and IV doubling piccolo), 5 oboes (oboes IV and V doubling English horn), 7 clarinets in A (clarinets IV and V doubling bass clarinet in B$^b$, and clarinets VI and VII doubling soprano clarinet in E$^b$), 3 bassoons, 2 contrabassoons, 10 horns in F (horns VII, VIII, IX, and X doubling Wagner tubas), 7 trumpets in F, B$^b$, and C, bass trumpet in E$^b$, 1 alto trombone, 4 tenor trombones, bass trombone, contrabass trombone, tuba, percussion (6 players - 6 timpani, glockenspiel, xylophone, large field drum, snare drum, bass drum, cymbals, tam-tam, triangle, ratchet, large chains), 4 harps, celeste, and strings (20 1st violins, 20 2nd violins, 16 violas, 16 cellos, and 12 doublebasses).

Reduced Instrumental Scoring: 3 or 4 flutes, 3 oboes, 4 clarinets, 3 bassoons, 4 to 6 horns, 3 or 4 trumpets, 3 or 4 trombones, tuba, percussion, 2 harps, celeste, harmonium, piano, and strings.

**First Performance:** 23 February 1913; Vienna; Vienna Philharmonic and Philharmonic Chorus, conducted by Franz Schreker.

**Edition:** *Gurrelieder* was originally published by Universal Edition. For both the original and reduced orchestrations, some of these materials are now distributed by Belmont, including a full score (BEL 1005) and a piano-reduction score (UE 3696) which are available for purchase. Performance materials are available from Belmont through rental. Full scores (UE 6300), piano-vocal scores (3696), and choral parts (3699A-H) are available for purchase from Universal Edition. The "Lied der Waldtaube" movement is available separately in three different reduced orchestrations, including one by Erwin Stein, all of which are available through rental from Universal Edition.

**Autograph:** The manuscript of the draft score of *Gurrelieder* is in the Schoenberg Institute at the University of Southern California. The manuscript of the full score is in the possession of Universal Edition in Vienna. This manuscript was published by Universal Edition in Facsimile in 1912. The manuscript was later marked with a number of alterations in scoring, and the eradication of a measure (the third bar after rehearsal number 109). The engraved score, published in 1920 reflects these and other changes. It should be noted that a piano-vocal score prepared by Alban Berg for publication concurrent with the facsimile score still contains the measure struck from the later version.

**Notes:** This score includes the first notated orchestral trombone glissando, and the first use of chains in an orchestral percussion section.[32] This is Schoenberg's first score which calls for spoken passages of approximate pitch, which he would later refine in his melodrama, *Pierrot Lunaire.*

**Performance Issues:** This is a brilliantly scored, chromatic, yet tonally secure composition following the musical traditions of Mahler and Richard Strauss. Like these models, the shear size and complexity of the instrumental forces presents unusual challenges to successful ensemble playing. The instrumental parts are technically demanding throughout the sections of the orchestra, but

---

32 Nicolas Slonimsky: *Music Since 1900*, fifth edition, 138. New York: Schirmer Books, 1994.

the greater challenge is dealing with the overall complexity of the orchestration. Expressive elements of time and dynamics require a very responsive orchestra. Generally, the scoring is well conceived in relation to the solo vocal parts, so that the balance between soloists and the orchestra should not be problematic. There is significant interplay of timbres within this score that will demand attention in rehearsal. The sonorities are rich and demand a suppleness of sound from the players, especially in the string parts. The bass trumpet can be played on euphonium, and the contrabass trombone could be doubled by a smaller bore tuba; however, all four harp parts must be present in the full version. There are string divisi by stand; although the score does not specify a number of doublebasses, there are passages for 4 doublebass soloists and a two-part division of the remaining players that suggests a minimum of 10 players. Similar numbered divisi suggest that the composer envisioned a mixed choir of 48 sopranos, 48 altos, 40, tenors, and 40 basses. There is no indication to suggest sizes for the men's choirs, but groups of 16 singers or more in each seems appropriate. The men's choirs do not enter until midway into the third act, and the mixed choir appears prominently only during the last six minutes of the score. The pitch material for the choirs is generally diatonic and well supported by the accompaniment. The choral singers must be capable of carrying over the large instrumental forces, but their parts are not otherwise demanding. **Soloists:** Speaker, this role requires a musically trained performer, all rhythms are specific and approximate pitches are indicated; Tove, range: b-b", tessitura: f-f", this role is dramatic and requires a rich and powerful voice, there is only one b" for which an optional pitch is offered, but a" appears a number of times; Waldtaube, range: a-g#", tessitura: f-e", this is a lyric and sustained role, although the tessitura is similar to that of Tove, Schoenberg's indication of a different vocal fach suggests that he desired a clear timbral difference between these two voices; Waldemar, range: B$^b$-b', tessitura: f-f', this is a dramatic heldentenor role requiring a large vocal presence throughout the range while remaining capable of clear pianissimo singing; Klaus-Narr, range: d-b', tessitura: g-e', this role calls for a clear and facile voice; Bauer, range: G#-g', tessitura: f-d', this role is sustained and lyric; **Choir:** medium difficult; **Orchestra:** very difficult.

**Discography:** Semser (Tove), Tangeman (Waldtaube), Lewis (Waldemar), Riley (Speaker); New Symphony Society of Paris

Chorus and Orchestra; conducted by Réné Liebowitz. Haydn Society: HSL 100 [LP].

Vreeland (Tove), Bampton (Waldtaube), Althouse (Waldemar), Robovsky (Speaker); Philadelphia Orchestra and Chorus; conducted by Leopold Stokowski. Victor: LCT 6012 [LP].

Jesse Norman (Tove), Tatiana Troyanos (Waldtaube), James McCracken (Waldemar), Werner Klemperer (Speaker); Boston Symphony and Tanglewood Chorus; conducted by Seiji Ozawa. Philips: 412511-2 PH 2 [ADD].

Inge Borkh (Tove), Hertha Töpper (Waldtaube), Herbert Schachtschneider (Waldemar), Lorenz Fehenberger (Klauss-Narr), Kieth Engen (Bauer), Hans Herbert Fiedler (Speaker); Bayerischen Rundfunks Chorus and Orchestra; conducted by Rafael Kubelik. Deutsche Grammaphon: D 293657 [ADD]. This is a live recording originally made in 1965 and remastered to compact disc.

Deborah Voigt (Tove), Jennifer Larmore (Waldtaube), Thomas Moser (Waldemar), Bernd Weikl (Klauss-Narr), Kenneth Riegel (Bauer), Klaus Maria Brandauer (Speaker); choirs from Dresden, Leipzig, and Prague; Dresden Staatskappelle; conducted by Giuseppe Sinopoli. Teldec: 2160000 [DDD].

*Lied der Waldtaube,* only:

Martha Lipton; New York Philharmonic; conducted by Leopold Stokowski. Columbia: ML 2140 [LP].

### Selected Bibliography

Berg, Alban: *Arnold Schönberg: Gurre-leider Führer* (Grosse Ausgabe Vienna, 1913; kleine Ausgabe 1914).

Nachod, H: "The Very First Performance of Schoenberg's Gurre-lieder," *Music Survey*, volume 3, number 3 (1950), 38.

Pahlen, Kurt: *The World of the Oratorio*, 286-289. Portland, Oregon: Amadeus Press, 1985.

Berger, Melvin: *Guide to Choral Masterpieces: A Listener's Guide*, 264-267. New York: Anchor Books, 1993.

# Die Jakobsleiter (1917-22)

**Duration:** ca. 60 minutes

**Text:** The text in German is by Schoenberg based upon the biblical tale of Jacob's dream of a heavenly ladder.

**Performing Forces: voices:** "Die Seele/The Soul"—high soprano, "Die Sterbende/He who is dying"—high soprano (speaking in a low voice), "Der Mönch/The Monk"—tenor (speaking), "Ein Aufrührerischer/One who is rebellious"—tenor (speaking), "Ein Berufener/One who is called"—tenor, "Ein Ringender/One who is struggling"—baritone (speaking), "Der Auserwählte/He who is chosen"—baritone, "Gabriel"—baritone (singing and speaking), soloists; SSMMAATTBarBarBB choir; **orchestra:** piccolo, 3 flutes (flute III doubling piccolo II), 3 oboes, English horn, clarinet in E$^b$, 3 clarinets in B$^b$, bass clarinet in B$^b$, 3 bassoons, contrabassoon, 3 trumpets in B$^b$, 4 horns in F, 3 trombones, tuba, timpani, percussion (3 players - glockenspiel, xylophone, 2 cymbals, tamtam, large side drum, triangle, wind machine), harp, celeste, piano, and strings.

2 additional sub-groups near the main orchestra: {H1: high soprano; harmonium, 6 solo violins}, {H2: 3 oboes, English horn, clarinet in B$^b$, bass clarinet in B$^b$, 3 trumpets in B$^b$, mandolin, celeste, harp, harmonium, 5 solo violins}.

2 additional sub-groups off-stage: {F1: "The Soul," 3 trumpets in B$^b$, 2 horns in F, harmonium, 6 solo violins}, {F2: 3 sopranos; 2 horns, 2 trombones, harmonium, 6 solo violins}.

**First Performance:** 16 June 1961; Vienna; given as part of the 35th Festival of the International Society for Contemporary Music.

**Edition:** *Jakobsleiter* is published by Universal Edition, full score (UE 13356). All materials are available through rental from Belmont.

**Autograph:** Schoenberg's manuscript of the draft score through measure 685, the manuscript of the complete text and other sketch materials are in the Schoenberg Institute at the University of Southern California.

**Notes:** *Jakobsleiter*, though begun in 1915, was left incomplete at Schoenberg's death. He had written to his former pupil, Karl Rankl (1898-1968), requesting that Rankl prepare a score based upon the detailed instructions included throughout the draft materials. Rankl later gave this letter to Schoenberg's widow who arranged for the score to be prepared for performance by another of the composer's pupils, Winfried Zillig (1905-63), following the composer's extensive instructions. Schoenberg authored the text between 1915 and 1917, completing it 26 May 1917. The published score is entirely at sounding pitch, including the piccolo and double basses which are indicated in their sounding octaves; however, the glockenspiel is printed at written pitch, sounding two octaves higher.

**Performance Issues:** A significant logistical issue is that the score calls for a second, distant orchestra and chorus. In a letter to Winfried Zillig in 1944, Schoenberg suggested that these groups be placed in a sound-proof place and broadcast into select locations in the performance space through loudspeakers. The score states that the *Sprechstimme* parts, although spoken in quality, must remain true to the indicated pitches. The individual instrumental parts are well-written for each instrument. Some of the glockenspiel passages are particularly difficult. The rhythmic material is not overly complex; however, although this is not a serial composition it is functionally atonal and presents a wide variety of pitch challenges for both the singers and instrumentalists. The score explores the many parameters of sevenths and ninths which are often spelled in ways that make them more difficult to perform accurately. The choral writing utilizes a variety of contrapuntal textures. While the solo vocal parts are often clearly supported by the accompaniment, the choral singers are required to be more independent of the instruments. There are sections of choral *Sprechstimme* which maintain a high level of pitch complexity. The only choral divisi occur at the choir's initial entrance (p. 6 of the full score). The range of the choral bass II part extends down to BB. **Soloists:** "Die Seele/The soul," range: a-f", tessitura: d'-b", this is a very sustained and ethereal, textless solo role; "Die Sterbende/He who is dying," this is a *Sprechstimme* role utilizing the lower register of the soprano voice, range: e-f#"; "Der Mönch/The Monk," this is a *Sprechstimme* role, range: G#-a'; "Ein Aufrührerischer/One who is rebellious," this is a *Sprechstimme* role, range: d-b'; "Ein Berufener/One who is called," range: c-c", tessitura: g-g', this is a sustained and lyrical role; "Ein Ringender/One who is struggling," this is a *Sprechstimme* role, range: G-f'; "Der Auserwählte/He who is chosen," range: G-ab', tessitura: d-d', this role requires broad melodic leaps and rapid articulation and control of sustained singing; "Gabriel," range: F-f', tessitura: e-d', this role combines sung passages with

*Sprechstimme*, and requires an articulate, declamatory, and clear voice; **Choir:** very difficult; **Orchestra:** very difficult.

**Discography:** Ortrun Wenkel, Mady Mesple, Siegmund Nimsgern, Kenneth Bowen, Ian Partridge, Paul Hudson, John Shirley-Quirk, Anthony Rolfe-Johnson; BBC Singers, BBC Symphony Orchestra; conducted by Pierre Boulez. SONY: SMK 48462 [ADD].

### Selected Bibliography

Pauli, H.: "Zu Schönbergs 'Jakobsleiter,'" *Schweizerische Musikzeitung*, volume 102 (1962), 350.
Wörner, K H: "Schönbergs Oratorium 'Die Jakobsleiter,': Musik zwischen Theologie und Weltanschauung," *Schweizerische Musikzeitung*, volume 105 (1965), 250, 333.
Pahlen, Kurt: *The World of the Oratorio*, 289. Portland, Oregon: Amadeus Press, 1985.

## Kol Nidre, op. 39 (1938)

**Duration:** ca. 15 minutes

**Text:** The text is an English translation and adaptation of the traditional Jewish prayer of atonement from the celebration of Yom Kippur.

**Performing Forces: voices:** Rabbi/speaker; SATB choir (6 to 8 sopranos, 6 altos, 6 tenors, 6 basses); **orchestra:** 2 flutes (flute II doubling piccolo), oboe, $E^b$ soprano clarinet, clarinet in A, bass clarinet in $B^b$, bassoon, 2 horns in F, 2 trumpets in $B^b$, 2 trombones, tuba, percussion (3 players - timpani, xylophone, tenor drum, bass drum, suspended cymbal, crash cymbals, tam-tam, flexatone, and a bell), and strings (6 to 9 violins I, 3 to 5 violins II, 3 to 4 violas, 3 to 4 cellos, and 2 to 3 basses).

**Edition:** *Kol Nidre* is published by Boelke-Bomart. The study score (B19177) and full score (B19175) are available for purchase; orchestral materials are available through rental. The full score is included in the series, *Arnold Schönberg: Sämtliche Werke*, Abteilung V: Chorwerk II, Reihe A, Band 19; edited by Josef Rufer and Christian Martin Schmidt; Vienna: Universal Edition/Mainz: B Schotts Söhne, 1975.

**Autograph:** The location of the fair copy blue-print score is unknown. The draft manuscript is held by the Schoenberg Institute at the University of Southern California.

**Notes:** This score is written with transposed parts, an unusual feature among Schoenberg's published works. The work was written for Rabbi Dr. Jakob Sonderling. At Sonderling's suggestion, Schoenberg added an introductory passage to the traditional prayer. Schoenberg used a number of traditional cantillations of this prayer as sources of motivic material.

**Performance Issues:** This is a tonally rooted, though very chromatic score. Much of the chromatic material seems to be inspired by Jewish cantillation with a conspicuous interplay of major and minor thirds. The choral parts combine unison singing, paired doubling and some free four-part counterpoint. In all cases they are well supported by the orchestra, follow traditional voice leading principles, and are rhythmically conservative. This is a very expressive score with much of the choral writing in a declamatory style. The orchestral parts are highly chromatic throughout. Although this is a tonally centered work there are frequent shifts in the tonal center with numerous cross-related chromatic scalar passages which will demand significant attention in securing good intonation. The rhythmic language for the orchestra is much more complex than that for the singers with intricate interplay between disparate sections of the ensemble. Schoenberg also exploits staggered entrances within the beat, and there is significant interplay between three and four-part divisions of the beat. All of the instrumental parts are idiomatically written. The trumpet I part requires dynamic control at the top of the staff and the horn I has some awkward and exposed solo passages. The woodwinds have a great amount of unison playing of rapid chromatic figures interspersed with sustained harmonies which are often voiced at a disadvantage for accurate intonation between the respective instruments. There are four-part divisi for the violas, cellos and the doublebasses, five-part divisi for the violins I, and two-part divisi for the violins II. The subtleties of the string parts and their dispensation will require careful preparation of the bowings before rehearsal. A separate string sectional is advisable. **Soloist:** Rabbi/speaker - This role combines free narration and male *Sprechstimme* requiring an expressive speaker who is musically literate. **Choir:** medium difficult; **Orchestra:** medium difficult.

**Discography:** Hans Jaray, narrator; Academic Chamber Choir, Vienna Symphony Orchestra; conducted by Hans Swarowsky. Columbia: ML 4664 [LP].
John Shirley-Quirk, narrator; BBC Singers, BBC Chorus, BBC Symphony Orchestra; conducted by Pierre Boulez. CBS: M 35882 [LP]; rereleased as Sony: S2K 44571 [ADD].

### Selected Bibliography

Schmidt, Christian Martin, editor: "Chorwerke II," *Kritischer Bericht* from *Arnold Schönberg: Sämtliche Werke*, division 5, part B, volume 19, 1-39. Mainz: B. Schtt's Söhne, 1977.

## Survivor from Warsaw, op. 46 (1947)

**Duration:** ca. 11 minutes

**Text:** The speaker's text by Schoenberg is in English with additional exclamations in German. The men's choir closes the work with a traditional Hebrew prayer.

**Performing Forces:** voices: speaker and TTBB choir; **orchestra:** 2 flutes (each flute doubling piccolo), 2 oboes, 2 clarinets in B$^b$, 2 bassoons, 4 horns in F, 3 trumpets in B$^b$, 3 trombones, tuba, percussion (5 players - timpani, bells, chimes, xylophone, military drum, bass drum, tambourine, cymbals, tam-tam, triangle, castanets), harp, and strings.

**First Performance:** 4 November 1948; Albuquerque, NM; Albuquerque Civic Symphony Orchestra, conducted by Kurt Frederick.

**Edition:** *A Survivor from Warsaw* is published in multiple editions. Boelke-Bomart publishes a piano-vocal score and choral parts which are available for purchase. A miniature score may be purchased from Philharmonia (53 478). Both publishers produce an edition revised by Jacques-Louis Monod in 1979. Orchestral materials are available through rental from Schotts. The full score is included in the series, *Arnold Schönberg: Sämtliche Werke*, Abteilung V: Chorwerk II, Reihe A, Band 19; edited by Josef Rufer and Christian Martin Schmidt; Vienna: Universal Edition/Mainz: B Schotts Söhne, 1975.

**Autograph:** The manuscript of *A Survivor from Warsaw* is in the Library of Congress. The Schoenberg Institute at the University of Southern California is in possession of a reproduction of this manuscript which contains a number of corrections in the composer's hand. The institute also possesses the manuscript of the row chart.

**Notes:** This work about the Holocaust is dramatized by shouts in German representing Nazi exterminators counting Warsaw Jews being sent to the gas chambers. It concludes with a traditional chanted Hebrew prayer. The score bears the inscription: "For the Koussevitsky Music Foundation. Dedicated to the Memory of Natalie Koussevitsky." The score is written at sounding pitch, including the piccolos and doublebasses, but not the bells and xylophone.

**Performance Issues:** This is a serial composition of great dramatic content and effect, executed with subtlety and sensitivity. Schoenberg suggests 10 violins I, 10 violins II, 6 violas, 6 cellos, and 6 double basses. There are solo passages for 3 first violins, 3 violas, 3 cellos, and 3 doublebasses. Individual instrumental parts are well conceived and accessible to college-level players. Some of the solo string passages are exposed and more difficult than the tutti writing. Rhythmic integration between sections of the orchestra will require attention in rehearsal, especially in the closing choral section. Farish[33] indicates that only four percussionists are needed, which is possible, but will cause some awkward transitions and doublings for the players, who must cover six instruments simultaneously in measures 79 and 80. This can be reasonably executed by five players. Schoenberg employs some extended instrumental techniques including flutter tonguing, playing on the bridge with the bow and playing *col legno*, string players are also asked to beat the string with the wood of the bow. There is a great deal of rubato and rhythmic flexibility indicated throughout the score. Much of this flexibility is the result of give and take between the speaker and the orchestra. The chorus portion of this work is brief (18 measures) and in unison. Pitch stability for the singers is greatly aided by the first trombone, which doubles the choir completely. The Hebrew text is phonetically transliterated in the score and quite accessible. **Soloist:** speaker, this role

---

[33] Margaret K. Farish: *Orchestral Music in Print*. Philadelphia, Pennsylvania: Musicdata, 1979.

requires a person of musical training who can portray a number of characters and have a strong vocal presence. The speaker's part is indicated with precise rhythms and specific relative pitches including accidentals and ledger lines; however, they are all written around a single-line staff rather than the conventional five-lined staff of the other parts. The speaker also has freely recited text. The role includes a first-person narrative in English and a portrayal of a concentration-camp sergeant in German. **Choir:** medium difficult, **Orchestra:** difficult.

**Discography:** Hans Jaray, narrator; Academic Chamber Choir, Vienna Symphony Orchestra; conducted by Swarowsky. Columbia: ML 4664 [LP].
John Horton, narrator; Festival Singers of Toronto (Elmer Iseler, chorus-master), CBC Symphony Orchestra; conducted by Robert Craft. Columbia: M2S-679 [LP].
Gunther Reich, narrator; BBC Singers, BBC Chorus, BBC Symphony Orchestra; conducted by Pierre Boulez. CBS: M 35882 [LP]; rereleased as Sony: S2K 44571 [ADD].

### Selected Bibliography

Craft, Robert: notes for the recording: *The Music of Arnold Schoenberg*, volume 1. New York: Columbia, 1963.
Schmidt, Christian Martin: "Schönbergs Kantate 'Ein Überlebender aus Warschaw,'" *Archiv für Musikwissenschaft*, vokume 33 (1976), 174.
_____, editor: "Chorwerke II," *Kritischer Bericht* from *Arnold Schönberg: Sämtliche Werke*, division 5, part B, volume 19, 60-81. Mainz: B. Schtt's Söhne, 1977.

## Moderne Psalm, op. 50c (1950)

**Duration:** ca. 7 minutes

**Text:** The text, in German, is by the composer. It is the first in a series of sacred poems written by him.

**Performing Forces: voices:** speaking voice; SATB choir; **orchestra:** 2 flutes (flute II doubling piccolo), 2 oboes (oboe II doubling English horn), soprano clarinet in $E^b$, clarinet in $B^b$ or A; bass clarinet in $B^b$, 2 bassoons, 2 horns in F, 2 trumpets in C, trombone, percussion (1 player - bells, bass drum, tam-tam), and strings (8 violins, 4 violas, 4 cellos, and 4 doublebasses).

**Edition:** *Moderne Psalm* is published by Schotts and Belmont; all materials are available through rental. The full score is included in the series, *Arnold Schönberg: Sämtliche Werke*, Abteilung V: Chorwerk II, Reihe A, Band 19; edited by Josef Rufer and Christian Martin Schmidt; Vienna: Universal Edition/Mainz: B. Schotts Söhne, 1975.

**Autograph:** The manuscript is in the Schoenberg Institute at the University of Southern California.

**Notes:** This composition was left incomplete upon the composer's death, but is included here because performing materials of the completed first seven minutes of the score have been made available. The score is published at sounding pitch for all instruments including the glockenspiel, but excepting the doublebasses which are to sound an octave below the notated pitch.

**Performance Issues:** This is a serially conceived composition which is organized to exploit some tonal implications through pitch repetition and the outlining of triadic structures within the row itself. There is consistent support of the vocal parts within the orchestra; however, there are often cross-related pitches in other instruments sounding concurrently. The individual orchestral parts are well written for their respective instruments, and are not technically demanding. The strings are often divided, and most of the string players must be capable of covering an independent part. All of the doublebasses are expected to play down to pedal CC. **Soloist:** The speaker is asked to approximate pitches placed around a single staff line. This, compiled with specific rhythms, requires a musically experienced executant for this role. **Choir:** difficult; **Orchestra:** medium difficult.

**Discography:** John Shirley-Quirk, narrator; BBC Singers, BBC Chorus, BBC Symphony Orchestra; conducted by Pierre Boulez. CBS: M 35882 [LP]; rereleased as Sony: S2K 44571 [ADD].
Gunther Reich, narrator; Slovak Philharmonic Choir (Pavol Prochazka, chorus-master), Southwest German Radio Orchestra; conducted by Michael Gielen, recorded in Munster Schwarzach on 1 July 1988. Wergo: WER 60185-50 [DDD].

## Selected Bibliography

Schmidt, Christian Martin, editor: "Chorwerke II," *Kritischer Bericht* from *Arnold Schönberg: Sämtliche Werke*, division 5, part B, volume 19, 111-134. Mainz: B. Schott's Söhne, 1977.

## Shostakovich, Dmitri (b. St. Petersburg, 25 September 1906; d. Moscow, 9 August 1975)

**Life:** Shotakovich was the most celebrated Russian composer of the Soviet era. He produced an enormous body of works in virtually every genre which have been quickly assimilated into the standard repertoire. He received his early music instruction from his mother. In 1919, he enrolled in the Petrograd Conservatory where he studied composition with Maximilian Steinberg. He graduated in piano in 1923 and composition in 1925. His graduation project was his Symphony No. 1, which was premiered by the Leningrad Philharmonic the following year to great public acclaim. His compositional career was plagued by official criticism for its worldly subject matter and progressive technical procedures, causing him to fall in and out of favor with the Soviet regime. At his peaks, he received numerous honors including: 3 Orders of Lenin, Hero of Socialist Labor, and Order of the October Revolution. Outside of the Soviet Union he was also heralded with an honorary membership in the American Institute of the Arts, and honorary doctorates from Oxford and Northwestern Universities. As the restrictions upon the arts in the Soviet Union relaxed, even Shostakovich's most controversial works were restored to the repertoire.

**Writings:** Following Shostakovich's death his memoirs were published in the west as *Testimony: The Memoirs of Dmitri Shostakovich*, Volkov, Solomon, editor. New York: Harper and Rowe, 1979. The authenticity of this text was the subject of some controversy, particularly in the Soviet Union, as it explores the composer's inner struggles by his creative incompatibility with the musical ideals of his government.

**Principal Works:** *opera - The Nose*, op. 15 *(1928), Lady Macbeth of the Mtensk, op. 29 (1932), Moskva, Cheryomushki*, op. 105 (1958); *ballets - The Age of Gold*, op. 22 (1930), *Bolt*, op. 27 (1931); *orchestral* - 15 Symphonies (no. 1 - op. 10, 1925; no. 2 - "To October," op. 14, 1927; no. 3 - "The First of May," op. 20, 1929; no. 4 - op. 43, 1936; no. 5 - op. 47, 1937; no. 6 - op. 54, 1939; no. 7 - "Lenningrad," op. 60, 1941; no. 8 - op. 65, 1943; no. 9 - op. 70,

1945; no. 10 - op. 93, 1953; no. 11 - "The Year 1905," op. 103, 1957; no. 12 - "The Year 1917," op. 112, 1961; no. 13 - "Babi Yar," op. 113, 1962; no. 14 - op. 135, 1969; no. 15 - op. 141, 1971), 2 piano Concertos (op. 35, 1933; op. 102, 1957), 2 Violin Concertos (op. 77, 1948; op. 129, 1967), 2 Cello Concertos (op. 107, 1959; op. 126, 1966), *Festive Overture*, op. 96 (1954), *October*, op. 131 (1967); *chamber* - 15 String Quartets (no. 1 - op. 49, 1938; no. 2 - op. 68, 1944; no. 3 - op. 73, 1946; no. 4 - op. 83, 1949; no. 5 - op. 92, 1952; no. 6 - op. 101, 1956; no. 7 - op. 108, 1960; no. 8 - op. 110, 1960; no. 9 - op. 117, 1964; no. 10 - op. 118, 1964; no. 11 - op. 122, 1966; no. 12 - op. 133, 1968; no. 13 - op. 138, 1970; no. 14 - op. 142, 1973; no. 15 - op. 144, 1974); *piano* - 2 Sonatas (op. 12, 1926; op. 61, 1943), 24 Preludes and Fugues, op. 87 (1951); *choral* - Ten Poems, op. 88 (1951), Loyalty, op. 136 (1970); and numerous songs and film scores.

## Selected Composer Bibliography

Blokker, Roy and Peter Reddaway: *The Music of Shostakovich: The Symphonies*. London: Tantivy Press, 1979.

Volkov, Solomon, editor: *Testimony: The Memoirs of Dmitri Shostakovich*. New York: Harper and Rowe, 1979.

Shostakovich, Dmitri: *Dmitri Shostakovich: About Himself and His Time*, edited by L. Grigoryev and Y. Platek. Moscow: Progress, 1980.

Sollertinsky, Dmitri and Ludmilla: *Pages from the Life of Dmitri Shostakovich*. New York: Hale, 1981.

MacDonald, Malcolm: *Dmitri Shostakovich: A Complete Catalogue*, second edition. London: Boosey and Hawkes, 1985.

MacDonald, Ian: *The New Shostakovich*. Boston: Northeastern University Press, 1990.

Hulme, Derek C.: *Dmitri Shostakovich: A Catalogue, Bibliography, and Discography*, second edition. Oxford: Clarendon Press, 1991.

# Symphony No. 2, op. 14 (1927)

**Duration:** ca. 20 minutes

**Text:** The text is the poem, "To October," by Alexander Bezymensky. It is in Russian. Singing translations have been published in German and English.

**Performing Forces: voices:** SATB choir; **orchestra:** piccolo, 2 flutes, 2 oboes, 2 clarinets in B$^b$, 2 bassoons, 4 horns in F, 3 trumpets in B$^b$, 3 trombones, tuba, timpani, percussion (4 players - glockenspiel, snare drum, bass drum, cymbals, triangle, factory whistle in F#), and strings.

The composer provides low brass cues for the four whistle blasts in the event that a facory whistle is unattainable.

**First Performance:** 5 and 6 November 1927; Leningrad Philharmonic Bolshoi Hall; Leningrad Philharmonic Orchestra, Academy Capella Choir; conducted by Nikolai Malko; as part of a festival commemorating the tenth anniversary of the 1917 Revolution.

**Edition:** Symphony No. 2 is published by Mezhdunaradnaja Kniga. The full score is available for purchase in the first volume of the collected works. Performance materials are available through rental. This score is reprinted by Kalmus (A2038), miniature score (1457); all materials are available for purchase and orchestral materials are also available through rental. Following the dissolution of the Soviet Union, the Russian edition materials have come under the proprietorship of the Russian Authors Society for whom G. Schirmer serves as the U.S. agent.

**Autograph:** The manuscript is in the Russian Archives of Literature and Art in Moscow.

**Notes:** This work is subtitled, *To October—A Symphonic Dedication*, and inscribed "Proletarians of the World, Unite." It was commissioned by the Soviet Government to commemorate the tenth anniversary of the October Revolution of 1917.

**Performance Issues:** The choir appears in the final third of the work. The choral passages are homophonically written with occasional two-part divisions for each section of the choir. The choral material is harmonically supported by the accompaniment of the orchestra, but this rarely includes direct doubling. The choral writing is scalar and diatonic. The orchestration requires a large choral ensemble. The factory whistle sounds at **69** and between **86** and **89**. It is probably not important that it be in f#, although that is the pitch center of the work when it sounds. The score is filled with devices of compositional virtuosity including a 9-part chromatic canon at the seventh, and polyrhythms combining simultaneous beat divisions of 2, 3, 4, 5, and 6. The orchestral writing is quite virtuosic for all parts. The woodwinds and strings have a great deal of rapid chromatic passage work which is not only a challenge to the coördination of the ensemble, but quite technically difficult in isolation. The tessitura of the brass parts is consistently high. The principal trumpet has significant passages above the staff throughout the work. The score begins with the 9-part canon which is an orchestral *tour de force* which will prove tricky to even the finest ensembles. **Choir:** medium easy; **Orchestra:** difficult.

**Discography:** Leningrad Philharmonic Orchestra, Krupskaya Institute Chorus (Ivan Poltavtsev, chorus-master); conducted by Igor Blazhkov, recorded in 1964. Melodiya: D 017953-4 [LP mono]. Reissued in the United States as Angel Melodiya: SR 40099.

Slovák Philharmonic Orchestra and Chorus; conducted by Ladislav Slovák, recorded in July 1967. Supraphon: SUA 10958 [LP mono].

Royal Philharmonic Orchestra and Chorus (John McCarthy, chorus-master; Igor Buketoff, chorus-director); conducted by Morton Gould, recorded in 1968. RCA Victor: LSC 3044 [LP mono].

Moscow Philharmonic Orchestra, RSFSR Academic Russian Chorus (Alexander Yurlov, chorus-master); conducted by Kirill Kondrashian, recorded in 1972. Melodiya: CM 03625-6 [LP]. Reissued in the United States as Angel Melodiya: SR 40236.

London Philharmonic Orchestra and Choir (John Alldis, chorus-master); conducted by Bernard Haitink, recorded in 1981. Decca: SXDL 7535 [digital LP], reissued as Decca: 421 131-2DH [DDD].

USSR Ministry of Culture Symphony Orchestra, Yurlov Republican Russian Choir (Rozaliya Peregudova (chorus-master); conducted by Gennadi Rozhdestvensky, recorded in 1984. Melodiya: A10 00119 002 [LP], reissued as Olympia: OCD 200 [ADD].

Royal Philharmonic Orchestra, Brighton Festival Chorus (Laszlo Heltay, chorus-master); conducted by Vladimir Ashkenazy, recorded in January 1989. London: D 103303 [DDD].

London Symphony Orchestra and London Voices; conducted by Mstislav Rostropovich. Teldec: 1156264 [DDD].

## Selected Bibliography

Lawson, Peter: "Shostakovich's Second Symphony," *Tempo*, no. 91 (winter 1969-70), 14-17.

Sabinina, Marina: *Shostakovich Sinfonist: Dramaturgiya, estetika, stil.* Moscow: Muzyka, 1976.

Ottaway, Hugh: *Shostakovich Symphonies*. London: BBC, 1978.

## Symphony No. 3, op. 20 (1929)

**Duration:** ca. 30 minutes

**Text:** The finale of this work features a choral setting of a poem by Semyon Kirsanov. It is in Russian.

**Performing Forces: voices:** SATB choir; **orchestra:** piccolo, 2 flutes, 2 oboes, 2 clarinets in B$^b$, 2 bassoons, 4 horns in F, 2 trumpets in B$^b$, 3 trombones, tuba, timpani, percussion (3 players - glockenspiel, xylophone, snare drum, bass drum, cymbals, gong, triangle), and strings.

**First Performance:** private concert: 21 January 1930; Moscow-Narva House of Culture, Leningrad; Leningrad Philharmonic Orchestra, Academy Capella Choir; conducted by Alexander Gauk.

official premiere: 6 November 1931; Leningrad; conducted by Alexander Gauk.

United States premiere: 30 December 1932; Philadelphia; Philadelphia Orchestra; conducted by Leopold Stokowski. This performance did not include the choral finale.

**Edition:** Symphony No. 3 is published by Mezhdunaradnaja Kniga. The full score is available for purchase in the first volume of the collected works. Performance materials are available through rental. This score is reprinted by Kalmus (A2032); all materials are available for purchase and orchestral materials are also available through rental. Following the dissolution of the Soviet Union, the Russian edition materials have come under the proprietorship of the Russian Authors Society for whom G. Schirmer serves as the U.S. agent.

**Autograph:** The manuscript is in the Russian Archives of Literature and Art in Moscow.

**Notes:** This work which is subtitled, "The First of May," celebrates the annual Day of International Labor.

**Performance Issues:** The choir appears only in the final quarter of the work. The choral material is melodically diatonic and scalar and is harmonically supported by the orchestra. The choral passages are exclusively in two-part textures.When all four sections of the choir sing together, the men's parts double the women's parts an octave lower. The string writing is idiomatic and lies well on the respective instruments. There is significant virtuosic passagework for all of the woodwinds. The tessitura of the trumpets is consistently high, especially the principal part. The score has a number of passages that feature rapid unison playing from the entire orchestra. There are also a number of quick synchopated homophonic sections which will demand careful attention for accurate ensemble playing. Some performances have deleted the final section, so as to avoid the chorus. If this were done, the work would conclude immediately before **98**, which is on a $B^b$ (The work ends in $E^b$); however, the choral material is so accessible that the deletion of the final section is difficult to justify. **Choir:** easy; **Orchestra:** difficult.

**Discography:** Leningrad Philharmonic Orchestra, Krupskaya Institute Chorus (Ivan Poltavtsev, chorus-master); conducted by Igor Blazhkov, recorded in 1964. Melodiya: D 017953-4 [LP mono]. Reissued in the United States as Angel Melodiya: SR 40099.

Royal Philharmonic Orchestra and Chorus (John McCarthy, chorus-master; Igor Buketoff, chorus-director); conducted by Morton Gould, recorded in 1968. RCA Victor: LSC 3044 [LP mono].

Moscow Philharmonic Orchestra, RSFSR Academic Russian Chorus (Alexander Yurlov, chorus-master); conducted by Kirill Kondrashian, recorded in 1972. Melodiya: CM 03625-6 [LP]. Reissued in the United States as Angel Melodiya: SR 40236.

London Philharmonic Orchestra and Choir (John Alldis, chorus-master); conducted by Bernard Haitink, recorded in 1981. Decca: SXDL 7535 digital LP], reissued as Decca: 421 131-2DH [DDD].

USSR Ministry of Culture Symphony Orchestra, Yurlov Republican Russian Choir (Rozaliya Peregudova (chorus-master); conducted by Gennadi Rozhdestvensky, recorded in 1984. Melodiya: A10 00119 002 [LP], reissued as Olympia: OCD 200 [ADD].

London Symphony Orchestra and London Voices; conducted by Mstislav Rostropovich. Teldec: 1156264 [DDD].

## Selected Bibliography

Calvocoressi, Michel Dmitri: "The First of May," *The Listener*, volume 15 (19 February 1936), 373.

Sabinina, Marina: *Shostakovich Sinfonist: Dramaturgiya, estetika, stil.* Moscow: Muzyka, 1976.

Ottaway, Hugh: *Shostakovich Symphonies.* London: BBC, 1978.

# The Song of the Forests [Pesn' o lesakh], op. 81 (1949)

**Duration:** ca. 33 minutes

**Text:** The text by Yevgeni Dolmatovsky is in Russian. A singing English translation has been prepared by Leo E. Christiansen.

**Performing Forces: voices:** tenor and bass soloists; SSAA boys' choir and SATB choir; **orchestra:** 3 flutes (flute III doubling piccolo), 2 oboes, English horn, 3 clarinets in $B^b$ and A, 2 bassoons, 4 horns in F, 3 trumpets in $B^b$, 3 trombones, tuba, timpani, percussion (4 players - glockenspiel, snare drum, cymbals, triangle), 2 harps, and strings.

The final movement has parts for an additional 6 trumpets in $B^b$ and 6 trombones.

**First Performance:** 15 November 1949; Vladimir Ivanovsky, Ivan Titov; Leningrad Philharmonic Bolshoi Hall, Leningrad; Leningrad Philharmonic Orchestra, Academy Choir; conducted by Yevgeni Mravinsky.

**Edition:** *The Song of the Forests* is published with a German text by Hinrichsen (P-4607) as *Das Lied von den Walden*. The piano-vocal score is available for purchase; orchestral materials are available through rental. An English singing translation is available as a piano-vocal score from Leeds Music. The full score is published in Russian by Muzgiz (no. 20914), and by Muzyka (full score - no. 11680, piano-vocal score - no. 11786). Following the dissolution of the Soviet Union, the Russian edition materials have come under the proprietorship of the Russian Authors Society for whom G. Schirmer serves as the U.S. agent.

**Autograph:** The manuscript is in the Russian Archives of Literature and Art in Moscow.

**Notes:** The text is written to proclaim a Soviet project of reforestation. It was awarded the Stalin Prize in 1950. The score was completed 15 August 1949. It is organized into seven sections as follows:

| I | When the war has ended | B soloist, ATB |
|---|---|---|
| II | Clothe the homeland with forests | SATB |
| III | Memories of the past | B soloist, SATB |
| IV | Pioneers plant the forests | boys' choir |
| V | Young Communists go forth | SATB |
| VI | A walk to the future | T soloist, SATB |
| VII | Slava—Glory | T and B soloists, boys' choir, SATB |

**Performance Issues:** The straightforward qualities of this score are, in part, a reaction to the 1948 Soviet decree against formalism in music. None-the-less, it is an attractive and impeccably well-crafted composition. There are two-part divisi for the top three sections of the choir. The basses have a three-part division in the first movement which includes a pedal C in the bottom part. Much of the choral singing is in unison or doubled two-part harmony. The remaining choral passages are homophonic in large block chords. All of the choral parts, for adults and children, are thoroughly reinforced by the orchestra. The orchestral parts are all written for strong players. There are numerous passages which are technically demanding for each section of the orchestra. The flute I part has some prominent solo passages. In the finale, the twelve extra brass players are two-on-a-part. The presence of two harps in the score is for balance as there is only one part, which they are to double. The final movement is quite bombastic and will require attention in order to achieve a musically satisfying balance. Because of this movement a large chorus and large children's chorus are mandatory. **Soloists:** tenor -range: f#-a', tessitura: f#-f', this role occurs in only two movements, it is declamatory and requires a voice capable of being heard over a large ensemble; bass -range: A-d', tessitura: c-c', this role appears throughout the work and requires a singer capable of being heard within a dense orchestral texture; **Choir:** medium easy; **Orchestra:** medium difficult.

**Discography:** I. Kilichevsky, Ivan Petrov; Moscow Philharmonic and Bolshoi Theater choirs and orchestras; conducted by Yevgeni Mravinsky, recorded in 1950. Recorded on 78s, this was rereleased in the United States as Colosseum: CRLP 118 [LP].

Vladimir Ivanovsky, Ivan Petrov; Moscow State Choral School Boys' Choir (Yuli Ulanov, chorus-master), RSFSR Academic Russian Choir, Moscow Philharmonic Orchestra; conducted by Alexander Yurlov, recorded in 1968. Melodiya: CM 02699-700 [LP]. Released in the United States as Angel Melodiya: SR 40214 [LP]; rereleased as Russian Disc: RD CD 11 048 [ADD].

Aleksei Maslennikov, Alexander Vedernikov; Moscow State Choral School Boys' Choir (Alexander Sveshnikov, chorus-master), Large Choir of Central Television and All-Union Radio (Klavdi Ptitsa, chorus-master), USSR Symphony Orchestra; conducted by Yevgeni Svetlanov, recorded 25 September 1978. Melodiya: C10 12415-6 [LP].

Royal Philharmonic Orchestra, Brighton Festival Chorus (Laszlo Heltay, chorus-master), New London Children's Choir (Ronald Corp, chorus-master); conducted by Vladimir Ashkenazy, recorded in January 1989. London: D 103303 [DDD].

### Selected Bibliography

Dolmatovsky, Yevgeni: "Music fills him to the brim," in *Dmitri Shostakovich: Articles and Materials*, 75. Moscow: 1976.

## The Sun Shines o'er Our Country [nad rodinoy nashey solntse siyayet], op. 90 (1952)

**Duration:** ca. 14 minutes

**Text:** The text by Yevgeni Dolmatovsky is in Russian.

**Performing Forces: voices:** SAA boys' choir and SATB choir; **orchestra:** piccolo, 2 flutes, 3 oboes, 3 clarinets in $B^b$, 2 bassoons, 4 horns in F, 3 trumpets in $B^b$, 3 trombones, tuba, timpani, percussion (3 players - glockenspiel, snare drum, cymbals, tam-tam, triangle), 2 harps, and strings.

The score calls for an additional band of 3 trumpets in $B^b$ and 3 trombones.

**First Performance:** 6 November 1952; Large Hall of the Moscow Conservatory.

**Edition:** The full-score of *The Sun Shines o'er Our Country* is published in Russian by Muzgiz (no. 20914), and by Muzyka (full score - no. 11680, piano-vocal score - no. 11786). Following the dissolution of the Soviet Union, the Russian edition materials have come under the proprietorship of the Russian Authors Society for whom G. Schirmer serves as the U.S. agent.

**Autograph:** The manuscript is in the possession of State Central Glinka Museum of Culture in Moscow.

**Notes:** The score was completed on 29 October 1952.

**Performance Issues:** Like *Songs of the Forests*, this score reflects Shostakovich's compliance with the 1948 Soviet decree against formalism in concert music, which remained dogmatically in effect until 1953 when Stalin died. There are two-part divisi for all of the choral parts and a brief section wherein the soprano part of the boy choir divides into two parts. All of the choral writing is either in unison or homophonic in large block chords. The choral parts are clearly supported by the accompanying instruments. The pitch material is diatonic throughout the work. The glockenspiel part is exposed and rather difficult. The presence of two harps in the score is for balance as there is only one part, which they double. The players in the brass band must play some long and highly exposed arpeggiated fanfares punctuated by  short bursts from the entire orchestra. The orchestra must make rapid and dramatic changes in dynamics. The principal brass section must be rhythmically concise and capable of clear articulations. There are a number of rapid unison passages between all of the winds and strings which will present some ensemble difficulties. This is a straightforward score best suited for a large symphonic choir. It is accessible to less-experienced vocal ensembles, but the orchestra is presented with a number of difficult passages for effective ensemble playing. **Choir:** medium easy; **Orchestra:** medium difficult.

**Discography:** RSFSR Russian Choirs, Moscow Philharmonic; conducted by Kirill Kondrashian. Melodiya: SR 40129 [LP].
Yurlov Russian Choir, USSR Symphony Orchestra; conducted by Konstantin Ivanov. Russian Disc: RD CD 11 048 [ADD].

## Selected Bibliography

Shostakovich, Dmitri: *Dmitri Shostakovich about Himself and His Time*, 140. Moscow: 1980.

# Symphony No. 13, "Babi Yar", op. 113 (1962)

**Duration:** ca. 60 minutes

**Text:** The text  by Yevgeny Yevtushenko is in Russian. The texts of movements 2, 3 and 5 were chosen from his collection, *A Wave of the Hand*; number 4 was penned at the composer's request; and "Babi Yar, the text of the first movement, was first published in the *Literaturnaya Gazeta*, 19 September 1961.

**Performing Forces: voices:** bass soloist; choir of bass voices; **orchestra:** piccolo, 2 flutes, 3 oboes (oboe III doubling English horn), 3 clarinets in B$^b$ and A (clarinet III doubling soprano clarinet in E$^b$ and bass clarinet in B$^b$), 3 bassoons (bassoon III doubling contrabassoon), 4 horns in F, 3 trumpets in B$^b$, 3 trombones, tuba, timpani, percussion (5 players - glockenspiel. xylophone, chime, snare drum, bass drum, tambourine, cymbals, tam-tam, triangle, rattle, castanets, whip, wood block), 2 to 4 harps, celeste, piano, and strings.

Shostakovich recommended a chorus of 40 to 100 bass voices, 16 to 20 violins I, 14 to 18 violins II, 12 to 16 violas, 12 to 16 cellos, and 10 to 14 doublebasses (indicating five-string doublebasses).

**First Performance:** 18 and 20 December 1962; Moscow Conservatory Bolshoi Hall; Vitali Gromadsky; basses of the Republican State and Gnessin Institute Choirs, Moscow Philharmonic Orchestra; conducted by Kirill Kondrashian.

**Edition:** Symphony No. 13 was initially engraved for publication by Muzyka in 1967, but its release was supressed by the Soviet government. The original version with a transliterated text is published by Leeds Music. The revised version is available for purchase from Kalmus (no. 528). Sikorski publishes an edition of the revised version with Russian and German texts. Muzyka publishes a revised edition from the *Collected Works*, which is available for purchase (full score - no. 10280, piano-vocal score - no. 11688). Following the dissolution of the Soviet Union, the Russian edition materials have come under the proprietorship of the Russian Authors Society for whom G. Schirmer serves as the U.S. agent. David Daniels lists the current publishing source as MCA.[34]

**Autograph:** The manuscript is in the possession of the Shostakovich family.

**Notes:** Shostakovich initially composed the first movement as a "symphonic poem" and then chose to use it as the beginning of a symphony. This is the first of his symphonies to use voices throughout. This work is organized as follows:

    I   Adagio — "Babi Yar"
    II  Allegretto — "Humor"
    III Adagio — "Women"
    IV  Largo — "Fears"
    V   Allegretto — "Career"

"Babi Yar" is a memorial to the Jews who were exterminated by the Nazis in 1941 at Babi Yar in Kiev. It came under some governmental criticism for isolating the plight of the Jews specifically when so many Russians of various backgrounds had died during the war.

**Performance Issues:** This score is metrically straightforward and while it is chromatically dissonant, the pitch material is generated along the lines of the common practice period. The choir is entirely in unison with the exception of the final sung note of the third movement which breaks into a three-note chord with the bottom pitch being pedal C. With the exception of this spot, the range of the choir is F# to e'. The choral writing is folk-like, being diatonically melodic and rhythmically simple. The vocal parts are not doubled by the orchestra, but the harmonic structure of the vocal line is always supported by the accompaniment. The chimes use the old-fashioned bass-clef notation. The orchestra parts are all

---

[34] David Daniels: *Orchestral Music: A Handbook*, third edition. Lanham, Maryland: Scarecrow Press, 1996.

technically demanding. The brass parts will present a challenge to the players' endurance. All four players of the horn section are featured prominently throughout the score. There is significant chromatic passagework for all of the woodwinds. The score calls for five-stringed basses, but a low CC extension is all that is required. The choral sections of this composition are well within the abilities of amateur choirs and men's glee club; however, the orchestral demands require a strong and experienced ensemble. This work would provide an opportunity for a professional orchestra to feature an amateur men's vocal ensemble. It is important to have at the very least, sixty singers. **Soloist:** bass - range: G-e'; tessitura: f-d', this role is featured prominently throughout the symphony, it requires a declamatory and dramatic voice; **Choir:** medium easy; **Orchestra:** difficult.

**Discography:** revised version: Vitali Gromadsky; RSFSR Academic Russian Choir (Alexander Yurlov, chorus-master), Moscow Philharmonic Orchestra; conducted by Kirill Kondrashian, recorded 20 November 1965.

Ruggero Raimondi; Rome RAI Symphony Orchestra and Male Chorus (Gianni Lazzari, chorus-master); conducted by Riccardo Muti, recorded 31 January 1970. Memories: HR 4101 [LP].

Artur Eizen; RSFSR Academic Russian Choir (Alexander Yurlov, chorus-master), Moscow Philharmonic Orchestra; conducted by Kirill Kondrashian, recorded in 1971. Melodiya: CM 02905-6 [LP]. Released in the United States as Angel Melodiya: SR 40212.

original version:

Tom Krause; Male Chorus of the Mendelssohn Club (Robert Page, chorus-master), Philadelphia Orchestra; conducted by Eugene Ormandy, recorded in January 1970. RCA Red Seal: LSC 3162 [LP].

Dimitre Petkov; Male Voice of the London Symphony Chorus (Richard Hickox, chorus-master), London Symphony Orchestra; conducted by André Previn, recorded 5 and 6 July 1979. HMV: ASD 3911 [LP].

John Shirley-Quirk; Bavarian Radio Male Chorus and Symphony; conducted by Kirill Kondrashian, recorded December 1980. Philips: LP 6514 120 [digital LP].

Marius Rintzler; Male Voice of the Concertgebouw Orchestra Chorus, Concertgebouw Orchestra; conducted by Bernard Haitink. Decca: 414 410-1DH2 [digital LP].

Anatoli Safiulin; Basses of the Yurlov Republican Russian Choir (Stanisleav Gusev, chorus director; Veniamin Kapitonov and Vladimir Sorokin, chorus-masters), Ministry of Culture Symphony Orchestra; conducted by Gennadi Rozhdestvensky. Melodiya: A10 00285 000 [digita LP], rereleased as Olympia: OCD 132 [DDD]. This recording includes a 22-minute interview, in Russian, with Yevtushenko.

Nikita Storojev; Men of the CBSO Chorus, City of Birmingham Choir, and the University of Warwick Chorus, City of Birmingham Symphony Orchestra; conducted by Okko Kamu, recorded 9 and 10 January 1987. Chandos: CHAN 8540 [DDD].

Nicola Ghiuselev; Men of the Choral Arts Society of Washington, National Symphony Orchestra; conducted by Mstislav Rostropovich, recorded in the Kennedy Center, Washington, DC, in January 1988. Erato: ECD 75529 [DDD].

Sergei Leiferkus; Men of the New York Choral Artists (Joseph Flummerfelt, chorus-master), New York Philharmonic; conducted by Kurt Masur, recorded in Avery Fisher Hall, New York, in January 1993. Teldec: D 145139 [DDD]. This "live" recording also includes a recording of the text recited by the author, Yevgeny Yevtushenko.

Film Soundtrack:

*Testimony Motion Picture Soundtrack.* John Shirley-Quirk; The Golden Age Singers, London Philharmonic Orchestra; conducted by Rudolf Barshai, recorded in 1987. Released on CD by Virgin: V2536 [DDD]. This recording includes an abbreviated version of the first movement, sung in English.

## Selected Bibliography

Ordzhonokidze, Givi: "Symphony No. 13," in *Dmitri Shostakovich*, edited by Vasilievich Danilevich. Moscow: Sovetskii Kompozitor, 1967.

Vishnevskaya, Galina: *Galina: A Russian Story*, translated by Guy Daniels, 349-61. London: Hodder and Stoughton, 1975.

Sabinina, Marina: *Shostakovich Sinfonist: Dramaturgiya, estetika, stil.* Moscow: Muzyka, 1976.

Ottaway, Hugh: *Shostakovich Symphonies*. London: BBC, 1978.

Shostakovich, Dmitri: *Dmitri Shostakovich: About Himself and His Time*, edited by L. Grigoryev and Y. Platek. Moscow: Progress, 1980.

# The Execution of Stepan Razin [Kazn' Stepana Razina], op. 119 (1964)

**Duration:** ca. 30 minutes

**Text:** The text, from *The Bratsk Hydro-electric Power Station* by Yevgeny Yevtushenko, is in Russian.

**Performing Forces:** **voices:** bass soloist; SATB choir; **orchestra:** piccolo, 2 flutes, 2 oboes, English horn, soprano clarinet in E$^b$, 2 clarinets in B$^b$ and A, bass clarinet in B$^b$, 2 bassoons, contrabassoon, 4 horns in F, 3 trumpets in B$^b$, 3 trombones, tuba, timpani, percussion (4 players - chimes, xylophone, snare drum, bass drum, tambourine, cymbals, tam-tam, triangle, whip) , 2 harps, celeste, piano, and strings (20 violins I, 18 violins II, 16 violas, 14 cellos, and 12 doublebasses).

Shostakovich indicated that there must be at least two harp players. The score also indicates the need for five-stringed doublebasses, but a four-stringed instrument with a low CC extension is all that is needed.

**First Performance:** 28 December 1964; Moscow Conservatory Bolshoi Hall; Vitali Gromadsky; RSFSR Academic Russian Choir, Moscow Philharmonic Orchestra; conducted by Kirill Kondrashian. This concert was repeated 10 January 1965 in the Minsk Philharmonic Concert Hall.

**Edition:** *The Execution of Stepan Razin* is published by MCA with a singing English translation made by Harold Heiberg. Sikorski published an edition with a German singing translation. The piano-vocal score, prepared by Carl A. Rosenthal, is available for purchase; orchestral materials are available through rental. The score is also available as part of the *Collected Works* from Muzyka (full score - no. 11680, piano-vocal score - no. 11786). Following the dissolution of the Soviet Union, the Russian edition materials have come under the proprietorship of the Russian Authors Society for whom G. Schirmer serves as the U.S. agent.

**Autograph:** The manuscript is in the Russian Archives of Literature and Art in Moscow.

**Notes:** Stepan Razin was a Russian dissident from Volga who rose up against the Czar in the 17th century. This score was awarded the Glinka State Prize in 1968.

**Performance Issues:** The indication of five-string doublebasses is to guarantee that a low CC be available. Shostakovich doubled the single harp part to ensure that it would be audible within this large orchestral palette. While this is more chromatic than most of Shostakovich's symphonic choral works, the vocal material is tuneful with its melodic material being triadic and/or scalar. There are a number of large choral glissandi between a sixth and an octave wide in parallel block harmonies. All of the choral material is supported by the accompanying instruments. Most of the choral writing is in two-part harmonies doubled in octaves between the men and women. The individual orchestral parts present some technical challenges within each section. The greatest challenges are in achieving overall ensemble. There are many sections which require short explosive gestures from the entire ensemble within a varied rhythmic scheme. The celeste has a number of important passages which may not project successfully within this large orchestra. The design of the work requires a very large chorus. This is another work, among the many by Soviet composers, which is suitable for a large amateur vocal ensemble, but which requires a professional-level orchestra. Unlike many of those other works, this benefits from a text which is suitable for use outside the realm of political propoganda. **Soloist:** bass - range: c-f', tessitura: a-d', this is a powerful and declamatory role which remains within the listed perfect-fourth tessitura throughout most of the work; **Choir:** medium easy; **Orchestra:** difficult.

**Discography:** premiere performance: Vitali Gromadsky; RSFSR Academic Russian Choir (Alexander Yurlov, chorus-master), Moscow Philharmonic Orchestra; conducted by Kirill Kondrashian. Melodiya: D 016471-2 [LP]. Released in the United States as Angel Melodiya: SR 40000.

Bohus Hanák; Slovák Philharmonic Orchestra and Chorus; conducted by Ladislav Slovák, recorded in 1968. Supraphon: SUA 10958 [LP].

Siegfried Vogel; Leipzig Radio Symphony Orchestra and Choir; conducted by Herbert Kegel, recorded in 1973. Philips Universo: 6585 012 [LP].

## Selected Bibliography

Shlifshteyn, Semyon: *"The Execution of Stepan Razin* and the traditions of Mussorgsky," in *Dmitri Shostakovich*, edited by Vasilievich Danilevich. Moscow: Sovetskii Kompozitor, 1967.

## Stravinsky, Igor (b. Oranienbaum, Russia, 17 June 1882; d. New York, 6 April 1971)

**Life:** Stravinsky is the most celebrated composer of the 20th century. The frequent changes in the character of his works perpetually reset the stylistic direction of music in the modern era. Stravinsky's father was a bass in the St. Petersburg Opera. Igor studied piano and harmony privately while he attended St. Petersburg University as a law student. He later became a private pupil of Nikolai Rimsky-Korsakov. His *Fireworks* attracted the attention of Sergei Diaghilev who contracted Stravinsky as a staff arranger for his Ballets Russes in Paris. When Liadov failed to submit a score for a proposed ballet, *The Firebird*, the commission was given to Stravinsky. *The Firebird* (1910) was an immediate success and was followed by *Pétrouchka* (1911) and the *Rite of Spring* (1913). The celebrated scandal created by the premiere of the latter is one of the most significant events in the history of western music. With these three ballets, Stravinsky had established himself as one of the most progressive and recognized composers of the time. Following World War I, Stravinsky, who had weathered the war in Switzerland, could not return to his homeland, where his family's estate had been seized by the Soviets. During this time, he began to explore methods of producing works for smaller ensembles and with sparser orchestration. He also began to explore elements of American jazz and European Baroque music in some of his works. During the 1920s and 1930s he integrated the structures, tonal centricities, and melodic features of the Classical period with the odd-legged rhythms and unresolved dissonances of the Modern era in a style which came to be known as neo-Classicism. Upon the advent of World War II, Stravinsky settled in the United States, living in New York and California, becoming a citizen in 1945. In the United States he established a fruitful collaborative relationship with the choreographer, George Balanchine. He later befriended the conductor and composer, Robert Craft, with whom he published numerous interviews, and who conducted many of Stravinsky's late works. Stravinsky had been outspoken against serialism until Schoenberg's death, at which time, he began composing works which used various serial methods. In 1962,

Stravinsky toured the Soviet Union where he was warmly received. Upon his death in New York, his remains were flown to Venice where he is buried in the Greek section of the cemetery island of San Michele next to his second wife, Vera (1893-1982) and near Diaghilev.

**Writings:** *Chroniques de ma vie.* Paris: 1936; revised and translated into English as: *An Autobiography.* New York: W.W. Norton, 1975. The Poetics of Music. Cambridge, MA: Harvard University Press, 1947.

With Robert Craft: *Conversations with Igor Stravinsky.* New York: Alfred A. Knopf, 1959. *Memories and Commentaries.* New York: Alfred A. Knopf, 1960. *Dialogues and a Diary.* New York: Alfred A. Knopf, 1961. *Expositions and Developments.* New York: Alfred A. Knopf, 1962. *Themes and Episodes.* New York: Alfred A. Knopf, 1966. *Retrospectives and Conclusions.* New York: Alfred A. Knopf, 1969.

**Principal Works:** *operas* - *Le Rossignol* (1914), *Renard* (1916), *Mavra* (1922), *Œdipus Rex* (1927), *The Rake's Progress* (1951); *ballets* - *The Firebird* (1910), *Pétrouchka* (1911), *Le Sacre du printemps* [Rite of Spring] (1913), *L'Histoire du soldat* (1918), *Pulcinella* (1920), *Les Noces* (1923), *Apollon Musagète* (1928), *Le Baiser de la fée* (1928), *Jeu des cartes* (1937), *Orpheus* (1947), *Agon* (1957); *orchestral* - *Fireworks*, op. 4 (1908), *Symphonies of Wind Instruments* (1920), *Dumbarton Oaks* (1938), Symphony in C (1940), *Circus Polka* (1942), Scherzo à la russe (1944), Symphony in 3 Movements (1945), *Ebony Concerto* (1945), *Variations: Aldous Huxley, In Memoriam* (1964); *chamber* - *Ragtime* (1918), Octet for Wind Instruments (1923); *piano* - Sonata (1924), Serenade in A (1925), Concerto for 2 Solo Pianos (1935), Sonata for 2 Pianos (1944); *vocal* - *Zvezdoliki* [King of the Stars] (1912), *Pribaoutki* (1914), *Pater Noster* (1926), *Symphony of Psalms* (1930), *Credo* (1932), *Perséphone* (1933), *Ave Maria* (1934), *Babel* (1944), *In Memoriam Dylan Thomas* (1954), *Canticum Sacrum* (1956), *Threni* (1958), *A Sermon, a Narrative, and a Prayer* (1962), *Elegy for J.F.K.* (1964), *Abraham and Isaac* (1964), *Introitus: T.S. Eliot in Memoriam* (1965), *Requiem Canticles* (1966), *The Owl and the Pussycat* (1966).

## Selected Composer Bibliography

Sutherland, Donald A.: *Stravinsky's Major Choral Works.* University of Michigan: Master's of Arts thesis, 1961.

Dale, Troy Lee, Jr.: *A Study of Igor Stravinsky as a Choral Composer.* Texas A. and M. University: Master's of Music Education thesis, 1965.

Harlow, Barbara Jean: *A Stylistic Analysis of the Choral Treatment of Igor Stravinsky.* California State University, Fullerton: Master's of Arts thesis, 1970.

Craft, Robert: *Stravinsky: Chronicle of a Friendship, 1948/1971.* New York: Alfred A. Knopf, 1972.

Stravinsky, Vera and Robert Craft: *Stravinsky: In Pictures and Documents.* New York: Simon and Schuster, 1978.

White, Eric Walter: *Stravinsky: the Composer and his Works.* Berkeley, California: University of California Press, 1966; revised and enlarged second edition, 1979.

Heintze, James R.: *Igor Stravinsky: An International Bibliography of Theses and Dissertations, 1925-78,* Detroit Studies in Music Bibliography, Number 61. Warren, MI: Harmonic Park Press, 1988.

# Svadebka—Les Noces [The Wedding] (1914-17, orchestrated 1921-23)

**Duration:** ca. 35 minutes

**Text:** Stravinsky derived these texts from traditional Russian folk-tales. The French version was prepared by C. F. Ramuz.

**Performing Forces: voices:** soprano, mezzo-soprano, tenor and bass soloists; 8-part mixed choir; **orchestra:** 4 pianos, percussion (5 players - timpani, xylophone, 1 bell (pitched b'), tambourine, triangle, 2 cymbals, 2 side drums, 2 drums, bass drum, crotales (c# and b)).

**First Performance:** 13 June 1923; Théâtre de la Gaieté Lyrique, Paris; Russian Ballet; conducted by Ernest Ansermet.

**Edition:** *Svadebka* is published by J. & W. Chester Ltd. and available in reprint from Kalmus. The piano-vocal score, choral parts, full score, and instrumental parts are available for purchase. This score contains singing texts for Russian and French.

**Autograph: The** J. & W. Chester Ltd., 1917 version was in the possession of Stiftung Rychenberg, Winterthur. The Stravinsky

Archive is in the possession of the Paul Sacher Foundation in Basle, Switzerland.

**Notes:** The score is dedicated to Serge Diaghilev. *Svadebka* was scored for full orchestra and singers in 1917, but Stravinsky was not satisfied with this combination, so he scored the 1923 version, which is the accepted final instrumentation. There is a certain element of primitivism in this score that reflects not only the rustic setting of the text, but also developments in music in Europe at this time. Works which would follow in the wake of *Svadebka* include Orff's *Carmina Burana* and Anteil's *Ballet Mechanique*. The work is organized as follows:

Part One

| | |
|---|---|
| Scene 1 | "At the Bride's House" |
| Scene 2 | "At the Bridegroom's House" |
| Scene 3 | "The Bride's Departure" |

Part Two

| | |
|---|---|
| Scene 4 | "The Wedding Feast" |

**Performance Issues:** This work is theatrical in conception, but works very well as a concert piece. Although the 1923 score is the composer's preferred version, there has been renewed interest in the 1917 version for full orchestra which has resulted in some performances and at least one recording (see Hungaraton: HCD-12989, below). In preparing for a performance of this work, an investigation into the original version may be helpful in determining some articulation choices. The choice of language is also an important issue to resolve. Robert Craft states that because the work is so deeply rooted in the traditions of Russian folk music, and so logogenic from its original Russian text, that this is the only satisfactory language for performance[35]; however, in the composer's own recording English was used so that it remained in the vernacular of the principal audience. The score is very rhythmic with frequent changes of meter, including the value of the beat unit. The pitch material for the singers is modally inflected, but diatonic. The accompaniment is generally supportive of the vocal

---

[35] Robert Craft: "*Svadebka*: An Introduction," *Stravinsky: Glimpses of a Life*, 335-357. New York: St. Martin's Press, 1992.

harmonies, although there are a significant number of passages wherein the choir and orchestra are in seconds with each other. The vocal rhythms are speech driven and much of the vocal material is quite comfortable from a singer's perspective. The singers must articulate rapid passages much more often than sustaining prolonged harmonies. At rehearsal 50, there is a brief solo for a "basso profundo from the choir" with a range of F to f. The percussion parts are technically quite accessible, but integrating them into the score will require some attention. The score is quite clear in assigning instruments to players. All four piano parts are quite challenging. Four instruments are required. A number of rehearsals should be planned with the pianists alone. The articulate nature of the score and the sonority of the instrumental contingent, suggests the use of a small choral ensemble of 16 to 24 members. **Soloists:** soprano - range: e'-b", tessitura: b'-g", much of this role is folk-like with a narrow and sustained tessitura; mezzo-soprano - range: a-f#", tessitura: e'-e", this is an articulate role with little sustained singing; tenor - range: c-a', tessitura: f-f', this is a declamatory role with many sustained high passages; bass - range: A-f#' (g' in falsetto), tessitura: d-d', this role has a number of falsetto passages and is generally declamatory; **Choir:** difficult; **Orchestra:** difficult.

**Discography:** Steingruber, Kenney, Wagner, Waechter; Vienna Chamber Choir; conducted by Rossi. Vanguard: VRS 452 [LP].

Addison, Okerson, Price, Burrows; Concert Choir; conducted by Margaret Hillis. Vox: PL 8630 [LP].

Mildred Allen, Regina Sarfaty, Loren Driscoll, Robert Oliver; American Concert Choir (Margaret Hillis, chorus-master); Columbia Percussion Ensemble; Samuel Barber, Aaron Copland, Lukas Foss, and Roger Sessions, pianists; (English) conducted by Igor Stravinsky, recorded in Hollywood, California on 21 December 1959. Sony Classical—Stravinsky Edition, volume 1: SM3K 46291 [ADD].

Ablaberdyeva, Ivanova, Martinov, Saflulin; Amadinda Percussion Ensemble, Savaria Symphony, Slovak Philharmonic Chorus (Russian); conducted by Eötvös. Hungaroton: HCD-12989 [DDD] Both 1917 and 1923 versions.

Jacqueline Brumaire, Denise Scharley, Jacques Pottier, José Van Dam; Orchestra and Chorus of the Théâtre Nationale Opera ; Geneviève Joy, Ina Marika, Jacques Delécluze, and Michel Quéval, pianists; (French) conducted by Pierre Boulez. Nonesuch: H-71133 [LP].

Mory, Parker, Mitchison, Hudson; English Bach Festival Orchestra and Chorus (Russian); conducted by Leonard Bernstein. DG: 423251-2 GC [ADD].

Quercia, Cooper, Capelle, Marinov; Strasbourg Percussion Ensemble Contemporaine; conducted by Hayrabedian. Pierre Vernay: PV-787032 [DDD].

## Selected Bibliography

Lindlar, H.: "Christ-kultische Elemente in Stravinskys Bauernhochzeit," *Melos* , volume 25 (1958), 63.

Stravinsky, Igor and Robert Craft: "Svadebka (Les Noces): An Instrumentation," *Retrospectives and Conclusions*, 117-122. New York: Alfred A. Knopf, 1969.

Imbrie, Andrew: "One Measure of Eternity," *Perspectives in New Music*, volume 9, number 2 - volume 10, number 1 (1971), 51.

Nijinska, Bronislava: *Création des "Noces,"* Gontcharov and Larionov, editors. Paris: T. Loguine, 1971.

Jackson, Isaiah Allen: *Changes: A Study of Stravinsky's Successive Re-Orchestrations of Firebird and Les Noces*. Juilliard School of Music: Ph.D. dissertation, 1973.

Craft, Robert: "Stravinsky's Svadebka," *Prejudices in Disguise*, 243. New York: Alfred A. Knopf, 1974.

_____: "Svadebka: An Introduction," *Stravinsky: Glimpses of a Life*, 335-357. New York: St. Martin's Press, 1992.

Stravinsky, Vera and Robert Craft: *Stravinsky: In Pictures and Documents*, 144-166. New York: Simon and Schuster, 1978.

White, Eric Walter: *Stravinsky: the Composer and his Works*, 250-261. Berkeley, California: University of California Press, 1966; revised and enlarged second edition, 1979.

Weinstock, Stephen Jay: "The Evolution of Les Noces," *Dance Magazine*, volume 15, number 4 (1981), 70.

_____: *Independence Versus Interdependence in Stravinsky's Theatrical Collaborations: The Evolution of the Original Production of The Wedding*. University of California, Berkeley: Ph.D. dissertation, 1982.

Newby, David L.: *Referential Pitch Structures in Igor Stravinsky's Les Noces*. Indiana University: Master's of Music thesis, 1984.

Jones, David, L.: *Igor Stravinsky's Les Noces: A Comparative Study of the 1917, 1919, and 1923 Versions*. University of Western Ontario: Master's of Arts thesis, 1987.

# Œdipus Rex (1926-27)

**Duration:** ca. 50 minutes

**Text:** The text is an adaptation of Sophocles made by Stravinsky and Jean Cocteau translated into Latin by Jean Daniélou. The narration is to be given in the vernacular of the audience. There is a complete English translation prepared by E.E. Cummings.

**Performing Forces:** voices: soloists: Œdipus - tenor, Jocasta - mezzo-sopano, Creon - bass-baritone, Tiresias - bass, Shepherd - tenor, Messenger - baritone, narrator; men's choir; **orchestra:** 3 flutes (flute III doubling piccolo), oboes, English horn, 3 clarinets in B$^b$ and A (clarinet III doubling E$^b$ soprano clarinet), 2 bassoons, contrabassoon, 4 horns in F, 4 trumpets in C, 3 trombones, tuba, timpani, percussion (2 players - snare drum, bass drum, tambourine, cymbals), piano, harp, and strings.

**First Performance:** 30 May 1927; Théâtre Sarah-Bernhardt, Paris; Ballets Russes, conducted by the composer.

**Edition:** *Œdipus Rex* was first published by Editions Russe, it is now available from Boosey and Hawkes. The piano-vocal score, choral score, and miniature score are available for purchase; orchestral materials are available through rental.

**Autograph:** The full score is with Boosey and Hawkes and the vocal manuscript is in the Library of Congress. The Stravinsky Archive is in the possession of the Paul Sacher Foundation in Basle, Switzerland.

**Notes:** The piano-vocal score was completed 14 March 1927, and the full score 10 May. Written as a twentieth-anniversary gift to the Diaghilev Ballet, it was revised in 1948. The initial performances of *Œdipus Rex* did not meet with much critical success, but the passage of time and successive performances have proven it to be one of the most significant symphonic works for men's choir.

In *Dialogues*, Stravinsky indicates that the narrator was Cocteau's idea, and that he felt that it presents problems of continuity. *Œdipus Rex* is subtitled, an "Opera-Oratorio in Two Acts after Sophocles." It was premiered as a concert work, but was first performed as an opera nine months later in Vienna on 23 February

1928. Stravinsky, in his *Dialogues*, suggests that the work is more successful when staged. The score also indicates that the roles of Creon and the Messenger may be sung by the same person. It is organized as follows:

## Act One

I. Speaker's Commentary

| | |
|---|---|
| "Cædit nos pestis" | choir |
| "Œdipus, adest pestis" | choir |
| "Liberi vos liberabo" | Œdipus |
| "Serva nos adhuc" | choir |
| "Uxoris frater" | Œdipus |
| "Vale, Creo!" | choir |

II. Speaker's Commentary

| | |
|---|---|
| "Respondit deus" | Creon |
| "Non reperias" | Œdipus |
| "Solve, Œdipus" | choir |

III. Speaker's Commentary

| | |
|---|---|
| "Delie, exspectamus" | choir |
| "Salve, Tiresia" | choir |
| "Invidia fortunam odit" | Œdipus |
| "Gloria" | choir |

## Act Two

IV. "Gloria" (repeated) — choir

Speaker's Commentary

| | |
|---|---|
| "Nonn'erubescite" | Jocasta |
| "Laius in Trivio" | Jocasta and choir |
| "Pavesco subito" | Œdipus and choir |
| "Ego senem cecidi" | Œdipus |
| Duet | Jocasta and Œdipus |
| "Volo consulere" | Jocasta, Œdipus and choir |

V. Speaker's Commentary

| | |
|---|---|
| "Adest omniscius pastor" | choir |
| "Mortuus est Polybus" | Messenger |
| "Falsus pater" | Messenger and choir |
| "Reppereram in monte" | Messenger |
| "Resciturus sum" | choir |
| "A patre, a matre" | Shepherd |
| "In monte reppertus est" | Shepherd, Messenger and choir |
| "Natus sum" | Œdipus |

VI. Speaker's Commentary - intercut with trumpet fanfares

| | |
|---|---|
| "Divum Jocastae" I | Messenger |
| "Mulier in vestibulo" | choir |
| "Divum Jocastae" II | Messenger |
| "Et ubi evellit" | choir |
| "Divum Jocastae" III | Messenger |
| "Sanguis ater" | choir |
| "Divum Jocastae" IV | Messenger |
| "Ecce regem" | choir |
| "Ellum regem" | choir |
| "Adest ellum" | choir |
| "Vale Œdipus" | choir |

**Performance Issues:** This is one of the first of Stravinsky's "neo-classical" works. The harmonic language is very similar to that of his *Symphony of Psalms*; however, here the texture of the vocal writing is less contrapuntally complex. The choral parts are divided in various ways, the largest being TTBB. The choral material is well conceived for the voices and in general the pitch material is clearly supported by the orchestra, but there are some brief *a cappella* passages. Much of the choral writing is homophonic, written in unison, octaves, or thirds. The few imitative sections are in two-part counterpoint. Virtually all of the instrumental parts have exposed soloistic passages. While there is some intricate passagework for the strings, especially the cellos and basses, it is idiomatically conceived and lies well on the instruments. Much of the writing for the woodwinds is more technically demanding and less idiomatic. There are difficult passages for all of the brass, but those for the principal horn are particularly treacherous. The trumpets have a number of fanfares which remain very high in their range. Although the percussion parts are nominal and do not require technically skilled players, the timpanist must be experienced as there are frequent and difficult pitch changes and a number of highly exposed passages. Among many divisi for the strings, there are parts for four solo cello players accompanied by a fifth line for the remaining cellists. **Soloists:** Œdipus - range: $e^b$-a', tessitura: a-f', this is a difficult, lyrical, and declamatory role which could be effectively performed by a young singer; Jocasta - range: a-a", tessitura: e'-e", this role suggests a powerful voice capable of sustained power in the lower range; Creon - range: $A^b$-f', tessitura: c-c', this role requires a powerful voice capable of sustaining long lines; Tiresias - range: F#-d', tessitura: A-a, this role is slow and declamatory, but not vocally challenging; the Shepherd - range: e-g', tessitura: g-f', the accompaniment of this solo is very light suggesting a more delicate voice than the other roles, it is quite chromatic with some awkward leaps; the Messenger - range: A-e', tessitura: f-d', this role is fairly short, but requires a singer who is musically independent as much of the solo is not directly supported by the accompaniment; **Choir:** moderately difficult; **Orchestra:** difficult.

**Discography:** Martha Mödl, Peter Pears, Heinz Rehfuss; Jean Cocteau, speaker; Cologne Radio Symphony Orchestra; conducted by Igor Stravinsky. Columbia: ML 4644 [LP].

Shirley Verrett. George Shirley, Loren Driscoll, Donald Gramm, Chester Watson, John Reardon; John Westbrook, narrator; Chorus and Orchestra of the Opera Society of Washington, D.C.; conducted by Igor Stravinsky, recorded in Washington on 20 January 1961. Sony Classical—Stravinsky Edition, volume 10: SM2K 46 300 [ADD].

Jesse Norman, Thomas Moser, Siegmund Nimsgern, Peter Bracht; Bavarian Radio Symphony and Chorus; conducted by Colin Davis. Orfeo: C-071831 [DDD].

video tape

Felicity Palmer, Neil Rosenheim, Claudio Desderi, Anton Scharinger; Jean Rochefort, speaker; Columbia Symphony Orchestra; conducted by Robert Craft. Produced in 1984, RM Arts Home Vision [VHS].

236  A Conductor's Guide to Choral-Orchestral Works, volume II

## Selected Bibliography

Cocteau, Jean: "La collaboration Œdipus rex," *La revue musicale*, number 212 (1952), 51 [special issue].

Weissmann, J. S.: Review of I. Stravinsky: Œdipus Rex , *The Music Review*, volume 13 (1952).

Mellers, Wilfred: "Stravinsky's Œdipus as 20th-century Hero," *Musical Quarterly*, volume 48 (1962), 300.

Zinar, Ruth E.: *Greek Tragedy in the Theatre Pieces of Stravinsky and Milhaud*. New York University: Ph.D. dissertation, 1968.

Dick, William Joe: *An Analysis of the Rhythmic Construction of Stravinsky's Œdipus Rex*. University of Texas: Master's of Music thesis, 1968.

Newman, Elaine Waxgiser: *Hero and Anti-Hero: The Œdipus Tyrannus of Sophocles in Twentieth-Century Music*. Case Western Reserve: Ph.D. dissertation, 1973.

Hirsbrunner, T.: "Ritual und Spiel in Igor Stravinskys Œdipus Rex," *Schweizerische Musikzeitung*, volume 117 (1974).

Armanini, Ronald: *A Study of Jean Cocteau's Collaboration with Igor Stravinsky in the Composition of Œdipus Rex*. Long Island University: Master's of Arts thesis, 1977.

Hansen, M.: "Igor Stravinskys 'Œdipus Rex,'" *Musik und Gesellschaft*, volume 28 (1978), 329.

Stravinsky, Vera and Robert Craft: *Stravinsky: In Pictures and Documents*, 264-272. New York: Simon and Schuster, 1978.

White, Eric Walter: *Stravinsky: the Composer and his Works*, 327-339. Berkeley, California: University of California Press, 1966; revised and enlarged second edition, 1979.

Möller, Dieter: *Jean Cocteau und Igor Stravinsky: Untersuchunger zur Ästhetik und zu Œdipus Rex*. Hamburg: Musikalienhandlung Wagner, 1981.

Vinay, G.: "Da 'Œdipus' a 'Œdipus rex' e ritorno: un itinerario metrico," *Rivista italiana di musicologia*, volume 17 (1982).

Craft, Robert: "Œdipus Rex, Perséphone, Zvezdoliki," *Stravinsky: Glimpses of a Life*, 383-395. New York: St. Martin's Press, 1992.

Walsh, Stephen: *Stravinsky: Œdipus rex*. Cambridge: Cambridge University Press, 1994.

# Symphony of Psalms (1930)

**Duration:** ca. 23 minutes

**Text:** The text is taken from the Book of Psalms in the Vulgate (Latin) Bible. The composer has insisted that it only be sung in Latin.

**Performing Forces: voices:** SATB choir; **orchestra:** 5 flutes (flute V doubling piccolo), 4 oboes, English horn, 3 bassoons, contrabassoon, 4 horns in F, trumpet in D, 4 trumpets in C, 2 tenor trombones, bass trombone, tuba, timpani, percussion (1 player - bass drum), harp, 2 pianos, cellos and doublebasses.

The composer has indicated that he would prefer the use of children's voices for the soprano and alto parts.

**First Performance:** actual first performance: 13 December 1930; Brussels. intended first performance: 19 December 1930; Boston; Boston Symphony Orchestra, conducted by Serge Koussevitsky. Since this work was commissioned to celebrate the 50th anniversary of the Boston Symphony, they were supposed to give the premiere, but illness postponed Koussevitsky's performance by a week.

**Edition:** *Symphony of Psalms* is published by Boosey and Hawkes. The piano-vocal score (LCB 13), full score (FSB 102), and miniature score (HPS 637) are available for purchase; orchestral materials are available through rental.

**Autograph:** The Stravinsky Archive is in the possession of the Paul Sacher Foundation in Basle, Switzerland.

**Notes:** The score is inscribed "This symphony, composed to the glory of God, is dedicated to the Boston Symphony Orchestra on the occasion of the fiftieth anniversary of its existence." The work is divided into three progressively longer movements, performed without break from the Vulgate psalm texts as follows:

    I    Psalm 38, verses 13 and 14
    II   Psalm 39, verses 2, 3, and 4
    III  Psalm 150, all

For reference, it should be noted that the numbering of the Vulgate psalter differs from that used in most other editions. The numbering in the King James Bible is psalms 39, 40, and 150.

**Performance Issues:**  This work is tonally centered and utilizes an assortment of traditional imitative techniques including canon and fugue. The choral writing is generally diatonic and aurally accessible. There are no divisi for the singers. Each section of the choir has exposed melodic material. For the tenors this is often in the upper range. There are a number of ostinato sections in which the sopranos sing in the passaggio range for a prolonged period of time, which will begin to wreak havoc with the intonation. The choral material is reinforced by the accompaniment. It is not always doubled directly, but there is conspicuous harmonic support. The exception to this is the reoccurring *a cappella* "alleluia" motto in the last movement, which stands on its own. The orchestral writing is melodically conceived and idiomatic, and all players have integral and exposed passages. The large fugue in the second movement will require careful attention to maintain clarity between parts. The orchestration of this work and the voicing of the harmonies within the score present numerous challenges to intonation. The brass parts are all articulate and technically demanding. The horns I and III have some very high passages, as do the trumpet I and trumpet in D. The strongest of the trumpeters should be given the D part, as it is the most difficult and the most prominent. The final movement between 3 and **20** is where the greatest challenges to ensemble cohesion occur. There are interplays between duple and triple divisions of the beat, frequent changes of meter, displaced downbeats, and non-concurrent, overlapping jagged melodic passages which are of varied hierarchical importance. This is a very effective work which is within the abilities of most collegiate choral ensembles, although the soprano part can be fatiguing for young adult singers. The orchestra's role is within the abilities of collegiate ensembles if secure players can be found for all of the wind parts. **Choir:** medium difficult; **Orchestra:** difficult.

**Discography:**  Radiodiffusion Chorus, National Orchestra; conducted by Jascha Horenstein. Angel: 35101 [LP].

London Philharmonic Orchestra and Chorus; conducted by Ernest Ansermet. London: LL 889 [LP].

St. Hedwig's Cathedral Chorus, RIAS Chorus and Orchestra; conducted by Ferenc Fricsay. Decca: DL 7526 [LP].

Festival Singers of Toronto (Elmer Iseler, chorus-master), CBC Symphony Orchestra; conducted by Igor Stravinsky, recorded in Toronto, Canada, on 2-3 December 1962. Sony Classical— Stravinsky Edition, volume 4: SM2K 46 294 [ADD].

New York Philharmonic Orchestra, Westminster Choir; conducted by Leonard Bernstein. CBS: MK-44710 [ADD].

Berlin Radio Symphony and Chorus (Ernst Senff, chorus-master); conducted by Riccardo Chailly, recorded in Jesus Christus Kirche, Berlin during February 1984. London: 14 078-1 [digital LP].

## Selected Bibliography

Mattei, Otto: *Igor Stravinsky's Symphony of Psalms: An Analytical Study*. Eastman School of Music: Master's of Music thesis, 1948.

Bass, Claude Leroy: *Phrase Structure and Cadence Treatment in Stravinsky's Symphony of Psalms and Honegger's Le Roi David*. University of Oklahoma: Master's of Music thesis, 1960.

Toplis, Gloria H.: *Igor Stravinsky's Symphony of Psalms (III): An Analytical Study*. King's College: Master's of Music thesis, 1975.

Stravinsky, Vera and Robert Craft: *Stravinsky: In Pictures and Documents*, 294-298. New York: Simon and Schuster, 1978.

Chamberlain, Bruce B.: *Igor Stravinsky's Symphony of Psalms: An Analysis for Performance*. Indiana University: Doctor of Musical Arts dissertation, 1979.

White, Eric Walter: *Stravinsky: the Composer and his Works*, 359-367. Berkeley, California: University of California Press, 1966; revised and enlarged second edition, 1979.

Berger, Samuel Max: *A Conductor's Guide to Stravinsky's Symphony of Psalms*. Central Washington University: Master's of Music thesis, 1980.

Berger, Melvin: *Guide to Choral Masterpieces: A Listener's Guide*, 280-284. New York: Anchor Books, 1993.

## Persephone  (1933-34)

**Duration:** ca. 56 minutes[36]

**Text:** The text by André Gide is in French.

**Performing Forces: voices:** tenor soloist (Eumolpus), narrator (Persephone); SATB choir, children's choir; **orchestra:** 3 flutes, 3 oboes, 3 clarinets in B$^b$, 3 bassoons, 4 horns in F, 4 trumpets in C, 3 trombones, tuba, timpani, percussion (1 player - xylophone), 2 harps, piano, and strings.

**First Performance:** 30 April 1934; Théâtre National de l'Opéra, Paris; Ballets Ida Rubinstein; conducted by the composer with Ida Rubinstein dancing and speaking the lead role. This program also contained the premiere of Jacques Ibert's *Diane de Poitiers*.

**Edition:** *Persephone* was first published by Édition Russe de Musique. It is now available from Boosey and Hawkes. The piano-vocal score and miniature score are available for purchase; orchestral materials are available through rental.

**Autograph:** The full score is in the possession of Victori Ocampo, Buenos Aires. The Stravinsky Archive is in the possession of the Paul Sacher Foundation in Basle, Switzerland.

**Notes:** The score was completed in Paris on 24 January 1934 and revised in 1949. It is divided into three scenes, each of which is divided into a number of subsections as follows:

Scene One - Perséphone ravie

    1.   "Déesse aux mille noms" - aria
    2.   a)  "Reste avec nous" - choir
          b)  "Ivresse matinale" - choir

---

[36]  Margaret K. Farish lists 45 minutes duration in *Orchestral Music in Print*. Philadelphia, Pennsylvania: Musicdata, 1979. The score also indicates this duration, and David Daniels indicates 48 minutes in his *Orchestral Music: A Handbook*, third edition. Lanham, Maryland: Scarecrow Press, 1996; however, the recording made under the composer's direction is 55 minutes and 34 seconds long.

    c)  "De toutes les fleurs" - solo and choir
    d)  "Je Vois sur des prés" - recitation
    e)  "Ne cueille pas cette fleur" - choir
    f)  "Viens, joue avec nous" [music of 2a] - choir
3. "Perséphone un peuple t'attend" - aria

## Scene Two - Perséphone aux enfers

4. Orchestra Introduction
5. "C'est ainsi nous raconte Homère" - aria
6.    a)  "Sur ce lit elle repose" - choir
    b)  "Les ombres ne sont pas malheureses" - choir
    c)  "Parle-nous du printemps" - choir and recitation
7. "Tu viens pour dominer" - aria
8. Orchestra Interlude
9. "Viens, Mercure" - choir
10. "Persephone confuse" - aria
11. "Si tu contemples le calice" - choir and recitation
12.    a)  "Pauvres ombres désespérées" - aria
    b)  "Ainsi l'espoir renaît" - choir and recitation
    c)  "Déméter, tu m'attends" - recitation

## Scene Three - Perséphone renaissante

13. Orchestra Introduction
14. "C'est ainsi nous raconte Homère" - aria
15.    a)  "Nous apportons nos offrandes" - choir
    b)  "Encore mal réveillée" - choir
    c)  "L'ombre encore l'environne" - choir of children
16. "Mère, ta Perséphone" - Recitation
17. "Ainsi vers l'ombre souterraine" - solo and choir

**Performance Issues:** The narrator, who portrays the title character, should be musically literate so that spoken passages will coördinate with concurrent musical passages in the score. The choral writing is triadic and homophonic. All of the vocal material is harmonically supported by the orchestra. The instrumental writing is some of Stravinsky's most conservative. The score uses functional tonal harmonies throughout. There are few metrical changes and the rhythmic material is quite straightforward. This work, while seldom performed, is an excellent example of neo-classicism, which serendipitously utilizes a classical subject in its texts. The score is well within the abilities of most amateur choral ensembles and many less-experienced orchestras. Much of the success of a performance is dependent upon the tenor soloist and the narrator. It is also a good introductory piece for conservative audiences to Stravinsky's symphonic choral music. **Soloist:** tenor - range: e-b', tessitura: g-f', this role is very lyrical and pervades most of the work; **Choir:** medium easy; **Orchestra:** medium easy.

**Discography:**  Vera Zorina, Michele Molese; Ithaca College Concert Choir, The Texas Boys Choir of Fort Worth, Gregg Smith Singers, Columbia Symphony Orchestra; conducted by Igor Stravinsky, recorded in Hollywood, California on 4-7 May 1966. Sony Classical—Stravinsky Edition, volume 10: SM2K 46 300 [ADD].

### Selected  Bibliography

Stravinsky, Igor and Robert Craft: *"Perséphone* (letters from André Gide)," *Memories and Commentaries*, 144-153. Berkeley, California: University of California Press, 1960.

Stravinsky, Vera and Robert Craft: *Stravinsky: In Pictures and Documents*, 313-319. New York: Simon and Schuster, 1978.

White, Eric Walter: *Stravinsky: the Composer and his Works*, 374-388. Berkeley, California: University of California Press, 1966; revised and enlarged second edition, 1979.

Truman, Philip A.: *Stravinsky's Approach to Opera*. Université de Bruxelles: doctoral thesis, 1982.

Craft, Robert: *"Persephone*: The Evolution of the Libretto," Appendix B in *Stravinsky: Selected Correspondence, volume 3*, 475-507. New York: Alfred A. Knopf, 1984.

_____: "Œdipus Rex, Perséphone, Zvezdoliki," *Stravinsky: Glimpses of a Life*, 383-395. New York: St. Martin's Press, 1992.

Slonimsky, Nicolas: *Music Since 1900*, fifth edition, 370-71. New York: Schirmer Books, 1994.

## Mass (1944-48)

**Duration:** ca. 16 minutes

**Text:** The text is taken from the Roman Catholic Eucharistic Rite.

**Performing Forces:** voices: men and boys choir; **orchestra:** 2 oboes, English horn, 2 bassoons, 2 trumpets in C, and 3 trombones.

**First Performance:** 27 October 1948; Teatro alla Scala, Milan, Italy; conducted by Ernest Ansermet.

**Edition:** *Mass* is published by Boosey and Hawkes. The piano-vocal score (LCB 17), full score (FSB 54), and miniature score (HPS 655) are available for purchase; orchestral materials are available through rental.

**Autograph:** The Stravinsky Archive is in the possession of the Paul Sacher Foundation in Basle, Switzerland.

**Notes:** "The immediate impulse to compose the *Mass* came in 1948, when Stravinsky picked up a used copy of some Mozart Masses in a bookshop on Los Angeles, where he was then living, and decided to 'write a Mass of [his] own, but a real one.'"[37]

**Performance Issues:** The score indicates that children's voices are to be used for the soprano and alto parts of the choir. It should be noted that the premiere recording of this work which was conducted by the composer uses adult women in these parts. This recording also includes some pitches altered from those in the published score. There are occasional two-part divisi for each section of the choir. The instrumental parts present few significant technical challenges to the players. The "Gloria" is the most rhythmically involved movement with some quintuple divisions of the beat. The primary performance issue for the instumentalists is clarity of rhythm and intonation within non-traditional harmonic structures. The composer integrates many elements of early music in this score including the contrast between solo and tutti passages. There are soprano and alto passages throughout the "Gloria" which are labeled "preferably a solo voice." In the "Sanctus" there are passages strictly labeled as solos for soprano, alto, two tenors, and a bass. All of these solos are conservative in range, well within the average compass of each voice type. Each solo part is melismatic and chromatically challenging, but throughout the work each solo line moves almost exclusively in scalar patterns of minor and

---

37   Berger, Melvin: *Guide to Choral Masterpieces: A Listener's Guide*, 285. New York: Anchor Books, 1993.

major seconds. Most of the work employs contrapuntal devices derived from Renaissance music including treatment of voices in pairs, cadential figurations, and imitative procedures. Many of the voice relationships within pairs of voices resemble species counterpoint; however, the pitch material of the combined pairs is in no way obedient to Palestrinian models. The individual vocal parts are logical and vocally accessible, but the harmonies generated from these simultaneous melodic events are often aurally challenging due to a preponderance of minor seconds and major sevenths between voices. The most difficult entrance pitches for the voices are generally cued by the instruments just before the singers must enter. There is also considerable doubling of the pitch centers of the vocal lines within the instrumental parts; however, there are extended *a cappella* passages for the singers, especially in the "Agnus Dei," in which there are only two beats of overlapping sound between the voices and instruments. The greatest challenge to the singers is intonation with cross relations compounding the difficulties of already demanding harmonic material. This work is less metrically complex than many of Stravinsky's works, and most of the rhythmic material is direct, although agogic and metric stresses are often at odds with the natural accents within the text. It should be noted that in the "Credo" there are more syllables than notes for the word "visibilium" in the eighth measure. This movement is contrapuntally different from the others in that the voices move homophonically in block chords declaiming the articles of faith. **Choir:** difficult, **Orchestra:** medium difficult.

**Discography:** Addison, Okerson, Price, Burrows; Concert Choir; conducted by Margaret Hillis. Vox: PL 8630 [LP].
Gregg Smith Singers, Columbia Symphony Winds and Brass; conducted by Igor Stravinsky, recorded in Hollywood, California, on 5 June 1960. Sony Classical—Stravinsky Edition, volume 11: SM2K 46 301 [ADD].

### Selected Bibliography

Moses, Don V: *A Conductor's Analysis of the Mass (1948) by Stravinsky; A Conductor's Analysis of the Mass (1963) by Hindemith*. Indiana University: Doctor of Music dissertation, 1968.
Dehning, William John: *A Study and Performance of Mass and Cantata by Igor Stravinsky*. University of Southern California: Doctor of Musical Arts dissertation, 1971.

Rower, Dennis D.: *Annotated Program Notes for Mass (1948) by Igor Stravinsky*. Bowling Green University: Master's of Music thesis, 1974.

Agawa, Victor: *Igor Stravinsky: Mass (1948). An Analysis of Some Aspects of Structure as Revealed by Pitch Organization*. King's College: Master's of Music thesis, 1978.

White, Eric Walter: *Stravinsky: the Composer and his Works*, 446-450. Berkeley, California: University of California Press, 1966; revised and enlarged second edition, 1979.

Vantine, Bruce Lynn: *Four Twentieth-Century Masses: An Analytical Comparison of Style and Compositional Technique*, 159-253. University of Illinois: Doctor of Musical Arts dissertation, 1982.

## Cantata (1951-52)

**Duration:** ca. 30 minutes

**Text:** The text is a collection of anonymous lyrics of the fifteenth and sixteenth centuries, in English.

**Performing Forces: voices:** soprano and tenor soloists; women's choir; **orchestra:** 2 flutes, 2 oboes (oboe II doubling English horn), and cello.

**First Performance:** 11 November 1952; Los Angeles, California; Los Angeles Chamber Symphony; conducted by Stravinsky.

**Edition:** *Cantata* is published by Boosey and Hawkes. The piano-vocal score and miniature score are available for purchase; instrumental materials are available through rental.

**Autograph:** The Stravinsky Archive is in the possession of the Paul Sacher Foundation in Basle, Switzerland.

**Notes:** The score is inscribed: "This *Cantata* is dedicated to the Los Angeles Symphony Society which performed it under my direction and for the first time on November 11th, 1952."

It is organized as follows:

     I   A Lyke-Wake Dirge (Versus I), Prelude: choir
    II   Ricercar I - 'The maidens came': soprano
   III   A Lyke-Wake Dirge (Versus II), 1st Interlude: choir

IV   Ricercar II - 'Tomorrow shall be...': tenor
V    A Lyke-Wake Dirge (Versus III), 2nd Interlude: choir
VI   Westron Wind: soprano and tenor
VII  A Lyke-Wake Dirge (Versus IV), Postlude: choir

A great deal of attention has been paid to the serial features of this work. Written in the year following Schoenberg's death, it is often described as Stravinky's first foray into serial music. In the Ricecar II of *Cantata*, Stravinsky has incorporated a number of pitch ordering procedures which are as firmly rooted in baroque counterpoint as they are in the serialization of pitch. Using a variety of canonic procedures with hexachordal sets and frequent pitch repetition Stravinsky's methods do more to emphasize pitch centers than generate tonal equity.

The text of "A Lyke-Wake Dirge" is also used by Benjamin Britten in his *Serenade for Tenor, Horn, and Strings*.

**Performance Issues:** The instrumental parts require musically independent players. Both oboe parts are particularly difficult because they are taxing to the player's endurance. The music for the nine verses sung by the choir is virtually the same. The last verse has some rhythmic alterations in it. There are written divisi for both sections of the choir, but the choral harmonies do not exceed three pitches at a time. The brevity of the choral passages combined with diatonic motion and substantial repetition make this a work well within the grasp of most women's choirs. Stravinsky has left the difficult vocal work for the soloists. **Soloist:** soprano - range: c'-g", tessitura: e'-c", the generally low tessitura of this role suggests the use of a mezzo-soprano soloist; tenor - range: e-a$^{b'}$, tessitura: g-e', this role is very sustained and demands subtle intonation adjustments to make cross-relations clear, the repetition of pitch material and scalar writing makes this musically accessible, but the repeated emphasis of the narrow tessitura makes it vocally fatiguing especially to younger singers; **Choir:** medium easy; **Orchestra:** difficult.

**Discography:** Jennie Tourel, Hugh Cuenod; Concert Choir, Philadelphia Chamber Ensemble. Columbia: ML 4899 [LP].
Adrienne Albert, Alexander Young; Gregg Smith Singers, Columbia Chamber Ensemble; conducted by Igor Stravinsky, recorded in Hollywood, California, between 27 November 1965 and 10

February 1966. Sony Classical—Stravinsky Edition, volume 11: SM2K 46 301 [ADD].

### Selected Bibliography

Lindar, H: "Igor Stravinsky: Cantata," *Tempo*, number 27 (1953), 29.

Cowell, Henry : "Current Chronicle," *Musical Quarterly*, volume 39 (1953), 251.

Mason, C: "Serial Procedures in Ricercar II of Stravinsky's Cantata," *Tempo* , numbers 61-62 (1962).

Schechter, John M.: *An Analysis of the Stravinsky Cantata: The Craft within the Suite.* Indiana University: Master's of Music thesis, 1970.

Dehning, William John: *A Study and Performance of Mass and Cantata by Igor Stravinsky.* University of Southern California: Doctor of Musical Arts dissertation, 1971.

Hatfield, Robert Benjamin: *A Conductor's Analysis of Laud to the Nativity by Ottorino Respighi and Cantata by Igor Stravinsky*, 89-142. Southwestern Baptist Seminary: Master's of Church Music thesis, 1973.

Beres, Albert T.: *An Analysis of Igor Stravinsky's Cantata for Soprano, Tenor, Female Chorus, and a Small Instrumental Ensemble.* Eastern Michigan University: Master's of Arts thesis, 1977.

Brantley: John Paul: *The Serial Choral Music of Igor Stravinsky.* University of Iowa: Ph.D. dissertation, 1978.

White, Eric Walter: *Stravinsky: the Composer and his Works*, 468-472. Berkeley, California: University of California Press, 1966; revised and enlarged second edition, 1979.

# Canticum Sacrum ad honorem Sancti Marci Nominis (1955)

**Duration:** ca. 17 minutes

**Text:** The text is from the Vulgate (Latin) Bible.

**Performing Forces: voices:** tenor and baritone soloists; SATB choir; **orchestra:** flute, 2 oboes, English horn, 2 bassoons, contrabassoon, 3 trumpets in C, bass trumpet in C, 2 tenor trombones, bass trombone, contrabass trombone, harp, organ, violas and doublebasses.

**First Performance:** 13 September 1956; St. Mark's Cathedral, Venice; conducted by the composer.

**Edition:** *Canticum Sacrum* is published by Boosey and Hawkes. The piano-vocal score, choral parts, full score, and miniature score are available for purchase; orchestral materials are available through rental.

**Autograph:** The full score is in the collection of Signora Adriana Panni, Accademia Filarmonica, Rome; the piano reduction is in the Library of Congress. The Stravinsky Archive is in the possession of the Paul Sacher Foundation in Basle, Switzerland.

**Notes:** The score is dedicated "To the City of Venice, in praise of its Patron Siant, the Blessed Mark, Apostle." Movements II, III, and IV are strictly serial. Movements I and V are palindromes of each other. The work is divided into five movements and a dedication as follows:

| | |
|---|---|
| Dedicatio | The dedication text [see: Notes] |
| I Euntes in mundum | Mark XVI.15 |
| II Surge, aquilo" | Song of Songs IV.16, V.1 |
| III Ad Tres Virtures | |
| a) Caritas | Deuteronomy VI.5, I John IV.7 |
| b) Spes | Psalms CXXV.1, CXXX.5-6 |
| c) Fides | Psalms CXVI.10 |
| IV Brevis Motus Cantilenae | Mark IX.23-4 |
| V Illi autem profecti | Mark XVI.20 |

**Performance Issues:** The score is notated at sounding pitch except for the doublebasses, contrabass trombone, and bass trumpet, all of which sound an octave lower than written. If necessary, the contrabass trombone could be covered by a tuba, and the bass trumpet, by a baritone horn. The choral writing uses a lot of paired doubling with occasional canonic treatments, but it is primarily homophonic. Throughout this work, Stravinsky integrates serial pitch material with the contrapuntal devices of the late Renaissance and early Baroque periods as established in Venice. The choral parts are well-related to each other and are generally independent of the instruments. There are a number of spots where optional string parts have been provided to assist a section of the choir if necessary. Much of the vocal material is transparently accompanied. Although the pitch material is challenging, the organization of the row and its arrangement between parts helps to keep this material accessible. There is a three-part divisi for solo doublebasses, so that three players is the minimum. The second movement, which features the principal tenor solo, is the most difficult; it includes the doublebass trio, which is all in harmonics, and a very difficult duet for flute and English horn. Outside of this movement, the instrumental parts are not particularly difficult. In the 6/4 sections of movements I and V, the rhythms are notated so that the placement of the beats within some measures is difficult to discern. It is advisable to mark the parts here to simplify the rehearsal of these movements. **Soloists:** tenor - range: d#-g#', tessitura: f-e", this role is rhythmic and articulate with wide leaps; baritone - range: B$^b$-e', tessitura: e-d', this is a lyrical part with many passages alternating half- and whole-step relationships; **Choir:** difficult; **Orchestra:** difficult.

**Discography:** Richard Robinson, Howard Chitjian; Los Angeles Festival Symphony Orchestra and Chorus; conducted by Igor Stravinsky, recorded in Hollywood, California, on 19 June 1957. Sony Classical—Stravinsky Edition, volume 11: SM2K 46 301 [ADD].

### Selected Bibliography

Craft, Robert: "A Concert for St. Mark," *The Score*, number 18 (1956), 35.

Stern, A.: "Igor Stravinsky's Canticum Sacrum ad honorem S. Marci nominis ," *Tempo*, number 40 (1956), 3.

Weissmann, J. S.: "Current Chronicle," *Musical Quarterly*, volume 43 (1957), 104.

Dailey, William Albert: *Techniques of Composition Used in Contemporary Works for Chorus and Orchestra on Religious Texts—As Important Representative Works of the Period from 1952 to 1962*. Catholic University of America: Ph.D dissertation, 1965.

Loeftelholz, K. von: "Igor Stravinskys Canticum Sacrum," *Neue Zeitschrift für Musik*, Jahrgang 128 (1968), 168.

Tykac, Phyllis Dianne: *Stravinsky and the Pursuit of Unity: A Study of Five Works from the Fifth Decade*. California State University at Northridge: Master's of Arts thesis, 1969.

Cook, Joseph Thomas: *A Conductor's Study of Igor Stravinsky's Canticum Sacrum, Introitus: T.S. Eliot in memoriam, and*

*Requiem Canticles.* Indiana University: Doctor of Music dissertation, 1976.

Stravinsky, Vera and Robert Craft: *Stravinsky: In Pictures and Documents*, 430-435. New York: Simon and Schuster, 1978.

Brantley: John Paul: *The Serial Choral Music of Igor Stravinsky.* University of Iowa: Ph.D. dissertation, 1978.

White, Eric Walter: *Stravinsky: the Composer and his Works*, 481-482. Berkeley, California: University of California Press, 1966; revised and enlarged second edition, 1979.

Berger, Melvin: *Guide to Choral Masterpieces: A Listener's Guide*, 286-290. New York: Anchor Books, 1993.

## Threni (1957-58)

**Duration:** ca. 35 minutes

**Text:** This Latin text is from the Vulgate Bible - The Lamentations of Jeremiah - Chapter I: parts of verses 1, 2, 5, 11, 20; Chapter III: verses 1-6, 16-27, 34-36, 40-45, 49-66*; Chapter V: verses 1,19, 21.

* In verse 59 "Judica Judicium meum" is omitted.

**Performing Forces: voices:** soprano, contralto, 2 tenor, bass and basso-profundo soloists; SATB choir; **orchestra:** 2 flutes, 2 oboes, English horn, 2 clarinets in B$^b$ and A (clarinet II doubling alto clarinet in F), bass clarinet in B$^b$, sarrusophone, 4 horns in F, contralto bugle in B$^b$, alto trombone, tenor trombone, bass trombone, tuba, timpani, harp, celeste, piano, and strings.

**First Performance:** 23 September 1958; Sala della Scuola Grande di San Rocco, Venice; conducted by the composer; given as the first concert of the International Festival of Contemporary Music in Venice.

**Edition:** *Threni* is published by Boosey and Hawkes. The piano-vocal score (VSB 97) and miniature score (HPS 637) are available for purchase; orchestral materials are available through rental.

**Autograph:** The Stravinsky Archive is in the possession of the Paul Sacher Foundation in Basle, Switzerland.

**Notes:** *Threni* is Stravinsky's first wholly serial composition. It was commissioned by, and is dedicated to North German Radio. It is organized as follows:

> Introduction
> I De Elegia Prima
> II De Elegia Tertia
> > 1. Querimonia
> > 2. Sensus Spei
> > 3. Solacium
> III De Elegia Quinta

**Performance Issues:** The alto clarinet in F is probably intended for basset horn; if a modern alto clarinet is used, the part will need to be transposed for the E$^b$ instrument. The sarrusophone part can be best doubled on contrabassoon; optionally, it could be covered by a bass saxophone which would require that the part be transcribed for a treble-clef B$^b$ transposition. Two measures of the "Sensus Spei" section calls for a solo alto and solo bass from the choir to join the solo quintet. The solo roles all have fairly low tessituri which makes possible the compelling idea of using an all-male quintet with countertenors singing the alto and soprano roles, which fall well within the range of most falsettists. The most contrapuntally complex vocal writing is reserved for the soloists. Much of the choral writing is in unison, or in four-part, turba-like, proclamations of the headings of each text sung by the soloists. The instrumental accompaniment does not directly support the choral parts, but there are clear interconnections between the instruments and voices. The instrumental writing is technically conservative, but there are a number of complicated metric combinations which will require careful attention. A large portion of the solo vocal material is unaccompanied, or accompanied only with occasional interjections from the trombones. Many of these vocal passages are unbarred, but delineated by implied metrical indications that are constantly in a state of flux. The orchestra must have a strong solo cellist and doublebassist. The horn quartet has a number of exposed passages for each player in the extremes of their ranges. Much of the organization of this composition is influenced by medieval and renaissance models, but with the introduction of atonal pitch sets in the place of church modes. If a strong quintet is available, this piece provides a good introduction of Stravinsky's later works to developing choral ensembles. **Soloists:** soprano - range: c'-f", tessitura: e'-d", this is a lyric role with very little high singing; alto - range: f#-e$^{b}$", tessitura: b-a', this role is lyric with some awkward melodic leaps; tenor I - range: c-a$^{b}$', tessitura: f-f', this is the largest of the solo roles, it is sustained; tenor II - range: c-g', tessitura: f-d', this is the smallest of the solo roles and is usually featured within ensemble sections; bass - range: G-d#', tessitura: B-b, this is a sustained role; basso profundo - range: E$^{b}$-b, tessitura: G-e, this is a prominent part of the piece, the singer must be able to make clear leaps between b$^{b}$ and E$^{b}$; **Choir:** medium difficult; **Orchestra:** medium difficult.

**Discography:** Bethany Beardslee, Beatrice Krebs, William Lewis, James Wainner, Mac Morgan, Robert Oliver; Schola Cantorum (Hugh Ross, chorus-master), Columbia Symphony Orchestra; conducted by Igor Stravinsky, recorded in New York on 5 and 6 January 1959. Sony Classical—Stravinsky Edition, volume 11: SM2K 46 301 [ADD].

## Selected Bibliography

Pauli, H.: "On Stravinsky's Threni," *Tempo*, number 49 (1958), 16.

Weismann, J. S.: "Current Chronicle: Italy," *Musical Quarterly*, volume 45 (1959), 104.

Tykac, Phyllis Dianne: *Stravinsky and the Pursuit of Unity: A Study of Five Works from the Fifth Decade*. California State University at Northridge: Master's of Arts thesis, 1969.

Klimisch, Sister Mary Jane: *The Music of the Lamentations: Historical and Analytical Aspects*, 118-140. Washington University: Ph.D. dissertation, 1971.

Dhont, J: "Lineaire Intervalstructuren in Stravinsky's 'Threni,'" *Mens en mélodie*, volume 32 (1977), 403.

Stravinsky, Vera and Robert Craft: *Stravinsky: In Pictures and Documents*, 443-454. New York: Simon and Schuster, 1978.

Brantley: John Paul: *The Serial Choral Music of Igor Stravinsky*. University of Iowa: Ph.D. dissertation, 1978.

White, Eric Walter: *Stravinsky: the Composer and his Works*, 497-504. Berkeley, California: University of California Press, 1966; revised and enlarged second edition, 1979.

Cowen, Graeme M.: *Igor Stravinsky's Threni: A Conductor's Study for Performance*. Indiana University: Doctor of Music dissertation, 1981.

Hogan, Clare: "'Threni': Stravinsky's Debt to Krenek," *Tempo*, number 141 (1982), 22.

_____: *An Examination of Stravinsky's Contribution to Serialism in Light of the Theories, Music, and Personality of Ernst Krenek, with Particular Reference to the Connection between Lamentatio Jeremiæ and Threni.* University of Keele: Master's of Arts thesis, 1982.

Waters, William Jerome: *An Analysis of Igor Stravinsky's Threni Based on Edward T. Cone's Principles of Stratification, Interlock, and Synthesis.* Flordia State University: Master's of Music thesis, 1984.

Berger, Melvin: *Guide to Choral Masterpieces: A Listener's Guide,* 290-296. New York: Anchor Books, 1993.

## A Sermon, a Narrative, and a Prayer (1960-61)

**Duration:** ca. 16 minutes

**Text:** Taken from St. Paul's Epistles, The Acts of the Apostles [Authorized Version]; and a prayer by Thomas Dekker; the text is in English.

**Performing Forces: voices:** alto and tenor soloists; speaker; choir; **orchestra:** flute in C, alto flute in G, 2 oboes, clarinet in B♭, bass clarinet in B♭, 2 bassoons, 4 horns in F, 3 trumpets in B♭, 2 tenor trombones, bass trombone, tuba, percussion (3 players - 3 tamtams), harp, piano, and strings (8-7-6-5-4).

**First Performance:** 23 February 1962; Basle, Switzerland; Basler Kammerorchester; conducted by Paul Sacher.

**Edition:** *A Sermon, a Narrative, and a Prayer* is published by Boosey and Hawkes. The piano-vocal score (LCB 124) and miniature score (HPS 133) are available for purchase; orchestral materials are available through rental.

**Autograph:** The Stravinsky Archive is in the possession of the Paul Sacher Foundation in Basle, Switzerland.

**Notes:** The Prayer movement is inscribed with "In memoriam Reverend James McLane (†1960)." *A Sermon, a Narrative, and a Prayer* was commissioned by, and is dedicated to, Paul Sacher. The score was completed 31 January 1961.

**Performance Issues:** This is a serial work. See: Stravinsky's *In Memoriam Dylan Thomas* for his treatment of a very similar tone row. The score is notated entirely in sounding pitches, including the doublebasses. There is a three-measure solo for a bass from the choir, beginning at measure 61. There are two-part divisi for each section of the choir. There are also short *Sprechstimme* figures for the choir. The vocal material is atonally conceived, but conservatively executed so that it remains fairly accessible. The choir sings in the first and third movements and their pitch material is not supported by the accompaniment. The instrumental writing is quite transparent with only three or four instrumental parts sounding simultaneously. There are frequent meter changes which also involve a change of the primary beat value. Rhythmic material includes three against four, five against four, six against four, and seven against four. These shifts of subdivision and beat value, compounded by rapidly shifting instrumentation, create significant challenges for entrances and a cohesive sense of ensemble playing and singing. The individual instrumental parts are not overly difficult. There are some challenging figures for the two flutists and the two clarinetists. The piano and harp parts are quite idiomatic, and within the abilities of most undergraduate players. The tam-tam parts could probably be played by a single player, but the rhythms between instruments and their overall size may make the use of three individual players more practical. **Soloists:** alto - range: g-e", tessitura: d'-c", this role is atonal, but with a traditional vocal contour; tenor - range: d-a', tessitura: f-f', this is a sustained and lyric role; **Choir:** medium difficult; **Orchestra:** difficult.

**Discography:** Shirley Verrett, Loren Driscoll, John Horton; CBC Symphony Orchestra; conducted by Igor Stravinsky, recorded in Toronto, Canada, on 29 April 1962. Sony Classical—Stravinsky Edition, volume 11: SM2K 46 301 [ADD].

### Selected Bibliography

Mason, C: "Stravinsky's New work," *Tempo*, number 54 (1960), 2.
Clifton, T: "Types of Symmetrical Relations in Stravinsky's 'A Sermon, a Narrative and a Prayer,'" *Perspectives in New Music*, volume 9, number 1 (1970), 96.
Brantley: John Paul: *The Serial Choral Music of Igor Stravinsky.* University of Iowa: Ph.D. dissertation, 1978.
Starnes, Erwin Stanley, Jr.: *A Conductor's Study of Igor Stravinsky's Babel and A Sermon, a Narrative and a Prayer, with a Survey of*

*His Serial Procedures through the Latter.* Indiana University:
Doctor of Music dissertation, 1978.

White, Eric Walter: *Stravinsky: the Composer and his Works,* 510-516.
Berkeley, California: University of California Press, 1966; revised
and enlarged second edition, 1979.

Nelson, John Douglas: *Serial Techniques and Analysis of Selected
Compositions Published after 1960 by Igor Stravinsky.* San Diego
State University: Master's of Arts thesis, 1984.

# Introitus: T. S. Eliot in Memoriam (1965)

**Duration:** ca. 4 minutes

**Text:** The text is extracted from the Latin *Missa pro defunctis.*

**Performing Forces: voices:** TB choir; **orchestra:** 2 timpanists,
percussion (2 players - 2 tam-tams), harp, piano, solo viola, and
solo doublebass.

**First Performance:** 17 April 1965; Chicago; Chicago Symphony
Orchestra, conducted by Robert Craft.

**Edition:** *Introitus* is published by Boosey and Hawkes. The full score
and study score (HPS 780) are available for purchase; instrumental
materials are available through rental.

**Autograph:** The Stravinsky Archive is in the possession of the Paul
Sacher Foundation in Basle, Switzerland.

**Notes:** This score is written entirely at sounding pitch, including the
doublebass part.

**Performance Issues:** This is a serial composition which uses
minimal forces to great dramatic effect. The individual instrumental
parts are not technically challenging and the slow tempo and
conservative rhythmic material minimize ensemble difficulties. The
pitch changes for the timpanists are somewhat perilous. There are
numerous chromatic changes for both players, many of which must
be executed in a brief amount of time. These players must have a
strong sense of relative pitch. Because of the time constraints and
minimalist scoring, timpani with mechanical pitch gauges are
advisable. Although the pitch material of the choir is not doubled
by the instruments, the composer is sympathetic in his

juxtaposition of concurrent statements of the tone row, so that minimal interference is presented to the singers. With the exception of some rhythmically spoken passages, half of the vocal material is in unison and the other half in two-part homophony. These homophonic sections are written in an aurally accessible manner allowing amateur singers to successfully comprehend a serial work. **Choir:** medium difficult; **Orchestra:** medium easy.

**Discography:** Gregg Smith Singers, Columbia Chamber Ensemble; conducted by Igor Stravinsky, recorded in New York, on 9 February 1966. Sony Classical—Stravinsky Edition, volume 11: SM2K 46 301 [ADD].

### Selected Bibliography

Stravinsky, Igor and Robert Craft: "Program Notes: Introitus: T.S. Eliot in Memoriam," *Themes and Episodes*, 62-63. New York: Alfred A. Knopf, 1966.
Cook, Joseph Thomas: *A Conductor's Study of Igor Stravinsky's Canticum Sacrum, Introitus: T.S. Eliot in memoriam, and Requiem Canticles.* Indiana University: Doctor of Music dissertation, 1976.
Brantley: John Paul: *The Serial Choral Music of Igor Stravinsky.* University of Iowa: Ph.D. dissertation, 1978.
White, Eric Walter: *Stravinsky: the Composer and his Works*, 538-539. Berkeley, California: University of California Press, 1966; revised and enlarged second edition, 1979.
Nelson, John Douglas: *Serial Techniques and Analysis of Selected Compositions Published after 1960 by Igor Stravinsky.* San Diego State University: Master's of Arts thesis, 1984.

# Requiem Canticles (1965-66)

**Duration:** ca. 15 minutes

**Text:** The text is taken from the Latin Mass for the Dead.

**Performing Forces:** voices: alto and bass soloists; SATB choir; **orchestra:** 3 flutes (flute III doubling piccolo), alto flute in G, 2 bassoons, 4 horns in F, 2 trumpets in C, 3 trombones, 2 timpanists, percussion (2 players - xylophone, vibraphone, bells), harp, celeste, piano, and strings.

**First Performance:** 8 October 1966; Princeton University; Princeton, New Jersey; conducted by Robert Craft.

**Edition:** *Requiem Canticles* is published by Boosey and Hawkes. The piano-vocal score (LCB 124), choral parts (LCB 71), full score (FSB 328), and miniature score (HPS 825) are available for purchase; orchestral materials are available through rental.

**Autograph:** The Stravinsky Archive is in the possession of the Paul Sacher Foundation in Basle, Switzerland.

**Notes:** The score is dedicated "To the memory of Helen Buchanan Seeger." The entire score is written at sounding pitch, including doublebass, with the exception of the piccolo which sounds an octave higher than written.

**Performance Issues:** This score suggests a profound influence from the works of Webern. Although a fairly complete orchestra is required, rarely does the composer employ more than two families of instruments at the same time. This scoring allows for a chamber-sized string section. There are concertato solo parts for each principal string player; however, there are two doublebass soloists whose solo playing never concurs with the very few passages marked tutti. The few divisi indicated for these solos are open fifths easily executed as double stops by a single player, allowing for only one double bass player in the orchestra. The score is serially conceived, but not strict in its execution. It is filled with meter changes and a spartan scoring that causes there to be entrances for instruments in nearly every measure. In addition to regularly altering the meter, Stravinsky frequently displaces the downbeat, further concealing a sense of metric order. There are exposed layerings of beat divisions, including 6 against 5 against 4, and 10 against 8 against 6 against 4 against 3. Despite the complexity of these relationships, the rhythmic material is highly ordered, requiring great precision of ensemble throughout the work. The choral pitches are often supported by the orchestra, but in some sustained passages the vocal and instrumental pitches are in dissonant opposition to each other. The choral passages are brief and fairly vocally logical within each part. The choir is given some rhythmically-spoken passages and one movement features a quartet from the choir singing homophonically with all the pitches doubled in the horns while the remaining chorus members speak an unrhythmed text against it. While presenting substantial pitch challenges to the choral singers, this score remains accessible to many choirs because of the brief choral passages and sensitive voice leading. All of the orchestral parts are musically and technically challenging, and above all else, exposed. Strong players are required on all instrumental parts and the integration of sporadic instrumental passages will require attention in rehearsal. **Soloists:** alto - range: a-c#", tessitura: d'-a', although only two minutes long, this role is rhythmically complex and exceptionally difficult in terms of pitch; bass - range: d-f', tessitura: g-c', this role is only about one minute long and though challenging in pitch content is somewhat supported by the accompaniment and cast in a clear ABA' form; **Choir:** difficult; **Orchestra:** very difficult.

**Discography:** Linda Anderson, Elaine Bonazzi, Charles Bressler, Donald Gramm; The Ithaca College Concert Choir (Gregg Smith, chorus-master), Columbia Symphony Orchestra; conducted by Robert Craft, under the supervision of Igor Stravinsky, recorded in New York on 11 October 1966. Sony Classical—Stravinsky Edition, volume 12: SM2K 46 302 [ADD].

## Selected Bibliography

Cook, Joseph Thomas: *A Conductor's Study of Igor Stravinsky's Canticum Sacrum, Introitus: T.S. Eliot in memoriam, and Requiem Canticles.* Indiana University: Doctor of Music dissertation, 1976.

Chance, Van Darnell, Jr.: *The Use of Borrowed Musical Materials in Benjamin Britten's War Requiem and Igor Stravinsky's Requiem Canticles.* University of Tennessee at Knoxville: Master's of Arts thesis, 1978.

Stravinsky, Vera and Robert Craft: *Stravinsky: In Pictures and Documents,* 476-482. New York: Simon and Schuster, 1978.

Brantley: John Paul: *The Serial Choral Music of Igor Stravinsky.* University of Iowa: Ph.D. dissertation, 1978.

White, Eric Walter: *Stravinsky: the Composer and his Works,* 539-542. Berkeley, California: University of California Press, 1966; revised and enlarged second edition, 1979.

Don, Gary William: *An Analysis of Stravinsky's Requiem Canticles.* University of Washington: Master's of Arts thesis, 1982.

Craft, Robert: "On the Chronology of the *Requiem Canticles,*" Appendix G in *Stravinsky: Selected Correspondence, volume 2,* 467-470. New York: Alfred A. Knopf, 1984.

**Thompson, Randall** (b. New York, 21 April 1899; d. Boston, MA, 9 July 1984)

**Life:** Thompson attended Harvard University (BA 1920, MA 1922) where he studied with Archibald T. Davison, Edward Burlingame Hill, Walter Spalding, and Ernest Bloch. He continued his studies at the Eastman School (1929-33). He taught at Wellesley College (1927-29, 1936-37), the University of California, Berkeley (1937-39), the Curtis Institute (1939-41), the University of Virginia (1941-46), Princeton University (1946-48), and Harvard University (1948-65). His pupils include Samuel Adler, Leonard Bernstein, Lukas Foss, Leo Kraft, and Ivan Tcherepnin. Thompson conducted an investigation of collegiate music programs under the auspices of the Association of American Colleges which produced the book *College Music* (1935). His many honors include two Guggenheim Fellowships (1929, 1930), a fellowship from the American Academy in Rome, Elizabeth Sprague Coolidge Award for Service to Chamber Music (1941), medals from the Signet Society and Glee Club of Harvard, 4 honorary doctorates, elected to the National Institute of Arts and Letters (1938), he was named "Cavaliere ufficiale al merito della Repubblica Italiana" by the Italian Government (1958), and laureate of the Contemporary Composers Festival at the University of Bridgeport (1983). Thompson's compositional output is marked by a large quantity of fine choral works. They show a keen understanding of the singing voice and a respect for the techniques of previous centuries. He has a masterful control of imitative counterpoint and vocal color.[38]

**Principal Works:** *opera* - *Solomon and Balkis: The Butterfly that Stamped* (1942), *The Nativity According to St. Luke* (1961); *orchestral* - 3 Symphonies (1929, 1931, 1947-49), *A Trip to Nahant* (1953-54); *choral* - *Five Odes of Horace* (1924), *Pueri hebraeorum* (1928), *Americana* (1932), *Tarantella* (1937), *The Last Words of David* (1949), *Requiem* (1957-58), *Frostiana* (1959), *The Best of Rooms* (1963), *The Passion According to St. Luke* (1964-65), *A Psalm of Thanksgiving* (1967), *A Hymn for Scholars and Pupils* (1973), *A Concord Cantata* (1975), and *Five Love Songs* (1978). Thompson's most performed work is the *a cappella* "Alleluia" (1940), which was

38  Harold Gleason and Walter Becker: "Randall Thompson," *Twentieth-Century American Composers*. Music Literature Outlines, series 4, 196-202. Bloomington, Indiana: Indiana University Press, revised 1981.

commissioned for the opening ceremonies of the Tanglewood Festival.

## Selected Composer Bibliography

Porter, Quincy: "American Composers, XVIII, Randall Thompson," *Modern Music*, volume 19 (1942), 237.

_____, James Haar, Alfred Mann, and Randall Thompson: "The Choral Music of Randall Thompson," *American Choral Review*, volume 16, number 4 (1974), 1-61.

McGilvray, B. W.: *The Choral Music of Randall Thompson: An American Eclectic.* University of Missouri, Kansas City: Dissertation, 1979.

Thompson, Randall: "On Choral Composition: Essays and Reflections," edited by D. F. Urrows, *American Choral Review*, volume 22, number 2 (1980), entire issue.

Gleason, Harold, and Walter Becker: "Randall Thompson," *Twentieth-Century American Composers.* Music Literature Outlines, series 4, 196-202. Bloomington, Indiana: Indiana University Press, revised 1981.

Benser, Caroline Cepin and David Francis Urrows: *Randall Thompson: A Bio-Bibliography.* New York: Greenwood Press, 1991.

## The Testament of Freedom (1943)

**Duration:** ca. 24 minutes

**Text:** The text is taken from the writings of Thomas Jefferson.

**Performing Forces: voices:** TTBB men's chorus; **orchestra:** 2 flutes, 2 oboes, 2 clarinets [written in C in the full score], 2 bassoons, 4 horns in F, 3 trumpets in C, 3 trombones, tuba, timpani (3 drums; 32", 29", 26" are best), percussion (2 players — snare drum, bass drum, cymbals), and strings.

**concert band version:** piccolo, 2 flutes, 2 oboes, 2 bassoons, 3 clarinets in $B^b$, alto clarinet in $E^b$, bass clarinet in $B^b$, 2 alto saxophones in $E^b$, tenor saxophone in $B^b$, baritone saxophone in $E^b$ [listed as "bass saxophone" in the score's front matter], 3 trumpets in $B^b$, 4 horns in F, 3 trombones, tuba, timpani, percussion {2 players—snare drum, cymbals, and bass drum}, and doublebass.

**First Performance:** 13 April 1943; Cabell Hall, the University of Virginia, Charlottesville, VA; Virginia Glee Club, the composer at the piano; conducted by Dr. Stephen D. Tuttle. This concert was broadcast nationally by the Columbia Broadcasting System and rebroadcast through the Armed Forces Network.

orchestra version: 6 April 1945; Boston, MA.

concert band version: 22 October 1960; Kresge Auditorium, Massachusetts Institute of Technology, Cambridge, MA; Massachusetts Institute of Technology Glee Club and Concert Band; conducted by the composer.

**Edition:** *The Testament of Freedom* is published by E. C. Schirmer. The piano-vocal score for men's chorus (E.C.S. 1410), mixed chorus (E.C.S. 3017), full score (E.C.S. 1410), band score (E.C.S. 1424), and miniature score are available for purchase; performance materials are available through rental.

**Autograph:** The manuscripts of the full score, piano vocal score and over 200 other items related to the work are in the University of Virginia's Special Collections in the Alderman Library.

**Notes:** *The Testament of Freedom* was written to commemorate the 200th anniversary of the birth of Thomas Jefferson. It is inscribed: "To the University of Virginia Glee Club, in memory of the Father of the University."

The work is in four movements with texts from the following sources:

   I  *A Summary View of the Rights of British America* (1774)
  II  *Declaration of Causes and Necessity of Taking up Arms* (1775)
  III  *Declaration of Causes and Necessity of Taking up Arms*
  IV  *Letter to John Adams, Monticello* (12 September 1821)

The first performance was given with piano accompaniment; the orchestration being written the following year. John Corley transcribed the work for men's chorus and concert band under the guidance of the composer, instrumentation and first performance information is given above.

**Performance Issues:** The performance issues below are based on the orchestral version; however, the band version is well within the grasp of a good high school wind ensemble. Although choral scores are published for SATB choir, this work was clearly conceived as a TTBB composition and functions within the orchestral setting best in the men's-choir version. The transcription is well conceived and with single or few players per part it will balance well with a full men's choir. A larger symphonic band will present a challenge for such balance. All of the parts are well written for each instrument. Some ornamental writing in the clarinets will challenge less experienced players because of the frequency of register shifts.

The choral writing is conservative and well written for younger voices. The vocal parts are diatonic and tonally centered. Although written for TTBB choir, much of the choral writing is in two parts. These are conceived homophonically or in pervasive imitation. The tessitura of the tenor I part in the final movement is fairly high, and quite sustained. The horn and trumpet parts require clear rhythmic articulation. The individual instrumental parts are well within the means of a good youth or college orchestra, making this an ideal work for student performance. The orchestration is typical of tonal American music written during the Second World War. The text is set in a declamatory fashion and the vocal parts will be easily learned by inexperienced ensembles. The accessibility of the musical material in this work should not dissuade conductors from programming it. In the years following the Second World War, *Testament of Freedom* was subject to significant criticism because of its unabashed attractiveness to the general public. The score is strong and well-crafted and it provides a quality work for programs with an American patriotic focus. **Choir:** medium easy; **Orchestra:** medium easy.

**Discography:** Eastman-Rochester Chorus and Orchestra; conducted by Howard Hanson. Mercury: MG 40000 [LP].

### Selected Bibliography

Downes, Olin: "New Trends in Composition: Thompson's 'Testament of Freedom' seen as an Expression of Our National Tradition and Spirit," *New York Times* (22 April 1945), x:4.

Brookhart, Charles Edward: *The Choral Music of Aaron Copland, Roy Harris, and Randall Thompson.* George Peabody College for Teachers: Ph.D. dissertation, 1960.

Stanley, Hildegard Jo: *The Major Choral Works of Randall Thompson with Particular Emphasis on Analyses of the "Testament of Freedom."* Southwestern Baptist Theological Seminary: Master's of Church Music thesis, 1962.

Berger, Melvin: *Guide to Choral Masterpieces: A Listener's Guide,* 306-308. New York: Anchor Books, 1993.

# Webern, Anton (b. Vienna, 3 December 1883; d. Mittersill, Austria, 15 September 1945)

**Life:** Webern's interpretation of the seriel techniques developed by his teacher Schoenberg created a body of highly organized miniature masterworks which became the intellectual models for many academic composers of the post-World War II generation. Webern's early musical education came from his mother and Edwin Komauer. He matriculated at the University of Vienna where his teachers included Guido Adler, Hermann Graedener, and Karel Navrátil. He completed a Ph.D. in musicology in 1906. Webern began his association with Schoenberg as a private composition pupil in 1904. From 1908 to 1938, Webern held various conducting posts in Austria, Czechoslovakia, and Germany. During World War II, Werbern supported himself by teaching privately and working as an arranger. He had just been offered a rewarding position, following the end of the war, to resume as conductor for Austrian Radio (a position he held from 1927 to 1938), when he was accidentally shot by an American soldier while stepping out on his son-in-law's front porch to smoke a cigar. Webern's music is typified by a sparse use of, often large, musical resources, creating works of literal minimalism, which are the result of assiduous organizational procedures combining serialism with intricate contrapuntal devices and a careful arrangement of timbral combinations.

**Writings:** *The Path to the New Music,* edited by Willi Reich, 56-58. London and Bryn-Mawr, Pennsylvania: Theodore Presser, 1963.

**Principal Works:** *orchestral - Passacaglia,* op. 1 (1908), *Six Orchestral Pieces,* op. 6 (1909), *Five Orchestral Pieces,* op. 10 (1913), Symphony, op. 21 (1928), *Variations,* op. 30 (1940); *chamber - 6 Bagatelles for String Quartet,* op. 9 (1913), Concerto for 9 Instruments, op. 24 (1934), String Quartet, op. 28 (1938), *vocal - Entflieht auf* *leichten Kähnen*, op. 2 (1908), *Five Sacred Songs*, op. 15 (1922), *Five Canons*, op. 16 (1924), and numerous songs.

## Selected Composer Bibliography

Webern, Anton: *Letters to Hildegard Jone and Josef Humplik*, edited by Josef Polnauer. Vienna: Universal Edition, 1959. In an English translation by Cornelius Cardew, Bryn Mawr, Pennsylvania: Theodore Presser, 1967.

McKenzie, Wallace: "Webern's Technique of Choral Composition," *Anton Webern Perspectives*, edited by Demar Irvine. Seattle: University of Washington Press, 1966.

Moldenhauer, Hans: *Anton Webern: A Chronicle of His Life and Work*. New York: Alfred A. Knopf, 1979.

Roman, Zoltan: *Anton Webern: An Annotated Bibliography*. Detroit, MI: Information Coördinators, 1983.

Bailey, Kathryn: *The Twelve-Note Music of Anton Webern: Old Forms in a New Language*. Cambridge: Cambridge University Press, 1991.

# Das Augenlicht [The Light of the Eye], op. 26 (1935)

**Duration:** ca. 10 minutes

**Text:** The text is by Hildegard Jone, from her *Viæ inviæ*, and is in German. The score includes a singing English translation by Eric Smith.

**Performing Forces: voices:** SATB choir **orchestra:** flute, oboe, clarinet in B$^b$, Alto saxophone in E$^b$, horn in F, trumpet in C, trombone, percussion (2 players - timpani, glockenspiel, xylophone, suspended cymbal), celeste, harp, mandolin, 8 violins, 4 violas, 4 cellos.

**First Performance:** 17 June 1938; London; the BBC Symphony Orchestra and Chorus, conducted by Hermann Scherchen; as part of the 16th Festival of the International Society for Contemporary Music.

**Edition:** *Das Augenlicht* is published by Universal Edition. The orchestral materials were first published in 1956, but a piano-vocal edition, prepared by Ludwig Zenk was first published by Universal

Eidition in 1938. A study score is available for purchase from Philharmonia (427), performance materials are available through rental from Schotts.

**Autograph:** The Webern Archive is in the possession of the Paul Sacher Foundation in Basle, Switzerland.

**Notes:** Webern was less dogmatic in his application of 12-tone techniques to this work, none-the-less, it is serially conceived. In the opening section of the choral writing, the name B-A-C-H is spelled musically within the row as stated in the soprano part and then in reverse in the tenor part four measures later. The score is notated at sounding pitch throughout. It is inscribed "meiner Tochter Amalie Waller."

**Performance Issues:** The greatest challenge in performing this piece is pitch accuracy. The orchestration is Spartan with considerable doubling between parts. Webern employs orthodox contrapuntal techniques throughout, including strict rhythmic canon, homophonic chorale writing, pervasive imitation, and simultaneous statements in prime and inverted forms. The small orchestra leaves many solo instrumental passages exposed. A single player could cover all of the percussion parts with the proper stage set-up. There is some intricate interplay between instruments, especially among the brass, which will require attention, but will be less troublesome than in a larger orchestration. The instrumental writing requires independence, but is within the abilities of moderately experienced players. The choral passages are in no way supported by the accompaniment, with vocal lines either *a cappella*, or musically independent of the orchestra. Even starting pitches of choral sections must be discerned through pitch relations. Most of the choral material is in two-part polyphony or four-part homophony. The choir must also be capable of rhythmic independence, as at times it is cross-metric with the orchestra. **Choir:** difficult; **Orchestra:** medium difficult.

**Discography:** John Alldis Choir (John Alldis, chorus-master), London Symphony Orchestra; conducted by Pierre Boulez, recorded in Banking Town Hall, London during 2-4 June 1969. Sony Classical: SM 3K 45 845 [ADD].

## Selected Bibliography

Smith, Eric: "Foreword" to Anton Webern's *Das Augenlicht*. Vienna: Universal Edition, 1956.

Immel, Ralph Conrad, Jr.: *The Relationship Between the Text and the Music in Anton Webern's "Das Augenlicht'*. University of Texas: Master's of Music thesis, 1966.

Miller, D. Douglas: *An Analysis for Performance of Anton Webern's Choral Works with Opus Numbers*. Indiana University: Doctor of Music thesis, 1973.

# Erste Kantate, op. 29 (1938-39)

**Duration:** ca. 8 minutes

**Text:** The German text is by Hildegard Jone. The text of movement I is taken from *Blitz und Donner*, found in *Enthülle Form*; movement II is from; *Fons hortorum*; and movement II from *Verwandlung der chariten*. The score includes a singing English translation by Eric Smith.

**Performing Forces: voices:** soprano soloist; choir; **orchestra:** flute, oboe, clarinet in B$^b$, bass clarinet in B$^b$, horn in F, trumpet in C, trombone, timpani, percussion (2 players - glockenspiel, bass drum, cymbals, tam-tam, triangle), harp, mandolin, celeste, and strings (with no doublebasses).

**First Performance:** 2 February 1947; London; Emelie Hooke; BBC Orchestra and Chorus; conducted by Karl Rankl.

**Edition:** *Erste Cantata* is published by Universal Edition under the Philharmonia line. The piano reduction (UE 12197) and miniature score (PH. 447) are available for purchase; performance materials are available through rental.

**Autograph:** The Webern Archive is in the possession of the Paul Sacher Foundation in Basle, Switzerland.

**Notes:** The second half of the tone row upon which the piece is composed is the retrograde inversion of the first half. The score is divided into three movements as follows:

| I | "Zündender Lichtblitz" | choir |
| II | "Kleiner Flügel" | soprano solo |
| III | "Tönen die seligen Saiten Apollos" | choir with |
| | | soprano solo in |
| | | the final 17 bars |

**Performance Issues:** Webern has organized his serial material in the vocal parts to create a sense of triadic motion; however, the choir may often be singing four consecutive chromatic pitches simultaneously. This does allow the singers to make some aural sense of this extremely dense musical fabric. Vocal dissonances are also tempered by octave separations. The choral passages in the first movement are all *a cappella* with no direct pitch preparation from the orchestra. In the third movement there is ample instrumental doubling of the choral parts. All of the parts sound as written in the score including the glockenspiel. The independent instrumental parts are not particularly difficult, but the interweaving of independent parts, and overall transparency of the score presents substantial difficulties in achieving ensemble and balance. All of the instrumental parts are disjunct with only a few notes at a time which contribute to a large melodic line formed by the interplay of disparate instrumental parts. **Soloist:** soprano - range: c'-b", tessitura: d'-f#", this solo exploits the entire range with broad leaps and disjunct melodic lines, it is musically very difficult; **Choir:** difficult; **Orchestra:** difficult.

**Discography:** Halina Lukomska; John Alldis Choir (John Alldis, chorus-master), London Symphony Orchestra; conducted by Pierre Boulez, recorded in Banking Town Hall, London on 3 June 1969. Sony Classical: SM 3K 45 845 [ADD].

## Selected Bibliography

Jone, Hildegard: "Eine Kantate," *Die Reihe 2* (1955), 14-15.

Rochberg, George: "Webern's Search for Harmonic Identity," *Journal of Music Theory*, volume 6, number 1 (Spring 1962) 109-122.

Miller, D. Douglas: *An Analysis for Performance of Anton Webern's Choral Works with Opus Numbers*. Indiana University: Doctor of Music thesis, 1973.

Konold, Wolf: "Anton Webern: Erste Kantate, op. 29," *Weltliche Kantaten in 20 Jahrhundert*, 120-123. Zürich: Möseler, 1975.

## Zweite Kantate, op. 31 (1941-43)

**Duration:** ca. 16 minutes

**Text:** The German text is by Hildegard Jone. The score includes a singing English translation by Eric Smith. The sources from Jone's work for the texts by movement are:

    I   *Strahl und Klang*, from the *Licht und Lied* cycle
    II  *Die Stille um den Bienenkorb*, from the *Das Feldpostpäcken* cycle
   III *Alle Glocken*, from the *Mohnkopf* cycle
   IV *Der Wind*, from the *Das Feldpostpäcken* cycle
   V  *Freundselig ist das Wort* from the *Freundseligkeit* cycle
   VI *Das Neueborene*, from the *Alltag* cycle

**Performing Forces: voices:** soprano and bass soloists; choir; **orchestra:** 2 flutes, 2 oboes, 2 clarinets in $B^b$, bassoon, alto saxophone $E^b$, horn in F, trumpet in C, trombone, tuba, percussion (1 player - glockenspiel, bells), harp, celeste, and strings.

**First Performance:** 23 June 1950; Brussels; festival of the International Society for Contemporary Music; Ilona Steingruber, Otto Wiener; NIR Chamber Orchestra and Chorus; conducted by Herbert Häfners.

**Edition:** *Zweite Cantata* is published by Universal Edition. The piano reduction (UE 11885), choral score (UE 11996), and miniature score (PH. 466) are available for purchase; performance materials are available through rental.

**Autograph:** The Webern Archive is in the possession of the Paul Sacher Foundation in Basle, Switzerland.

**Notes:** Webern divided this cantata into two sections each of which contains all 48 permutations of its fundamental tone row stated a single time. This is the last composition which he completed. The original order of composition was IV - V - VI - I - II - III. The arrangement of the work into six movements is as follows:

    I   "Schweigt auch die Welt"       baritone solo
    II  "Sehr tiefverhalten"          baritone solo

| III | "Schöpfen aus Brunnen" | SSA choir and soprano solo |
| IV | "Leichteste Bürden" | soprano solo |
| V | "Freundselig ist da Wort" | SATB choir and soprano solo |
| VI | "Gelockert aus dem Schosse" | SATB choir in a canonic chorale |

**Performance Issues:** The organization of the tone-row creates a number of triadic formulations which aid the singers in accessing the pitch material. All of the parts sound as written in the score including the glockenspiel and doublebasses. The choral passages in movement V are unaccompanied, but brief. The final movement is comprised of thorough doubling between the vocal and instrumental parts, and in movement III the choral parts are doubled throughout, but the solo is not. The final movement is modeled on medieval polyphony and has as many as four different meters, sharing the same beat value, occuring simultaneously, so that there are non-concurrent down beats between parts. The instrumental parts are somewhat technically demanding, more importantly, they require great control of dynamics and articulations. Some of the harp notation is impractical and must be enharmonically respelled. As with much of Webern's orchestral music, the greatest challenge lies in the integration of widely diverse instruments providing two or three notes to a melodic line within a sparse musical texture. There are frequent changes of meter and tempo which compound the difficulties in achieving cohesive ensemble. **Soloists:** soprano - range: $b^b$-c#''', tessitura: f#'-g'', this is a disjunct solo with broad leaps, the singer must be capable of pianissimo singing on c#'''; bass - range: G-g', tessitura: B-e', this role requires a singer who can make a legato phrase from a set a wide melodic leaps; **Choir:** very difficult; **Orchestra:** very difficult.

**Discography:** Halina Lukomska, Barry McDaniel; John Alldis Choir (John Alldis, chorus-master), London Symphony Orchestra; conducted by Pierre Boulez, recorded in Walthamstow, London on 28 May 1969. Sony Classical: SM 3K 45 845 [ADD].

## Selected Bibliography

Smith, Eric: "Foreword" to Anton Webern's *Zweite Cantata*. Vienna: Universal Edition, 1956.

Castiglioni, Niccolo: "Sul rapporto tra parole e musici nella Seconda Cantata di Webern," *Incontri Musicali*, number 3 (August 1959), 112-127.

Spinner, Leopold: "Anton Weberns Kantate Nr. 2, Opus 31. Die Formprinzipalen der kanonische Darstellung (Analyse des vierten Satzes)," *Schweizerische Musikzeitung*, volume 101, number 5 (1961), 303-308.

Miller, D. Douglas: *An Analysis for Performance of Anton Webern's Choral Works with Opus Numbers*. Indiana University: Doctor of Music thesis, 1973.

**Weill, Kurt** (b. Dessau, Germany, 2 March 1900; d. New York, 3 April 1950)

**Life:** Weill's work in developing the genre of musical theater in the 20th century has produced a diverse body dramatic pieces reflecting a wide range of styles which often combine elements of western-classical music with jazz and other popular-music styles. Weill attended the Berlin Hochschule für Musik (1918-19), studying counterpoint with Friedrich Koch and composition with Engelbert Humperdinck. He then studied at the Prussian Academy of Arts (1920-23) with Ferruccio Busoni and Busoni's protegé, Philipp Jarnach. Weill achieved early success writing satirical and politically motivated works for theater. In a number of these socially progressive projects he worked with the librettist, Berthold Brecht. Fleeing the Nazi's, Weill settled in the United States in 1935, becoming a citizen in 1943. In the United States, Weill engaged in a successful career writing works of substance for Hollywood films and the stages of Broadway. Weill's wife, Lotte Lenya, was the star of many of his staged works in Europe and the United States. His music is marked by a natural assimilation of popular music styles, an unusual sensitivity to language, and a focus upon themes of human dignity and the struggle against social injustice.

**Principal Works:** *operas/musicals - Der Protagonist* (1925), *Die Dreigroschenoper* (1928), *Aufstieg und Fall der Stadt Mahagonny* (1929), *Happy End* (1929), *Der Jasager* (1930), *Die Bürgschaft* (1931), *Der Silbersee* (1933), *Johnny Johnson* (1936), *Knickerbocker Holiday* (1938), *Lady in the Dark* (1940), *One Touch of Venus* (1943), *The Firebrand of Florence* (1944), *Street Scene* (1946), *Love Life* (1947), *Down in the Valley* (1948), *Lost in the Stars* (1949); *ballet - Die sieben Todsünden der Kleinbürger* (1933); *film scores - You and Me* (1938), *Where Do We Go from Here?* (1944), *Salute to France* (1944); *orchestral* - Symphony No. 1, *Berliner Sinfonie* (1921), *Sinfonia* *sacra* (1922), Symphony No. 2, *Pariser Sinfonie* (1933); **vocal - *Der Neue Orpheus*** (1925), *Vom Tod im Wald* (1927), *Song of the Railroads* (1938), *Kiddush* (1946).

## Selected Composer Bibliography

Sanders, Ronald: *The Days Grow Short: The Life and Music of Kurt Weill*. New York: Holt, Rinehart, and Winston, 1980; reprinted, New York: Limelight Editions, 1985.

Jarman, Douglas: *Kurt Weill: An Illustrated Biography*. Bloomington, Indiana: Indiana University Press, 1982.

Drew, David: *Kurt Weill: A Handbook*. Berkeley, California: University of California Press, 1987.

Schebera, Jürgen: *Kurt Weill: An Illustrated Life*, translated by Caroline Murphy. New Haven, Connecticut: Yale University Press, 1995.

Weill, Kurt and Lotte Lenya: *Speak Low (When You Speak of Love): The Letters of Kurt Weill and Lotte Lenya*, edited and translated by Lys Symonette and Kim H. Kowalke. Berkeley, California: University of California Press, 1996.

# Das Berliner Requiem (1928)

**Duration:** ca. 21 minutes[39]

**Text:** The text is a compilation of poems, in German, by Bertold Brecht, selected and organized for this purpose by Brecht and Weill.

**Performing Forces: voices:** tenor and baritone soloists; TBarB men's choir; **orchestra:** 2 clarinets in $B^b$, 2 bassoons, 2 alto saxophones in $E^b$ (saxophone II doubling tenor saxophone in $B^b$), 2 horns in F, 2 trumpets in $B^b$, 2 trombones, tuba (optional), timpani, percussion (1 player -snare drum, suspended cymbal), guitar, and organ or harmonium.

The composer indicates that this work may be sung by tenor, baritone, and bass soloists alone.

**First Performance:** 22 May 1929; as a Frankfurt Radio broadcast; Hans Grahl (tenor), Johannes Willy (baritone), Jean Stern (bass),

---

[39] The score indicates ca. 21 minutes; however, the Atherton recording is 18'38".

Reinhold Merten (organ); Frankfurt Radio Orchestra; conducted by Ludwig Rottenberg.

**Edition:** *Das Berliner Requiem* is published by Universal Edition. The piano-vocal score (UE 09786), choral parts (UE 13429A-C), and study score (UE 16630) are available for purchase; performance materials are available through rental.

**Autograph:** All but a few fragments of the original manuscript have been lost. A fair copy of the score with some missing pages survives.

**Notes:** This work was commissioned by Reichs-Rundfunkgesellschaft and is dedicated to Frankfurt Radio. It was originally conceived for three male voices and wind band. Some time following the premiere, Weill adapted the score to include two soloists and male choir. Due to the disappearance of the manuscript materials, the transformation is not fully clear. Additional fragments of the revised full score have also been lost. A contemporary performing edition has been prepared for Universal Edition by David Drew (see above). The original, seven-movement version included a bass solo, "Vom tod im Wald," which served as the opening movement. The work is now in six sections as follows:

  I   "Grosser Dankchoral"
  II  "Ballade vom ertrunkenen Mädchen"
  III "Marterl" changed by Weill in 1929 to "Grabschrift 1919"
  IV  "Berichte über den unbekannten Soldaten I
  V   "Berichte über den unbekannten Soldaten II
  VI  "Grosser Dankchoral" [da capo of movement I]

This work was conceived during the celebrations commemorating the tenth anniversary of the end of WWI. The strong antiwar sentiments caused the radio officials to postpone its premiere broadcast. The premiere was not broadcast in Berlin, but only in southern Germany.

**Performance Issues:** With the exception of the first eight measures of movement IV, and a melismatic cadential extension at the close of movement II, all of the vocal ensemble writing is in block-chord homophonic style. The entire work is text driven, in terms of meaning and rhythm. All of the vocal rhythms are logogenic, reflecting the prosody of the naturally spoken text. Because of this, it is difficult to justify performing this work in translation, yet the directness of the text's presentation suggests a need for it to be clearly understood by the audience. The harmonic language is often quite dissonant, but the voice leading reflects tonal traditions. Generally, less conventional harmonic sequences are repeated a number of times. The pitch material for the singers is always clearly supported by the instrumental accompaniment. The score indicates that the trombone part in movement III may be played on tuba if available; however, it should be noted that this part stays on the staff, so a smaller tuba or a euphonium, should be employed. The percussion part is fairly inconsequential: a two-beat snare drum roll and two strikes on a suspended cymbal in movement IV. This may be covered by a member of the choir, but not the timpanist. The instrumental parts are accessible to players of moderate experience. The guitar part consists of strummed chords, which are notated without tablature. The second movement is choir accompanied by guitar alone. The guitar and banjo parts can be played by the same person as they appear in different movements. The organ parts would be most effective on a reed organ, or an instrument akin to a Hammond B-3. **Soloists:** tenor - range: d-g', tessitura: f#-e', this is a lyric role with some sustained singing; baritone - range: A-e$^{b\prime}$, tessitura: f-d', this is a speech-like solo which stays almost exclusively within the indicated tessitura; **Choir:** easy, **Orchestra:** medium easy.

**Discography:** Philip Langridge, Benjamin Luxon, Michael Rippon; London Sinfonietta; conducted by David Atherton, recorded in 1975. Polygram: D 172783 [ADD].
Ensemble Musique Oblique; conducted by Philippe Herreweghe, recorded in 1992. Harmonia Mundi: 901422 [DDD].

### Selected Bibliography

Weill, Kurt: "Notiz zum Berliner Requiem," *Der deutsche Rundfunk* 7 (17 May 1929).
Drew, David: "Forward" and "Revisionsbericht" to Kurt Weill: *Das Berliner Requiem*, revised. Vienna: Universal Edition, 1976.
_____: *Kurt Weill: A Handbook*, 207-211. Berkeley, California: University of California Press, 1987.
Schebera, Jürgen: *Kurt Weill: An Illustrated Life*, translated by Caroline Murphy, 128-129, 131-132. New Haven, Connecticut: Yale University Press, 1995.

# Der Lindberghflug (1929)

**Duration:** ca. 40 minutes

**Text:** The text for *Der Lindberghflug* was written specifically for this work by Bertold Brecht. It is in German with some amusing American proper nouns.

**Performing Forces:** voices: tenor (Lindbergh), baritone, and bass soloists; SATB choir; **orchestra:** 2 flutes, 2 clarinets in B♭, 2 bassoons, 2 trumpets in B♭, 2 trombones, percussion, piano, and strings.

**First Performance:** radio broadcast: 28 July 1929; Kurhaus, Baden-Baden; Betty Mergler, Josef Witt, Johannes Willy, Oskar Kalman; Hugo Holles Madrigal Society, Frankfurt Radio Orchestra; directed by Ernst Hardt and conducted by Hermann Scherchen; on the final concert of the *Musiktage*; with Hindemith listed as co-composer.

first public concert: 5 December 1929; Krolloper, Berlin; Erik Wirl; Preußische Staatskapelle (Karl Rankl, chorus-master); conducted by Otto Klemperer; with Hindemith's contributions withdrawn, and Weill listed as sole composer.

United States premiere: 4 April 1931; Philadelphia Orchestra; conducted by Leopold Stokowski. This was in an English translation made by George Antheil.

**Edition:** The revised version of *Der Flug des Lindberghs* is available as *Ozeanflug* from Universal Edition. The 1930 score is now available in reprint from Universal Editioin (U.E. 9938). All materials are available through rental. An authoritative reference score of the original version is being prepared by Rudolf Stephan in the Paul Hindemith, *Sämtliche Werke, Band 1, 6, Szenische Versuche*. Mainz: B. Schott Söhne, 1982.

**Autograph:** The manuscript of the sections of the original score composed by Weill are in the Universal Edition Archive. The portions composed by Hindemith are in the possession of the Paul Hindemith Institute.

**Notes:** Commissioned by Deutsche Kammermusik, Baden-Baden, Weill originally composed this work with Paul Hindemith from a radio score under the title, *Der Lindberghflug*. This was premiered in Baden-Baden on 28 July 1929. Weill rescored the piece making it entirely his own. This version was premiered in Berlin on 5 December 1929. He revised the score again in 1930 changing its title to *Der Flug des Lindberghs*. Weill later retitled the work *Der Ozeanflug* in protest of Lindbergh's public expressions of neutrality toward Nazi Germany. Neither Hindemith, nor Weill sought to have the original version published; it will appear in print for the first time as part of the Hindemith *Collected Works*. The work is in fifteen sections centered around the first transatlantic flight with the choir personifying fog, a storm, and the plane's engines, all of which converse with the pilot as follows:

|   |   |   |
|---|---|---|
| I | Inviting an American pilot to fly across the ocean | choir |
| II | Introducing the pilot Charles Lindbergh | T solo |
| III | Lindbergh's departure from New York to fly to Europe | T solo |
| IV | New York City interviews the craft | Bar solo, SA |
| V | Almost at the beginning of the flight the pilot must battle fog | T solo, TTB |
| VI | In the night a snowstorm comes | T solo, S |
| VII | Sleep | B and T solos |
| VIII | Nearly all of the flight, the American papers tell of Lindbergh's perpetual luck | Bar solo, SATB |
| IX | Thoughts of Luck | orchestra |
| X | The French papers write: So he flies, over the storm, across the sea, under the shadows | SATB |
| XI | Lindbergh speaks to his motor | T solo |
| XII | Finally, near Scotland, Lindbergh sees a fisherman | Bar and B solos |
| XIII | At the Bourget Airport in Paris, in the night of 21 May 1927, at 10 o'clock in the evening, the American pilot is awaited by a great crowd | T solo, SATB |
| XIV | The arrival of the pilot, Charles Lindbergh to the Bourget Airport in Paris | orchestra |
| XV | Report of the unattainable | T, Bar, and B solos, SATB |

**Performance Issues:** This is an interesting work of social realism. It is quite accessible to less experienced performers. The soloists have the most challenging pitch language, which remains tonal, but with some imaginative uses of chromaticism. The entire composition is pervaded with a cosmopolitan assimilation of American jazz elements similar to the music in the Brecht/Weill operas, *Mahagonny* and *Die Dreigroschenoper*. It is important that the instrumentalists and soloists be able to perform in this style. The choral portions are less conspicuously jazz-based. The score uses many ostinati in the orchestra and choir. The choral writing is comprised primarily of unison singing and homophonic block-chord motion. The vocal parts are very clearly supported by the accompaniment, except for movement X, which is *a cappella*. The orchestration is fairly exposed similar to a theater orchestra. The instrumental writing remains very practical for the players and for achieving successful ensemble. **Soloist:** tenor - range: c-a$^{b'}$, tessitura: f-d', this is a lyric role with some rapid text declamation; baritone - range: A-f', tessitura: e-c', this is a declamatory role with sustained singing in the upper range; bass - range: A-c', tessitura: d-a, this is a lyric and fairly brief role; **Choir:** medium easy, **Orchestra:** medium easy.

**Discography:** Shellac recordings of the original version from Cologne Radio: ensembles of Cologne Radio; conducted by Hermann Scherchen, recorded 18 March 1930.

University Chorus and Academic Orchestra Association of Göttingen; conducted by Hermann Fuchs, recorded in 1978. Thorofon: MTH 118 [LP].

Pro Musica of Cologne, Cologne Radio Orchesta; conducted by Jan Latham-König, recorded in 1990. Capriccio: 10250 [DDD].

### Selected Bibliography

Einstein, Alfred: review of the concert premiere, *Berliner Tageblatt* (6 December 1929).

Urban, Erich: review of the concert premiere, *Berliner Zeittung am Mittag* (6 December 1929).

Kowalke, Kim H.: *"Der Lindberghflug*: Kurt Weill's Musical Tribute to Lindbergh," *Missouri Historical Society Bulletin* (April 1977).

Stephan, Rudolf: "Kritische Bericht" for Paul Hindemith: *Sämtliche Werke, Band 1, 6, Szenische Versuche*. Mainz: B. Schott Söhne, 1982.

Heyworth, Peter: *Otto Klemperer: His Life and Times*, volume 1: 1885-1933, 292-297. Cambridge: Cambridge University Press, 1983.

Drew, David: *Kurt Weill: A Handbook*. Berkeley, California: University of California Press, 1987; 212-217.

Schebera, Jürgen: *Kurt Weill: An Illustrated Life*, translated by Caroline Murphy. New Haven, Connecticut: Yale University Press, 1995; 132-138, 140, 143, 239.

# APPENDIX I

# SOURCES, AUTHORS, AND TRANSLATORS OF TEXTS

**Antolsky, Pavel** (1896-1978) was a Soviet Russian poet. He studied at Moscow University, and in 1943 joined the Communist Party. His works include the poetry collections: *The Son* (1943), and *The Ocean* (1950); and the book, *The Strength of Vietnam* (1960). [found in: Prokofiev - *Ballad of a Boy Who Remained Unknown*].

**Arnold, Robert Franz** (1872-1938) was an Austrian scholar of literary history. He studied at the Universities of Berlin and Vienna, and then served on the faculty at the University of Vienna (1906-36). He was a guest scholar at Stanford University in 1936, and for the last two years of his life served as president of the Goethe-Gesellschaft. [found in: Schoenberg - *Gurrelieder*]

**Augustine, St. Aurelius Augustinus** (354-430) was one of the most significant leaders of the early Christian church. He was born in what is now Tunisia, studied in Carthage, and then taught in Rome and Milan. In 386, he converted to Christianity and was baptized, with his son, by St. Ambrose. He returned to northern Africa and became Bishop of Hippo in 396, a position he retained for the remainder of his life. He was a prolific author of philosopical works which have had a profound influence upon the majority of philosophers and theologians since his time. His principal works are *The Confessions* (400) which is an autobiographical spiritual odyssey, and *The City of God* (412-427), a 22 book study of the spiritual history and destiny of mankind. [found in: Martin - *Golgotha*]

**Balmont, Konstantin** (1867-1943) was a Russian essayist, poet and translator. A prominent member of the Russina Symbolist movement, his works are often marked by exotic themes. [found in: Rachmaninov - *Kolokola* (translator of Poe's text of *The Bells* into Russian)]

**Barbour, John** (c. 1316-1396) was a Scottish poet, theologian, and scholar. He is regarded as the "father of Scottish history and poetry." He was educated in Oxford and Paris, served as Archdeacon in Aberdeen, and was a clerk under King Robert II of Scotland. His writings include *The Bruce* (1375), which is an epic poem on the life of Robert the Bruce. [found in: Copland - *Canticle of Freedom*]

**The Beatitudes** are also known as "The Sermon on the Mount," an address attributed to Jesus Christ and recorded in the *Gospel of Matthew*, 5:3-11. [found in: Martin - *In terra pax*]

**Bechstein, Ludwig** (1801-60) was German poet, novelist, and collector of folktales. He was librarian of the Ducal Library in Meiningen and later served as its archivist. His works include: *Die Haimonskinder* (1830), *Faustus* (1833), *Das Tolle Jahr* (1833), and *Fahrten eines Musikanten* (1836-37). [found in: Mahler - *Das klagende Lied*]

**Bédier, Charles Marie Joseph** (1864-1938) was a French scholar of medieval literature. His works include: *Les Fabliaux* (1893), *Roman de Tristan et Iseult* (1900), and *Les Légendes épiques* (1908-13). [found in: Martin - *Le Vin herbé*]

**Benedictbeuren Monastery** This monastery was a prominent place of learning in the middle ages. It became the repository for a body of 12th- and 13th-century secular poetry written by the Goliard scholars and students there which have come to be known as the *Carmina Burana*, or "Songs of Beuren." These texts reached a much broader audience through their use in Carl Orff's work of the same name. [found in: Orff - *Carmina Burana*]

**Benn, Gottfried** (1886-1956), a German expressionist writer and physician, Benn was the only prominent author in Germany to openly support the Nazi party. He later broke from them and was expelled from the Reichsschrifttumskammer. [found in: Hindemith - *Das Unaufhörliche*]

**Bernsten, Aage** (1885-1952) was a Danish physician and poet from the Funen region. He attended the University of Copenhagen. His father was a Danish politician who introduced Carl Nielsen to Copenhagen society in 1883. [found in: Nielsen - *Fynsk Foraar*]

**Bezymensky, Alexander** (1898-1973) was a poet and prominent figure in Soviet Russian literature. He studied at the Kiev

Commercial Institute. Having joined the Communist Party in 1916, he served on the first Central Committee of the Russian Communist Youth. His works are dedicated to the furtherance of Soviet political ideals. He was never censured by the government. His works include *October Dawns* (1920), *The Smell of Life* (1924), *Tragic Night* (1930), and *Angry Lines* (1949). [found in: Shostakovich - Symphony No. 2]

**The Bible** is comprised of the Old and New Testaments which respectively serve as the principal texts supporting the faiths of Judaism and Christianity. [see also text sources under: *The Beatitudes, Lamentations of Jeremiah, The Psalms, Revelation of St. John the Divine*] [found in: Martin - *Golgotha*; Penderecki - *Passio et Mors Domini Nostri Iesu Christi Secundum Lucam, Kosmogonia, Canticum Canticorum Salomonis*, Schoenberg - *Jakobsleiter*, Stravinsky - *Canticum Sacrum, A Sermon, a Narrative, and a Prayer*]

**Brecht, Bertold** (1898-1956) was a poet and the most significant German playwright of the 20th century. He studied philosophy and medicine. His early works helped to shape the expressionist movement, which he gradually imbued with elements of Marxism. He viewed his works as the theater of the people. He fled the Nazis and settled in Hollywood in 1941. In 1946, he was brought before the Senate sub-committee on un-American activities where he denied having membership in the Communist Party. He was offered his own theater company in East Germany, which he accepted in 1948. There he continued his experiments in drama. His works include: *Mann ist Mann* (1926), *Mahagonny* (1927, opera with Weill), *Die Dreigroschenoper* (1928, opera with Weill), *Mother Courage* (1941), *Der Aufhaltsame Aufstieg der Arturo Ui* (1948). [found in: Weill - *Das Berliner Requiem, Der Lindberghflug*]

**Bruno, Giordano** (1548-1600) Originally ordained a Roman Catholic priest, Bruno grew to doubt the teachings of the church and fled to the Calvanist city of Geneva, revoking his holy orders. He taught and wrote in France, England , and Germany. He was invited to Venice by Giovanni Mocenigo who turned him over to church authorities. He was imprisoned, refused to recant, and was burned at the stake 17 February 1600 in the Campo dei Fiori in Rome where a statute now memorializes his martyrdom. [found in: Henze - *Novae de Infinito Laudes*, Penderecki - *Kosmogonia*]

**Catullus, Gaius Valerius** (c.84-c.54 BC) was a Roman lyric poet. He is best known for his love verses to the married Roman, "Lesbia." [found in: Orff - *Catulli Carmina, Trionfo di Afrodite*]

**Claudel, Paul** (1868-1955) was a French essayist, playwright, and poet. His work is characterized by a strong Roman Catholic predilection. His works include: *L'Annonce fait à Marie* (1892), *Partage de Midi* (1905), *Le Soulier de Satin* (1921), *Cinq Grandes Odes* (1922), *Christophe Colombe* (1930, opera with Milhaud). [found in: Hindemith -*Triumphsgesang, Custos quid de nocte*, and *Cantique de l'espérance*; Honegger - *Jeanne d'Arc au Bûcher*]

**Cocteau, Jean** (1889-1963) was a French playwright, film director, critic, artist, actor, and poet. He worked in a wide variety of creative circumstances and in as many varied roles. He was a prominent champion of *Les Six*, Stravinsky, de Chirico, and Picasso. His works include the novels: *La Lampe d'Aladin* (1909), *Le Grand Ecart* (1923), *Les Infants terribles* (1929); the plays: *Orphée* (1926), *L'Aigle à deux têtes* (1946); and the films: *Le Sang du poète* (1932), and *La Belle et la bête* (1945). [found in: Stravinsky - *Œdipus Rex*]

**colinde** are a genre of Rumanian folktales and folksongs on themes surrounding Christmas. [found in: Bartok - *Cantata Profana*]

**Copernicus, Nicolas** (1473-1543) was a Polish astronomer. The nephew of the Bishop of Ermeland, he was educated in science at the University of Krakow, in canon law in Bologna, and in medicine in Padua, and was made doctor of canon law at Ferrara. A diverse intellect, and public official, he proved that the earth revolved around the sun in his *De Revolutionibus* (1530) for which he is considered to be the founder of modern astronomy. [found in: Penderecki - *Kosmogonia*]

**Cummings, E[dward] E[stlin]** (1894-1962) was an American poet. He was educated at Harvard and served as an ambulance driver in France during World War I. At this time, he was mistakenly imprisoned, the experience of which became the basis of his novel, *The Enormous Room* (1922). He attained great success as a poet of short verse which gained celebrity for its expressive spirit and its use of visual arrangements of characters using a typewriter. [found in: Stravinsky - *Œdipus Rex* (translator)]

**Daniélou, Jean** (1905-74) was a Roman Catholic Bishop, Cardinal, and a Jesuit patristic scholar. He was the author of many religious studies including: *Bible and Liturgy* (1950) and *Theology of Judeo-Christianity* (1958). He served as an expert council to the Vatican II. [found in: Stravinsky - *Œdipus Rex* (translator)]

**Dekker, Thomas** (c.1570-c.1541) was a British playwright. Among his works are: *The Bachelor's Banquet* (1603), *The Wonderful Year* (1603, pamphlet), *The Honest Whore*, parts I and II (1604, 1607),

*Westward Ho!* (1607), *The Witch of Edmonton* (1623). [found in: Stravinsky - *A Sermon, a Narrative, and a Prayer*]

**Dolmatovsky, Yevgeni** (b. 1915) was a popular Soviet Russian poet. He studied at the Gorky Literary Institute and, in 1934, joined the Communist Party. He attacked the anti-Stalin movement even after Stalin's death. He won the Stalin Prize in 1949. His works are direct and traditionally metric. [found in: Shostakovich - *The Song of the Forests*; Prokofiev - *Songs of Our Days, Flourish, Our Mighty Land* ]

**Eastern Orthodox Liturgy** the various Orthodox Christian rites, primarily centered in eastern Europe which split from Roman Catholicism in 1054. These religious sects accept only the doctrines of the seven Ecumenical Councils (325-787). [found in: Janacek - *Msa Glagskaja*; Penderecki - *Untrenja*]

**Eisenstein, Serge Mikhailovich** (1898-1948) was a great Russian filmmaker. He was initially trained as a scenery painter, but established his fame as the director of Soviet propaganda films. His works include: *The Battleship Potemkin* (1925), *Ten Days That Shook the World* (1928), *Alexander Nevsky* (1938), and *Ivan the Terrible* (1944). [found in: Prokofiev - *Ivan the Terrible*]

**Engels, Friedrich** (1820-95) was a German-born socialist reformer. He spent a portion of his life in England where he wrote *Conditions of the Working Classes in England in 1844* (1845). He met Karl Marx in 1844, and assisted him in writing *The Communist Manifesto* (1848). Following Marx's death, Engels dedicated his remaining years to editing and translating Marx's work. [found in: Prokofiev - *Cantata on the 20th Anniversary of the October Revolution*]

**Euripides** (c.484-406 BC) was a great Greek playwright. Of 80 works that survive only 18 are complete. Among them are: *Alcestis, Andromache, Electra, Iphigenia in Aulis, Iphigenia in Tauris, Medea,* and *Orestes.* [found in: Orff - *Trionfo di Afrodite*]

**Gagarin, Yuri** (1934-68) was the Soviet cosmonaut who became the first man to travel into space in 1961. He was killed while flying in a training exercise. [found in: Penderecki - *Kosmogonia*]

**Gide, André** (1869-1951) was a French novelist, poet, diarist, and translator. He wrote in nearly every genre and published over 50 books. In the early 20th century he became the voice of French youth. He received the Nobel Prize for literature in 1947. [found in: Stravinsky - *Persephone*]

**Glenn, John** (b. 1921), an astronaut and politician, he was the first man to orbit the earth in 1962. He became a U.S. senator representing Ohio in 1975. Of some musical interest, he was a grand-prize winner on the 1950s television program, "The $64,000 Question" with popular music as his topic. [found in: Penderecki - *Kosmogonia*]

**Goethe, Johann Wolfgang von** (1749-1832) is considered to be one of the greatest writers in the history of the German Language. He was a playwright, poet, scientist, and court official. At his father's insistence, he studied law at the University of Leipzig (1765-68) and Strasbourg (1770). He served as councillor to the Duke of Weimar (1776-86). He published significant studies in human anatomy and botany. He established a friendship with Schiller with whom he maintained an important correspondence, and near whom he is buried. His large literary output includes many fine poems and the following larger works: *Egmont* (1788), *Wilhelm Meisters Lehrjahre* (1796), *Wilhelm Meisters Wanderjahre* (1821-29), and a two-part adaptation of Marlowe's *Faust* (1808, 1832). [found in: Mahler - Symphony No. 8]

**Heiberg, Johan Ludvig** (1854-1928) was a Danish classical scholar. He taught philology at the University of Copenhagen (1896-1925), and edited many works from Greek antiquity, especially in the fields of mathematics and medicine. [found in: Nielsen - *Hymnus Amoris*]

**Isakovskogo, M.** (1900-73) was a Soviet Russian poet and journalist. After joining the Communist Party in 1918, he worked as a journalist in Smolensk (1921-31) and then moved to Moscow in 1931. He won the Stalin Prize in 1942 and 1948. His works had a broad following throughout the Soviet Union. He wrote little after 1953. [found in: Prokofiev - *Songs of Our Days*]

**Jacobsen, Jens Peter** (1847-85) was a Danish novelist and poet whose works combine elements of naturalism and impressionism. His works include: *Fru Marie Grubbe* (1876), *Niels Lyhne* (1880), and translations of Dickens into Danish. [found in: Schoenberg - *Gurrelieder*]

**James, Edward** (1907-84) was a French poet and journalist whose work appeared in the journal *Minotaur*. [found in: Poulenc - *Sécheresses*]

**Jefferson, Thomas** (1743-1826) was the third president of the United States, and one of that nation's greatest intellects. He was elected to the House of Burgesses in 1769, participated in the first Continental Congress in 1774, and drafted the *Declaration of Independence* in 1776. He was governor of Virginia (1779-81), congressmen (1781-84), a delegate and then minister to France (1784-89), and was appointed first Secretary of State by Washington (1789-94). After a brief retirement, he was called to become Vice-President in 1797, and was elected President (1801-1809). He helped to draft the Constitution of the state of Virginia, oversaw the Louisiana Purchase, and founded the University of Virginia. [found in: Thompson - *Testament of Freedom*]

**Jewish Liturgy** is based upon recitations from the *Torah* and Psalms of the Old Testament of the Bible combined with a series of traditional Hebrew prayers which vary in age from the time of King Solomon to the present day. [found in: Ernest Bloch - *Avodath Hakodesh*, Schoenberg - *Kol Nidre*]

**Jone, Hildegard** (1891-1963) was a poet and artist, born in Sarajevo, who is best remembered for her contributions of texts to the works of her close friend, Anton Webern. He husband was the sculptor, Josef Humplik. Her works include: *Ring, mein Bewurstein* (1918), and *Anima. Gedicht des Gottesjahr* (1948). [found in: Webern - *Das Augenlicht, Erste Kantate, Zweite Kantate*]

**Jørgensen, Johannes** (1866-1956) was a Danish poet and novelist who spent most of his life in Assisi, Italy. He converted to Roman Catholicism in1896. His works include biographies of St. Francis of Assisi (1907), St. Catherine of Siena (1915), St. Birgitta (1941-43), and an autobiography (1916-28). [found in: Nielsen - *Søvnen*]

**Kirsanov, Semyon** (1906-72) was an avant-garde Soviet Russian poet. He studied at the Odessa Institute for Public Education after which he began working with Mayakovsky in Moscow. His experimental techniques brought about attacks for formalism. He won the Stalin Prize in 1950. His works include: *A Poet's Poem* (1939), *The Sky Above the Homeland* (1947), *The Seven Days of the Week* (1956), and *Quests* (1967). [found in: Shostakovich - Symphony No. 3]

**Klopstock, Friederich** (1724-1803) was a German poet of religious works which include *Der Messias* (1773), and *Die deutsches Gelehrtenrepublik* (1774). [found in: Mahler - Symphony No. 2]

***Des Knaben Wunderhorn.*** (The Boy's Wonderful Horn, volume I, 1805; volume II, 1808; volume III, 1818) is a collection of German folk songs edited by Clemens Brentano and Achim von Arnim. [found in: Mahler - Symphony No. 2, Symphony No. 3]

**Lamentations of Jeremiah** is a book from the Old Testament of the Bible. Attributed to the prophet, Jeremiah, its five poetic sections lament the misery of the destruction of Jerusalem and pray for its restoration through the mercy of God. [found in: Penderecki -*Passio et Mors Domini Nostri Iesu Christi Secundum Lucam*, Stravinsky - *Threni*]

**Lebedev-Kumach, V.** (1898-1949) was an immensely popular Soviet Russian poet who joined the Communist Party in 1940. He began his career writing pro-revolutionary poems in newspapers. He worked for the journal, *Krokodil* (1922-34) after which he concentrated on nationalist song lyrics. His best known work, "Song of My Homeland," sold over 20 million copies. [found in: Prokofiev - *Songs of Our Days*]

**Lenin, Vladimir Ilyich** (1870-1924) was a Russian revolutionary and the first leader of the Soviet Union. After studying the works of Karl Marx, he spent the years of 1894 to 1917 organizing opposition to Czarist rule, which reached fruition in the "October Revolution." He is regarded as the founder of the Soviet Union. [found in: Prokofiev - *Cantata on the 20th Anniversary of the October Revolution*]

**Leonardo da Vinci** (1452-1519) was a great Renaissance painter, scientist, engineer, inventor, and architect. He is credited with developing oil painting and modern hydraulic irrigation. His detailed studies of anatomy and mechanics were far ahead of his time and remain of great interest to this day. He is best known for his paintings of the *Mona Lisa*, *The Last Supper*, and *The Virgin on the Rocks*. [found in: Penderecki - *Kosmogonia*]

**Lincoln. Abraham** (1809-65) was the 16th president of the United States. Famed for his honest ways and humble background, he distinguished himself in public life as a gifted orator, first achieving national attention for his debates with Stephen A. Douglas in 1854. He was elected president in 1860 as the victor of a four-way race. During his first year in office, South Carolina seceded from the Union and the Civil War began. He was assassinated shortly before the war's end by John Wilkes Booth. His best known speeches are *The Emancipation Proclamation* (1862) and *The Gettysburg Address* (1863). [found in: Diamond - *This Sacred Ground*]

**Lord's Prayer** is a prayer attributed to Jesus Christ and occurs in two places in the New Testament of the Bible: the Gospel of St. Matthew, 6:9-13 as part of the Sermon on the Mount (see: Beatitudes), and the Gospel of St. Luke 11:2-4. [found in: Martin - *In terra pax*]

**Lucretius** (c.99-55 BC) is a Roman poet and philosopher best known for his six-volume epic poem, *De Natura Rerum*. [found in: Penderecki - *Kosmogonia*]

**Lugovskoi, Stikhi V.** (1901-57), a Soviet Russian poet, was the son of a literature professor and a singer. He attended Moscow University, served in the Red Army, and became a leading figure in the constructivist movement in the 1930s. He published 36 books during his lifetime, but his fame was achieved gradually following his death. In 1937, he was criticized by the government and spent years in depression and fallow creativity, until a rich creative outburst following Stalin's death. [found in: Prokofiev - *Alexander Nevsky*, *Ivan the Terrible*]

**Marshak, Samuel** (1887-1964) was a prominent Soviet Russian author of children's literature. He lived with Gorky's family (1904-06) and later worked in child welfare (1914-22). He moved to Petrograd/Leningrad in 1922, and in 1924 was appointed director of children's literature for the State Publishing House. He was an outstanding translator of English works into Russian, and a prolific writer of children's stories and texts for political posters. [found in: Prokofiev - *Songs of Our Days*, *On Guard for Peace*]

**Marx, Karl** (1818-83) was a German philosopher and economic and social theorist. He is credited with the foundation of modern communism. While in exile he met Engels who assisted him in writing the *Communist Manifesto* (1848) and *Das Kapital*, in 3 volumes as completed by Engels (1867, 1884, 1894). The basic tenet of his writings is that the masses must overthrow their capitalist oppressors and establish equitable self rule. His theories are often misrepresented by his detractors, but have exerted significant influence on 20th-century society. [found in: Prokofiev - *Cantata on the 20th Anniversary of the October Revolution* ]

**Mashistov, Aleksei Ivanovich** was a Soviet Russian author. [found in: Prokofiev - *Flourish, Our Mighty Land*]

**Morax, René** (1873-1963) was a Swiss dramatist who produced a number of innovative works for the theater including significant collaborations with Honegger. [found in: Honegger - *Le Roi David*]

**Nekrasov, Nikolai A.** (1821-78) was a Russian journalist, critic, and poet. His works address the plights of the peasant class. [found in: Rachmaninov - *Vesna*]

**Nietzsche, Friedrich** (1844-1900) was a German nihilist philosopher, and author. He was the son of a Lutheran minister, and studied in Leipzig and Bonn. He was appointed to the faculty of the University of Basle (1868-78). In 1889, he collapsed and was sporadically insane and infirm for the remainder of his life. Between 1872 and 1888, he produced a large body of brillant and provocative writings which include: *Die Geburt der Tragödie* (1872), *Also Sprach Zarathustra* (1883-92), and *Ecce homo* (1888). [found in: Mahler - Symphony No. 3]

**Olrik, Axel** (1864-1917) was a Danish folklorist who is best known for his studies in Norse mythology. [found in: Nielsen - *Hymnus Amoris*]

**Ovid** (43 BC- 17 AD) was the most prolific of the Roman Latin poets. He is best known for his works: *Medea, Heroides, Amores, Metamorphoses, Ars Amandi,* and *Tristia.* [found in: Penderecki - *Kosmogonia*]

**Poe, Edgar Allan** (1809-49) was an American author best known for supernatural poems and short stories. His best known works include: *The Fall of the House of Usher* (1839), T*he Murders in the Rue Morgue* (1841), *The Pit and the Pendulum* (1842), *The Tell-Tale Heart* (1843), *The Purloined Letter* (1845), *The Raven* (1845), and *The Bells* (1848). [found in: Rachmaninov - *Kolokola* [The Bells]]

**Prichelyitz, A.** was a Soviet Russian author. [found in: Prokofiev - *Songs of Our Days*]

**The Psalms** are a body of 150 sacred poems, originally in Hebrew, which make up the nineteenth book of the Old Testament of the Bible. Many of these are attributed to King David. [found in: Bernstein - *Chichester Psalms,* Kodaly - *Psalmus Hungaricus,* Stravinsky - *Symphony of Psalms*]

**Ramuz, Charles-Ferdinand** (1878-1947) was a Swiss novelist. Among his 20 novels are: *Le Règne de l'ésprit malin* (1917), *Présence de la mort* (1922), and *Derborence* (1936). [found in: Stravinsky - *Svadebka*]

**Reinhart, Hans** (1880-1963) was a very prolific German author. He studied at the Universities of Heidelberg, Berlin, Leipzig, Zurich, and Paris. He traveled to India to study eastern theology. He was a prolific writer of poetry, drama, and literary criticism. [found in: Honegger - *Le Roi David* (translator)]

***Revelation of St. John the Divine*** is the final book of the New Testament of the Bible. It describes the visions its author had while exiled on the island of Patmos, of the second coming of Jesus Christ and the last judgement of the world. It is also called "The Apocalypse." [found in: Martin - *In terra pax*]

**Roman Catholic Liturgy** includes a large body of rituals and sacred texts which serve as the offices of the day and those of the liturgical year. Those which are included in the works above are: **Mass,** the texts of the Eucharist, or communion service based upon the Last Supper of Jesus Christ and his Apostles. [found in: Kodaly - *Missa Brevis,* Poulenc - *Gloria,* Stravinsky - *Mass*]; **Passion Liturgy** is the drama of Jesus Christ's betrayal, crucifixion, burial, and resurrection, as recorded in the New Testament of the Bible. [found in: Penderecki -*Passio et Mors Domini Nostri Iesu Christi Secundum Lucam*]; **Requiem,** Latin for "grant them rest," it is the name given to the Mass for the Dead which expands the traditional communion service with additional texts praying for eternal rest for the departed and speculating upon the Last Judgement of the world. [found in: Duruflé - *Requiem*, Ligeti - *Requiem*, Penderecki - *Dies Irae*, Stravinsky - *Introitus*, *Requiem Canticles*]; **Stabat Mater** is a 13th-century sacred poem describing the suffering of the Virgin Mary at the Cross of Jesus Christ's crucifixion; it is often attributed to a Franciscan friar, Jacopone da Todi. [found in: Poulenc - *Stabat Mater*]; **Te Deum** is a traditional song of praise which myth attributes to the occasion of St. Ambrose baptizing St. Augustine, whereupon the two saints are said to have spontaneously sung this text. [found in: Kodaly - *Te Deum of Budavár*]

**Rusak, Adam** was a Soviet Russian author. [found in: Prokofiev - *Songs of Our Days*]

**Sappho** (b. 612 BC) was a lyric poet from the Isle of Lesbos. Her works survive in fragments which display great poetic skill and emotional intensity. Many of her poems are addressed to members of a circle of girls of which she was the leader. She is said to have thrown herself into the sea having been rejected by the young Phaon. This legend has been the subject of numerous dramatic works from ancient Rome to the present day. [found in: Orff - *Trionfo di Afrodite*]

**Schnabel, Ernest** (b. 1913) is a well-known author and radio and television personality. Following World War II, he gained a strong following for his broadcasts on North-German and West-Berlin radio and television. He is a prolific writer whose works reflect his vast travel experience, and include: *Nachtwind* (1942), *Sie sehen dem Marmor nicht* (1949), *Der sechste Gesang* (1956), *Fremde ohne Souvenier* (1961), and *Hurricane* (1972). [found in: Henze - *Das Floss der Medusa*]

**Sophocles** (c.496-405 BC) was a great Greek playwright. His best known works are: *Ajax, Antigone, Œdipus Tyrannus, Œdipus Coloneus, Philoctetes*, and *Trachinæ*. [found in: Penderecki - *Kosmogonia*]

**Stalin, Joseph** (1879-1953) was a Russian revolutionary and Soviet leader. He succeeded Lenin as the leader of the Soviet Union in 1924. During his rule, he banished Trotsky, and established a series of unsuccessful organizational objectives known as the five-year plans. His leadership was dictatorial and millions of Russians died at his command. He demanded purges of the artists and intelligentsia, stifling the intellectual culture of his people. His brilliant strategies at the Yalta and Potsdam conferences led to the

Sovietization of eastern Europe following World War II and fostering the birth of the cold war. [found in: Prokofiev - *Cantata on the 20th Anniversary of the October Revolution* ]

**Vég, Mihály** (16th century) was a Magyar author of sacred verse. [found in: Kodaly - *Psalmus Hungaricus*]

*Veni Creator Spiritus*, "Come Creator Spirit," is an 18th-century Latin hymn text by an anonymous author. [found in: Mahler - Symphony No. 8]

**Virgil** (70-19 BC) was a great Roman poet and gardener. As a court poet to Mæcenas, he was able to enjoy an affluent lifestyle. His great masterpiece is the *Æneid* which was completed in the year of his death. [found in: Henze - *Die Muzen Siziliens*]

**Wilkerson, [Lancelot] Patrick** (1907-85) was a classics scholar at Cambridge University. His works include: *Horace and His Lyric Poetry* (1945), *Letters of Cicero* (1949), *Ovid Recalled* (1955), *The Roman Experience* (1974). [found in: Britten - *Cantata Misericordiam*]

**Wordsworth, William** (1770-1850) was the most prolific of all English poets. He studied at Cambridge (1787-91). After some brief investigations into radical social philosophy, he found his calling as a poetic chronicler of English country life. He befriended Coleridge with whom he published *Lyric Ballads* (1798), and settled in Grasmere in his native Lake District where he undertook a productive career. He was made poet laureate in 1843. Among his most celebrated works are: *Tintern Abbey* (1798), *Intimations of Immortality* (1807, inspired by Coleridge's young son), and *The Excursion* (1814).[ found in: Finzi - *Intimations of Immortality*]

**Wyss, Bernard** was a Swiss scholar and an officer of the University of Basle. [found in: Britten - *Cantata Academica*]

**Yevtushenko, Yevgeny** (b. 1933) was the most prominent Russian poet of the young post-Stalinists. He was an outspoken supporter of Solzhenitsyn and an advocate of human rights. His best known works are: *The Third Snow* (1955), *The Promise* (1957), *Babi Yar* (1962), *A Wave of the Hand* (1962), *A Precocious Autobiography* (1963), *Love Poems* (1977), *Ivan the Terrible and Ivan the Fool* (1979), and *Berries* (1981). [found in: Shostakovich - Symphony No. 13, *The Execution of Stepan Razin*]

# APPENDIX II

# A LIST OF MUSIC PUBLISHERS AND DISTRIBUTORS

**Artia**, Ve Smeckcah 30, Prague 2, Czech Republic
Rentals are distributed in the United States and Great Britain by
Boosey and Hawkes.

**Belmont Music Publishers**, P. O. Box 49961, Los Angeles, CA
90049

**Belwin-Mills Publishing Corp.**, 25 Deshon Drive, Melville,
NY 11747
distributed by Theodore Presser

**Boelke-Bomart Publications**, Hillsdale, NY 12529

**Boosey and Hawkes**, 200 Smith Street CSB6, Farmingdale, NY
11735
phone: 212-979-1090, ext. 26

**Alexander Broude Inc.**, 225 West 57th Street, New York, NY
10019

**Broude Bros. Ltd.**, 141 White Oaks Road, Williamstown, MA
01267
phone: 413-458-8131

**Rolf Budde Musikverlag,** Hohenzollerndam 54 A, D-1000 Berlin 33, Germany

**Carisch S.p.A.,** Via General Fara 39, 20124 Milan, Italy
distributed by Boosey and Hawkes

**Éditions Chant du Monde**
distributed by MCA

**Dover Publications Inc.,** 31 East 2nd Street, Mineola, NY 11501

**Durand et Cie**
distributed by Elkan-Vogel through Theodore Presser

**Educational Music Service,** 13 Elkay Drive, Chester, NY 10918
phone: 914-469-5790

**Elkan-Vogel Inc.,** Presser Place, Bryn Mawr, PA 19010
distributed by Theodore Presser

**European American Music Corp.,** 2480 Industrial Boulevard, Paoli, PA 19301
phone: 610-648-0506

**Carl Fischer, Inc.,** 56-62 Cooper Square, New York, NY 10003
phone: 800-762-2328

**Fürstner Ltd.**
distributed by Boosey and Hawkes

**Wilhelm Hansen Musik-Forlag**
Sales are distributed by Alexander Broude and Magnamusic. Rentals are distributed by G. Schirmer.

**Hinrichsen Editions Ltd.**
distributed by C.F. Peters

**Alphonse Leduc,** 175 rue Sainte-Honoré, 75040 Paris Cedex 01, France
Rentals are distributed by Theodore Presser.

**Magnamusic-Baton Inc.,** 10370 Page Industrial Boulevard, St. Louis, MO 63132

**MCA**, 445 Park Avenue, New York, NY 10022, a division of Belwin-Mills and distributed by Theodore Presser Company

**Mezhdunaradnaja Kniga,** Moscow
distributed by G. Schirmer

**Hermann Moeck Verlag**
distributed by Belwin-Mills through Theodore Presser

**Novello and Co.,** Fairfield Road, Borough Green, Sevenoaks, Kent TN15 8DT England
distributed by Theodore Presser Company

**Peer International Corp.,** 1740 Broadway, New York, NY 10019
phone: 212-265-3910

**C. F. Peters Corp.,** 373 Park Avenue South, New York, NY 10016
phone: 212-686-4147

**Philharmonia** is a division of Universal Edition
available through European American Music

**Plymouth Music Co., Inc.,** 17 West 60th Street, New York, NY 10023

**Theodore Presser Co.,** Presser Place, Bryn Mawr, PA 19010
phone: 610-525-3636

**Francis Salabert Éditions**
distributed by G. Schirmer

**E. C. Schirmer Music Co.,** 112 South Street, Boston, MA 02111
phone: 617-236-1935

**G. Schirmer, Inc.,** 866 Third Avenue, New York, NY 10022
phone: 914-469-2271

**B. Schotts Söhne,** Weihergarten 5, Postfach 3640, D-6500 Mainz, Germany
distributed by European American Music Corp.

**Staff Music Publishing Co., Inc.**
distributed by Plymouth Music

**Summy-Birchard Co.,** 1834 Ridge Avenue, Evanston, Illinois 60204

**Edition Supraphon,** Palckeho 1, 112 99 Prague 1, Czech Republic
Rentals are distributed by Boosey and Hawkes.

**Universal Edition**
distributed by European American Music

# GENERAL BIBLIOGRAPHY

## General Reference and Biography

Anderson, E. Ruth: *Contemporary American Composers: A Biographical Dictionary.* Boston: G. K. Hall, 1976.

Apel, Willi, editor: *The Harvard Dictionary of Music,* second edition. Cambridge: Belknap Press of Harvard University Press, 1972.

*Arthur Honegger Werkverzeichnis.* Zurich: Schweizerisches Musik-Archiv, 1975.

Austin, William W.: *Music in the Twentieth Century from Debussy through Stravinsky.* New York: W.W. Norton, 1966.

Benser, Caroline Cepin, and David Francis Urrows: *Randall Thompson: A Bio-Bibliography.* New York: Greenwood Press, 1991.

Berger, Melvin: *Guide to Choral Masterpieces: A Listener's Guide.* New York: Anchor Books, 1993.

Briscoe, James R.: *Claude Debussy: A Guide to Research.* New York: Garland Press, 1990.

Burton, Humphrey: *Leonard Bernstein.* New York: Doubleday, 1994.

Cooper, Martin, ed.: *New Oxford History of Music, volume X. The Modern Age, 1890-1960.* London: Oxford University Press, 1974.

Copland, Aaron, and Vivian Perlis: *Copland: 1900 through 1942.* New York: St. Martin's Press, 1984.

_____: *Copland since 1943.* New York: St. Martin's Press, 1989.

Drew, David: *Kurt Weill: A Handbook.* Berkeley: University of California Press, 1987.

Durant, Will and Ariel: *The Story of Civilization.* 11 volumes. New York: Simon and Schuster, 1975.

Eagon, Angelo, ed.: *Catalog of Published Concert Music by American Composers,* second edition. Metuchen, NJ: Scarecrow Press, 1969. Supplement, 1971; Second Supplement, 1974.

Evans, Ivor H., ed.: *Brewer's Dictionary of Phrase and Fable,* Centenary Edition, revised. New York: Harper and Row, 1981.

Gleason, Harold, and Walter Becker: *20th-Century American Composers.* Music Literature Outlines, series 4. Bloomington: Indiana University Press, revised in 1981.

Greene, Richard: *Holst: The Planets.* Cambridge: Cambridge University Press, 1995.

Heintze, James R.: *Igor Stravinsky: An International Bibliography of Theses and Dissertations, 1925-78,* Detroit Studies in Music Bibliography, Number 61. Warren, MI: Harmonic Park Press, 1988.

Heyworth, Peter: *Otto Klemperer: His Life and Times,* volume 1: 1885-1933. Cambridge: Cambridge University Press, 1983.

Hitchcock, H. Wiley: *Music in the United States: An Historical Introduction,* revised edition. Englewood Cliffs, NJ: Prentice-Hall, 1974.

Holst, Imogen: *The Music of Gustav Holst,* third edition; and *Holst's Music Reconsidered.* 1 volume. Oxford: Oxford University Press, 1986.

_____: *A Thematic Catalogue of Gustav Holst's Music.* London: Faber and Faber, 1974.

Hulme, Derek C.: *Dmitri Shostakovich: A Catalogue, Bibliography, and Discography,* second edition. Oxford: Clarendon Press, 1991.

Kasak, Wolfgang: *Dictionary of Russian Literature Since 1917.* New York: Columbia University Press, 1988.

Keck, George R.: *Francis Poulenc: A Bio-Bibliography*. New York: Greenwood Press, 1990.

Kennedy, Michael, editor: *The Concise Oxford Dictionary of Music*, third edition. London: Oxford University Press, 1980.

King, Charles W.: *Frank Martin: A Bio-Bibliography*. New York: Greenwood Press, 1990.

Kushner, David Z.: *Ernest Bloch: A Guide to Research*. New York: Garland Publishing, 1988.

La Grange, Henry-Louis de: *Mahler*, volume I. Garden City, NY: Doubleday and Co., 1973.

_____: *Gustav Mahler: Vienna: The Years of Challenge (1897-1904)*. Oxford: Oxford University Press, 1995.

Magnusson, Magnus, ed.: *Cambridge Biographical Dictionary*. Cambridge: Cambridge University Press, 1990.

Miller, Mina F.: *Carl Nielsen: A Guide to Research*. New York: Garland Publishing, 1987.

Moldenhauer, Hans: *Anton Webern: A Chronicle of His Life and Work*. New York: Alfred A Knopf, 1979.

Morgan, Robert P.: *Twentieth-Century Music*. New York: W.W. Norton, 1991.

Morton, Brian and Pamela Collins, editors: *Contemporary Composers*. Chicago: St. James Press, 1992.

Pahlen, Kurt: *The World of the Oratorio*. Portland, Oregon: Amadeus Press, 1985.

Palmieri, Robert: *Sergei Vasil"evich Rachmaninov: A Guide to Research*. New York: Garland Publishing, 1985.

Peinkofer, Karl, and Fritz Tannigel: *Handbook of Percussion Instruments*, translated by Kurt and Else Stone. New York: Schott, 1976.

Perkins, George, Barbara Perkins, and Phillip Leininger, eds.: *Benét's Reader's Encyclopedia of American Literature*. New York: Harper Collins, 1991.

Peyser, Joan: *Bernstein: A Biography*. New York: Beechtree Books, 1987.

Robinson, Harlow: *Sergei Prokofiev*. New York: Viking, 1987.

Robinson, Ray: *Krsysztof Penderecki: A Guide to His Works*. Princeton, NJ: Prestige Publications, 1983.

Roman, Zoltan: *Anton Webern: An Annotated Bibliography*. Detroit, MI: Information Coördinators, 1983.

Rufer, Josef: *The Works of Arnold Schoenberg: A Catalogue of his Compositions, Writings, and Paintings*, translated by Dika Newlin. New York: Free Press of Glencoe, 1963.

Sadie, Stanley, ed.: *The New Grove Dictionary of Music and Musicians*. 20 volumes. London: Macmillan, 1980.

Salzman, Eric: *Twentieth-Century Music: An Introduction*, second edition. Englewood Cliffs, NJ: Prentice-Hall, 1974.

Schmidt, Carl B.: *The Music of Francis Poulenc (1899-1963): A Catalogue*. Oxford: Clarendon Press, 1995.

Schwinger, Wolfram: *Penderecki: Begegnungen, Lebensdaten, Werkkomentare*. Stuttgart: Deutsche Verlagsantalt, 1979. Published in English translation by William Mann as: *Krzysztof Penderecki: His Life and Work*. London: Schott, 1989.

Slonimsky, Nicolas: *Baker's Biographical Dictionary of Musicians*, eighth edition. New York: Schirmer Books, 1992.

_____: *Music Since 1900*, fifth edition. New York: Schirmer Books, 1994.

DeVenney, David P., ed.: *Source Readings in American Choral Music*. Missoula, MT: College Music Society, 1995.

Stevens, Halsey: *The Life and Music of Bela Bartok*, revised. New York: Oxford University Press, 1964.

Thomson, Virgil: *American Music Since 1910*. New York: Holt, Rinehart, and Winston, 1971.

*Webster's Biographical Dictionary*. Springfield, MA: G. and C. Merriam, 1964.

White, Eric Walter: *Stravinsky: the Composer and his Works*. Berkeley: University of California Press, 1966; revised and enlarged second edition, 1979.

Wingfield, Paul: *Janácek: Glagolithic Mass*. Cambridge: Cambridge University Press, 1992.

### Repertoire

Aronowsky, Solomon: *Performing Times of Orchestral Works*. London: Ernest Benn Limited, 1959.

Daniels, David: *Orchestral Music: A Handbook*, third edition. Lanham, MD: Scarecrow Press, 1996.

Daugherty, F. Mark, and Susan H. Simons, eds.: *Secular Choral Music in Print*, second edition, 2 volumes. Philadelphia: Musicdata, 1987.

Dox, Thurston: *American Oratorios and Cantatas: A Catalog of Works Written in the United States from Colonial Times to 1985*. 2 volumes. Metuchen, NJ: Scarecrow Press, 1986.

Eslinger, Gary S., and F. Mark Daugherty, eds.: *Sacred Choral Music in Print*, second edition, 2 volumes. Philadelphia: Musicdata, 1985.

Farish, Margaret K.: *Orchestra Music in Print*. Philadelphia: Musicdata, 1979.

Robertson, Alec: *Requiem: Music of Mourning and Consolation*. London: Praeger Press, 1985.

Ulrich, Homer: *A Survey of Choral Music*. New York: Harcourt, Brace, and Jovanovich, 1973.

Young, Percy M.: *The Choral Tradition*. New York: W.W. Norton, 1971.

## *Discographies*

*CD Plus: Compact Disc Catalogue*, various issues.

Cohn, Arthur: *The Collector's Twentieth-Century Music in the Western Hemisphere*. Philadelphia: J. B. Lippincott, 1961.

Halsey, Richard Sweeney: *Classical Music Recordings: For Home and Library*. Chicago: American Library Association, 1976.

Kolodin, Irving: *The New Guide to Recorded Music*, International edition. Garden City, NY: Doubleday and Company, 1950.

_____: *The Guide to Long-Playing Records: Orchestral Music*. New York: Alfred A. Knopf, 1955.

Miller, Philip L.: *The Guide to Long-Playing Records: Vocal Music*. New York: Alfred A. Knopf, 1955.

*Musical Heritage Society Master Catalogue* (1991).

Oja, Carol J.: *American Music Recordings: A Discography of Twentieth-Century U.S. Composers*. Brooklyn, NY: Institute for Studies in American Music, 1982.

*Schwann Catalogues* (including: *Schwann Long Playing Record Catalog*, *Schwann Compact Disc Catalog*, and *Opus*). Boston: W. Schwann, 1949-1996.

U.S. Library of Congress: *Library of Congress National Union Catalogue, Music and Phonorecords*. Washington, DC: Library of Congress, 1953- .

# ABOUT THE AUTHOR

JONATHAN D. GREEN (BMus, Fredonia School of Music at SUNY Fredonia; MMus, University of Massachusetts; DMA, University of North Carolina Greensboro) is Director of Ensembles at Sweet Briar College in Virginia. He has previously held conducting posts at Williams College, Amherst College, Hampden-Sydney College, and Elon College, and served as Music Librarian at Bennington College. He continues to lead summer graduate seminars in conducting at the University of North Carolina at Greensboro. An active composer, he has written over ninety works to date, including six symphonies, five song cycles and many choral works. He is the recipient of numerous commissions, an Ornest Fellowship, an ASCAP Composer's Award, a Composition Fellowship to the Virginia Center for the Creative Arts, and he was made an Excellence Fellow of the University of North Carolina Greensboro. Green is a member of the American Choral Directors' Association, the American Symphony Orchestra League, ASCAP, the Conductors Guild, the Southeastern Composers' League, the College Music Society, and Phi Mu Alpha Sinfonia. He currently resides in Greensboro, NC, with his wife, Lynn Buck.